Books are to be returned on or before
the last date below

LIBREX–

Intending Scotland

For Conan

INTENDING SCOTLAND

Explorations in Scottish Culture since the Enlightenment

Cairns Craig

Edinburgh University Press

Edinburgh University Press Ltd
22 George Square, Edinburgh
www.euppublishing.com

Typeset by the Research Institute for Irish and Scottish Studies,
University of Aberdeen
Printed and bound in Great Britain
by CPI Antony Rowe,
Chippenham and Eastbourne

A CIP record for this book is available from the British Library

ISBN 978 0 7486 3713 3 (hardback)

Arts & Humanities
Research Council

Some of the research contained in this title
was supported by the Arts and Humanities Research Council
through the AHRC Centre for Irish-Scottish Studies,
University of Aberdeen

Contents

Preface   vi

Introduction   1

1. In Tending Scotland   13

2. When Was the Scottish Enlightenment?   77

3. Beyond Reason: Hume, Seth, Macmurray   145
        and Scotland's Postmodernity

4. Intended Communities: MacIver, Macmurray   179
        and the Scottish Idealists

5. Telephonic Scotland: Periphery, Hybridity, Diaspora   203

6. Identifying Another Other   245

    Afterword   271

    Index   273

Preface

The chapters of *Intending Scotland* reflect – and reflect on – changes in Scotland since the establishment of the Scottish parliament, whose reshaping of Scotland's future requires a fresh understanding of its past. It deals with three groups of neglected Scottish thinkers. The first are the scientists – William Thomson, Peter Guthrie Tait, Macquorn Rankine and James Clerk Maxwell – who revolutionised physics by their discoveries in thermodynamics. The second is a group of biblical and classical scholars – John Ferguson McLennan, William Robertson Smith and Sir J. G. Frazer – whose work shaped the new science of anthropology from the 1860s till the 1920s. And the third – Andrew Seth, Robert Morrison MacIver, John Macmurray and Norman Kemp Smith – not only transformed the understanding of the history of Scottish philosophy but helped define the emergent discipline of sociology. I had hoped to include a chapter on Scottish women intellectuals of the nineteenth- and early-twentieth centuries but that project has grown so large it will need (and deserves) a book to itself.

Some of this book was researched while I was still at the University of Edinburgh, where I benefited from extended sabbatical leave, in part funded by a grant from the Arts and Humanities Research Council. I would like to thank both the AHRC and the University for their support, and to thank (again) my former colleagues in the English Literature Department for providing such a stimulating environment to work in. Since moving back to the University of Aberdeen, where I first taught in the 1970s, I have had the privilege of being Director of the AHRC Centre for Irish and Scottish Studies, and I have learned a great deal from those who have been involved in the Centre's work: I would particularly like to thank Edna Longley, Fran Brearton, Peter MacKay, John Kirk, Graham Walker and John Thomson in Queen's University, Belfast; David Dickson, Jane Ohlmeyer, Ian Campbell Ross, Terence Brown and Micheal O'Siochru in Trinity College, Dublin; and John Morrill of Cambridge University, as well as John MacKenzie, formerly of Lancaster University, and Karen Corrigan of Newcastle University. In Aberdeen, I have benefited both from the groundbreaking research and from the good humour of Patrick Crotty, Michael Brown, Andrew MacKillop, Ralph O'Connor, Rosalyn Trigger, Steve Dornan and Paul Shanks.

Some sections of the following chapters have previously appeared in journals or in books and I would like to thank the editors for their assistance: portions of Chapter 1 derive from 'Constituting Scotland', *The Irish Review,* No. 28 (2001); a version of Chapter 3 was first published in Gavin Miller and Eleanor Bell's *Scotland in Theory* (Amsterdam: Rodopi, 2004); sections of the 'Introduction' appeared in Caroline McCracken-Flesher's *Culture, Nation and the New Scottish Parliament* (Lewisburg: Bucknell University Press, 2007); Chapter 5 is based in part on 'Centring on the Peripheries', in Bjarne Thomsen, *Centring on the Peripheries* (Norwich: Norvik, 2007); versions of the sections of Chapters 1 and 4 dealing with Benedict Anderson were first developed in Alistair McCleery and Benjamin Brabon's *The Influence of Benedict Anderson* (Edinburgh: Merchiston, 2007), and those on Homi Bhabha and hybridity in a chapter in Gerard Carruthers, David Goldie and Alastair Renfrew's *Beyond Scotland* (Amsterdam: Rodopi, 2004).

I owe particular debts to Jack Costello of Regius College, University of Toronto and David Fergusson of the University of Edinburgh for the insights they have provided into the writings of John Macmurray; to Gavin Miller for introducing me to the work of Scottish psychology before R. D. Laing; to Tom Nairn, David McCrone and Christopher Harvie for debating my criticisms of their work in a spirit of shared commitment to Scottish causes; and to John Brewer of the University of Aberdeen for bringing the work of Robert Morrison MacIver to my attention. To Craig Beveridge and Ronald Turnbull I am particularly indebted for doing so much to prepare the ground which I have tried to tend in these chapters.

My thanks also go to the staff of the National Library of Scotland, and to the librarians of the universities of Edinburgh, Aberdeen, Columbia and Toronto without whose assistance the following chapters would not have been possible. And, as always, to Jackie Jones and the editorial team at Edinburgh University Press for their persistence and patience.

Without the passion of my father and mother, Bill and Jean Craig, for gardening, I would never have learned the pleasure of tending my own garden with my son Conan, and never have discovered the pleasure of researching Scottish gardens and gardeners. Linda has made our visits to those gardens a delight, and my deepest thanks go to all of them.

Introduction

The phenomenon of the Scottish Enlightenment has become the focus of such a vast scholarly industry, as well as being extolled as a political and cultural icon in Scotland and in North America, that it is easy to lose sight of just how recently it was identified as a specific historical occurrence. As Charles Withers and Paul Wood pointedly remind us in *Science and Medicine in the Scottish Enlightenment*, the first book-length study on the Scottish Enlightenment was only published in 1976[1] and the term only came into general use in the previous decade. Indeed, we can probably date the inauguration of the Scottish Enlightenment as a historical happening – and a historical issue – to Hugh Trevor-Roper's address to the Second International Congress on the Enlightenment at St Andrews in 1966.[2] What this date implies, however, is that the period of the emergence of the Scottish Enlightenment as a matter of intellectual concern is identical with the period of the emergence of modern Scottish nationalism, since the Scottish National Party went from having no MPs in 1964 to having eleven in 1974. Such a conjunction between the rise of the Scottish Enlightenment and the rise of Scottish nationalism is deeply ironic, since the Enlightenment has been regarded by nationalists, at least until recently, as a distinctly Unionist phenomenon, whose major proponents, such as Trevor-Roper, were committed to resisting Scottish self-government. Indeed, Trevor-Roper's original account of the Enlightenment emphasised that it was only made possible by breaking down 'the barricades of a defensive nationalism',[3] an achievement which he was in turn to defend by putting up barricades to the establishment of a devolved Scottish parliament

---

[1] Charles W. J. Withers and Paul Wood, *Science and Medicine in the Scottish Enlightenment* (East Linton: Tuckwell, 2002). The book was Anand C. Chitnis, *The Scottish Enlightenment: A Social History* (London: Croom Helm, 1976).

[2] Published in Theodore Besterman (ed.), *Studies on Voltaire and the Eighteenth Century,* Vol. LVIII (1967), 1635–58.

[3] Ibid., 1643.

in the 1970s.[4] What has come to be seen as one of Scotland's most significant contributions to world culture has, paradoxically, been treated with deep suspicion by nationalists, precisely because it has been so enthusiastically supported by anti-nationalists as proof that nationalism in Scotland would be incapable of producing a culture of world significance. The emphasis of Enlightenment historiography has been, according to nationalists, on the fact that the Scottish Enlightenment was produced not from native resources but from external – and, especially, English – influences. Put crudely, the Union was the fundamental cause of the Scottish Enlightenment and therefore any challenge to the Union is a betrayal of Scotland's greatest intellectual achievements. What is true of its modern supporters was also assumed to have been true of its original *dramatis personae*: they were committed not to the development of Scotland's national culture but to its suppression, and to the promotion of the virtues of Anglicisation as the effective route to intellectual and cultural distinction. As Colin Kidd has put it, 'nationalists found the theoretical detachment of Enlightenment social science to be a matter for reproach, and condemned the Scottish Enlightenment for its rootless, cosmopolitan betrayal of Scottish cultural distinctiveness'.[5]

Nonetheless, the increasing prominence of the Scottish Enlightenment and the rise of Scottish nationalism have in fact gone hand-in-hand: by 2002, when American historian Arthur Herman was to claim that the Scottish Enlightenment represented nothing less than the 'Invention of the Modern World',[6] construction had begun on the new Scottish parliament building next to Holyrood Palace, at the foot of Edinburgh's Royal Mile. The rise and rise of the international prominence of the Scottish Enlightenment did not provide the bulwark against nationalism that Trevor-Roper had hoped for. While nationalist historians, such as William Ferguson, would continue to insist that the Enlightenment thinkers 'were regressive', and 'impeded the triumph of record scholarship on which historical science depended',[7] the Enlightenment was itself becoming an element in the national distinction

---

[4] H. R. Trevor-Roper, 'Scotching the Myths of Devolution', *Times*, 28 April 1976, 14.

[5] Colin Kidd, 'Lord Dacre and the Politics of the Scottish Enlightenment', *Scottish Historical Review*, Vol. LXXXIV, 2, No. 218 (October 2005), 202–20, at 204.

[6] Arthur Herman, *The Scottish Enlightenment: The Scots' Invention of the Modern World* (London: Fourth Estate, 2002).

[7] William Ferguson, *The Identity of the Scottish Nation* (Edinburgh: Edinburgh University Press, 1998), 206–7.

on which nationalist claims were founded. So while Iain Gray, on his election to the leadership of the Labour group in Holyrood in 2008, could claim anti-nationalist credentials on the basis that he had studied 'natural science in the academic home of the enlightenment',[8] Alex Salmond had no compunction in asking his supporters to reflect on and to take inspiration from 'Scotland's proud record of invention and our huge contribution, through the Enlightenment, in the development of the ideas that form the foundation of our modern world'.[9]

The notion of the Scottish Enlightenment has not only fundamentally changed the understanding of Scottish history since the 1960s, but has played a crucial role in the redefinition of modern Scotland's conception of its contemporary identity – and, therefore, of its possible future. In exploring Scottish culture since the Enlightenment, I am therefore invoking a double perspective: one focused on the consequences of that upsurge of Scottish innovation which we have come to call the Enlightenment – and whose historical lineaments have been attributed by Paul Wood to Dugald Stewart's account of his eighteenth-century predecessors[10] – and the other, the impact of the concept in Scottish cultural studies (and Scottish cultural politics) in the period since the 1960s. The major issue with which these two perspectives confront us is whether there is any continuity between the eighteenth-century Enlightenment and contemporary Scotland. For Trevor-Roper, the promotion of the Scottish Enlightenment was also the negation of all that had come to be accepted as Scottish culture in the intervening period, when not only Scotland but the rest of the world was seduced by the 'fantasies' of Walter Scott. The romantic Scotland promoted by Scott was, to Trevor-Roper, nothing less than a self-deluding evasion of the real nature of modern, progressive, industrial Scotland. For Scotland to fulfil its real identity, it had to resist the glamour of Scott's construction of its 'national' past in favour of the values of Enlightenment 'progress', this being the very discovery which was the greatest achievement of Scotland's eighteenth-century thinkers: 'Before sinking into the past as the raw material

---

[8] http://www.sundaymail.co.uk/news/scottish-news/2008/09/14 (accessed December 2008).

[9] http://news.bbc.co.uk/2/shared/bsp/hi/pdfs/20_04_08_salmond.pdf (accessed December 2008).

[10] Paul Wood, 'Dugald Stewart and the Invention of "the Scottish Enlightenment"', in Paul Wood (ed.), *The Scottish Enlightenment: Essays in Reinterpretation* (Rochester, NY: Rochester University Press, 2000), 'Introduction'.

of the new romanticism, they had helped to stimulate that analysis of human progress which is the peculiar contribution of the Scottish Enlightenment.'[11] 'Progress' was both the key discovery of and the principal value of the Enlightenment, and it was identical with the beneficial effects of the Union and of Anglicisation. Contemporary Scotland's progress would likewise depend on retaining its commitment to those Enlightenment values, proof as they were of the illusory attractions of Scottish nationalism.

When the new Scottish parliament was convened on 12 May 1999, however, a very different kind of continuity was asserted when Winnie Ewing – the oldest member and the one whose victory for the Scottish National Party in the safe Labour seat of Hamilton in 1967 (just a few months after Trevor-Roper's address in St Andrews) had indicated the unexpected surge in support for nationalism – declared that 'The Scottish Parliament, adjourned on the twenty-fifth day of March 1707, is hereby reconvened'. It was, in strictly legal terms, untrue, for the modern Scottish parliament is devolved from the Westminster parliament rather than being the old Scottish parliament reconstituted, but what that assertion did was to present the years of a single British parliament as the interruption of a narrative which had now been resumed. For Trevor-Roper, on the other hand, this could represent only the recovery of a world in which 'Scotland was a by-word for irredeemable poverty, social backwardness, political faction' and in which the Scots would return 'to reiterate their atavistic war-cries: to remember Bannockburn, or to debate, for the thousandth time, the admittedly very debatable virtues of Mary Queen of Scots'.[12]

Which narrative did modern Scotland belong to? The relevance of the question, provoked initially by the emergence of the SNP in the 1960s, was to be sharpened by the failure of the Labour government's devolutionary proposals in 1979, which resulted in Mrs Thatcher's domination of British politics for the following thirteen years. For many, the Thatcherite revolution was seen as the imposition of alien values on Scottish society – even if Malcolm Rifkind, her Scottish Secretary of State, declared these to be the values of the Scottish Enlightenment.[13] That Scots consistently voted against the Conservatives but became the testing ground for many of their most radical initiatives (such as the 'Poll Tax') only increased the sense of living in

---

[11] Trevor-Roper, 'The Scottish Enlightenment', 1658.

[12] Ibid., 1636–7.

[13] Christopher Harvie, *Scotland and Nationalism: Scottish Society and Politics 1707–1994* (London: Routledge, 1994; 2nd edn), 202–3.

a narrative of someone else's invention. It is a condition which I described in the 1980s as being 'out of history' – that is, being cut off from any narrative which could connect the national present in a meaningful way to the national past. I attributed the beginnings of this contradiction to David Hume and the other historians of the Enlightenment in whose works the narrative of 'progress' represented the fundamental virtue of English history, an English history to which events in Scotland had been irrelevant. Insofar as Scotland had joined the history of 'progress', it had to accept that its historical origin was not in its native development but in the development of the structures of English society.[14] Being 'out of history', both in the Enlightenment construction of 'British' history and in the practical politics of the Thatcherite 1980s, proved, however, to be the prologue to an outpouring of historical writing in Scotland, involving a radical remaking of Scotland's past, and culminating in 2007 in an orgy of historiographic production to mark – and to contest – the three hundredth anniversary of the Union.[15]

The irony of this great upsurge in Scottish historical writing since the 1960s – sufficient to inspire 'one American observer', Michael Lynch tells us in the introduction to his 'new history' of Scotland, 'to write of a second Enlightenment'[16] – is that it has responded to the foundering of the narrative of Scottish history by effectively dispensing with the need for narrative. As Michael Fry has noted, the major event of nineteenth-century Scotland, the Disruption of the Church of Scotland in 1843, is almost unknown to the modern population of the country and almost inexplicable in contemporary historiography.[17] In place of narrative explanation, the histories which accompanied the intensifying debate over a Scottish parliament turned increasingly

---

[14] See, *Out of History: Narrative Paradigms in Scottish and English Culture* (Edinburgh: Polygon, 1996), which collected essays from the 1980s.

[15] See, for instance, T. M. Devine (ed.), *Scotland and the Union: 1707–2007* (Edinburgh: Edinburgh University Press, 2008); Michael Fry, *The Union: England, Scotland and the Treaty of 1707* (Edinburgh: Birlinn, 2007); Allan I. Macinnes, *Union and Empire: The Making of the United Kingdom in 1707* (Cambridge: Cambridge University Press, 2007); John Robertson (ed.), *A Union for Empire: Political Thought and the British Union of 1707* (Cambridge: Cambridge University Press, 2008); Jeffrey A. Stephen, *Scottish Presbyterians and the Act of Union* (Edinburgh: Edinburgh University Press, 2007); Christopher A. Whatley, *The Scots and the Union* (Edinburgh: Edinburgh University Press, 2007).

[16] Michael Lynch, *Scotland: A New History* (London: Pimlico, 1991), xv.

[17] Michael Fry, 'The Disruption and the Union', in Stewart J. Brown and Michael Fry (eds), *Scotland in the Age of the Disruption* (Edinburgh: Edinburgh University Press, 1993), 31.

instead to economic analysis. If Scotland had any kind of historical narrative it had to be dug out of its economic base rather than its political superstructure, which, as Richard Finlay commented in the conclusion to his *Modern Scotland 1914–2000*, 'has been largely directionless'.[18] Statistics rather than the state formed the basis of the major histories produced by economic and social historians from T. C. Smout in the 1960s to T. M. Devine in the 1990s – the social rather than the personal, the institutional rather than the individual.

Insofar as these histories did, however, invoke an underlying narrative structure, it was one that continued to be firmly tied to the traditional structures of English historiography. T. M. Devine's best-selling account of *The Scottish Nation 1700–2000* might have asserted the continuity of the Scottish 'nation' in terms appropriate to the opening of the new parliament, but the argument of the book effectively transferred to Scotland the assumed pre-eminence in industrial development that had always been part of the narrative of English history. While the conception of an 'Industrial Revolution' had faded in English historiography, Devine tells us, 'north of the Border there truly was an Industrial and Agricultural Revolution. In fact, recent research on comparative urban development in Europe suggests that the explosive Scottish rate of town and city growth was the fastest of any region in Britain or the Continent between 1750 and 1850.'[19] Thus England's leading role as the first truly urban society is displaced by Scotland's much shorter and therefore more intense experience: '... the Scottish rate of urban growth after *c.* 1760 was significantly faster than England's and the process of economic change more intense and convulsive than that of her southern neighbour. Here indeed was a society *par excellence* in which traditional religious structures must have been powerfully challenged by the enormous force of industrialization.'[20]

What once had been the uniquely distinctive narrative of English history has, in this account, become the distinguishing feature of Scottish history. Thus Engels's analysis of English industrial society is presented as being 'even more valid for Scotland', as Scotland becomes, in Devine's account, the paradigm case of modernisation in nineteenth-century Europe.[21] It is an

---

[18] Richard Finlay, *Modern Scotland 1914–2000* (London: Profile, 2004), 397.
[19] T. M. Devine, *The Scottish Nation 1700–2000* (Harmondsworth: Penguin, [1999] 2000), 107–8.
[20] Ibid., 364.
[21] Ibid., 487.

account in which Scotland takes over the lineaments of the whig view of history that had itself been transposed, in the 1950s and 60s, into the New Left conception of the unbroken continuity of the 'long revolution' wrought by the English working-class, and which Devine finds in the 'Scottish radical tradition': 'The values of justice, fairness, morality, self-help and the conviction that all men should work together for the common good, which Chartism inherited and refined, profoundly influenced the Labour movement of the later nineteenth century and beyond. Despite successive failures, there was a remarkable thread of continuity in the radical tradition.'[22] Scotland is reunited with its forward historical trajectory by becoming the real medium of the progressive structure once accorded to England's working-class radicalism and recovers its relationship with a general conception of progressive history by domesticating the English narrative that had previously been used to demonstrate Scotland's historical *lack* of significance. The difficulty this poses to Scottish historians seems to be acknowledged by Devine in his later book, *Scotland's Empire 1600–1815*, when he notes how, on key issues such as relationship of imperial wealth to industrial development, a real understanding of the dynamics of the Scottish situation has been hampered by the fact that 'Scottish historiography has been influenced by English thinking on empire and industrialization'.[23] Scottish history, in other words, like the Scottish parliament whose areas of responsibility were far less than those of German *länder* or Canadian states, continued to be a *domestic* history which operated within fundamentally anglocentric structures.

The economic emphasis in contemporary presentations of Scotland's national history – which reflects, indeed, the economistic orientation of even nationalist politics in contemporary Scotland – ignores the extent to which the real driving force of Scottish difference and of Scottish *distinction* was not in the brute fact of its economic development, nor in the profound social problems which that development left to the modern nation, but in the power of its cultural response to those economic developments. It is not the dramatic upsurge of the Scottish economy in the eighteenth century that makes Scotland internationally important but that Scotland, through those institutions which the Union had left intact – the law, the universities, the church – as well as through its very productive publishing industry, retained a context in which it was possible to interpret its economic transformation in

---

[22] Ibid., 280.

[23] T. M. Devine, *Scotland's Empire 1600–1815* (London: Allen Lane, 2003), 327.

radically new ways.[24] Equally, it was the reproduction of elements of Scotland's distinctively different cultural infrastructure that made its contribution to the British Empire more than just a repetition of English cultural forms.

It is the sustained nature of that cultural achievement, however, that has been put in question by accounts of the Scottish Enlightenment which are premised on the fact that Enlightenment in Scotland did not only come to end but had no continuing influence on the development of later Scottish culture. These narratives present Scotland as a country in precipitous decline from its once internationally acknowledged eminence, and make the Enlightenment an isolated event that simply underlines the mediocrity of what follows on from it. And yet the period of the rise in interest in the Enlightenment is also the period of one of the greatest outpourings of Scottish creativity – in literature, in the visual arts, and in popular culture – since the beginning of the nineteenth century. What those creative achievements suggested – against the wishes of promoters of Enlightenment like Trevor-Roper – was that Scotland had, long before the new parliament became the 'settled will of the Scottish people', effectively declared cultural independence.

That the arrival of the parliament has not – or not yet, at any rate – made the issue of Scotland's relationship to its past, and to the nature of history-as-progress, irrelevant is suggested by the terms of a review of Neal Ascherson's *Stone Voices*, written by the Scottish novelist and columnist Andrew O'Hagan in October 2002. *Stone Voices* is a meditation on the matter of Scotland, focused around Ascherson's experiences as a journalist for the *Scotsman* newspaper in the period leading to the devolution referendum of 1979, and then again in the run-up to the referendum of 1997, when he was part of a touring group of writers and artists campaigning for a 'yes' vote. O'Hagan praised Ascherson's work only when the latter was analysing the 'Scottish trauma' of 'self-doubt' that represented a 'deep geological fault running underneath national self-confidence', but attacked him for not seeing that,

> Free-falling anxiety about Scottishness has a tendency among Scots, not only to turn into hatred of others, but into hating bad news about the country itself, and seeing critics as traitors. There are few European nations in which the intellectuals are so willing to serve as soft-pedalling merchants of 'national character,' handmaidens to the tourist

---

[24] As Colin Kidd, points out, it was precisely the uniqueness of Scotland's response to the experience of 'progress' that Trevor-Roper had emphasised in 1966; 'Lord Dacre and the Politics of Scottish Enlightenment', 207–10.

industry: broadcasters, academics, lawyers, some of the poets too, sell pride and tears, spiritual laxity and pawky good humour in place of inquiry.[25]

There is a profound irony in this attack since there are in fact few European nations where the intellectuals, from Hugh MacDiarmid and Edwin Muir in the 1920s and 30s, to Tom Nairn and others of the New Left such as Colin McArthur in the 1970s and 80s, have spilled so much ink on excoriating attacks on the history of their national culture. For O'Hagan, 'Scotland should have outgrown its own pantomime by now', but has not because 'nationalism in Scotland is a place where good men and women busy themselves shaking the dead hand of the past'. It is O'Hagan, however, rather than Scotland, who is shaking the dead hand of the past, a past in which decades of Scottish intellectuals have maintained a relentless attack upon the versions of Scottish culture produced by the success of Burns's poetry or Sir Walter Scott's *Waverley* novels.

What O'Hagan finds most unacceptable is Ascherson's presentation of Scotland through its landscape of stone: the poetry of stone, he suggests, 'appeals to those who are more taken with essence than experience, those who, for good reasons not bad, wish for an overarching grandeur, a galvanising truth, something in the Scottish character that can live up to the landscape. It is part of what Ibsen called "the saving lie".'[26] The reference to Ibsen's play 'The Wild Duck' is presumably intended to confront Scottish falsity with the sternness of a European realism, but Ibsen's work has been so often performed in Scotland – and so often in Scots – over the last fifty years that he is almost an honorary Scottish writer. Scottish audiences would certainly have a more subtle conception of the ironies of Ibsen's 'saving lie' than O'Hagan's opposition implies. 'Ascherson's stones', he concludes, 'are interesting, they are not as interesting as people.'[27] But for Ascherson the special quality of the Scottish landscape is that it is an appropriate context for trying to find 'a new way to understand humanity's integral place in creation',[28] one that will replace a Faustian conception of humanity's dominating role in relation

---

[25] Andrew O'Hagan, 'A Beast of a Nation', *London Review of Books*, 31 October 2002, 12.

[26] Ibid., 11.

[27] Ibid., 12.

[28] Neal Ascherson, *Stone Voices: The Search for Scotland* (London: Granta, [2002] 2003), 29.

to its environment. Ascherson's meditation on Scotland's re-engagement with history through the establishment of its parliament is founded not on a recovery of Scottish history – though there is plenty of that in his book – but on a sense of Scotland that stretches beyond the boundaries of knowable history. Indeed, one of his starting points is a vision of Edinburgh from the Fife coast when 'you ought to see, straight across the water, the capital city of Edinburgh itself, the port of Leith and the coastal towns of East Lothian. But in certain lights a shadow effaces them all, and an almost uninhabited country is revealed over there.'[29] It is the moment when Scotland is 'out of history', a moment replicated in the structure of the new Museum of Scotland, in which, for Ascherson, the emphasis on 'objects' rather than narrative gives priority to the most ancient items:

> In the silence, the objects from before 1200 steal the show. Imagination flies straight to them, and stays there with the 'barbaric' jewellery, the undeciphered rock inscriptions, the stone faces with their narrow noses and bulging lentoid eyes, the vivid and yet utterly lost language of Pictish carved symbols. And yet this new rush into ancient identities cannot even claim to give Scotland a new 'when'. For almost all of them relate to times before Scotland had been invented.[30]

A Scotland which reaches beyond history is, for Ascherson, the foundation for a historical Scotland that will not be merely subservient to the needs of our current historical epoch nor determined by its economic priorities; its connection to values beyond those defined by the 'progress' of modern history will sculpt both its special character among nations and its potential offering to the world's future.

O'Hagan and Ascherson stand in confrontation, one demanding that Scotland re-enter the real history of the modern world, the other asking that it remain conscious of what lies beyond that history; one insisting that Scotland is out of history because it is trapped in the past; the other that it is out of history because it challenges the limitations within which modern history is understood. In trying to get beyond these confrontations we are faced by the fact that the key concepts by which we construct our historical past, such as 'nation', 'culture' and, indeed, 'identity', already come freighted with meanings in which England's historical experience has assumed a privileged

---

[29] Ibid., 28.
[30] Ibid., 45.

role – or with meanings which derive from the equally privileged role of contemporary 'theory' in France. As a result, the terms of our debates about Scotland's past are profoundly shaped by conceptual formulations which are reflections of these privileged traditions, traditions which are assumed to be somehow independent of the national contexts from which they derive.

The chapters of *Intending Scotland* are attempts, therefore, to rethink some of these fundamental formulations and their implications in Scottish culture. The chapters have three inter-related objectives. First, they explore certain cultural developments in Scotland since the eighteenth century – like the concept of the Scottish Enlightenment – and try to challenge the ways in which Scotland's cultural history has traditionally been described. Second, they test the development of contemporary theories of the nation and of national identity – such as Benedict Anderson's concept of 'imagined communities' – against Scottish experience. And, thirdly, they try to bring into focus neglected aspects of Scottish history – such as the Scottish contribution to the physics of energy – and try to extrapolate how these might help us understand other aspects of Scotland's cultural history. They therefore attempt to *tend* forgotten elements of Scotland's cultural past; and do so by focusing, in part, on the prominent place of *intention* in the development of modern Scottish thought, and on the nation as an outcome of our *intending*.

All history, of course, is written from the perspective of the present, and my concern with the nature of 'intention' and of 'agency' reflects the changed relationship of Scots to their political intentions that has been brought about by the agency of the Scottish parliament. Retrospectively, what this throws into relief is the extent to which, in the period when Scotland would seem to have been least in control of its national destiny, its most important philosophers and sociologists were deeply concerned with issues of intention and agency. It is nowadays assumed that to understand the eighteenth century in Scotland, historians have to have some understanding of the philosophical and social theories of Hume, Smith and Ferguson – of the intellectual achievements of the Scottish Enlightenment – but exactly the opposite assumption is made about the nineteenth and twentieth centuries – the philosophies of Edward Caird and A. S. Pringle-Pattison, or of Norman Kemp Smith and John Macmurray, (not to mention the theologies of Robert Flint or T. F. Torrance) go unmentioned in recent histories. And yet these were thinkers who not only exerted a powerful influence on the political decision-making of their own time but on the political thinking of subsequent generations of British politicians.[31] Their absence from contemporary histories of Scotland is indicative not only of a narrowing of the perspective of what counts as historically significant in the modern world but indicative, too, of a refusal to engage with what was culturally significant in modern Scottish history. The fact that a scientist such as James Clerk Maxwell, whose work constitutes the very foundations for everything that we, now, experience as modernity, barely merits mention in many of the major histories of Scotland of the last twenty years is symptomatic of how little of Scotland's real contribution to the modern world has actually become part of our contemporary conception of the Scottish past; the complete absence of its modern philosophers and social thinkers an indication of how etiolated is the conception of cultural significance in the perspectives of contemporary historiography.

The title, *Intending Scotland*, takes its place in what is now a considerable line of titles that have attached 'Scotland' to a present participle – David McCrone's *Understanding Scotland* (1992), Jonathan Hearn's *Claiming Scotland* (2000), Eleanor Bell's *Questioning Scotland* (2004) most notably. The need for the present continuous in such titles suggests the speed with which Scotland itself has been changing over the past thirty years, a speed that has demanded a regular updating of our conceptions of the nation – as, for instance, in the change of David McCrone's subtitle from 'the sociology of a stateless nation' in its first edition to 'the sociology of a nation' in later editions. 'Scotland' is a rapidly changing concept. As such, the ambiguity in these titles as to whether 'Scotland' is the object or the subject of its verb – whether we are engaged in *understanding* or *claiming* or *questioning* Scotland or whether it is indeed Scotland that is doing the understanding, claiming and questioning – underlines the extent to which 'Scotland' has become the site of a new agency (and a new urgency) since the recovery of its political narrative. Reading that agency back into the Scottish past, the chapters which follow are not a history but rather a prolegomena to a history, a series of excavations whose consequences are tested against some contemporary theories of the nation and against some recent accounts of the nature of Scottish culture. They are, therefore, like the devolutionary politics from which they emerge, provisional: part of a narrative whose implications we are only just beginning to discern.

---

[31] One of Kemp Smith's referees when he applied for the Edinburgh chair in philosophy was US President Woodrow Wilson; the influence of John Macmurray's Christian socialism on Tony Blair was briefly the topic of journalistic concern after the Labour victory in the 1997 general election.

1   In Tending Scotland

I   Delving for Scotland

In the autumn of 1966, Ian Hamilton Finlay and his wife Sue took over an abandoned croft in the Southern uplands of Scotland. For Finlay, a poet, short-story writer and editor, best known for his poems in Glasgow dialect, *Glasgow Beasts, an a Burd* (1961), and for the *avant garde* internationalism promoted by his journal *Poor. Old. Tired. Horse.*, the setting seemed an unlikely one. The croft was called Stonypath, a name all too appropriate to its environment, set as it was in a landscape of rough pasture that had been ravaged by two hundred years of grazing sheep. The Finlays' empty croft might have been an emblem of the Scotland which, even more dramatically than the rest of the UK, had declined from the 'workshop of the world' before the First World War to the 'sick man of Europe' after the Second. Uniquely, Scotland had the same population in 2000 as it had in 1900, a lack of growth matched by its low economic performance.[1] Abandoned crofts in the countryside, slums in the cities, identically endless housing estates in the suburbs: Scotland was Europe's 'hard case', a place where housing was worse than in the communist states of Eastern Europe, a place where inner-city deprivation was among the worst in Western Europe, a place as resistant to art as its climate was to fertility – a place recollected in 1999 in Andrew O'Hagan's *Our Fathers*:

> In my father's anger there was something of the nation. Everything torn from the ground; his mind like a rotten field. His country was a country of fearful men: proud in the talking, paltry in the living, and every promise another lie. My father bore all the dread that came with

---

[1] Finlay, *Modern Scotland*: 'from 1954 to 1965 Scotland's per capita GDP declined from 90.6 per cent to 88.4 per cent of the GDP of the United Kingdom', at a time when the UK economic performance 'was deemed to compare badly with that of other nations' (257–8).

the soil – unable to rise, or rise again, and slow to see the power in his own hands. Our fathers were made for grief. They were broken-backed. They were sick at heart, weak in the bones. All they wanted was the peace of defeat.[2]

A country incapable of growth, 'a rotten field' – like the croft that the Finlays took over, Scottish culture through much of the century was imaged as derelict. After the First World War it became a commonplace among cultural critics that Scotland was a place in which the garden of culture could not be made to flourish, and in which all growth was warped and deformed by a hostile environment. Hugh MacDiarmid's 'Scottish Renaissance' movement of the 1920s took as its slogan 'Not Burns, Dunbar', but the effort to reconnect with an earlier Scotland implied that the last real flowering of Scottish culture had been in the late middle ages – which is why the other slogan was 'Not traditions, precedents', since Scotland was a country which had failed the test of 'tradition'. The underlying implication of this failure of Scottish culture is clear in an essay of Neil Gunn's from the 1920s, challenging those who rejected MacDiarmid's agenda:

> Artistically in the modern world Scotland doesn't exist. No music, no drama, no letters, of any international significance. Why is this all-round sterility so complete, so without parallel in the life of any modern nation? Should not an honest attempt be made to answer that question before attacking the very movement that is trying to do so?[3]

Ireland had its 'Revival' but in Scotland it was a 'Renaissance' that was required – not a return to life but a completely new birth to displace the corpse which the nation had become. Hugh MacDiarmid launched his journal *The Voice of Scotland* in 1938 with the poem 'The Glen of Silence':

> Where have I "heard" a silence before
> Like this that only a lone bird's cries
> And the sound of a brawling burn today
> Serve in this desolate glen but to emphasize?

---

[2]   Andrew O'Hagan, *Our Fathers* (London: Faber and Faber, 1999), 8.
[3]   Neil Gunn, 'Defensio Scotorum', *Scots Magazine*, 1928; quoted from Alistair McCleery (ed.), *Landscape and Light: Essays by Neil Gunn* (Aberdeen: Aberdeen University Press, 1987), 150.

Every doctor knows it – the stillness of foetal death,
The indescribable silence over the abdomen then!
A silence literally "heard" because of the way
It stands out in the auscultation of the abdomen.

Here is an identical silence picked out
By a bickering burn and lone bird's wheeple
– The foetal death in this great "cleared" glen…

Not only the culture of the Highlands had died, however: the Scottish nation, too, was dead, its death inscribed in the makar's tongue in which it had last been fully alive:

Set in golden letteris then this ressoun
"Pride of Earth's landis, Scotland, Europe's croun,
Sumtyme countit the floo'er of Nationheid
Under this stane, late lipper, lyis deid."[4]

For MacDiarmid, Scotland represented 'The tragedy of an unevolved people', where 'everything is morbid, hopeless and inert'.[5]

It was a theme which was to be taken up by major accounts of Scottish literature from the 1940s to the 1960s. John Speirs's *The Scots Literary Tradition* (1940), for instance, had begun as a series of articles in *Scrutiny*, the journal founded by F. R. Leavis, and Speirs approached writers in Scots by testing them against the Leavisite standard of the quality of their language, 'both locally and as a cumulative organic whole'.[6] Speirs's aim was to reveal potentialities in early Scots poetry that were missing in conceptions of poetry as they had developed in nineteenth-century romanticism – a regular target of Leavisite indignation – but what his analyses actually demonstrated was the inevitable degeneration of poetry in Scots: Dunbar's is 'a poetry that is medieval and European and at the same time Scots',[7] while Burns is 'provincial in

---

[4] *The Voice of Scotland*, Vol. I, No. 1 (1938), 1, 3; the final quotation is from Robert Henryson's 'The Testament of Cresseid', with Scotland substituting for Cresseid.

[5] Ibid., 1–2.

[6] John Speirs, *The Scots Literary Tradition* (London: Chatto and Windus, 1940), 150.

[7] Ibid., 152.

comparison' – not because of Burns's own character but because 'the Scotland of Burns no longer formed part of the European background',[8] and Hugh MacDiarmid 'is a forlorn and isolated figure, the European background having vanished, and Scotland with it'.[9] Twenty years later, David Craig's *Scottish Literature and the Scottish People, 1680–1830* (1961) saw the story of the whole of Scotland's culture in the same terms that Speirs had seen its poetry:

> This glorification of Scotland's 'Golden Age' does not explain the cultural impasse which followed: the use of the native language became embarrassed, poetry ran shallow and dried up, the novel was provincial from the start, many of the most original minds emigrated. Hence the historian is left calling Victorian culture in Scotland '*strangely* rootless', whereas a more critical sense of the eighteenth century would have seen that some sort of disintegration was already visible even in the best Scots poetry and in the way the language was being used.[10]

In this construction, the major figures of the Scottish tradition have to be revealed – in Edwin Muir's phrase from his poem 'Scotland 1941' – as 'sham bards of a sham nation'. Muir traced this national failure to what he saw as its source in his account of John Knox, whose life becomes for Muir a synecdoche of the culture which he 'fathered':

> The life of John Knox is broken in two. For the first forty years we can vaguely discern a devout Catholic; for the next twenty-seven we see another character, with the same name, the same appearance, and probably the same affections and passions, but with entirely different opinions. This new figure is born at the age of forty, and seems to have no ancestry. For Knox left no record either of his early life or of his conversion: the one is like an absolute event which had existed from eternity, the other is as if it had never been.[11]

Scotland, like Knox, does not 'develop': its history is broken by the Reformation and as a consequence it has no 'tradition' and its major artists are deformed

---

[8] Ibid., 153.
[9] Ibid., 153.
[10] David Craig, *Scottish Literature and the Scottish People, 1680–1830* (London: Chatto and Windus, 1961), 13.
[11] Edwin Muir, *John Knox : Portrait of a Calvinist* (London: Cape, 1929), 11.

by the lack of one. For MacDiarmid, Burns may be 'the most powerful lyrical poet the world has ever seen', but only in order to underscore how Scotland itself was responsible for distorting and repressing that genius:

> It is in keeping with the cultural history of Scotland that such a Pegasus should have had to work in double harness with the clumsiest of cart-horses, that Burns's wonderful power of song should have been so prosaically shackled, that his unique gift should have had to manifest itself behind such an irrelevant array of trite platitudinisation. And it is in keeping too with the cultural history of Scotland that even yet he should be most esteemed for the orthodox externalities of his work, for all that is irrelevant to, most opaque to, and most disfiguring of his genius rather than for the essence of that genius in itself.[12]

These words of the 1920s were to be reasserted thirty years later when MacDiarmid published, in *The Voice of Scotland*, an essay by David Craig on 'Burns and Scottish Culture':

> In a culture so thin and so badly placed as the Scottish there were few conflicts in society that did not lead to waste and confusion. Much of the national spirit, often in rabid form, went into the Low Kirk religion, but its spirit…was irreconcilable with the cultivated ethos…it led directly to the Disruption of 1843. This is another of the deep dis-unities which ran off the energies of 18th century Scotland into dispute and partisan bitterness, anyway characteristic of the race, which made for a stultifying monotony of idiom, religious, political, poetic,–an inhumane extreme of partiality, in which positions defined themselves more by violence of opposition than by their positive natures.[13]

And Muir, famously, summed up the condition of Scotland by attributing to it the failure of Walter Scott, his 'enormous genius' warped by the fact that 'he spent most of his days in a hiatus, in a country, that is to say which was neither a nation nor a province, and had, instead of a centre, a blank, an Edinburgh, in the middle of it'.[14]

---

[12] Hugh MacDiarmid, *Contemporary Scottish Studies* (Edinburgh: *Scottish Educational Journal,* n.d.), 114.

[13] *The Voice of Scotland*, Vol. VII, Nos. 3–4 (October 1956–January 1957), 28.

[14] Edwin Muir, *Scott and Scotland* (London: Routledge, 1936), 11.

And yet, twenty years after the Finlays moved into their derelict croft, the desolate hillside around Stonypath had been transformed into a garden rich not only in flowers and shrubbery and trees but in statuary and inscriptions—'a garden of ideas and poetry', as Jessie Sheeler describes it, 'a hidden oasis of fruitfulness and refreshment'.[15] It was a transformation of the landscape that equalled in its radicalism—in going, quite literally, to the root—the choice of a Scottish poet, in the late twentieth century, to make a garden the focus of his creative endeavour. A modern Scottish poet in welly boots, wheeling a barrow, would have seemed as likely as a poet returning to rhyming couplets in the manner of Alexander Pope.

Forty years earlier, however, another Scottish writer, the novelist John Buchan, had envisaged a similar transformation of the landscape where the Finlays were working: his novel *Witchwood* (1927) opens with a scene in which twentieth-century Scotland, dominated by 'the colliery headgear on the horizon, the trivial Moorish hill-tops, the dambrod pattern fields', suddenly gives way to a vision of the place as it would have been three hundred years earlier: 'bounded and pressed in upon by something vast and dark, which clothed the tops of all but the highest hills, muffled the ridges, choked the glens and overflowed almost to the edge of the waters', the village is surrounded by 'that most ancient forest where once Merlin harped and Arthur mustered his men'.[16] The Finlays' garden enacts in material reality the transformation that Buchan's novel had imaginatively invoked—the recovery of a Scotland not yet despoiled, still forested. In the eighteenth century Scotland's treelessness had been regularly noted by travellers such as Samuel Johnson: 'From the bank of the Tweed to St. Andrews I had never seen a single tree, which I did not believe to have grown up within the present century…The variety of sun and shade is here utterly unknown. There is no tree for either shelter or timber. The oak and the thorn is equally a stranger, and the whole country is extended in uniform nakedness.'[17] This very nakedness, however, was already being celebrated at the time of Johnson's tour in the 1770s as one of the

---

[15] Jessie Sheeler, *Little Sparta: The Garden of Ian Hamilton Finlay* (London: Frances Lincoln, 2003), 11.

[16] John Buchan, *Witchwood* (Edinburgh: Canongate, [1927] 1988), 1. For the mythic nature of this forest see T. C. Smout, *Nature Contested: Environmental History in Scotland and Northern England since 1600* (Edinburgh: Edinburgh University Press, 2000), Ch. 2.

[17] Ian McGowan (ed.), *Journey to the Hebrides* (Edinburgh: Canongate, 1996), Samuel Johnson, *A Journey to the Western Islands of Scotland* (1775), 8.

essential features that made the Scottish highlands such a dramatic experience to its visitors:

> Long tracts of mountainous desert, covered with dark heath, and often obscured by misty weather; narrow vallies, thinly inhabited, and bounded by precipices resounding with the fall of torrents; a soil so rugged, and a climate so dreary, as in many parts to admit neither the amusements of pasturage, nor the labours of agriculture…a lonely region, full of echoes, and rocks, and caverns.[18]

James Beattie's description emphasises both the emptiness of the Highlands and its resistance to human appropriation in an aesthetic that Peter Womack has dubbed the 'negative sublime', and traced to James Macpherson's Ossianic poems of the 1760s.[19] The 'paucity of imagery' in Ossian's poetry was justified by Macpherson's supporter, Hugh Blair, as appropriate to 'the desert uncultivated state of the country, which suggested to him few images beyond natural inanimate objects in their rudest form'.[20] The aesthetic interest of this 'desert' Scotland intensified as it was made increasingly more empty by clearance and by emigration, and long after the romantic taste for 'The Land of Mountain and of Flood'[21] had been reduced to cliché, the effort to confront and master this 'negative sublime' remained a powerful imperative for Scottish artists. Edwin Muir's *Scottish Journey* of 1935, for instance, encounters the Highlands as a place where 'there was not a human habitation in sight [and not] in all the expanse of tree-less deer forest could I see a single movement to betray the presence of a living creature';[22] and it reaches its climax in a vision of the highest mountains as inducing 'the same feeling one might have if one could have a glimpse of an eternal world, such as the world of mathematics, which had no relation to our human feelings, but was composed of certain shapes which existed in complete and changeless autonomy'.[23] And many of Hugh MacDiarmid's greatest meditative poems

---

[18] James Beattie, *Essays on Poetry and Music*, 3rd edn (1779), 169.

[19] Peter Womack, *Improvement and Romance* (London: Macmillan, 1989), 78.

[20] Hugh Blair, 'A Critical Dissertation on the Poems of Ossian', in Howard Gaskell (ed.), *The Poems of Ossian and Related Works* (Edinburgh: Edinburgh University Press, 1996), 384.

[21] Hamish MacCunn's orchestral work of this title, taken from Walter Scott's 'The Lay of the Last Minstrel', was first produced in 1887.

[22] Edwin Muir, *Scottish Journey* (Edinburgh: Mainstream, [1935] 1979), 214.

[23] Ibid., 213.

are engaged, precisely, with such a 'negative sublime', whether focused on the emptiness of mountain tops or the barrenness of raised beaches.

Buchan's vision in *Witchwood* of an earlier, forested Scotland opposed the tradition of the 'negative sublime' with an alternative version of Scotland as a place of fertile *excess* rather than awe-inspiring deprivation, as a place where nature is threateningly abundant rather than stultifyingly impoverished. A Scotland characterised by fertility rather than lack, by propagation rather than barrenness was a Scotland with a very different history – and therefore with a very different future potential – from the Scotland of noble savagery amidst stark scarcity which had come to be so valued by the European imagination.

This vision of Scotland as overflowing with aboriginal woodland was not, however, simply inspired by tales of an ancient Caledonian forest but was in part a response to a new and influential theory of art history that had been proposed by Wilhelm Worringer in his *Formprobleme der Gotik (Form in Gothic)*, first published in 1918 and translated in the year of *Witchwood*'s composition by Herbert Read, briefly a lecturer at the University of Edinburgh. For Worringer, Gothic was the natural form of northern European art, because its sweeping columns and patterned roofs represented the sculptured equivalent of the vast forests in which northern European culture had originally developed and which still shaped the psychology of Northern European artists. Just as Buchan's historical novel was a return, in the 1920s, to the form that Scott had initiated in the 1810s, Scotland's nineteenth-century Gothic literature – given sculptural form in the monument to Walter Scott in Edinburgh's Princes Street Gardens – could be envisaged as the ghostly exhalation of its once-forested landscape that had been so conspicuously removed to create the very 'Athens of the North' in which Scott's Gothic monument was sited.

The opposition between the neo-classical of Edinburgh's New Town and the Gothic of Scott's and Buchan's fiction is one which Worringer himself would have seen as an opposition between culture and nature, between imitative artifice and aboriginal fertility, and it is tempting to see Finlay's garden as a place which has allowed the natural to flourish again, but it is precisely such oppositions that Finlay's garden is designed to challenge. Since Adam and Eve's expulsion from Eden, gardens have often symbolised a place of recovered natural fertility,[24] but what Finlay's garden emphasises is that

---

[24] See Andrew Cunningham, 'The Culture of Gardens', in N. Jardine, J. A. Secord and E. C. Spray, *Cultures of Natural History* (Cambridge: Cambridge University Press, 1996), 38ff.

gardens are the artifice of nature; they flourish because of human intervention, and their richness comes from the cultivation of plants that are not natural to the place. Scotland's early gardens, like David Lyndsay's at Edzell Castle, imported their designs from Italy and from France, their plants from Holland and from the Mediterranean, and, possibly, a symbolism from the memory systems of Giulio Camillo's 'Theatre of Memory'.[25] A garden may be a place *of* nature but it is not a place *in* nature, which is why Finlay's garden, like those on which it is modelled, is full of statuary, of inscriptions, and of natural things *named* in order to emphasise their incorporation into a human environment: inscribed stones declare that what one is encountering is 'The Shady Grove, The Murmuring Stream'; trees stand behind sculpted plaques with the names of historical figures – Michelet, Corot – with whom they are to be associated; and carved into the bar of a gate is the word 'picturesque', at once defining and questioning how we are to respond to the landscape it looks on to.[26]

Finlay's tree-filled landscape is dedicated not to an aboriginal Gothic, nor to the rational neo-classicism of the 'Athens of the North': it is designed to recall the gardens of the gods in classical Greece and Rome. It is dedicated to a classicism rich in the protean myths that Socratic rationalism would have banished from the ideal Republic: 'as they gazed in astonishment, and wept for the fate of their people, their old cottage, which had been small, even for two, was changed into a temple: marble columns took the place of its wooden supports, the thatch grew yellow, till the roof seemed to be made of gold.'[27] But it is a classicism in history rather than in nature, a classicism which, if still in touch with the primitive powers of nature, nonetheless translates them into modernity: 'To Apollo: His Music: His Missiles: His Muses' is the inscription on the front of the 'temple' which Finlay created from one of the outbuildings of the croft. The garden is a place of transformation of the past into the present, a place of re-enactment in which the past becomes present. Just as individual gardens re-enact themselves in the annual cycle of growth and decay, so the Finlays' garden-as-art is a scene of historical re-enactment in which contemporary Stonypath becomes an ancient 'Little Sparta', the site of Finlay's long-running defiance of the bureaucracy of

[25] See Sheila Mackay, *Early Scottish Gardens: A Writer's Odyssey* (Edinburgh: Polygon, 2001), 120ff.

[26] See Sheeler, *Little Sparta*, 79, 96, 110.

[27] Quoted from Ovid's *Metamorphoses*, Book VIII, in Yves Abrioux, *Ian Hamilton Finlay: A Visual Primer* (London: Reaktion Books, [1985] 1992), 19.

Strathclyde Region,[28] and a place in which the memory of a classical and Mediterranean Arcadia blossomed in defiance of its northerly as well as its political location. In its change of name, Finlay's croft announces itself as devoted to the rich magic of translation: a Scottish croft transformed into a Greek temple symbolically repeating the cultural translation that allows the Mediterranean laurel (*laurus nobilis*) – used in classical times to honour poetic achievement – to flourish in Scottish gardens.

The rapidity of the transformation achieved by Finlay's garden might be taken as a metaphor of the transformation of Scotland itself in the same period. Between 1966, when the Finlays moved into their abandoned croft, and October 2004, when the Scottish parliament moved into its new, purpose-built and award-winning building, Scotland was a nation translated from provincial decline and decay into a place of internationally recognised creative fertility. In poetry, in the novel, in the visual arts, in music and in popular culture, the 70s, 80s, and 90s in Scotland saw an explosion of creative activity that was deeply rooted in the local (the Glasgow of Alasdair Gray's *Lanark* or the Edinburgh of Ian Rankin's Rebus series), in the vernacular (from Liz Lochhead's plays to Irvine Welsh's *Trainspotting*), and in the invocation of Scottish traditions (from the music of Runrig to Calum Colvin's Ossian exhibition).

These were testimony to a culture as flourishing as the Finlays' garden, and along with it went a radical rewriting of the nation's past that challenged the notion of a failed tradition. In Alexander Broadie's *The Tradition of Scottish Philosophy* (1990), the Enlightenment was presented as the outcome of a Scottish philosophical tradition stretching back to the medieval Scottish philosophers Duns Scotus and John Major; in Duncan Macmillan's *Scottish Art 1460–1990* (1990), visual art in Scotland was seen as the unfolding of a communal vision rooted in the Reformation; in John Purser's *Scotland's Music* (1992) the Scottish musical tradition of the pre-Reformation period was recovered and reconnected with modern Scottish music; and in the *History of Scottish Literature* (1987–9) which I edited, the continuities rather than the discontinuities of writing in Gaelic, Latin, Scots and English were insisted upon. This renewed sense of Scottish traditions which had resisted all efforts to reduce the nation to dereliction was to be raised in stone when the new Royal Museum of Scotland was opened, inviting its visitors to connect the

---

[28] Strathclyde Region refused to acknowledge that Finlay's garden contained a religious 'temple' which therefore exempted it from the payment of the local taxation known as the 'rates'.

Declaration of Arbroath of 1320 at its doorway with the bric-a-brac of contemporary Scotland on its upper floor. The political breakthrough of the Devolution Referendum of 1997, reversing that of 1979 and leading to the establishment of the Scottish parliament, was no more than the belated acknowledgment that Scotland had already declared cultural independence. When Tom Devine's *The Scottish Nation 1700–2000* became a best-seller in 1999, its title was a confident assertion of both the survival and the Scottishness of the nation whose passage through the Union, as through industrialisation and de-industrialisation, it charted.

The derelict nation, 'the rotten field', had become a nation tended and flourishing. But gardens decay: 'Gardens, it is true, are republics', Finlay writes, 'but they are also, alas, Empires, which wax and wane.'[29] Gardens need to be turned over, replanted, weeded if they are to continue to flourish. Gardens not only have to be tended but have to be constantly *in*tended, the labour of each season being directed towards the intended outcomes of the next. Because it is maintained only by our active intention, by our constant tending, nothing decays as quickly as an untended garden.

II   The Scottish Garden

To choose a *garden* as one's artistic statement for the last decades of the twentieth century was a challenge both to the history of art – to which gardens had become increasingly irrelevant – and to the history of gardens – dedicated to the domestic virtues of the 'beautiful' rather than the ultimate aesthetic challenge of the 'sublime'. As William Howard Adams has suggested, 'The garden as a work of art, an aesthetic composition beyond the pursuit of horticulture, therapy or extravagance in support of power, has all but disappeared from the modern world'.[30] Indeed, modern art, as initiated in the twentieth century by the cubism of Picasso and Braque or by the architecture of Le Corbusier, was founded on a rejection of the forms of the natural world as the basis of the forms of art. As an early critic of modernism put it:

---

[29] Ian Hamilton Finlay, 'More Detached Sentences on Gardening', *Proposal for a Garden Built on a Slope* (Edinburgh: Morning Star Publications, 1991).

[30] Quoted in Stephanie Ross, *What Gardens Mean* (Chicago: University of Chicago Press, 1998), 189, from William Howard Adams, *Nature Perfected: Gardens through History* (New York: Abbeville Press, 1991), 329.

It is in the garden that the modernist finds himself stuck. That is where his interpretation of functionalism breaks down. Walls, steps, balustrades, and pavements – even hedges and windscreens – are functional features that may be treated as such. Nobody will dispute my statement, however, that most of the garden that we see is pure decoration for its own sake…We need only once glance at the modernist's pitiful attempts out of doors to know that he is stuck. In most cases he has thrown up his hand and done nothing…[31]

Modernism was an art in search of a time-transcending, time-defying fixity – the 'abstract', the 'image', the 'epiphany', the 'verbal icon', Eliot's 'stillness, as a Chinese jar still/Moves perpetually in its stillness'[32] – but a garden is necessarily an art in motion, a procession through time, an assertion not of art's sublime transcendence of nature but of its continuity with the natural world. As John Dixon Hunt has expressed it:

Art, it is claimed, transcends time; yet garden art, supremely vulnerable to the depradations of time, must actually invoke time in its most successful creations – time in which plants, shrubs and trees may grow, seasonal change which alters the whole appearance of a garden four times a year, and even the length of time during which the full extent of a garden's riches is discovered by its visitor.[33]

The garden is a work of time – indeed, it is the product of continuous work *in time* – but it is precisely this submission to temporality that has undermined the 'garden' as an object of significant aesthetic value in an era when modernism committed itself to non-natural abstract forms.

Finlay's garden is thus a work of defiance: gardens may traditionally invoke the world of 'nature' when set over against the built environment of our urban spaces but, as one of Finlay's 'Unconnnected Sentences on Gardening' prompts us, 'Certain gardens are described as retreats when they

---

[31] H. B. Dunnington-Grubb, 'Modernismus Arrives in the Garden – To Stay?', quoted in Dorothée Imbert, *The Modernist Garden in France* (New Haven: Yale University Press, 1993).

[32] T. S. Eliot, *Collected Poems 1909–1962* (London: Faber and Faber, 1963), 194.

[33] John Dixon Hunt, *Garden and Grove: The Italian Renaissance Garden in the English Imagination: 1600–1750* (London: Dent, 1986), 90.

are really attacks.'[34] To fulfil its attack on modernism's separation of art and nature, Finlay's garden is a recollection of the history of European gardens: from its Roman and Greek gardens to its allusions to those arts which tried to capture in permanent form the passing shape of gardens, as in the images from *Nature Over Again After Poussin* (1979), Finlay's is a meta-garden, able to contain and to mimic the whole history of the European culture of gardens – all of it *taking place* under a Scottish sky and in a Scottish climate. The ability to produce and *reproduce* the traditions of European temple gardens becomes, in itself, a defiant image of the fertility and productivity of Scottish soil and the potential of Scottish landscape, on whose northern flourishing is *grafted* the classical culture of the Mediterranean.

In accounts of Finlay's garden the northernness of its environment is almost always presented as hostile: it is an enemy to be overcome. The garden is not natural to a place like Scotland, and that an art-garden like Finlay's should appear in Scotland can only be an accident of individual genius. As Charles Jencks puts it,

> These literary gardens [in China], in which calligraphy and poetic inscription play such a key role, are so close to his own in spirit that they might have inspired Little Sparta, had Finlay not first responded to Western, eighteenth-century classical gardens, to Stowe and Stourhead, with their Temple of Ancient Virtue and Pantheon. His model is actually the idyllic Roman campagna, reconstituted in Scottish vernacular and cow-byres.[35]

The models of gardening to which Finlay's work is connected are always 'elsewhere' – that this is a *Scottish* garden tended by a *Scottish* gardener is incidental rather than fundamental; and if, as Finlay insists, 'Garden sculpture ought to have roots, as garden plants do',[36] Finlay's own roots must be envisaged as reaching tentacularly beyond Scotland through European culture to classical sources rather than being rooted in Scotland itself. But as Murdo MacDonald has pointed out, classicism was the mode of Scotland's eighteenth-century art, and the 'ploughman poet' who is Scotland's national

---

[34] Quoted in Abrioux, *Ian Hamilton Finlay*, 40.

[35] Charles Jencks, 'Aphorisms on the Garden of an Aphorist', in Alec Finlay (ed.), *Wood Notes Wild: Essays on the Poetry and Art of Ian Hamilton Finlay* (Edinburgh: Polygon, 1995), 108.

[36] Finlay, 'More Detached Sentences on Gardening'.

bard was not an identity created especially for Burns: 'It has a long history and relates as much to the classical conception of the rural as it does to eighteenth-century Scotland. It links Burns to the Roman poet Virgil.'[37] Far from being an isolated gesture, Finlay's recuperation of classicism connects his work to a Scottish tradition which sees Scottish nature as a home for classical virtues, and in which Burns, far from being the poet of a sentimental ruralism, is in fact not only the inheritor of but a modern representative of classical traditions.

This much was evident to the gathering which met in the Freemason's Tavern in London in 1819 to commemorate Burns's work and to raise funds for a national memorial to him, for the only monument appropriate to his poetic status was a classical temple:

> as a Monument to BURNS, the Committee should think proper to select and restore some one of those ancient works which have excited the enthusiastic admiration of all ages, it would associate with the memory of our favourite Poet, all that is refined and beautiful in art. One such Building, placed on the Calton-hill, might lead to the erection of others, until it should become the Acropolis of the Northern Athens, and Edinburgh be called the City of Temples and of Taste.[38]

If we picture Burns as the classical pastoral poet of a new Athens, then Finlay's classicism can be seen to derive from the central tradition of eighteenth-century Scottish poetry that runs from Allan Ramsay's *The Gentle Shepherd* to Burns's 'The Vision' and 'The Cotter's Saturday Night'. And if, for Finlay, 'Jacobinism is a form of pastoral',[39] then Burns's radical politics, in which Jacobitism can be a cover for Jacobinism, would be the logical outcome of his role as 'rustic Bard'. Those who have recently (re-)read Burns's poetry as the product of a potentially revolutionary Jacobin have, in effect, been reading him as precursor of Hamilton Finlay, whose temple of the muses

---

[37] Murdo MacDonald, 'Wood Notes Wild: A Tale of Claude', in Finlay (ed.), *Wood Notes Wild*, 128.

[38] Festival in Commemoration of Robert Burns; and to promote a subscription to erect a National Monument to his Memory at Edinburgh: held at the Freemason's Tavern in London, on Saturday, 5 June, 1819 (London: printed by B. McMillan, Bow-Street, Covent-Garden, Printer to His Royal Highness the Prince Regent). The proposal was made by Andrew Robertson.

[39] Finlay, 'More Detached Sentences on Gardening'.

is dedicated to the ultimate sign of the Revolution – the guillotine.[40] The ploughman poet who turns over the earth is, in the punning imagery of Finlay's 'Autumn Poem' (1966), already engaged in revolution:

> Turn
> -ing
> o-
> ver
>
> the
> earth

These lines are set in a faded square of earth clods and leaves, while below them, in a circle that looks like cloud and land on an earth seen from space, are inscribed:

> the
> earth
>
> turn
> -ing
> o-
> ver[41]

It is the revolution of the earth that makes the garden possible but the gardener's turning over of the earth each year is itself a model for *revolution*. That is why, for Finlay, 'Garden Centres must become the Jacobin Clubs of the new Revolution'.[42] Gardens are havens of peace based on permanent revolution, revolution carried out in acts of violence – pruning, shearing, uprooting – which have their historical correlate in Finlay's image of the guillotine as a trellis over which honeysuckle is growing, and under which we are informed, 'Both the garden style called "sentimental", and the French

[40] See, for instance, the 'Introduction' to Andrew Noble and Patrick Scott Hogg (eds), *The Canongate Burns* (Edinburgh: Canongate, 2001), and Liam McIlvanney, *Burns the Radical: Poetry and Politics in Late Eighteenth-Century Scotland* (East Linton: Tuckwell Press, 2002).
[41] Abrioux, *Ian Hamilton Finlay*, 280.
[42] Ibid.

Revolution, grew from Rousseau. The garden trellis and the guillotine are alike entwined with the honeysuckle of the new "sensibility".[43] For Finlay, the nation – whether it be the United States, France, Scotland, Ireland or England – is as rooted in the garden of revolution as it is in the revolution of the garden.

Finlay's garden may represent a revolutionary achievement in modern art, but what the intersection between Finlay's art and Burns's brings into prominence is not only a classicism that has been domesticated and become 'native' to Scotland, but a tradition of the garden as a key mode of Scottish artistic expression. Finlay is fond of populating his gardens and his designs for public spaces with sundials – there is one in the town square at Biggar, and one in the Royal Botanic Garden in Edinburgh[44] – but these sundials are not merely reminders of a pre-mechanical, natural temporality: they recollect a crucial moment in the recovery of the tradition of the Scottish garden. In 1883, Thomas Ross conducted a survey of Scottish sundials, and in his view these now freestanding sundials were 'among the most important class of monumental object bequeathed to this century by the seventeenth century and it is only when we come to realise how numerous they are and that many of them are fine works of artistic and scientific skill that we perceive how widespread must have been the appreciation of the sculptor's art as combined with that of the landscape gardener'.[45] Ross's sundials have been used as an indicator of the number of early Scottish gardens which have disappeared or been overbuilt, and as testimony to a Scottish culture which, in the seventeenth and early eighteenth centuries, did not identify Scotland with a sublimely barren and nobly savage landscape but with its ornate, productive and well-tended gardens. In 1600 Henri Duc de Rohan was surprised by the fact that there were a hundred country seats within a two-league radius of Edinburgh and in 1661 Jorevin de Rocheford noted the large garden filled with fruit trees near to Glasgow University.[46]

Far from being 'desert', Scotland's was a well-tended landscape and, as Patrick Geddes was to insist in the context of trying to revitalise the Old Town of Edinburgh in the 1890s, its urban architecture had, until population growth squeezed them out, always included gardens. James Gordon of

---

[43] Ibid., 275.

[44] Ibid., 232ff.

[45] Forbes W. Robertson, *Early Scottish Gardeners and their Plants 1650–1750* (East Linton: Tuckwell Press, 2000), 144–5.

[46] Ibid., 11.

Rothiemay's 'Bird's Eye View of Edinburgh' (1647), for instance, shows the city's famous tenements not as a cluster of stone structures defiantly resisting the world of nature, but as thrusting skywards from their roots in formal gardens. Despite all the aspersions on its climate and on its treeless, desert condition, Scotland, it appears, has always been a country of gardens and gardeners.

It is a tradition whose significance can be traced in the life of one of Burns's contemporaries, Thomas Blaikie, born at Corstorphine in 1751. Blaikie's father was a market gardener, supplying fruit and vegetables to Edinburgh at a time when it was, in Tobias Smollett's famous gardening phrase, a 'hot-bed of genius' ('hot-beds' being boxes with deep layers of manure to generate heat and bring on plants not native to the Scottish climate). Blaikie seems to have trained at Edinburgh's Botanic Garden,[47] originally developed from the 'physic garden' of Holyrood House, and then moved on to London's Kew Gardens, whose role as a botanic garden was inspired by the botanic interests of John Stuart, the Third Earl of Bute (1713–92), prime minister to George III. It was Bute who established Kew Gardens as a centre of botanic knowledge – his own contributions included the nine-volume *Botanical Tables Containing the Families of British Plants* (1785), published at a cost of some £12,000 and containing 654 hand-coloured plates – and, as in so many other areas of political patronage, he employed a Scot, William Aiton (1731–93), as director. Aiton had previously worked at the Chelsea Physic Garden which had been overseen for many years by another Scot, Philip Miller (1691–1771), who was said to be resented by local London workmen for his inclination to employ fellow Scots. The Chelsea garden under Miller developed one of the richest collections of plants in Europe and, under Aiton, Kew established itself as the pre-eminent botanic garden in Britain.

Blaikie's work at Kew led to his being chosen by Joseph Banks, Aiton's successor and President of the Royal Society, to collect plant specimens in the Alps: 'So well does the Seriousness of a Scotch Education fit the mind of a Scotsman to the habits of industry, attention and frugality', wrote Banks, 'that they rarely abandon them at any time of life and I may say never while they are young.'[48] Banks had previously chosen another Scot, Francis Masson,

---

[47]   Patricia Taylor, *Thomas Blaikie: The 'Capability' Brown of France* (East Linton: Tuckwell Press, 2001), 11ff.

[48]   Quoted in Taylor, *Thomas Blaikie*, from H. C. Cameron, *Sir Joseph Banks* (London: Angus and Robertson, 1966), 100, fn. 52.

to undertake the collection of plants in South Africa,[49] but his choice of Blaikie was at the particular recommendation of another Scotsman, James Lee of the Vineyard Nursery, Hammersmith, who, with his partner Lewis Kennedy, ran the most influential nursery in London, introducing around 135 new plants to cultivation in England.[50] So important was the firm of Lee and Kennedy to the transmission of plants from around the world that they continued to trade with the Empress Josephine during the Napoleonic wars, and the strength of the firm's French connections resulted in Blaikie's return to France in 1776 with plants for the Comte de Lauragais, an introduction which was then to lead to his spending the rest of life in France and becoming the country's foremost landscape designer.

Noted for his skill in grafting trees – his technique came to be known as the *greffe Blaikie* – Blaikie was responsible for grafting the 'jardin paysage' (ironically to become more commonly known as the *jardin anglais*) on to French culture,[51] and such was his prominence that he became not only a confidante of Marie Antoinette before the Revolution but, in its aftermath, worked on the design of the Empress Josephine's favourite country retreat at Malmaison. In between, Blaikie was both a witness to the events of the French Revolution and threatened with Revolutionary justice, and yet continued to be employed by the French élite, whether the new élite of Napoleon's Empire or, after 1815, by the restored aristocrats of the Bourbon monarchy. Blaikie's and Finlay's gardens, therefore, form strange mirror images to one another: Blaikie promotes a garden which is apparently 'natural' but which forms the backdrop to a French Revolution that sees itself as the re-enactment of classical prototypes; Finlay's classical garden, dedicated to the foregrounding of artifice, has at its centre a 'temple' dedicated to that same Revolution as a product of the new philosophy of 'nature'.

The connections which took Blaikie to France reveal how important gardens and gardeners were in Scotland between the sixteenth and the nineteenth centuries, and underline their ability to find work not only in England

---

[49] See John MacKenzie, *The Scots in South Africa* (Johannesburg: Wits University Press, 2007), 31 ff.

[50] Taylor, *Thomas Blaikie*, 16. Lee actually turned Blaikie down for another assignment, that of accompanying Captain Cook on his last voyage to the Pacific, a post which went to another Scottish botanist, David Nelson.

[51] His biographer, Patricia Taylor, describes him as the '"Capability" Brown of France' but this underestimates the extent to which the 'jardin anglais' was also the 'jardin écossais'.

but across Europe. The neglect of the cultural impact of Scotland's gardeners has allowed historians to assume that early modern Scotland was a country more or less without gardens: '…travellers' tales of the half-century after the Restoration continue to tell of a rough and hard way of life…the equivalent of the smaller type of English manor house or parsonage with its often productive and interesting garden scarcely existed.'[52] And it has encouraged the assumption that Scotland's climate imposed on its population the most limited natural fare, both nutritional and visual. And yet the flow of Scottish gardeners to England – in the mid-eighteenth century a society was established by English gardeners who pledged to refuse employment to Scots[53] – suggests that there were plenty of opportunities for Scots gardeners to become skilled in their profession in Scotland. And Blaikie was by no means the only Scottish gardener in France: indeed, Alexander Howatson, from Leadhills in Lanarkshire, who was head gardener at Malmaison, had been previously employed by the revolutionary government to maintain the hothouses formerly belonging to the Duc d'Orléans. The training for such gardeners, as Forbes W. Robertson has shown, came from 'a very large number of country houses, castles and seats occupied by the gentry in Scotland', the great majority of which 'were embellished with gardens, orchards, "yeards" and often avenues',[54] and those gardeners' success in England was noted by Andrew Carlisle who, on a tour of English estates in 1758, 'discovered the truth of what I have often heard that most of the head gardeners of English noblemen were Scotch'.[55]

Having left in 1776, Blaikie did not return to Scotland till 1822 – the year in which George IV made his (in)famous visit to a tartan-clad Edinburgh, orchestrated by Walter Scott. Much has been made of George IV's visit as a symbol of the falsity of the culture with which Sir Walter invested Scotland, but much more significant as an image of Scottish culture is the celebration of Blaikie's return, dined by 200 members of the Caledonian Horticultural Society, and presented with a bound copy of the *Memoirs of the Caledonian Society*.[56] Those members of the Society were the people who were *tending* the Scottish land, rather than, like George IV, merely attending their Scottish lands. And unlike George, it had always been Blaikie's intention to return

---

[52] Quoted in Mackay, *Early Scottish Gardens*, 1.
[53] Ibid., 12.
[54] Robertson, *Early Scottish Gardeners*, 143.
[55] Ibid., 188.
[56] Taylor, *Thomas Blaikie*, 218.

to Scotland, to take up again his father's gardening business and to share in his tending of a Scottish garden. It was an intention defeated in the end by the fact that his French government pension could not be transferred out of France, but in compensation he became, in his old age, a correspondent of an offshoot of the Caledonian Society, *The Gardener's Magazine*, edited by the Scottish landscape gardener and architect, John Claudius Loudon (1783–1843), whose influence over public taste in gardens and houses in Victorian Britain was as great as Blaikie's in France – so much so that his biographer chose as the title of his biography, *Mr Loudon's England*.[57]

Loudon, born in Cambuslang, trained in gardening in and around Edinburgh, and had attended classes in botany, chemistry and agriculture at Edinburgh University. Dr Coventry, Professor of Agriculture at Edinburgh, provided him with an introduction to Sir Joseph Banks, at Kew, through whom he became a member of the Linnean society and began to receive commissions for landscape design, the most significant being the Palace Gardens at Scone in Perthshire. At the same time, he was publishing a series of treatises on gardens and estate development, which culminated in 1809 in a pamphlet entitled *The Utility of Agricultural Knowledge to the Sons of the Landed Proprietors of England, and to Young Men intended for Estate-Agents; illustrated by what has taken place in Scotland*. Scotland's estates and gardens were intended by Loudon to be the model for England's, and he followed this pamphlet with another entitled *Observations on laying out Farms in the Scotch Style adapted to England*.[58] Far from being a country of agricultural and horticultural backwardness, Scotland's gardening traditions allowed Loudon to amass a fortune by teaching the English how to apply Scottish models. Having lost much of that fortune in business ventures, including inventing new ways of constructing iron-framed greenhouses which helped make possible the great public greenhouses of the mid-Victorian period, he turned entirely to authorship and by 1822 had collected the vast amount of information necessary to publish an *Encyclopaedia of Gardening*, whose success required a new edition by 1824, and selections from which were published in French in 1825. Loudon, a phenomenon of literary productivity, had by

---

[57] John Gloag, *Mr Loudon's England: The Life and Work of John Claudius Loudon, and his influence on architecture and furniture design* (Newcastle-upon-Tyne: Oriel Press, 1970).

[58] Details from 'A Short Account of the Life and Writings of John Claudius Loudon', written by his wife Jane after his death, and reprinted in Gloag, *Mr Loudon's England*, Appendix II, 182ff.

this time published *The Green-House Companion* and was about to publish his *Encyclopaedia of Agriculture,* amounting to more than 1,200 pages, itself to be followed in 1829 by the *Encyclopaedia of Plants.* He founded *The Gardener's Magazine* in 1826, and visited Blaikie several times in Paris in order to report on developments in French gardening. Through such publications Loudon exerted a significant influence on the development of Victorian gardening, but through another encyclopaedia – *of Cottage, Farm and Villa Architecture and Furniture* (1833) – and his *Suburban Gardener and Villa Companion* (1838), Loudon also shaped the design of much of Victorian domestic building, including the development of the semi-detached villa. Just as Blaikie had set the pattern for gardens in France in the 1780s and 90s, so Loudon helped reshape the English suburban landscape in the 1830s and 40s, and, perhaps, as John Gloag suggests, 'helped to change the face of England during the last two thirds of the nineteenth century'.[59]

The remarkable careers of Blaikie and Loudon are testimony not only to the international influence exerted by the Scottish tradition of gardening and garden design in the eighteenth and nineteenth centuries but, in their interaction with places such as Kew, indicate the key role that Scots played in the development of botanical science. A symbol of that contribution might be the moment in 1828 when Robert Brown (1773–1858), whom Joseph Banks had appointed as ship's surgeon and botanist on the Flinders expedition to Australia (1801–5), made a visit to the country seat of the Duc d'Orléans at Blois. Brown, who had taken over Joseph Banks's library and herbarium and would integrate it into the British Museum, had just published the pamphlet on his microscopic investigations of the movement of particles in liquid – called 'Brownian motion', though not fully understood till Einstein's work on it in 1905 – and was rapidly becoming recognised as the foremost botanist in Europe. His trip to Blois was both botanical and patriotic since it was to allow him to look at 'the botanic garden over which our countryman Morrisson presided'.[60] Robert Morison (as the name was actually spelled, 1620–83) was a graduate of Marischal College, Aberdeen who had gone into exile in France after being wounded in the royalist cause in the 1640s. He became physician and gardener to the Duc d'Orléans and returned to Britain with Charles II in 1660 as royal physician, before taking up his post as the first Professor of Botany at Oxford in 1669. In their different periods, Morison and Brown

---

[59] Ibid., 17.
[60] D. J. Mabberley, *Jupiter Botanicus: Robert Brown of the British Museum* (London: British Museum, 1985), 282.

were both botanical pioneers, trained in Scottish universities, who developed new systems of plant classification and used their gardens to develop and test the properties of previously unknown plants. Morison's role in France underlines the long association of the Ducs d'Orléans with Scottish physicians and gardeners, and Brown's at Kew and at the British Museum the central role played by Scots in the development of botany in England. The reasons for this prominence lay in the close connection of gardening in Scotland with its universities. Under Dr John Hope (1725–86), who was professor of both medicine and botany at Edinburgh University, medical students were expected not merely to study the medicinal properties of plants but to develop an understanding of their cultivation in the botanic garden. The relative openness of the Scottish university system also allowed gardeners (like Loudon) to attend botany lectures, providing a route by which those who were not studying for a degree could still become informed of the latest scientific developments. It was this combination that made for botanically educated gardeners and plant collectors (like Blaikie) and also made Scots so often the preferred choice as ship's surgeons on voyages of discovery, acting as doctors when at sea and as plant collectors when on land.

Hope's close connections with Joseph Banks at Kew meant that in the eighteenth century Edinburgh was a major centre for the collecting and documenting of the plant species being discovered across the new territories of Empire, as well as for their onward transmission to other botanic gardens to allow their commercial potential to be tested in different environments. Many of Hope's students went on to found or run botanic gardens in various parts of the Empire, the first of which had been established at Kingstown, on the island of St Vincent in the West Indies, in 1765, by General Robert Melville (1723–1809), a graduate of Glasgow and Edinburgh universities. In 1765, when he had risen to be Governor of St Vincent, he was concerned both to provide plant specimens for use in Britain and to test the effects of deforestation on the local climate.[61] Similarly, William Roxburgh (1751–1815) – one of Hope's students – developed the extensive botanic garden in Calcutta, which he took over in 1793, and where, among much else, he tested various forms of jute for their possible industrial use.[62]

---

[61] Richard Grove, *Green Imperialism: Colonial expansion, tropical island Edens and the origins of environmentalism, 1600–1860* (Cambridge: Cambridge University Press, 1995), 269.

[62] See Tim Robinson, *William Roxburgh: The Founding Father of Indian Botany* (Chichester: Phillimore, 2008), 153ff.

The continuing prominence of Scots in the development of the botanic garden in the nineteenth century can be seen closer to home in the Glasnevin Botanic Gardens in Dublin, where Ninian Niven (1799–1879) was appointed curator in 1834. Niven, born in Glasgow, was one of the earliest to use seeds sown 'broadcast' rather than in the strict lines and, as Keith Lamb and Patrick Bowe point out in their *History of Gardening in Ireland*, 'such was Ninian Niven's genius that in 1993 two gardens designed by him were chosen as worthy of restoration by the European Union under the "Gardens of Historic Interest" scheme. These were the Iveagh Gardens, Dublin, laid out for the Great Exhibition of 1865, and that at Hilton Park, County Monoghan.'[63] Niven's successor at Glasnevin was David Moore (1808–79), who had been apprenticed to the Earl of Camperdown's gardener and worked at James Cunningham's nurseries at Comely Bank in Edinburgh. Moore had arrived in Ireland as assistant to another Scot, James Townsend Mackay, from Kirkcaldy, who was the first manager of Trinity College's botanic gardens. The global reach of these Scottish networks is underlined by the fact that Moore's brother, Charles, was responsible for laying out the Botanic Gardens in Sydney, Australia.

From Wellington, New Zealand, where James Hector from Edinburgh designed the botanic garden in the 1860s, to British Columbia, where John Davidson from Aberdeen developed the University of British Columbia's botanic garden, Scottish gardeners were engaged in the investigation of the native flora and fauna of the lands where they settled – in Dublin, Townsend Mackay was the author of *Flora Hibernia* (1836) and Roxburgh's *Flora Indica; or Descriptions of Indian Plants* was published in 1820, five years after his death. The gardens they oversaw, however, were designed not as places of environmental protection for local plants but as places of cultural and environmental exchange, and as places to test the local possibilities of plants collected in other parts of the world. James Hector, in Wellington, for instance, planted a huge variety of trees to test their potential for replacing New Zealand's rapidly declining forest areas, and discovered that the Monterey Pine, usually stunted and warped in its native California, rose rapidly to majestic heights in its new habitat.

The interaction of the work in botanical gardens with those in 'pleasure gardens' can be seen in John Claudius Loudon's development of the notion

---

[63] Keith Lamb and Patrick Bowe, *A History of Gardening in Ireland* (Dublin: National Botanic Gardens, 1995), 116.

of the 'gardenesque', a style of gardening which concentrated on setting exotic species together with a deliberate emphasis on the artificiality of the arrangement of its plants and on their 'unnatural' contingency. Loudon's 'gardenesque' was to become the model of the suburban garden as a miniature version of the botanic garden, a domestic garden based on the availability of plants exchanged across the globe between botanic gardens.

Hamilton Finlay believed that there were only two kinds of gardens: art gardens and botanical gardens.[64] What they share is their emphasis on the garden as a place of cultural exchange, of cultural translation. For Finlay, 'A garden is not an object but a process',[65] and so too is his classicism: rather than the recreation of a fixed style derived from a particular point in the past, Finlay's classicism involves an ironic interplay between various historical renditions of classical forms as they traverse between cultures – as, for instance, in the 1984 Emblem whose text reads 'For the Temples of the Greeks/ Our homesickness lasts for ever', two lines which are separated by a diagrammatic etching of a modern warship. Finlay has set the emblem form, so common in the Renaissance, travelling through the modern world, with a message which insists on how far we must always be from a cultural origin that is unified and at one with itself. The condition of culture, in the modern world, is a condition in which an exchange of cultures has always already occurred, in which only past exchanges make possible the garden's present flourishing. The garden is an image of a Scotland where foreign seeds flourish in native soil.

III Invented Nations

The Finlays' arrival in Stonypath coincided with the sudden and unanticipated rise of Scottish nationalism: between 1962 and 1966 the membership of the Scottish National Party increased from 2,000 to 42,000;[66] in 1967 Winifred Ewing won the Hamilton by-election for the SNP, overturning a Labour majority of 16,000;[67] and although she would lose her seat at the following election in 1970, by the general election of February 1974 the SNP's total number of seats would rise to seven, and then to eleven at the election

---

[64] Abrioux, *Ian Hamilton Finlay: A Visual Primer*, 40.
[65] Ibid.
[66] Harvie, *Scotland and Nationalism*, 176.
[67] Ibid., 176.

in October of that year. Even more significant, it gained over 30 per cent of the popular vote. Nationalism in Scotland had become powerful enough for both the Tory and the Labour parties to bring forward proposals for some form of devolved government for Scotland.

This sudden flourishing of Scottish nationalism defied contemporary theories of nationalism. Elie Kedourie's influential account in *Nationalism* (1960) emphasised that, 'in nationalist doctrine, language, race, culture, and sometimes even religion, constitute different aspects of the same primordial entity, the nation', and that nationalism 'divides humanity into separate and distinct nations, [and] claims that such nations must constitute sovereign states'.[68] Kedourie, however, had argued that because neither Britain nor America could be defined in terms of an exclusivist ideology of language, race or religion, neither could be described as 'nationalist'. Since Scotland, equally, had no overriding demands of language, race or religion to justify its secession from the United Kingdom, it had none of the prerequisites that Kedourie regarded as essential for nationalist politics.

The lack of fit between emergent Scottish nationalism and the theoretical understanding of the subject was even clearer in relation to Ernest Gellner's influential account of the nation, first proposed in *Thought and Change* in 1964, and elaborated in *Nations and Nationalisms* in 1983. For Gellner, nationalism was a response to the pressure of 'modernization': tidal waves of modernity, as they pass outwards from the more advanced industrial countries, create a pattern of uneven development which can only be resisted in less developed countries by the establishment of their own national economies, justified in their autonomy by national cultures, and, in the end, by national languages. Nationalism is at once a defence against domination by more advanced societies and, at the same time, the means by which local resources can be mobilised to 'catch up' in the race towards modernity. This is why educational systems are, for Gellner, central to modern nations: they create a linguistic and cultural community in which it is impossible for people to be 'horizontally mobile' and so prevent them being able to move from one language area to another. A people, locked into its 'own' territory, becomes the resource on which a modern nation can be built, though only by convincing its people that modernisation is actually the fulfilment of an ancient right to separate and independent existence. This fundamental paradox of

<hr/>

[68] Elie Kedourie, 'Nationalism and Self-Determination', in John Hutchinson and Anthony D. Smith, *Nationalism* (Oxford: Oxford University Press, 1994), 49.

nationalism – its need to achieve modernisation while gathering its people within the narrative of an ancient history – was not the paradox posed by Scottish nationalism, for Scotland was already as fully industrialised as any country in the world. And far from promoting a national culture, its educational system was, in general, designed to *prevent* Scots coming into contact with their local cultures and so to ensure their linguistic mobility across the Anglophone world. Except for the tiny percentage of monolingual Gaelic speakers, horizontal movement to England, or to former territories of the British Empire, such as Canada, Australia and New Zealand, was only too easy, as the massive migrations from Scotland in the nineteenth century and through much of the twentieth century proved.

It was a problem that Tom Nairn sought to solve in *The Break-up of Britain* (1977) by dubbing the Scottish variety a 'neo-nationalism', a phenomenon so novel that although it was 'in some ways comparable to trends in Brittany, Catalonia, Wales, and other regions of Western Europe', it was in other ways 'unique', because 'nowhere else has the transformation been so abrupt, or so extensive'.[69] Scotland's problem, according to Nairn, was twofold. First, it had avoided the typical nationalism of the nineteenth century because it did not have to modernise in *resistance* to outside forces but was able to modernise in harmony with those forces: 'there are many stateless nationalities in history, but only one Act of Union.'[70] What the Union produced was 'a nationality which resigned statehood but preserved an extraordinary amount of the institutional and psychological baggage normally associated with independence – a decapitated national state, as it were, rather than an ordinary "assimilated" one'.[71] Secondly, that initial modernisation had, by the second half of the twentieth century, exhausted itself, and Scotland's industrial decline meant that it was once again subject to the effects of 'uneven development'. Nairn's 'neo-nationalism', therefore, reinforced the Gellnerite account of nationalism by showing how modernisation is not a singular event, a once-and-for-all rite of passage, but an ongoing process, in which the 'modernised' may slip back into being again the 'underdeveloped'.

Gellner's 'modernist' version of nations and nationalisms continues to be the ground on which most current accounts of nationalism are constructed. Its emphasis on the absolute modernity of the nation has, however, been

---

[69] Tom Nairn, *The Break-up of Britain: Crisis and Neo-nationalism* (London: Verso, [1977] 1981), 127.

[70] Ibid., 129.

[71] Ibid.

challenged by what has come to be known as 'ethno-symbolism', associated with the work of Anthony Smith,[72] which argues that the modernist version cannot explain why, if nations are simply 'inventions' of modernity, some groups are better able to 'invent' their nation than others. For the ethno-symbolists, the foundations of the nation rest on a pre-modern inheritance of 'myths, memories, traditions, and symbols of ethnic heritages', which provide 'a popular living past' that 'has been, and can be, rediscovered and reinterpreted by modern nationalist intelligentsias'.[73] Nations are indeed modern, but they can only succeed on the basis of a set of cultural resources – an *ethnie* – which pre-dates the modernity that calls them into being. The irony of Scotland's situation, according to Nairn, is that unlike the invented 'folk' cultures of nineteenth-century nationalism, Scotland's storehouse of 'myths, memories and symbols', its 'national-popular tradition', is 'unconnected with a "higher" or normal, nationalist-style culture' and so 'evolved blindly':[74]

> Headless aberration or not, the Scottish sub-culture is far more than most other submerged ethnic groups in Europe have to start from. Cramped, stagnant, backward-looking, parochial – all these and others are the epithets traditionally and rightly ascribed to modern Scottishness. But deformed as they are, these constitute none the less a strong, institutionally guaranteed identity.[75]

Scotland's neo-nationalism may have the same characteristics as other nationalisms but instead of being the 'revival' of an 'authentic' popular folk culture, Scotland's culture is parodic in form, since it is founded on an *ethnie* which is an 'assemblage of heterogeneous elements, neurotic double-binds, falsely honoured shades and brainless vulgarity', all still claiming to be constitutive of a 'national culture'.[76] The implication was that the underlying conditions that led to neo-nationalism might be a repetition of the original contradictions which produced nineteenth-century nationalism, but its cultural significance would be entirely different because the resources that it had to work with were not those of a pre-modern folk culture but the debased culture of

---

[72] Anthony D. Smith, *Myths and Memories of the Nation* (Oxford: Oxford University Press, 1999).
[73] Ibid., 9.
[74] Nairn, *Break-up of Britain*, 162.
[75] Ibid., 131.
[76] Ibid., 168.

an already modernised industrial working-class – a popular mass culture as incapable of providing the basis of oppositional proletarian resistance to capitalism as it was to producing an authentic national 'high' culture.

What is characteristic of all of these theories of the nation is the theorists' lack of sympathy with – indeed, profound repugnance for – the nationalisms they were studying (epitomised in Nairn's recoil from that 'insanely sturdy' beast, the 'tartan monster'[77]). To liberals who saw the future in terms of an increasing convergence of shared civic values, to neo-conservatives who saw the nation as an impediment to the spread of free trade and therefore of liberty, and to Marxists who believed the nation to be simply the 'false-consciousness' that masked bourgeois domination of the proletariat, the nation represented an *ancien régime* which ought to become increasingly irrelevant to humanity's future. A resurgence of nationalism would represent – as proven by the consequences of German nationalism in the 1930s – a reversion to atavistic beliefs that belonged to – and ought not to have returned from – a primitive past. What had to be explained by the theory of nationalism was, therefore, nationalism's inherent backwardness, its *pastness*, its resistance to the progress of civilisation. As such, the new Scottish nationalism could only represent a repetition of what Trevor-Roper described as Walter Scott's deliberate rejection of 'historic Scotland, his own Lowland Scotland' in favour of 'romantic Celtic fantasies' that had produced and would again produce 'a bizarre travesty of Scottish history, Scottish reality'.[78] Nationalism could only lead Scotland back into the primitive and superstitious darkness from which Union had redeemed it.

Scotland's apparently unique neo-nationalism was not, however, what it seemed to be in the 1960s – neither the nation's belated arrival at the juncture it had missed in the nineteenth century nor a strange mirror image in the homeland of the new nationalisms produced by the 'End of Empire'. Rather, it was the harbinger of a new Europe which, after the collapse of communism in 1989, saw a multitude of 'old' nations rise from their immersion in Marxist universalism to claim again their right to independent existence. When the revolutions of that and the succeeding years had played themselves out, the soil of Europe had been turned over to reveal how shallow had been the adopted identity of the Soviet Empire. Suddenly what had to be explained was not nationalism's atavism, its denial of historical progress, but its survival,

---

[77] See Nairn, *The Break-up of Britain*, 165.
[78] Eric Hobsbawm and Terence Ranger (eds), *The Invention of Tradition* (Cambridge: Cambridge University Press, 1983), 29–30.

its longevity, its success, its continuing ability to resist dictatorship and to promote democracy. The unexpected novelty of Scotland's 'belated' nationalism had foreshadowed something that nation theory had not anticipated – far from being the past, nations and nationalisms were the future.

IV   Imagined Communities

The text that came to encapsulate this moment of crisis in the theory of the nation was Benedict Anderson's *Imagined Communities*, first published in 1983 but reissued in an extended version in 1991 after the collapse of communism. That publishing history is significant, because the first edition of Anderson's book was written to come to terms with something that had gone largely unacknowledged in the aftermath of American withdrawal from Vietnam:

> Perhaps without being much noticed yet, a fundamental transformation in the history of Marxism and Marxist movements is upon us. Its most visible signs are the recent wars between Vietnam, Cambodia and China. These wars are of world-historical importance because they are the first to occur between regimes whose independence and revolutionary credentials are undeniable, and because none of the belligerents has made more than the most perfunctory attempts to justify the bloodshed in terms of a recognizable *Marxist* theoretical perspective.[79]

Marxism, even where successful, had failed to make the nation historically redundant. Marxism, which had claimed the copyright on modern revolution, was forced to confront the fact, 'that since World War II every successful revolution had defined itself in *national* terms' (*IC*, 12). This overturning of the West's conception of proletarian revolution in the national conflicts of the 'far East' prophetically anticipated events in the West: 'Who can be confident that Yugoslavia and Albania will not one day come to blows?' (*IC*, 12). Class had failed to displace the nation as the defining structure of modernity.

Since what these nationalist conflicts betokened was the failure of a *rational* history as predicted by Marxism, in which the nation state would wither away to be replaced by the international solidarity of the working classes,

---

[79] Benedict Anderson, *Imagined Communities* (London: Verso, [1983] 1991), 1. Hereafter cited in the text as *IC*.

the perseverance of *national* history must be the consequence of a power which was the antithesis of Marxism's rational teleology – the power of the imagination. For Anderson, nationalism's success derived from the fact that it was rooted in the imagination, a faculty which could appeal much more easily to the mass of human beings than the cold calculations of reason. To Anderson, the disenchanted Marxist, the imagination enchants nations into existence and maintains them by illusions too powerful for the mere force of reason to overthrow. To be properly understood, nationalism has to be taken out of the domain of politics and placed in the territory of those forms of human belief which do not require rational justification:

> …if one tries to imagine, say, a Tomb of the Unknown Marxist or a cenotaph for fallen Liberals [is] a sense of absurdity avoidable? The reason is that neither Marxism nor Liberalism are much concerned with death and immortality. If the nationalist imagining is so concerned, this suggests a strong affinity with religious imaginings. (*IC*, 10)

Nationalism is historically regressive because its ethos belongs not to the world of secular political debate but to the world of religion which secular politics thought it had overthrown: 'what I am proposing is that nationalism has to be understood by aligning it, not with self-consciously held political ideologies, but with the large cultural systems that preceded it, out of which – against which – it came into being' (*IC*, 12). Nations and nationalism are thus paradoxically poised between the premodern and the modern: they are created by the onset of secular modernity but only by transfusing modernity with the devotional spirit of its predecessor. Nationalism, like the religions whose ghosts give it substance, is a matter of belief, not of argument: it is beyond the boundary of reason. And however inevitable nations and nationalism might be to modernity, they remain part of the pre-Enlightenment world from which, unfortunately, we have not been redeemed by the powers of rational reflection.

If the 'magic of nationalism' (*IC*, 12) is produced by refusing scientific rationality, what gave an almost magical power to Anderson's concept of 'imagined community' – which became, in the 1980s and 90s, a talismanic means of solving almost all cultural problems – is that it draws on the tradition in Western aesthetics which sees in the imagination the faculty by which human beings are able to reach transcendental truths unapproachable by reason. In one of the most famous of such formulations, Samuel

Taylor Coleridge described the power of the imagination as being twofold: 'it dissolves, diffuses, dissipates' but only 'in order to recreate; or where this process is rendered impossible, yet still, at all events, it struggles to idealize and to unify'.[80] In the transition to modernity, the imagination, for Anderson, does the same: it dissolves the structures which held together earlier forms of human community – based on 'face to face' contact – and replaces them with structures in which 'the members of even the smallest nation will never know most of their fellow-members, meet them, or even hear of them, yet in the minds of each lives the image of their communion' (*IC*, 6). The underlying force of modernisation, which rends people from the traditional forms of life and of relationship, is compensated by the transcendental experience of nationalism as 'it struggles to idealize and unify'. In the nation the isolated individual self of modernity is transformed by a sense of shared identity and participation in a higher unity, an experience Anderson describes as 'unisonance':

> …there is a special kind of contemporaneous community which language alone suggests – above all in the form of poetry and song. Take national anthems, for example, sung on national holidays. No matter how banal the words and mediocre the tunes, there is in this singing an experience of simultaneity. At precisely such moments, people wholly unknown to each other utter the same verse to the same melody. The image: unisonance…How selfless this unisonance feels! If we are aware that others are singing these songs precisely when and as we are, we have no idea who they may be, or even where, out of earshot, they are singing. Nothing connects us but imagined sound. (*IC*, 145)

Inclusion in the song gives each individual the sense of belonging to a greater totality, the kind of unified totality, or 'organic whole', that Coleridge attributed to great works of art.

Anderson distinguishes his theory from the duplicitous 'invention of tradition' that his predecessors had seen in nationalism by insisting that where Gellner 'assimilates "invention" to "fabrication" and "falsity"', a proper understanding of 'imagination' would align it with 'creation', so that 'communities are to be distinguished not by their falsity/genuineness, but by the

---

[80] Samuel Taylor Coleridge, *Biographia Literaria, or biographical sketches of my literary life and opinions*, ed. George Watson (London: Dent, 1965), 167.

style in which they are imagined' (*IC*, 6). Nations, therefore, are fundamentally aesthetic constructs, and vehicles of our creativity. But as such they suffer from the same inner contradiction which haunted the romantic conception of the imagination: do they truly allow us access to *ideal unities* or are those unities only deceptive fictions? Have we really transcended our isolated individualism or have we only succumbed to an illusion of community?

Whatever his initial distinction between the imagination as 'fabrication' and the imagination as 'creation', Anderson's 'imagined communities' slide relentlessly into 'imaginary communities'. This can be seen in his description of what he takes to be the driving force behind the creation of these 'imagined communities'–print capitalism. The increasing literacy associated with modernity creates communities of readers whose vernacular languages will define the boundaries of the nation. But the product of print capitalism, and of the entry of the masses into reading, is, for Anderson, a world in which reality is insistently displaced by fiction, dramatised in his account of the role played by newspapers in the modern nation:

> The obsolescence of the newspaper on the morrow of its printing – curious that one of the earlier mass-produced commodities should so prefigure the inbuilt obsolescence of modern durables – nonetheless, for just this reason, creates this extraordinary mass ceremony: the almost precisely simultaneous consumption ('imagining') of the newspaper-as-fiction.

Newspaper-reading encourages the 'fiction' of a shared community, even though its readers will never know one another, so that newspapers become a compensatory illusion for the isolation which modernity imposes on us:

> We know that particular morning and evening edition will overwhelmingly be consumed between this hour and that, only on this day, not that…The significance of this mass ceremony–Hegel observed that newspapers serve modern man as a substitute for morning prayers–is paradoxical. It is performed in silent privacy, in the lair of the skull. Yet each communicant is well aware that the ceremony he performs is being replicated simultaneously by thousands (or millions) of others of whose existence he is confident, yet of whose identity he has not the slightest notion. Furthermore, this ceremony is incessantly repeated at daily or half-daily intervals throughout the calendar. (*IC*, 35)

The 'silent privacy, in the lair of the skull' in which each of us is actually trapped is apparently transcended by a 'mass ceremony' whose regularity assures us that we are not alone. Through the newspaper we imagine a community which is actually denied by the very isolation of our act of reading, and indulge ourselves in the fiction of community while the world in which we live is increasingly fragmented and atomistic: we read on so that we may be 'continually reassured that the imagined world is visibly rooted in everyday life' but it is an everyday life in which 'fiction seeps quietly and continuously into reality, creating that remarkable confidence of community in anonymity which is the hallmark of modern nations' (*IC*, 36).

It is not by accident that Anderson exemplifies the nature of 'imagined community' by reference to a novel, José Rizal's *Noli Me Tangere*, a novel that 'today is regarded as the greatest achievement of modern Filipino literature' as well as being the first novel written by an 'Indio' (*IC*, 26):

> ... right from the start the image (wholly new to Filipino writing) of a dinner-party being discussed by hundreds of unnamed people, who do not know each other, in quite different parts of Manila, in a particular month of a particular decade, immediately conjures up the imagined community ... The casual progression of this house from the 'interior' time of the novel to the 'exterior' time of the [Manila] reader's everyday life gives a hypnotic confirmation of the solidity of a single community, embracing characters, author and readers, moving onward through calendrical time. (*IC*, 27)

Although what Anderson seems to approve of in Rizal's description is the 'realism' of his presentation of an 'imagined community', its reconstruction of a reality which will be recognised by the book's readers as an accurate version of their own social world, such realism is itself a form of magic: the description 'immediately *conjures up* the imagined community', it produces 'a *hypnotic* confirmation of the solidity of a single community'. Fiction is not just the medium by which an 'imagined community' is documented: the 'imagined community' is itself only bound together by fiction – those fictions which seep into it from newspapers and novels. National societies are, in effect, structured like novels: nationalism succeeds because its imaginary longings are ideally suited to the unreal world generated by print capitalism, while Marxism fails because it tries to point towards a real world which is being ever more insistently concealed from us by fiction.

There are, however, some 'real' literary and historical problems with the world that Anderson is here describing. First, *Imagined Communities* talks about fiction as though fiction is, in itself, an unproblematic category. After quoting the opening paragraphs of *Noli Me Tangere*, Anderson says, 'Excessive comment is surely unnecessary' (*IC*, 27) – the novel, as it were, speaks for itself. But in a chapter entitled 'Hard to Imagine' in his later *Spectres of Comparison* (1998) he acknowledges that what he quoted in the original edition of *Imagined Communities* came from the translation by Leon Maria Guerrero, which the 'revised' edition of *Imagined Communities* of 1991 replaces with Anderson's own translation, footnoting only that when he had originally written the chapter he had had 'no command of Spanish', and was 'unwittingly led to rely on the instructively corrupt translation' (*IC*, 27) of Guerrero. Anderson, however, does not see any need to change his own analysis of the novel because of the change in the nature of the text under analysis: it still 'immediately conjures up the imagined community', despite the fact that its tone is completely changed by the new translation. Far from being a traditional realist novel, Rizal's text is revealed as one which plays ironically with its own fictionality. What could be described in 1983 as a Balzacian realist fiction has become, by 1991, something much more experimental but the changes in the text under analysis do not affect Anderson's own treatment of it: his analysis, apparently, remains true even though it is an analysis of a text which has been recognised as corrupt. The work of fiction from which the idea of 'imagined community' was derived turns out itself to have been even more profoundly fictional than Anderson supposed – an illusion created by a mistranslation.

Second, this fictional foundation for Anderson's 'imaginary nations' points us to the equally uncertain definitions from which his argument begins. He first defines the nation as an 'imagined *political* community' (*IC*, 6) but then elides the 'political' element in the contracted form of the 'imagined community'. Because 'political' disappears from the definition, politics also disappears from the community and erases opposition, conflict and dispute. Anderson's 'imagined communities' are not places of debate, they are places of religious communion: 'regardless of the actual inequality and exploitation that may prevail in each, the nation is always conceived as a deep, horizontal comradeship' (*IC*, 7). Anderson acknowledges in his original definition of 'imagined community' that 'all communities larger than primordial villages of face-to-face contact (and perhaps even these) are imagined' (*IC*, 6), but fails to acknowledge that this means the term 'community' itself already contains, of necessity, the requirement that it be 'imagined'. What the emphasis on 'imagined community' – rather than simply 'community' – allows Anderson to do is to exploit – and to confuse – three different possibilities of the meaning of 'imagination':

(1) 'imagined' as it refers to the process by which we relate ourselves to, or recollect, real things which are not present in immediate perception: we bring it before our minds as an 'image';

(2) 'imagined' as it refers to our ability to envisage future events which have, as yet, no existence but which we may sometime turn into realities;

(3) 'imagined' as it refers to our ability to entertain events which can have no reality, such as unicorns, characters in novels etc.

In *Imagined Communities,* the synchronic power of imagination to align ourselves with our absent fellow nationals (sense 1) is turned into a set of purely imaginary relations with those fellow nationals (sense 3), so that a real community of people with real connections to one another – if only because they are defined by the same forms of citizenship – is turned into a fictional community in which there are only unreal relationships. And the imaginings by which the community envisages its possible futures (sense 2) are turned no less insistently into fictions (in sense 3) none of which will ever become realities.

However inadequate the notion of 'imagined community' was to the real nature either of communities or of the imagination, its emphasis on the ways in which nations and nationalisms already reflect or will strive towards the ultimate unity implied by romantic accounts of the creative imagination powerfully reinforced fundamental assumptions about the key role of cultural coherence in modern theories of the nation. It was a conception by which Scotland, as a (potential) nation, would necessarily be found wanting. If nations, like works of art, are to be evaluated by the unity they have achieved, then Scotland – as a country with three linguistic traditions, competing religious commitments, and a large immigrant community that over several generations continued to see itself as defined by another homeland – could never represent the unity which the concept of the nation required. Indeed, Anderson's brief account of Scottish history in *Imagined Communities* – drawn largely from Nairn – reveals just how inappropriate to his conception of the nation is the juxtaposition of 'Scottish' and 'nationalism':

The key point here is that already in the early seventeenth century large parts of what would one day be imagined as Scotland were English-speaking and had immediate access to print-English, provided a minimal degree of literacy existed. Then in the early eighteenth century the English-speaking Lowlands collaborated with London in largely exterminating the Gaeltacht. In neither 'northward thrust' was a selfconscious Anglicizing policy pursued – in both cases Anglicization was essentially a byproduct. But combined, they had effectively eliminated, 'before' the age of nationalism, any possibility of a European-style vernacular-specific nationalist movement. (*IC*, 90)

If nations are defined by their vernacular print language, and if that language in Scotland from the seventeenth century onwards has been English, on what possible basis could there arise 'what would one day be imagined as Scotland'? In terms of Anderson's theory, Scotland would have been simply unimaginable. And Scottish nationalism would not only *not* have arisen in the age of nationalism, it would have been, like the country itself, an absolute impossibility.

Scotland's continuing existence and its flourishing neo-nationalism reveal, however, that it is not the nationalist's 'shrunken imaginings of recent history' (*IC*, 7) that are the problem, but the shrunken conceptions of recent theories of nationalism and the nation. What Gellner, Nairn and Anderson each assume in their different ways is that the language of one phase of nationalism – the drive towards territorial unification, as in Germany and Italy, or the demand for a spiritual unification, as in Ireland – actually defines the nature of the nations that are the eventual outcomes of those nationalist movements. Unity and homogeneity are the key indices of the right to be considered as a nation. In reality, however, as Roman Szporluk, has noted, 'national identity is a subject of intranational contestation and the ideological sphere is a battlefield in the struggle for hegemony within the nation'.[81] Those who have been active in nationalist politics know that there is nothing so fissiparous as nationalist movements – 'unity' may be a shared ideological aim but that unity, and the road to its fulfilment, are defined in such radically different ways that it is a utopian horizon forever receding before those

---

[81] Roman Szporluk, 'Thoughts about change: Ernest Gellner and the history of nationalism', in John A. Hall (ed.), *The State of the Nation: Ernest Gellner and the Theory of Nationalism* (Cambridge: Cambridge University Press, 1988), 34.

who march towards it. And what is true of nationalisms is as true of the nations they create. As John Hutchinson puts it, 'the modernist assumption that national cultures tend to homogenisation underplays the role of cultural wars within nationalism as protagonists look to alternative pasts as inspiration to their programmes';[82] and if the 'nation-state' implies a state whose boundaries are coterminous with those of a culturally coherent nation then, as Charles Tilly has argued, few European states have ever qualified as genuine 'nation states', and 'Great Britain, Germany and France – quintessentially national states – have never met the test'.[83] The 'unity' of the nation is a response not to the reality of nations but to the rhetoric of certain nationalisms as they struggled towards statehood: theory, in other words, has allowed its construction of the nation to be defined by the very 'romantic' nationalism which the theorists themselves believe to be nothing but falsification. However useful this might be in allowing those theorists to attack the falsehoods of nationalist traditions, it locks them into an equal blindness as to the reality of nations – which are never 'organic wholes', never homogeneous, and held together as much by internal dissonance as by their 'unisonance'. Most nations are, in effect, suspended civil wars. Scotland, that non-unified non-state, provides us, perhaps, with an alternative model of how we might conceptualise the nature of the nation.

Let us return to the origin of Anderson's argument about the role of print capitalism and the establishment of vernacular reading communities as the basis that makes possible the emergence of the nation. For Anderson,

> These print-languages laid the bases for national consciousness in three distinct ways. First and foremost, they created unified fields of exchange and communication below Latin and above spoken vernaculars. Speakers of a huge variety of Frenches, Englishes, or Spanishes, who might find it difficult or even impossible to understand one another in conversation, became capable of comprehending one another via print and paper. In the process, they gradually became aware of the hundreds of thousands, even millions, of people in their particular language-field, and at the same time that *only those* hundreds of thousands, or millions, so belonged. (*IC*, 44)

---

[82] John Hutchinson, *Nations as Zones of Conflict* (London: Sage, 2005), 4.

[83] Quoted in David McCrone, *The Sociology of Nationalism: Tomorrow's Ancestors* (London: Routledge, 1998), 85; Charles Tilly, *Coercion, Capital and European States, AD 990–1992* (Oxford: Blackwell, 1992), 3.

Printed vernacular languages produce 'unified fields of exchange' to which only certain people belong–the 'embryo of the nationally imagined community'. The 'unity' which is central to Anderson's vernacular communities of embryonic nationalism looks very different, however, if we trace it back to what appears to be its source in Marshall McLuhan's *Understanding Media*, first published in 1964: for McLuhan, nationalism is the direct product of the technology of movable 'type', which allows people to be trained as 'individuals' of a certain 'type':

> Of the many unforeseen consequences of typography, the emergence of nationalism is, perhaps, the most familiar. Political unification of populations by means of vernacular and language groupings was unthinkable before printing turned each vernacular into an extensive mass medium. The tribe, an extended form of a family of blood relatives, is exploded by print, and is replaced by an association of men homogeneously trained to be individuals. Nationalism itself came as an intense new visual image of group destiny and status, and depended on a speed of information movement unknown before printing.[84]

The nation itself becomes a 'mass medium', a circuit which makes possible the rapid transmission of information. That information circuit, however, does not, for McLuhan, result in Anderson's 'unified fields of exchange', each locked in their own inner psychic realm: at the same time that it produces nations, typography 'extended the minds and voices of men to reconstitute the human dialogue on a world scale that has bridged the ages'.[85] What typography made possible was not only the consolidation and expression of a new vernacular consciousness: it was the possibility of *translation* on a massive scale; it was the relentless demand for the exchange of texts *between* cultures. 'Until 1700', McLuhan notes, 'more than 50 per cent of all printed books were ancient or medieval.'[86]

The establishment of vernacular print cultures required, by the very limitation of their cultural reach, both in time and in space, the translation into them of all the knowledge that they lacked: the Bible, the classics, the sciences and literatures of other cultures. The 'imagined community' of belonging,

---

[84]   Marshall McLuhan, *Understanding Media: The Extensions of Man*, ed. W. Terence Gordon (Core Madera, CA: Gingko Press, [1964] 2003), 192–3.

[85]   Ibid., 233.

[86]   Ibid.

of 'unified fields of exchange', is also, and necessarily, the environment of exchange between fields which are *not* unified, which are now separated by historical (Greek, Latin) or linguistic (French, German, Spanish) boundaries. The language which is the medium of national unity is also, and at the same time, the medium that makes inevitable *non*-unified fields of exchange. The very singularity of national vernaculars requires their engagement in a process of cultural translation and cultural exchange which is every bit as dynamic as the exchange of goods across borders which drives the development of capitalism and imperialism. If nationalism is the product of the 'tidal wave of modernity', each emergent national culture begins with what Hamilton Finlay calls the 'Great Wave of Translation'.[87] And if, as McLuhan argued, the 'medium is the message', the medium of the nation founded in vernacular print culture was in fact the medium of translation. Far from being closed environments, those vernacular print cultures were precisely, for increasing masses of people who had been excluded from the world of Latin learning in the Middle Ages, the medium by which they could encounter that which did not belong within, and was not native to, their own vernacular environment. The emergence of national cultures, drawing into literacy larger and larger proportions of their populations, makes possible a previously undreamed of exchange of cultural information from beyond the boundaries of the nation.

By laying their emphasis on the inner homogeneity of the nation, the modernist and ethno-symbolist accounts of the nation have neglected what was, in fact, fundamental to its development: its dependence on translation; its transfer into the body of its own culture of what was 'different', 'alien' or 'other', and the translation outwards of its 'own' cultural products into other languages. If we think of nations not as the sites of vernacular unity and bounded belonging but as the medium of a new kind of cultural exchange which was unnecessary in the age when Latin represented the universal language of Christianity, a cultural exchange which – like the transfer of plants that formed the basis of medical practice in the Renaissance – is the very life-blood of cultural development, we will come closer, perhaps, to the real nature of the nation.

If nations are founded not in unity but in exchange, both exchange within a national territory whose boundaries are largely arbitrary, and exchange with

---

[87]   Ian Hamilton Finlay, *Wave, Solitary Wave, Great Wave of Translation* (Dunsyre: Wild Hawthorn Press, 1979).

cultures that are other to them in time or in space, then those bugbears of Scottish cultural history – Lowland Scotland's adoption of the iconography of a Highland Celtic identity and the country's increasing 'Anglicisation' – can be read not as the signs of failed nationhood but as the evidence of a nation which has grasped that its real resources are generated by its capacity for cultural export, translation and assimilation. That Lowland Scots would adopt the symbols of its contiguous Highland culture as an expression of their distinction from the English culture whose language they were at the same time assiduously cultivating is no more strange than that French aristocrats engaged in a worldwide struggle with Britain for economic, military and cultural dominance should employ a Scottish gardener to turn their parks into *jardins anglais*. Rather than being a failed version of a nation, Scotland is an index of the failure of nation theory to account for the nature of the nation.

V   Essential Nations

In 1962 Ian Hamilton Finlay and Hugh MacDiarmid were involved in an acrimonious exchange of letters in *The Scotsman*, provoked, initially, by an article by the Scottish poet Edwin Morgan in which he complained that the Scottish literary establishment was ignoring new literary developments such as Beat poetry in America, or the experimentalism of Finlay's Wild Hawthorn Press publications. MacDiarmid's defence was to query whether 'progress to any desirable end will be achieved under the impetus of a group of teddyboy poetasters who have in any case written little enough in justification of their own attitude'.[88] In return, Hamilton Finlay and his co-publisher, Jessie McGuffie, accused MacDiarmid of being a Stalinist trying to ignore the 'thaw' represented by younger writers. For many, the Scottish agenda of MacDiarmid's Renaissance movement had become a barrier rather than a boon to Scotland's creativity, the desire for *national* self-expression a halter on the nation's contemporary *self*-expression. In a Beatnik issue of the Edinburgh University student publication *Jabberwock*, the editor, Alex Neish, declared that 'Scotland lies in creative stagnation' because, 'by confining itself so exclusively to dialect, [poetry] has lost all contact with the public'. The dominance of the Renaissance agenda, based on 'dialect poetry and a

---

[88] Alan Bold (ed.), *The Letters of Hugh MacDiarmid* (London: Hamish Hamilton, 1984), 813.

commitment to Nationalism', had led directly to 'a loss of reality and sterility'.[89] It was a complaint taken sufficiently seriously that Maurice Lindsay,
one of the so-called 'second generation' of the Renaissance movement,
prefaced his *Snow Warning and Other Poems* of 1962 with an acknowledgment
that the Lallans movement initiated by MacDiarmid had failed: 'It is utterly
unthinkable that this poor wasted and abandoned speech, however rich in
theory its poetic potential, can possibly express what there is to be expressed
of the Scottish *ethos* in the age of the beatnik and the hydrogen bomb'.[90]
MacDiarmid's response to Finlay was to declare that 'all these productions'
which were 'purportedly "international"' were 'not really international, however, but simply cosmopolitan'.[91] The relation of 'Scottish' to 'International'
was to be a defining characteristic of the period: in 1945, MacDiarmid had
greeted the announcement of an international festival of music in Edinburgh
to which 'every distinguished composer and executant might be attracted'
as an occasion which would only 'emphasize the absence of their peers in
Scotland itself and the better the programmes the more ghastly would yawn
the abyss between them and the utter inability of the Scottish people to
assimilate and profit by anything of the sort, let alone be stimulated even
to try to produce anything of comparable worth on their own part'.[92] An
'international' festival, for MacDiarmid, would simply have foregrounded
Scotland's failure to develop the kind of *national* culture which would make
a real *inter*-nationalism possible. Without such a nationalist revival, 'internationalism' could only be a rootless and placeless 'cosmopolitanism'.

The tension between these two visions of Scotland's internationalism was
to prove to be as inherent in the content as it was to the title of the most
important cultural magazine of the 1960s, *Scottish International*, launched in
1968. In a letter to the magazine in April 1973, Tom Nairn described what he
perceived to be the problem with the 'romantic-nationalist view' of Scotland:
in comparison with the Enlightenment's 'critical ability to rise above a relatively weak national inheritance in a manner at once intellectual and universal
in its aim', romantic nationalism continued to assert that 'true liberation consists in knowing ourselves primarily *as* Scots', despite the fact that 'Scottish

---

[89] Quoted in *Lines Review*, No. 16 (Winter 1960), editorial by Albert Mackie,
5–6.
[90] Maurice Lindsay, *Snow Warning and Other Poems* (Arundel: Linden Press,
1962), 7.
[91] Bold (ed.), *The Letters of Hugh MacDiarmid*, 815.
[92] *The Voice of Scotland*, Vol. II, No. 2 (December 1945), 29.

culture was (as a consequence of the failures of the old monarchy) inchoate, heterogeneous, and "backward" '. It is romantic nationalism which produces 'irrepressible gloom in our land' because it knows 'how unpropitious the terrain has always been in Scotland for such imagined "nationalist phases", whether in music or anything else':[93]

> Barrenness, cold, lack of living 'roots', marginality in relation to Europe: these have always been the despair of the nationalist imagination. It feels that nothing can be done until this infertile ground is broken, planted, and tended by a great predominantly inward-looking cultural effort.[94]

The assumption that 'tending' the 'infertile ground' can only be achieved by an 'inward-looking cultural effort' is a typical expression of the belief that nationalism – and, indeed, the nation – exists only to defend what is 'native', 'indigenous', 'local'. The gardening metaphor that Nairn invokes, however, undermines the very point he is trying to make: far from being the site of 'inward-looking cultural effort', the tended garden is precisely the site of that global exchange of cultures, that cross-polli*nation*, which Scotland's gardeners had been engaged in from at least the time of the Roman invasion. For Nairn, 'the cultural nationalist invariably sees a fruitful culture as rooted in an internal wealth and psychological development: in the inner depths of the national personality's *Id*, as it were. For him, it's roots or nothing.'[95] The question is, however, 'whose roots?' Fruitful cultures are fruitful precisely because they are not 'rooted in an internal wealth' but because they have been enriched by their ability to cultivate and to naturalise the exotic. Take, for instance, the case of the strawberry, one of the prime products of the east of Scotland's fruit industry and a native European fruit, known to the Romans and found over much of northern Europe, but little regarded as a food before the seventeenth century because of the small size of its berries. A significant increase in the size of strawberries was first achieved by Jean de la Quintinie, gardener to Louis XIV: indeed, the king was so enamoured of strawberries that he created a poetry contest on their merits. Quintinie's efforts, however, were to be outdone by nature when Amédée-François Frézier returned from Chile with specimens of a strawberry the size of a walnut. Efforts to grow these in Brittany (whose climate was judged to be

---

[93] *Scottish International* (April 1973), 7.
[94] Ibid., 8.
[95] Ibid., 8.

similar to Chile's) failed until they were accidentally crossed with another imported variety from Virginia – it turned out that all of Frézier's strawberries had been of the same sex and could not pollinate. It is from this crossing of South and North American cultures with the tastes developed by Europe's gardening expertise that Scotland's cultivated strawberries derive – a crossing already embedded in Frézier's name, since it is the French version of Frazer, itself possibly deriving from 'fraise', the French for strawberry.[96]

Far from 'a fruitful culture' being 'rooted in an internal wealth', fruitfulness is the product of cultural crossings, of the adaptation of exotic species to new environments, of the creation of a wealth which nature has not and cannot provide by itself. Of course, that fruitfulness will come to nothing if the land itself is not tended but it is precisely such tending that Nairn took to be unnecessary: the route forward for the Scots is that pointed by the 'one great "non-national", one people of no country' who 'had acted for over a century as the leaven of European culture: the Jews'.[97] The destruction of Jewish culture in Europe by the Nazis meant that Europe had 'lost its former natural power to overcome the paralysis of all its different nationalisms and provincial cultures', and it is that rootless, non-nationalism to which the Scots ought to aspire: by imitating the cosmopolitanism of the Jews, the Scots could overcome Europe's nationalisms and regain the role they had played 'in the brief era of cosmopolitanism before nationalist cultures were entrenched everywhere'.[98]

Nairn's assumption about the necessary introversion of cultural nationalisms, and of the superiority of 'cosmopolitanism', has been regularly taken up in recent theorising about Scotland. Eleanor Bell, for instance, in *Questioning Scotland*, challenges those who would read Scottish writing in terms of its 'Scottishness' because 'such approaches tend to perpetuate the introversion of a discipline that in actuality needs to expand its conceptual boundaries'.[99] In her opening chapter she declares that

> It may seem a peculiar divergence to discuss Bhabha and Braidiotti when the focus of this chapter is the predicament of the Scottish writer. Yet,

---

[96] See 'The History of the Clan Fraser', http://myducksoup.com/scotland/fraser.shtml.

[97] *Scottish International*, January 1968, 8.

[98] Ibid., 8.

[99] Eleanor Bell, *Questioning Scotland: Literature, Nationalism, Postmodernism* (London: Palgrave, 2004), 2.

in some ways this is *why* these critics have been introduced. Critics of Scottish literature and culture have often been guilty of falling into this trap of essentialism, where they have perpetuated and encouraged fixed depictions of nationhood, 'its' boundaries, in order to justify and verify their own political positions. In doing so, critics have replaced the image of the nation as an 'imagined community', as the assimilation of its arbitrary signs, with a more closed, structured system.[100]

'Essentialism', by this account, is a failure to engage with writers and thinkers outside the boundaries of 'fixed depictions of nationhood', or to accept the 'imagined' – and therefore arbitrary and flexible – nature of the nation, and Bell, like several others, takes Beveridge and Turnbull's *The Eclipse of Scottish Culture* (1987) and *Scotland after Enlightenment* (1997) as the symptomatic texts of such introversion. Beveridge and Turnbull's insistence on the importance of neglected Scottish traditions of thought, which includes, according to Bell, 'George Davie, Alasdair MacIntyre, John Anderson and R. D. Laing', is taken to be indicative of

> an obsessive need to defend Scottishness from outsiders, from other ideas which might not be 'inherently' Scottish. This kind of position, however, is generated at the expense of excluding potentially more interesting accounts of Scottishness, and clearly Scotland does not exist in isolation where ideas can be organically or particularly Scottish. For Beveridge and Turnbull, though, thinkers and philosophers who are not Scottish are therefore not of fundamental interest to the Scottish tradition, their relevance is for the most part discounted, and once again the national tradition is given a parochial and introverted turn.[101]

Bell herself acknowledges, however, even if only in passing, that Beveridge and Turnbull's argument in fact begins from the work of Frantz Fanon – hardly a thinker who would normally have been in 1987 considered as of 'fundamental interest to the Scottish tradition' – and a brief look at the European and American names in the Index to either book would be enough to dismiss the accusation that they are concerned only with a Scotland 'in isolation'.

---

[100] Ibid., 34.
[101] Ibid., 75.

Equally, Beveridge and Turnbull's insistence on the importance of Augustinianism (not usually regarded as inherently Scottish) is reduced by Bell to 'a desperation...where important thinkers who happen to have been born in Scotland must somehow provide an explanation for the nature of lived Scottish reality and its "psyche"' – the philosopher concerned being Alasdair MacIntyre. The desperation, however, is on Bell's side, for in her desire to prove that 'Scotland is often problematically essentialised'[102] by an act of parochial introversion, she ignores the fact that Beveridge and Turnbull's concern is with MacIntyre not as in some sense a 'native' Scot – he himself, in any case, insists on his Irishness – but as someone who has 'drawn attention to the ways in which some of the central ideas of thinkers like Smith and Hume can be seen as secular expressions of fundamental Calvinist doctrines'.[103] MacIntyre's *engagement* with the Scottish philosophical tradition is what is important – and it is undeniable: major works such as *Three Rival Versions of Moral Enquiry* place Scottish Enlightenment thought as one of the three major strands of European tradition, and one of MacIntyre's earliest publications was an edition of *Hume's Ethical Writings* (1965). Bell's refusal to *engage* with Beveridge and Turnbull's argument about MacIntyre's engagement with Scottish tradition (MacIntyre does not figure in the Index to her book) and her reduction of their engagement with it to a matter of MacIntyre's having been 'born in Scotland' (which he was), is simply an evasion on her own part of what are, to some at least, 'potentially more interesting accounts of Scottishness'. MacIntyre's conclusion, after all, is far from being a cultural nationalist one, since he sees the development of the Scottish Enlightenment as symptomatic of the *failure* of enlightenment in general to meet the ethical demands of the modern world.

What Bell refuses to acknowledge is that Beveridge and Turnbull's effort to come to terms with MacIntyre's work is driven not by a cultural nationalist desire to incorporate him into a Scottish tradition but, as the opening section of their essay makes clear, to come to terms with something for which the Western media, with their secularist views of the world, have been unable to explain – 'the power and "relevance" of traditions of thought and action which are completely alien to the pragmatism and ethical premisslessness of liberal modernity', a power and relevance revealed in the fact that 'in Romania, it was the moral intransigence (or, in liberal code, "fanaticism")

---

[102] Ibid.

[103] Craig Beveridge and Ronald Turnbull, *Scotland After Enlightenment* (Edinburgh: Polygon, 1997), 82.

of a Calvinist pastor in Timosoara which set the popular revolt against Ceaucescu in motion'.[104]

According to Bell, Scottishness is a concept which Beveridge and Turnbull do not want to be 'scrutinised, for in doing so this invariably induces forms of inferiorism and undesirable formulations of Scottish culture in their overall picture'.[105] This is such a prejudicial misreading of their work that it can only stand as an implicit critique of Bell's own position rather than of theirs. What Beveridge and Turnbull want is precisely *more* scrutiny of Scottish culture, not less: it is the inferiorised condition of the Scottish intelligentsia that means they turn their eyes away from Scottish culture rather than scrutinising it, and in doing so are in no position either to praise or condemn its achievements. The essay on MacIntyre which Bell finds to be 'a clear example of this peculiar need to assert Scottishness'[106] is in fact an essay in which they try to tease out the views of George Davie as expressed in his *Crisis of the Democratic Intellect* (another book not in her Index), views which they state will be 'at first sight, no doubt, startling, even absurd', to the effect that 'what is most distinctive and valuable about twentieth-century Scottish contributions to theory involves a re-working, in more or less secular form, of the nation's theological inheritance'.[107] There is no sense here that Scottish culture must not be scrutinised because 'this invariably induces forms of inferiorism': what the scrutiny of Scottish culture reveals is the translation of value systems from one Scottish tradition, the theological, to another, the philosophical, a translation which opens the way in their text to a critical examination of the Marxism of Hobsbawm and Eagleton, of the communitarian theories of Taylor and Habermas, of the social theories of the Frankfurt school, and of the implications, for modern societies, of the decline of socialism. It is in this context that MacIntyre is invoked as a resource by which we may come to terms with the failure of the Enlightenment – and therefore of one important strand of Scottish tradition – and the rediscovery of a critical stance from which we may begin to escape from the 'moral-intellectual impoverishment' into which it has led us. If this should encourage us to return to those Scottish philosophers in whom Davie found 'a re-working…of the nation's theological inheritance' that is not the conclusion of their essay: rather, it is that MacIntyre challenges us with finding the resources – in Aristotle or in

---

[104] Beveridge and Turnbull, *Scotland After Enlightenment*, 115.
[105] Bell, *Questioning Scotland*, 76.
[106] Ibid.
[107] Beveridge and Turnbull, *Scotland After Enlightenment*, 116.

Aquinas, if necessary – by which 'we can now best confront the emptiness of liberalism and the exhaustion of modern sources of critique'.[108] The aim of this essay is patently *not* to 'assert Scottishness' but to explore alternatives to the dominant discourses of a liberalism which has proved incapable of providing us with a philosophy capable of ethical discrimination.

As someone who proclaims the importance of the 'ethical' as 'the underlying spur which generates this apparent need for clearer insights, the impulse for morality itself',[109] Bell ought to be grateful to Beveridge and Turnbull for demanding an answer as to how we are to establish a basis for that 'impulse for morality itself': instead, in the typical response of the believer in the value of the 'cosmopolitan', she refuses to engage with the local (even when the local is engaging with European and American thinkers), dismissing it as irrelevant to the larger concerns of supposedly 'international' movements of thought: 'As has been suggested', she tells us, 'it is this move towards postmodern conceptions of the self, often disregarded in Scottish studies, that have elsewhere gained increasing prominence and credibility.'[110] This, however, assumes that because certain conceptions have gained acceptance 'elsewhere', they are necessarily of more value, or more correct, than values to be discovered or developed at home – a tactic which evades debate in exactly the fashion that Bell wants to accuse others of doing. If we care to look up anthologies of postmodernism we will find that Alasdair MacIntyre's account of tradition, from *After Virtue* (1984), is one of the most regularly anthologised,[111] but is so precisely because it challenges the apparently empty relativity of postmodernism with a much more radical relativity – the relativity of different and competing traditions of moral enquiry, each of which has its own rationality. Bell's version of 'postmodernism' is something outside of Scottish culture, to be introduced into it by escaping from Scottish cultural traditions, but it is precisely that engagement between inherited traditions and external developments that is at issue in Beveridge and Turnbull's discussion. For Bell, 'Scottish studies should be encouraged to emerge from its often comfortable position of traditionalism in order to embrace, or at least to become more conversant in, contemporary theoretical discourses',[112] but what else is Beveridge and

---

[108] Ibid., 134.

[109] Bell, *Questioning Scotland*, 127.

[110] Ibid., 134.

[111] See, for instance, Lawrence Cahoone (ed.), *From Modernism to Postmodernism: An Anthology* (Oxford: Blackwell, 1994), 534.

[112] Bell, *Questioning Scotland*, 3.

Turnbull's engagement with MacIntyre but an engagement with an extremely important 'contemporary theoretical discourse', an engagement much more radical than Bell's own? It is an engagement, too, in which 'tradition' is the very reverse of 'comfortable'.

In Bell's work, the intellectual world is riven by the same kind of Manichean divide that shaped Nairn's early writings: a tradition-trapped Scottishness is utterly cast out from a theory-informed cosmopolitanism, with the consequence that a liberating non-national pluralism is always threatened by reabsorption into a monological and repressive nationalism. Bell believes that what she is attacking is the 'essentialism' of Scottish cultural nationalists but what she fails to acknowledge is that Beveridge and Turnbull's argument is itself precisely an argument against 'essentialism', the essentialism that has reduced Scottish culture to the limits of 'Scotch myths', and which can see in Scottish culture nothing but provincial backwardness. If their argument against such an essentialism is flawed because it necessarily generates another, opposite essentialism, it is an outcome which applies equally to her own argument, which advocates the 'postmodern'–postmodern conceptions of the self, of society, of globalisation–as the 'essential' context for understanding our postnational identities. To suggest that the 'postmodern' cannot be an 'essence' because it is inherently 'open', while tradition is 'closed', is to misread the whole nature of the idea of 'tradition' in modern thought, from T. S. Eliot's 'Tradition and the Individual Talent' to Alasdair MacIntyre's *After Virtue*. Traditions involve a constant negotiation between patterns of inheritance into which we are born and the reorganisation of that past from the perspective of, and from the needs of, the present.[113] The choice is not between a mobile conception of identity as defined by postmodernism and a static one defined by tradition, but between different versions of mobility, different orientations towards the values of the past and the possibilities of the future. Bell suggests that 'while there has been an impulse within Scottish literature to experiment with these new possibilities of identity, in criticism there has been a repeated recourse to more traditional forms of identity, an anxiety about potentially losing hold of the bedrock of tradition'.[114] Insofar as philosophical issues of identity are concerned, it would be absurd to hold that the tradition of Scottish criticism has had 'recourse to more traditional forms of identity', since the

---

[113] Bell also fails to acknowledge Beveridge and Turnbull's discussion of tradition in *Scotland After Enlightenment*, 168ff.

[114] Bell, *Questioning Scotland*, 139.

dissolution of the idea of personal identity is at the very heart of David Hume's philosophy – the so-called 'bundle' theory of the self – no less than of Stevenson's *Jekyll and Hyde*, and those problems of identity have, in turn, been central to debates about the contemporary relevance of Scottish literary and philosophical traditions.

The anxiety expressed by Beveridge and Turnbull, as by George Davie, is *not* about 'losing hold of the bedrock of tradition', nor is it – as their discussion of MacIntyre and Charles Taylor shows – about evading 'new possibilities of identity' (after all, what is their nationalism but the effort to create a new identity for the nation?): their anxiety is about the fact that some Scottish traditions have been so forgotten or denigrated that they have been lost as visible elements in the Scottish past and, therefore, as contributing possibilities to a Scottish future. The *Scottishness* of these traditions is not that they belong to some 'essence' of a timeless Scottish nation – some unchanging 'bedrock' – but that they were, once, part of the institutional processes – from Church or education to fiddle music and storytelling – by which a Scottish identity was recognised and (re)produced. Such traditions are constantly remade as they encounter new historical circumstances: new historical circumstances involve a constant reinterpretation of past tradition. In Scotland, however, those traditions ceased to be recognised, reproduced and reconfigured – have ceased to be *tended* – because they ceased to be the objects of institutional attention, and they have ceased to be the objects of institutional attention because of the need, on the part of certain elements in Scotland as well as under the pressure of hegemonic forces in England, to ensure Scotland's integration into the unified culture of a United Kingdom.

Cultural nationalism is not about holding to the 'bedrock of tradition' and remaining within a comfort zone that resists 'new possibilities of identity': it is about remaining aware of traditions which have played a significant role in the national culture which has shaped the environment – the intellectual environment, the built environment, the ecological environment – in which we now live, traditions which are not to be maintained out of an antiquarian desire for something 'Scottish' but out of the need to have alternative possibilities with which to address our current dilemmas, to have modes of resistance to incorporation into patterns of thought which are simply the expression of the power of the dominant economic and political forces in our present historical epoch.

Bell takes her cue for the possibility of a 'postmodern' Scotland from the work of sociologist David McCrone, who, she says, 'evidently has no time for sentimental depictions of Scottishness, and instead exposes such constructions as anachronistic and unable to adequately reflect modern Scotland'.[115] Apart from the fact that this ignores the extent to which cultural nationalists have spent much time on berating sentimental Scottishness, and have also been determined to expose those constructions which are anachronistic and unable to reflect modern Scotland, it ignores entirely McCrone's acknowledgment of his own commitments in the 'Preface' to his study of *The Sociology of Nationalism*, drafted symbolically on St Andrew's Day 1997: 'To the accusation that the author is a nationalist, one would have to reply that, since the British general election of 1997 at which the self-defined Unionist party in Scotland (and Wales) was wiped out, we are all nationalists now – to some degree or another.'[116] What Bell takes from McCrone, and what she believes Beveridge and Turnbull fail to address, is that 'monoculturalism is no longer an acceptable foundation on which to base the frameworks of national identity'.[117] It is a strange argument to make against a Scottish nationalism which has always had to acknowledge its debt to a heritage in Scots and in Gaelic as well as to its practical operation in English, but it also ignores McCrone's insistence that not only are all 'modern societies indubitably, if implicitly, nationalist'[118] but that 'the modern state is faced continuously with legitimating itself before its citizens' and this 'ultimately makes nationalism more, not less, important'.[119] The modern 'rise of nationalism', according to McCrone, is based on the power of nationalism 'to reconfigure personal identities and loyalties in a way more in tune with the social, cultural and political realities'[120] of the modern age.

Far from being antitheses, postmodernism and nationalism are in fact profoundly implicated with one another – which is why the era of postmodernism is *also* the era of resurgent nationalism. If such reconfigurations do 'not imply that ethnic identity will have priority over other forms of social identity',[121] that merely reiterates what has almost always been acknowledged within Scottish nationalism, not only because Scotland has always been

---

[115] Ibid., 77.

[116] McCrone, *The Sociology of Nationalism*, ix.

[117] Bell, *Questioning Scotland*, 78.

[118] David McCrone, *Understanding Scotland: the Sociology of a Stateless Nation* (London: Routledge, 1992), 159.

[119] Ibid., 160.

[120] McCrone, *Sociology of Nationalism*, 183.

[121] Ibid.

heir to multiple *ethnies*, but also because the territory of Scotland consists of very strong regional and local identities, as well highly focused religious identities.

In a passage which Bell quotes with approval, Berthold Schoene describes the activities of 'Scottish intellectuals', even when they acknowledge that there are plural Scotlands, as directed towards an object which is 'still a territorial, historically pre-coded and hence potentially essentialist term which serves to identify, isolate and exclude both internal and external "aliens" by clearly distinguishing what is Scottish from what is un-Scottish'.[122] To propose that some element of a tradition is *distinctively* Scottish is not, however, to claim that there are no other traditions in Scotland or that all Scots have to be participants in that tradition: it is to claim that particular conditions in Scotland have shaped a tradition which could not have developed in the same way in any other place. It does not mean that it owes nothing to other places, or that it is essentially 'native'; nor does it mean it refuses to engage with anything that has come from beyond the boundaries of Scotland or with anything that is 'un-Scottish' (think of Scottish rhododendron gardens). To suggest that the effort of cultural nationalists to call attention to Scottish traditions which have been ignored as a consequence of the failure of the Scottish educational system to tend things Scottish is somehow a monocultural denial of 'difference' ignores the fact that it is precisely the recognition of difference – the difference of Scotland, of difference in Scotland – to which many varieties of cultural nationalism have sought to direct our attention. Any argument about the cultural past is, in part, an argument about what constitutes a canon worthy of our effort in revisiting it, and in revising it, but to *propose* a canon does not mean that one is *imposing* a canon: a canon, like the nation, is a place of debate.

Bell's argument about monoculturalism, and about Scottish cultural nationalism's 'uncritical dependency on essentialist notions in order to justify the Tradition',[123] is aimed, in other words, at a target that does not exist. This is equally true of another often quoted challenge to Beveridge and Turnbull by Laurence Nicoll, who argues that 'by attempting to render philosophy an essential aspect of nation,… [they] simply fail to see, or fail to accept, that within any given country, any given community, any given university, an individual or a group of individuals might adopt a particular conception

---

122 Quoted in Bell, *Questioning Scotland*, 143; originally in *Scottish Literary Journal*, Vol. 25, No. 1 (May 1998), 55.
123 Bell, *Questioning Scotland*, 146.

of philosophical enquiry purely because it is felt, or more likely reasoned, to be a better conceptual or explanatory tool or to offer a more convincing depiction of the good life'.[124] Beveridge and Turnbull, Nicoll suggests, subscribe to the view that certain methods of philosophical enquiry are valuable because they are Scottish,[125] and as a consequence seek to 'operate a philosophical customs' point where a crude check – Continental equals "good"; English equals "bad" – determines what philosophies may be happily admitted into Scotland'. The consequence, Nicoll believes, is that Beveridge and Turnbull's argument enacts 'at an individual level' what 'it seeks to combat at a national level, for it colonises' by insisting that the individual must 'adopt, maintain and valorise a pre-cast "national" form' of thought.[126] Such appeals against the thought police of a future Scotland of repressive, indeed totalitarian monoculturalism – Beveridge and Turnbull's prose is described as trying to 'frog-march the reader'[127] – threaten us with the return of that repressive Scottish cultural past from which, according to the cosmopolitan view, we have barely yet escaped.

However, if we return to Beveridge and Turnbull's own text the issues that Nicoll raises are given a very different construction. First, the distinction between 'English' and 'Continental' philosophy is not theirs: it comes from a quotation they give from Oxford philosopher Geoffrey Warnock's account of the differences between the status of philosophy in England – 'an academic discipline, a subject with its own problems and own standards, capable of proceeding quite independently, in a sense, of what was going on in the world at large' – and of philosophy in Continental Europe, which is 'looked to for what one might call comment on the human predicament'.[128] This is a distinction Beveridge and Turnbull see as substantiated by A. J. Ayer's dismissive account of Heidegger in *Language, Truth and Logic*, one of the most influential books of philosophy in England in the 1930s.

This is not, as Nicoll would have it, simply a geographical division with no philosophical content: Beveridge and Turnbull's point is that these are two

---

124   Laurence Nicoll, 'Philosophy, Tradition, Nation', in Eleanor Bell and Gavin Miller (eds), *Scotland in Theory: Reflections on Culture and Literature* (Amsterdam: Rodopi, 2004), 217.

125   Ibid., 216.

126   Ibid., 218.

127   Ibid., 225.

128   Craig Beveridge and Ronald Turnbull, *The Eclipse of Scottish Culture: Inferiorism and the Intellectuals* (Edinburgh: Polygon, 1989), 69.

different kinds of philosophy with large-scale implications for the role of philosophy in the contemporary world. Philosophy as conducted on the lines advocated by Warnock or Ayer is, they contend, 'banal', and the fact that it is the dominant philosophical mode in the English-speaking world – as identified not by them but by thinkers like Gellner, in his *Words and Things*, and by the Radical Philosophy movement – has resulted in its achieving a prominent role in Scottish universities. Their argument is not with the *Englishness* of this particular form of Anglophone philosophy but with its lack of significant philosophical content, and with the fact that the tradition of philosophy in which it trains its students fails to acknowledge that any other tradition is relevant in the Anglophone world.

The irony of such a situation, as they see it, is that a Scottish tradition of philosophical enquiry that actually shares with the so-called 'Continental philosophy' a concern with 'the human predicament' has thereby been rendered invisible to those practising or learning philosophy in Scotland. The important issue is not one of the nationality of the philosophy or philosopher but of the mode of philosophy to be engaged in, though this choice, in Scotland, has been pre-empted by the suppression of certain kinds of philosophy precisely because they are Scottish:

> In both of the dominant philosophical traditions – logical positivism and ordinary language analysis – *philosophy becomes a specialism*, divorced from other forms of inquiry. The reduction of philosophy to the logic of science in the one, and to semantic analysis in the other, cuts it off from general social, political and moral issues, and excludes the conception that philosophy stands in a direct relation to conduct.[129]

They follow George Davie's argument in *The Democratic Intellect* (1961) that this very different and generalist tradition of Scottish philosophy was central both to the role of philosophy in the Scottish universities and to the distinctiveness of Scottish intellectual life in the eighteenth and nineteenth centuries, which makes the issue of *which* philosophy is to be practised in Scotland more than a matter of just philosophical consequence in a narrow disciplinary sense. Submission to the dominant positivist or linguistic philosophy changes the role of philosophy not only in the universities, in terms of the relationships between disciplines, but in the broader society

---

[129] Ibid., 68.

they serve. Nicoll cites R. D. Anderson's critique of Davie to suggest that Davie's work simply 'laid the groundwork for a number of misunderstandings of Scotland'.[130] Anderson's critique, however, is largely about how 'democratic' Scottish universities actually were and about the detail of the various curricula of the Scottish universities, not about the role of philosophy as providing a general overview for the other disciplines or about its role in relation to the rest of the society. Here, Davie's argument can be confirmed by historians of science, such as Crosbie Smith, who suggests that the generality of the scientific theories produced by Scotland's major scientists, including Lord Kelvin and James Clerk Maxwell, were a product of their philosophical training, which provided the bridge between their theological views and the aims of their experimentation,[131] and that this was a particular strength of the Scottish universities as compared with Oxford and Cambridge. Given the past distinctiveness of the Scottish universities in this respect, and the fact that such distinctiveness had been steadily eroded to make Scottish students more acceptable to the requirements of UK institutions, it is at least arguable that the role of philosophy in modern Scotland, and the kind of content that is taught in philosophy courses, is indeed an issue of *national* significance.

For Nicoll, Beveridge and Turnbull conflate nation and philosophy in order to impose on everyone a single tradition which will limit individual freedom by replacing 'Anglicisation' with 'Scotticisation', 'a move which is neither democratic, nor particularly intellectual'.[132] But nowhere in their text do Beveridge and Turnbull propose a closed system of only 'Scottish' philosophical ideas: indeed, they note that Scotland has been a centre for Kant scholarship and that Scots had played a key role in 'translating and interpreting the world of such figures as Martin Buber, Dietrich Bonhoffer, Karl Barth, Rudolf Bultmann and Martin Heidegger',[133] and therefore that the notion of an alien 'Continental' philosophy makes no sense in the Scottish context. What they propose is that attention in Scotland to some of the Scottish philosophers who were, in the 1980s, and still are, nearly thirty years later, ignored within a curriculum dominated by the 'analytical' tradition, would bring alternative philosophical questions into play and would allow

---

[130] Nicoll, 'Philosophy, Tradition, Nation', 219–20.
[131] Crosbie Smith and M. Norton Wise, *Energy and Empire: A Biographical Study of Lord Kelvin* (Cambridge: Cambridge University Press, 1989), 352ff.
[132] Nicoll, 'Philosophy, Tradition, Nation', 218.
[133] Beveridge and Turnbull, *Eclipse of Scottish Culture*, 91.

philosophy again to engage with 'the dimensions of experience, knowledge and reality which are beyond the scope of scientific reasoning'.[134] If French or German or American philosophers made such a proposal about neglected thinkers within their national philosophical canons, would it be regarded as a betrayal of philosophy by nationality? Of course, no such proposal would be necessary, because, unlike Scotland, these are all countries that take it for granted that the nation's philosophical traditions will be represented in their philosophical teaching – indeed, despite Nicoll's amazement, it may only be in Scotland that philosophy and nationality are *not* 'somehow conjoined'.

What drives Nicoll so insistently to misrepresent Beveridge and Turnbull's arguments is not their specific philosophical content but the fact that they are made as part of an explicitly cultural nationalist agenda which Nicoll believes makes 'identity a product of purely national difference' and which will therefore 'obviate difference at the level of the individual: nations are – supposedly – culturally different, but the individuals within them, in order to be "authentic", should all exhibit and seek to maintain this supposedly homogeneous culture'.[135] Like its gardens, the 'homogeneity' of the nation is, in fact and theory, an illusion: but so too is that isolated, autonomous, self-directing individual whom Nicoll sets out to defend from imposed homogeneity. Nicoll believes Beveridge and Turnbull's cultural nationalism 'amounts to the assertion that an individual ought to adopt a cultural practice simply because he or she is contingently born within the contingent borders of the contingent geographical space in which these contingent cultural practices arose',[136] whereas their position develops from the recognition that human beings live in communities of relationship and that individuals remain in relationship with their communities even when they reject or resist their values. What they ask is not that each individual becomes a version of a single national type but that neglected parts of the past of this-community-called-Scotland should be represented in its institutions in a way that allows Scots (and others) – if they choose – to make them an aspect of their relation to that past and, therefore, an element in the values by which they define their intentions towards the future.

This 'search for Scottish culture' in which Beveridge and Turnbull are engaged is, for David McCrone as for Nicoll, a false one, relying on Enlightenment conceptions in which 'the role of intellectuals…has been

---

[134] Ibid., 111.
[135] Nicoll, 'Philosophy, Tradition, Nation', 218.
[136] Ibid.

to identify the "essential character" of a people, and to give it political expression',[137] a character which, if it ever did exist, cannot, according to McCrone, continue to exist in the modern age:

> Being black, Glaswegian and female can all characterise one person's cultural and social inheritance without one aspect of that identity being paramount (except in terms of self-identification). What is on offer in the late twentieth century is what we might call 'pik 'n mix' identity, in which we wear our identities lightly, and change them according to circumstances.[138]

This is a passage which Beveridge and Turnbull have subjected to particularly caustic analysis as promoting a notion of the 'self' which, to any earlier age, would have represented a profound failure of the potentialities of being human.[139] It is, in any case, an unfortunate example, since at least two and possibly all three of the terms by which this person is categorised are ones which certainly cannot simply be 'picked' or easily changed: whatever they might signify, they are not identities that can simply be cast off lightly. I am more interested, however, in what happens if we add 'Scottish' to 'black, Glaswegian and female' – does 'Scottish' just add another element into the 'mix' or does it do something else? If, for example, the case was 'black, Glaswegian, female and American' (not an impossible outcome when the Firth of Clyde provided the forward defence of America's homeland territory), then one would be dealing with a person who had rights which someone 'black, Glaswegian, female and Scottish' would not have – right of domicile in the USA, for instance – while the American, equally, might not have access to some of the same rights as her Scottish-born equivalent – the automatic right, for instance, to free tertiary education. For two people otherwise describable in the same terms, being 'Scottish' provides and prevents certain possible developments of individual identity. Interestingly, the law, through which such rights are defined, makes almost no appearance in *Understanding Scotland*, despite the fact that the preservation of Scots law has always been taken to be one of the pillars of Scotland's ongoing identity after the Union, and despite the fact that lawyers are a highly influential sector of Scottish society, a sector which one would have thought of interest

---

[137] McCrone, *Understanding Scotland*, 190.
[138] Ibid., 195.
[139] Beveridge and Turnbull, *Scotland After Enlightenment*, 168–70.

to sociology.[140] That the law should be virtually absent from an attempt to understand Scotland is particularly significant given that the law contributes so directly to the texture of Scottish society, from the age at which Scots are able to marry to the hours at which they are able to consume alcohol; from the mode of purchase and possession of their homes to their rights to walk across land; from their ability to smack their children without prosecution to their access to nursing care in old age. And what is interesting about the absence of the law in McCrone's book is that Scotland in the modern world is, first and foremost, a legal entity, the product of a Treaty between states which recognised each other as such, and which guaranteed the continued operation of 'national' Scottish institutions: where Scots law is the law of the land, the land is Scotland.

This mutual implication of the nation and its laws signals the special role of institutions in the nation. Too often, discussions of the nation pass from the individual to the national without going by way of the institutions which, for all of us, are the forms in which the nation actually presents itself to us. Even advocates of so-called 'civic nationalism' – as a nationalism built not on ethnic identity but on the rights of anyone who is a participant in a particular society – tend to separate 'civil society' from the nation and to present it as a realm of relative individual autonomy, beyond the imprint of the nation or state. The importance of civic institutions, however, is that they provide what may be described as a 'feedback mechanism' by which the 'nationness' of the nation is reinforced. Institutions whose remit in Scotland is coincidental with the territory of the law are institutions whose remit is Scotland itself, from the Confederation of Scottish Business or the Scottish Trades Union Council to the Scottish Arts Council or the Scottish Football Association. It is through such channels that the people of the nation encounter the nation-in-action, and through which they can see their own intentions becoming elements of national action.

As such institutions go about their business, they reinforce the sense of the nation's presence in communal life because their activity is dependent on 'national' authority. The community thus comes to be informed in its daily life

---

[140] McCrone suggests that 'Scotland's professional classes – lawyers, doctors, teachers, churchmen – while socially conservative, embody the institutional survival of a distinctive Scottish "civil society" and can be considered as the keepers of native institutions, and hence incipient "nationalists"' (*Understanding Scotland*, 143), but gives no evidence for the social or political views of these groups.

by the nation, and therefore comes to see its life as representative *of* the nation. Such institutions perform a double function. On the one hand they embody specific intentions of the national past which are thereby given enduring solidity within the fabric of the nation: they are, in Alasdair MacIntyre's resounding phrase, 'an historically extended, socially embodied argument',[141] the continuation of a previous debate in an ongoing organisational structure. Such embodied institutional arguments shape the environment in which we live and give it a historical specificity which is not simply a product of antiquarianism or of the heritage industry: like the streets of our cities which are the product of someone else's decision and which shape the journeys we can take, the institutions of our national environment shape the way we walk through our lives. On the other hand, they provide the means by which we, as members of the nation, are able to direct our intentions towards the nation and reshape the ways in which it orders our communal existence. Cultural nationalists have always recognised the power of this feedback loop, since their primary activity has always been – from the founding of newspapers and theatres to the creation of museums and festivals – the inauguration of institutions which will feed back into the nation a heightened sense of the significance of its own status and an intensified awareness of the 'presence' of the nation in the community. 'Presence' here does not, of course, mean 'essence': it means an intentional object, the object of our intentions, the medium by which our intentions turn into actions and by which our actions are embodied in new institutions. It means the generation of difference, since it is fundamental to these institutions that in fulfilling their role they maintain the distinction – both in the sense of 'distinctiveness' and in the sense of claiming high value – of the legal entity from which they derive their authority.

It is the absence of such institutions from McCrone's account of Scotland in *Understanding Scotland* that makes him regard the search for Scottish culture a pointless task. There is, for McCrone, a choice only between the search for a 'real' Scottish culture which is 'inevitably retrospective and romantic',[142] and an acceptance that in the modern world cultures are all pretty much the same – that 'if we set out to look for what is distinctive in Scotland, we run the risk of focusing on the trivial and epiphenomenal, which will be found only in the past and in the museum'.[143] Museums, of course, are not

---

[141] Alasdair MacIntyre, *After Virtue* (London: Duckworth, 1985), 222.
[142] McCrone, *Understanding Scotland*, 192.
[143] Ibid., 194.

in the past: they are very much in the present, they are contemporary arguments embodied in material realities. McCrone presents the choice as being
between an impossible search for a 'real' Scottish identity which could only
have existed, if anywhere, in the past, or the acceptance of a Scotland which
is substantially indistinguishable from England or the United States. This
is what we might term the 'normalising' account of Scotland: Scotland is
simply a normal, developed country whose economy and social structure are
very little different from most other developed countries. In the aftermath
of the argument about Scotland's pathologically distorted condition, this is
seemingly attractive. But in making the 'difference' between nations 'trivial'
it makes it impossible to understand what it is that makes people *value* their
nation – value it enough, on occasions, to die for it. And the issue of *value*
disappears out of McCrone's analysis because he fails to acknowledge the
crucial role of the institutions which are the carriers of value.

The difference between nations (even nations which may share very similar economic structures) are the product of their very different institutional
structures, structures which are themselves the products of, and retain the
impress of, particular junctures in their history and of the on-going debates
between their various traditions. The differences between nations, even in a
globalised world, are not accidental – they are the product of past arguments
which are embodied in and through their institutions and in the intentions
which those structures project as possible futures for the nation. What makes
Scotland 'different' is not its national *geist* but a whole host of Scottish institutions whose intentions and actions bring to bear on the Scottish present sets
of values derived from the Scottish past – like the possibility of 'not proven'
as the outcome of a trial; like entitlement to qualify for university in the fifth
year of secondary school; like the right to education in a state-supported
Catholic school. These institutions, precisely because of the past arguments
about value which they continue to embody, and the intentions which their
values continue to shape, *generate* difference, because the equivalent institutions in other countries have developed at different historical junctures, and
in a different context of debate, than they did in Scotland, and so produce a
different set of relationships as the defining context of the nation.

A simple example of this is the Scottish Football Association: it exists
because of the decision of a small number of Scottish clubs, in 1873, not to
join the football association being formed in England, an association which
was specifically *not* called the English Football Association by its founder, a
Scot by the name of MacGregor, because he wanted the Scottish teams to

participate. In choosing not to join the FA but to form the SFA, they created an institutional structure which each year produces and reproduces a different context for football and, as a consequence, a kind of football which is recognisably *Scottish*. It also puts Scottish footballers in a context different from those elsewhere in the world, since Scotland (along with Wales, Northern Ireland and England) are the only countries allowed to enter 'international' competition without being recognised nation states. The possibility of access to 'international' football for players of this 'national' game has often led critics to suggest that football is a surrogate for nationhood in Scotland. In fact, it is an exemplary case of how an institutional structure, aligned with and operating in its own domain as part of the legal framework of the nation, produces difference, and reproduces the nation as a system of identifiable values. Rather than Scotland's nationalism having 'developed without the encumbrance of a heavy cultural baggage' because 'Scots have decided to travel light', Scottish cultural difference and the nationalism which develops from it are the product in part of Scotland's increasingly organised institutional structures for the support of its culture: the 'lightness' of Scottish cultural baggage in McCrone's account is the result of not having weighed the developing institutions – the Scottish National Library, the Scottish Arts Council, the Scottish Academy, Scottish National Galleries, the Royal Scottish Academy of Music and Dance, the Scottish National Orchestra, Scottish Opera, Creative Scotland, the National Museum, the Association for Scottish Literary Studies, the Scottish Folk Festival, the Scottish Qualifications Authority, the Scottish Poetry Library, Universities Scotland (to name but a few) – which exist to collect, record, promote and develop a 'distinctive' – and, hopefully, 'distinguished' – national culture. And if individual artists – like Hamilton Finlay – develop by resisting these established institutions, their argument with the establishment provokes an equally distinctive set of Scottish debates.

If Scotland's political nationalism has, as McCrone believes, developed as a 'political manifestation which is not tied to a specific *cultural* divergence' that can only be so by laying such emphasis on 'specific' that it means 'singular', as in, for instance, a nationalism of 'language politics'. But Scotland's cultural divergence from England in the period since the 1970s has been enormous and it is in the context of Scotland's revitalised cultural richness, both institutional and creative, that Scottish nationalism (with a small 'n') has flourished. Far from Scotland's neo-nationalism representing 'almost a cultureless, post-industrial journey into the unknown', and the new Scottish politics being the expression of a concern simply 'with the practicalities of decision-making and control',[144] Scotland's parliament has been built on the foundations of a revolution in the nation's culture – a turning over of its past which has also been an overturning of its past. Like many other nationalisms, Scotland discovered that remaking its culture was the best way of intending a new nation.

VI   Tended Nations

In 1924, Patrick Geddes, Scottish biologist, publisher, town-planner and theorist of human evolution, by then aged 70, took up residence on a hillside above the town of Montpellier in the south of France. In the 1890s, in Edinburgh, Geddes had been responsible for the development of halls of residence for students, reclaiming decaying parts of Edinburgh's Old Town and turning them into examples of how the redevelopment of traditional buildings, and their shared areas of garden, might enhance the sense of community and overcome the degrading effects of urbanisation and industrialisation. In 1900, as a way of inducting Scottish students into recent developments in French culture,[145] he had proposed the revival of the Scots College in Paris, which had, from 1325 until the Reformation, provided an institutional base for young Scots studying in France, and had thereafter, until its closure by the Revolutionary government in 1793, been a focus for Scottish Catholicism and Jacobitism. This, like many of Geddes's profligate ideas, had come to nothing but in his old age he set out to recreate in Montpellier a version of that Parisian Collège des Écossais.

Because of its geographical position, Montpellier had always been a crossing point between cultures, and since at least the twelfth century, it had been a centre for the biological and botanical sciences. Fundamental to those disciplines was its botanical garden, which was the oldest in France, having been founded in 1593, and the centrepiece of Geddes's College was also to be its garden. Geddes's professorship in Dundee had been in botany, and since Dundee did not have a botanic garden, Geddes had had to design his own and much of his teaching actually took place in the garden. To his American acolyte, Lewis Mumford (who always addressed him in letters as 'Master'), Geddes

---

[144]   Ibid., 196.
[145]   Philip Mairet, *Pioneer of Sociology: The Life and Letters of Patrick Geddes* (London: Lund Humphries, 1957), 60.

wrote on 17 May 1931: 'I have written about gardens, and it passed: but this fullest of Flowering-Paradises of the seasons will survive me – & always be exuberant with time – Life more abundantly – Life in evolution – thus in fact and deed, and not merely in words!'[146] The garden, in what might have been a prophecy of the career of Ian Hamilton Finlay, was to be the ultimate statement of his philosophy, because writing could never displace the need to act: 'I can't accept, in short, the idea of sociological writing unassociated with action'.[147] For Geddes, the garden of the Scots in France was an image of a possible international future: 'I see this growing place as a definitely possible academic league of nations – a junior Geneva'.[148] And the point of this Scottish garden was its comprehensiveness:

> Though the making of this garden has taken much time these two past winters, and again will next, it is also very helpful. For though there are bigger ones of every possible kind, and I have made some myself, never before, so far as I know, has there been an attempt to express the essentials of so *many kinds* of garden – e.g. from nature-reserve for formal garden, and evolutionary botanic garden; from ordinary cultivation to desert reclamation, and foresting sample; and so on concretely. Furthermore, beyond ordinary aspects, scientific, aesthetic and practical, there is the attempt to work out the expression of *philosophy peripatetically readable* – as from the classification of sciences, laid out in squares of pavement on the house terrace, to gardens of Olympus, the Muses etc.; and all in such forms as may be intelligible to the Boy Scouts, yet also stimulating to the professor.[149]

A garden 'of every possible kind' but created within the denomination of a Scots college; a universal philosophy created in Scotland but readable in the south of France. Geddes's Mediterranean garden enacts in reverse the transfer of plants, the transfer of cultures, by which the Scottish garden came to flourish in the sixteenth and seventeenth centuries. Despite its location, Geddes's garden is a Scottish garden, like Hamilton Finlay's, which, in tending the soil, tends the nation, and through it intends the world. Like Little Sparta,

---

146 Frank G. Novak, Jr (ed.), *Lewis Mumford and Patrick Geddes: The Correspondence* (London and New York: Routledge, 1995), 322.
147 Ibid.
148 Ibid., 240.
149 Ibid.

Geddes's Scots College – his 'Little Scotland' – contains plaques and inscrip-tions which offer commentary on its scenic effects; one of them, entitled 'un jardin de l'espérance', reads,

> Past joys revive young oaks
> And vines climb over past
>   inspirations
>   to flower
>   anew
> We learn again through
>   the leaves

In tending the garden that it may 'revive' and 'climb over past' versions of itself we have a symbol for the nation: we 'learn again' from what it 'leaves' to us, allowing 'past inspiration to flower anew' in the process of translation and transposition which makes both garden and nation possible.

2   When Was the Scottish Enlightenment?

I   Finding Enlightenment

In the 'Introduction' to their *Origins and Nature of the Scottish Enlightenment*, published in 1982, R. H. Campbell and Andrew Skinner note that 'interest in the Scottish Enlightenment is comparatively recent',[1] and they date the inauguration of that interest to W. C. Lehmann's *Adam Ferguson and Modern Sociology*, published in 1930, and to Gladys Bryson's *Man and Society: The Scottish Enquiry of the Eighteenth Century*, which appeared in 1945. The interest of both these writers was in establishing that 'social scientists of the twentieth century may properly regard them [the Scottish Enlightenment thinkers] as forerunners in the effort in which we are engaged',[2] and, therefore, as defining influences on the development of contemporary social science. Bryson, however, does not see her topic as an analysis of an event called 'The Scottish Enlightenment' but rather as an analysis of Scottish thinkers who 'were at home in the intellectual climate of the late Enlightenment when secular interest once again commanded attention'.[3] Her interest, in other words, is in the case of 'Enlightenment in Scotland' rather than 'Scottish Enlightenment', one in which Adam Ferguson, for instance, is seen as 'a central figure in the Scottish group of [the] "enlightened",'[4] as though that group was quite cut off from its surrounding – and presumably unenlightened – society.

More recently, John Robertson has assigned the commencement of the concept of the Scottish Enlightenment to the work of Duncan Forbes and Hugh Trevor-Roper in the 1960s, and particularly to the course on 'Hume,

---

[1] R. H. Campbell and Andrew Skinner, *Origins and Nature of the Scottish Enlightenment* (Edinburgh: John Donald, 1982), 1.
[2] Gladys Bryson, *Man and Society: The Scottish Enquiry of the Eighteenth Century* (Princeton: Princeton University Press, 1945), 11.
[3] Ibid., 5.
[4] Ibid., 30.

Smith and the Scottish Enlightenment' run by Forbes at Cambridge, and attended by many of the influential participants in Enlightenment studies in the following thirty or forty years – most notably, perhaps, by Nicholas Phillipson and Quentin Skinner. The emphasis in Forbes's account shifts from the 'enlightened' to the process of 'enlightenment' as a European social phenomenon: 'As the title of the course indicates, Forbes's Scottish Enlightenment was an intellectual movement to which others besides Hume and Smith had made important contributions, and which had concentrated upon the understanding of society and its development; it was also a cosmopolitan movement, whose frame of reference extended well beyond Britain';[5] while in Trevor-Roper's case the emphasis is on 'enlightenment' as the product of 'the country's experience of unusually rapid economic and social development'.[6] Trevor-Roper's socio-economic explanation laid the ground for the study of the Enlightenment 'in its national context' which, since Anand Chitnis's first book-length study of *The Scottish Enlightenment* in 1976, has proved such productive territory for scholars seeking to demonstrate the breadth and depth of 'enlightenment' in eighteenth-century Scotland, and its fundamental shaping by those cultural institutions – religion, law, education – which had retained their autonomy despite the political Union with England in 1707. It is a 'nationalising' of Enlightenment – both in the emphasis on its economic underpinnings in Scottish commerce and on its general dispersal through many sectors of Scottish society – which some, including Robertson, believe to have gone too far in cutting off the Scottish Enlightenment from the broader European movement, and which others, such as Roy Porter, see as falsifying the ways in which the Scots were integral participants in a wider British Enlightenment fundamentally shaped by developments in England.[7]

The centrality of the Scottish Enlightenment to the (re)construction of modern Scottish history and to the presentation of modern Scottish identity is underlined by the way it has been presented in works such as Arthur Herman's *The Scottish Enlightenment* (2000) – originally subtitled in the United States as 'the true story of how Western Europe's poorest nation created our world & everything in it' – and in Tom Devine's *The Scottish Nation* (1999), in which the Enlightenment sets Scotland up to fulfil those transformations

---

5 Ibid.
6 Ibid.
7 Roy Porter, *Enlightenment: Britain and the Creation of the Modern World* (London: Allen Lane, 2000).

of agriculture and industry that English history used to claim were unique to English development. According to Devine, the 'currently favoured view of English modernization, [is] a process characterized by cumulative, protracted and evolutionary development', but the case is very different in Scotland: 'North of the border there truly was an Industrial and Agricultural Revolution.'[8] The characteristics that had once justified England's exceptional place among European nations and explained its pre-eminence in economic development have been transferred to Scotland – Europe's truly revolutionary society despite its apparent political quiescence throughout the nineteenth century.

It is a vision of Scottish primacy which took on significant political overtones in the aftermath of the establishment of the Scottish parliament in 1999. In the following years newspaper articles regularly asked whether there could be a 'second Scottish Enlightenment' or whether, indeed, in the light of major contemporary Scottish scientific achievements – such as the cloning of Dolly the sheep – we were already living through a second Scottish Enlightenment. And the Enlightenment – which for many years had been regarded as having betrayed Scottish culture by its Anglicising tendencies – was rapidly adopted as the true foundation of modern Scottish identity. In 2006, the then first minister, Jack McConnell, chose to make the Enlightenment the theme of his Tartan Day address at Princeton University, deliberately attempting to relocate Scotland's national identity from 'romantic tartan' to 'enlightened science': Scots who migrated to the United States were 'the shock troops of modernisation – ordinary people who helped make America what it is today' – because at their back stood the Scottish Enlightenment philosophers who 'taught the world how to think scientifically; set out the laws of modern market economics; and helped create the modern, civilised values that the United States and the rest of the democratic world now upholds'. Despite the establishment of 'Tartan Day' as the iconic celebration of Scots in America, Scotland's future identity, like its past, was to be focused on 'enlightenment' rather than 'tartan' because, according to McConnell, 'there are some who think Scotland could become home to a second enlightenment'.[9]

The destabilising rapidity of this rise to prominence of the Scottish Enlightenment – and of the consequent rise of eighteenth-century Scotland

---

[8] Devine, *The Scottish Nation*, 107.

[9] Reported at http://www.scotland.gov uk/News/News-Extras/princeton (accessed September 2008)

to a new international significance – produced an initial uncertainty about what the nature of the phenomenon under discussion might be. This can be seen, for instance, in one of the earliest efforts to account for the Enlightenment, Nicholas Phillipson and Rosalind Mitchison's *Scotland in the Age of Improvement: Essays in Scottish History in the Eighteenth Century* (1970). The choice of 'improvement' over 'enlightenment' to define 'the Age' is itself indicative, and if 'the Age of Improvement' is characterised in the editors' introduction as 'the time of the Scottish enlightenment, that remarkable out-burst of intellectual life in which, almost overnight, Scotland was snatched from the relative cultural isolation in which she had passed the seventeenth century and placed in the centre of the thinking world',[10] the passive grammar of 'was snatched' suggests that Scotland itself had little to do with this transformation. If there was enlightenment in Scotland it was not necessarily an enlightenment stemming *from* Scotland. One chapter within the collection suggests not only an alternative way of reading Scotland's eighteenth-century history, but an alternative terminology: John Clive's essay raises the 'question of the origin of the "Scottish Renaissance" – that remarkable efflorescence of the mid-eighteenth century, with its roll call of the great names' which represents 'one of those historical problems which have hitherto stubbornly resisted a definite solution'.[11] The terminology of the 'Renaissance' can hardly, in 1970, have avoided associations with Hugh MacDiarmid's 'Scottish Renaissance' of the 1920s and its claim to reconnect modern Scottish writing with the great period of Scottish poetry in the fifteenth and sixteenth centuries. To describe the eighteenth century as a 'Renaissance' implies a continuity in Scottish culture not contained within the concept of an 'Enlightenment'. As Clive acknowledges in a footnote, however, the terminological difference is the result of the fact that 'This essay was first written some years ago, as a part, eventually not published, of the author's *Scotch Reviewers: The Edinburgh Review, 1802–1815* (London 1957)': its terminology, in other words, reflected the fact that it was produced before the general acceptance of the notion of a Scottish Enlightenment.[12]

The same was true on the other side of the Atlantic where, in 1961, a book entitled *The Story of Scottish Philosophy* was published in New York. Edited by

---

[10] Nicholas Phillipson and Rosalind Mitchison (eds), *Scotland in the Age of Improvement: Essays in Scottish History in the Eighteenth Century* (Edinburgh: Edinburgh University Press, 1970).

[11] Ibid., 227.

[12] Ibid., 225.

Daniel Somner Robinson, it tells the story of eighteenth- and nineteenth-century Scottish thought without making any mention of Enlightenment, and presents the climax of the story of Scottish thought as the work of James McCosh (1811–94), President of Princeton College and author of *The Scottish Philosophy* (1875).[13] For Robinson, the importance of the story of Scottish philosophy derives from its being the source of contemporary American pragmatism, a source which Americans both need to know and to acknowledge if they are to understand the presuppositions of their own tradition. The Enlightenment makes no appearance in Somner's Scottish story because it makes no appearance in McCosh's account of Scottish philosophy: for McCosh, Scottish philosophy is defined as a national tradition in which individual philosophers represent 'family members', so that although 'by the close of the [eighteenth] century, the fathers and elder sons of the family have passed away from the scene',[14] the family business will inevitably be continued by the younger sons and their heirs. What is significant about this philosophical family, however, is that it does not include the figure who, by the twentieth century, was to be central to the notion of the Enlightenment in Scotland. For Peter Gay, in his groundbreaking account of the Enlightenment in the 1960s as 'the rise of modern paganism', David Hume stood as the embodiment of 'The Complete Modern Pagan';[15] for McCosh, on the other hand, what was Scottish about Scottish philosophy was defined precisely by its *resistance* to Hume. Hume might be part of the story but he was not part of the tradition of Scottish philosophy, for that tradition was defined by its ability to provide answers to Hume's scepticism: 'It has been the aim of the Scottish school, as modified and developed by Reid, to throw back the scepticism of Hume.'[16] While accepting that all later philosophy has been required to address the challenge of Hume's philosophy, McCosh's belief is that Scottish philosophy's importance lies in the fact that it has found an adequate basis on which this 'foe', this outsider, 'might be repelled'.[17] Clearly, as long as Hume – the Scottish thinker most central to a European conception

---

[13]   McCosh is eulogised in McConnell's Princeton address on the Enlightenment with no indication of his failure to identify with any conception of 'enlightenment'.

[14]   James McCosh, *The Scottish Philosophy: Biographical, Expository, Critical, from Hutcheson to Hamilton* (London: Macmillan, 1875), 248.

[15]   Peter Gay, *The Enlightenment: An Interpretation: Volume 1, The Rise of Modern Paganism* (New York: Knopf, [1966] 1977), Ch. 7, sect. 3.

[16]   McCosh, *The Scottish Philosophy*, 146.

[17]   Ibid., 147.

of Enlightenment – remains outside of the Scottish tradition of philosophy, there can be no *Scottish* Enlightenment: Scottish philosophy is, in effect, defined as the refusal of Enlightenment.

In more recent accounts, these hesitations about the nature of 'Enlightenment' in Scotland, and about its origins, have been matched by an equal uncertainty about when it ended, though there is widespread agreement that it did disappear, leaving nothing in its wake. Enlightenment in Scotland, it appears, bequeathed nothing to its successors, and produced no Scottish succession. This is the conclusion of popular accounts such as Herman's *The Scottish Enlightenment*: 'As the nineteenth century waned, the intellectual capital of the Scottish Enlightenment waned with it', he suggests, as though the capital had failed to be invested in an ongoing business: 'Scotland's days as the generator of Europe's most innovative ideas were over.'[18] More academic analyses concur: Gordon Graham's version of nineteenth-century Scottish philosophy in Alexander Broadie's *Cambridge Companion to the Scottish Enlightenment* (2003), insists that 'the nineteenth century . . . saw the unravelling of the great philosophical project that had animated the eighteenth'.[19] It is a view based on the most influential account of nineteenth-century Scottish philosophy, George Davie's *The Democratic Intellect* (1961), which charts how 'the democratic intellectualism which had distinguished Scottish civilisation was being allowed to disappear' because Scots were no longer concerned to maintain 'national pretensions to intellectual independence'.[20]

The Enlightenment may now be the great glory of Scottish history but it is a glory whose fading leaves Scotland in a condition not dissimilar from that from which the Enlightenment was supposed to have saved it. That division is clearly marked in T. C. Smout's two major works. The first volume rises towards a culmination in 'The Golden Age of Scottish Culture', which recounts the take-off of industrialisation as a consequence of Enlightenment and an early entry into the world of potential plenty which it promises; the second volume tells of the failure of Scotland to benefit from that industrialisation, producing the iron age of Victorian poverty to which 'culture' is almost irrelevant. Smout's first volume concludes with the question, 'How can we account for the unprecedented cultural achievements of the Scots in

---

[18] Herman, *The Scottish Enlightenment*, 347.

[19] Alexander Broadie (ed.), *The Cambridge Companion to the Scottish Enlightenment* (Cambridge: Cambridge University Press, 2003), 338.

[20] George Davie, *The Democratic Intellect: Scotland and her Universities in the Nineteenth Century* (Edinburgh: Edinburgh University Press, 1961), 336–7.

the century after 1740?',[21] as though Scotland's achievement of any kind of cultural success is a miracle unlikely to be susceptible of rational explanation; while the second begins,

> The age of great industrial triumphs was an age of appalling social deprivation…I am astounded by the tolerance, in a country boasting of its high moral standards and basking in the spiritual leadership of a Thomas Chalmers, of unspeakable urban squalor, compounded of drink abuse, bad housing, low wages, long hours and sham education.[22]

To describe a country riven in 1843 by the Disruption of the Scottish Church, a disruption initiated by Chalmers, as '*basking* in [his] spiritual leadership', as though it was committed to nothing more than spiritual passivity, reveals the rhetorical disjunction not just between the earlier and later volumes of Smout's history but between such historical writing and the real conflicts of a society deeply concerned with the relation between its spiritual and material values. In such accounts, nineteenth-century Scotland is a country plunged again into the benightedness from which it had (only too briefly) emerged, its public life overtaken by religious commitments which Enlightenment ought to have made redundant. Later accounts, such as Alexander Broadie's, hesitate between the fact that the Scottish Enlightenment 'was one of the greatest moments in the history of European culture' and that, therefore, 'it is natural to think it a great pity that it came to an end',[23] and a longer view in which 'Enlightenment' defines not 'the complex set of relations within a group of geniuses and of other immensely creative people'[24] but a society which 'encourages autonomous thinking' and in which there is a 'high moral value attached to toleration'. In this context, for Broadie, 'nothing much has changed', so that it is possible to argue that Scotland 'is no less enlightened now than it was in the eighteenth century'[25]–even if the age of the group of geniuses which initiated it has indeed ended.

[21] T.C.Smout, *A History of the Scottish People 1560–1830* (London: Collins, [1967] 1972), 2.
[22] T.C.Smout, *A Century of the Scottish People 1830–1950* (London: Collins, 1987), 2.
[23] Broadie, *Cambridge Companion to the Scottish Enlightenment*, 5.
[24] Alexander Broadie, *The Scottish Enlightenment: The Historical Age of the Historical Nation* (Edinburgh: Birlinn, 2001), 219.
[25] Ibid., 220.

II   Scotland's Self-Enlightenment

In one sense, then, the Scottish Enlightenment began in the 1720s when Francis Hutcheson started lecturing – and lecturing in English rather than Latin – and ended somewhere around the 1780s or early 90s, or at best, staggered on till the 1820s; in Broadie's second sense, however, that of living in an 'enlightened' society, enlightenment has been a continuous Scottish experience, though it represents a continuity of no significant change, since it has produced no new 'extraordinary constellation of genius'.[26] As we have seen, however, there is also a sense in which the Scottish Enlightenment, as a concept of historical analysis rather than as a living constellation of geniuses, comes into focus only in the 1960s. Paradoxically, though, it was precisely in the period which historians of philosophy such as Davie and Graham have identified as the *end* of the Scottish philosophical tradition, the period of the late nineteenth century, that eighteenth-century philosophy in Scotland was first identified as an Enlightenment: this is now generally acknowledged to have been in W. R. Scott's study of Francis Hutcheson, published in 1900. That the concept should have been introduced at this particular point in time suggests that something significant was happening in Scottish intellectual life in the latter part of the nineteenth and early part of the twentieth centuries to make possible such a clarification of the historical landscape.

What was happening, I suggest, was a Scottish enlightenment of a very different kind – Scotland's *self-enlightenment* as to the nature and development of its own history and of its own past cultural achievements, and also a *self-enlightenment* as to the relevance of those national traditions to the issues confronting a modern society. Such signs of Scotland's self-enlightenment in the latter part of the nineteenth century are evident in the founding of key institutions dedicated to understanding and promoting the Scottish past: the Scottish Text Society was founded in 1882 to 'publish in each year about 400 pages of printed matter' that would be 'illustrative of Scottish Language and Literature before the Union';[27] the building of the Scottish National Portrait Gallery commenced in 1885 and was completed in 1900; the Scottish History Society was founded in 1886 on the instigation of Lord Roseberry, who wrote to the *Scotsman* on 3 February 1886 to propose a Scottish Manuscript Society on the lines of the Text Society, whose purpose would be 'to preserve the

---

[26] Ibid., 222.
[27] Alexander Law, *The Scottish Text Society 1882–1982* (Edinburgh: Scottish Text Society, 1983), 2.

perishable; it would form a collection valuable to the literature of the whole world, but profoundly attractive to Scotsmen; and it would raise a national monument, even more consistent and durable than those spectral and embarrassed columns which perplex the tourist on Calton Hill'.[28] The founding committee of the Society was presided over by David Masson, who was to become Historiographer Royal in 1898 but who had then held the Chair of Rhetoric and English Literature at the University of Edinburgh since 1865, a position which has been described as the first professional academic literary appointment in Britain.[29] Despite the title of his chair, however, Masson was deeply committed to the significance of Scotland's cultural achievement: in 'The Scottish Contribution to British Literature', for instance, he considered just how many influential Scottish writers overlapped with the life of Burns and declared that 'in reading the writings of such men, one is perpetually reminded, in the most direct manner, that these writings are to be regarded as belonging to a strictly national literature'.[30] This is confirmed in his study of *British Novelists and their Styles*, which is centred on the influence and achievement of Walter Scott – 'as, since Shakespeare, the man whose contribution of material to the hereditary British imagination has been the largest and most various'.[31] Indeed, for Masson, Scott's 'influence is more widely diffused through certain departments of European and American literature than that of any individual writer that has recently lived',[32] with the result that he has 'Scotticized European literature'.[33]

Such promotion of the Scottish achievement in literature had been increased by the gradual accumulation of properly edited texts of the 'medieval makars', most prominently those by David Laing, secretary to the Bannatyne Club (which had been formed in 1823 under the Presidency of Sir Walter Scott himself), whose editions of Lyndsay (1826), Dunbar (1834) and *Works of John Knox* in six volumes (1846–64) provided complete and scholarly editions

---

[28] W. C. Dickinson, 'Scottish History Society: Fifty Years, 1886–1936', in *The Court Book of the Barony of Carnwath, 1523–1542* (Edinburgh: T. and A. Constable, 1937), 4.

[29] See Chris Baldick, *Criticism and Literary Theory 1890 to the Present* (London: Longman, 1996), 13–14.

[30] David Masson, *Essays Biographical and Critical* (Cambridge: Cambridge University Press, 1856), 399.

[31] David Masson, *British Novelists and their Styles* (London: Macmillan, 1859), 195.

[32] Ibid., 195–6.

[33] Ibid., 204.

of the major writers for the first time. Particularly important was his edition of Henryson (1865), since Henryson – now considered one of the greatest of Scottish writers – had been unknown until the late eighteenth century except for the mention of his name in Dunbar's 'Lament for the Makars'. The greatest period of Scottish literature might have been its late medieval flowering but this could only be known and acknowledged in the last half of the nineteenth century, and it was this massive foundation of editorial recovery that made possible the first major histories of Scottish literature – John Merry Ross's *Scottish History and Literature to the Period of the Reformation* (1884), Hugh Walker's *Three Centuries of Scottish Literature* (1893) and James Hepburn Millar's *History of Scottish Literature* (1903) – a recovery which underlined Masson's belief that 'the rise and growth of Scottish literature is as notable a historical phenomenon as the rise and growth of the Scottish philosophy'.[34]

The 'rise and growth of the Scottish philosophy' might have preceded the 'rise and growth of Scottish literature' but its Scottish significance was also to be reinterpreted in this period. Masson had himself been a significant contributor through his book on *Recent British Philosophy*, published in 1865, in which he wrote:

> If I have mentioned Mill, Carlyle, and Hamilton as the persons in whom, if any, there was the likelihood, thirty years ago, of a new movement in British philosophy, I have not done so without good reason. Whatever other men, seniors or coevals of these three, may be named as having co-operated with them, … certain it is that it is to Carlyle, Hamilton and Mill that all would point as having been the most prominent leaders of free or uncovenanted British speculation during the last thirty years.[35]

Modern 'British philosophy', in other words, was fundamentally Scottish. The significance of this can be seen in the debates about the truth of the Christian religion initiated by the publication of Darwin's *Origin of Species* in 1859. Darwin's work itself had significant Scottish roots, since Darwin, like his father and grandfather, had been a student at Edinburgh, and since the publication of the discovery of the theory of natural selection was organised

---

[34] Masson, *Essays,* 408.
[35] David Masson, *Recent British Philosophy, A review with criticisms, including some comments on Mr. Mill's answer to Sir William Hamilton* (London: Macmillan, [1865] 1867), 7.

by the Scottish geologist, Sir Charles Lyell. It had come to Lyell's attention that Alfred Russel Wallace was about to announce his sudden insight into the process of natural selection and, determined that Darwin should not be denied recognition for his years of work on the topic, Lyell organised a joint presentation of the discovery at the Linnaean Society. In the aftermath of that announcement, however, ideas from the Scottish tradition were to be crucial to the ways in which Darwin's theories were interpreted and applied. T. H. Huxley, for instance, invented the term 'agnosticism' to define the position of those who did not believe it was possible for human beings to have a justifiable belief in God. Huxley's arguments drew heavily on both sides of the Scottish tradition, depending not only on Hume's critique of metaphysics but on Sir William Hamilton's most influential essay, 'Philosophy of the Unconditioned' (1829), which Huxley declared to be 'the original spring of Agnosticism'.[36] Hamilton's refusal of a philosophy of the Absolute, on the basis that 'the recognition of human ignorance is not only the one highest, but the one true, knowledge',[37] was used by Huxley as the fundamental first principle of his agnosticism – 'metaphysical nescience', the restraint of the intellect from passing beyond the limited but positive truths of science.[38] On the other side of the debate, however, Hamilton was also invoked by H. L. Mansel in his *The Limits of Religious Thought* (1858), as justifying the fact that we could not know God by means of reason but only through revelation, and was also the source of the theory of the Unknowable in Herbert Spencer's *A System of Philosophy* (1860).

Hume, Carlyle, Hamilton and Mill represent, as it were, the boundary positions within which late Victorian thought struggled with the consequences of its new scientific knowledge, and if even Huxley learned from Carlyle 'that a deep sense of religion was compatible with the entire absence of theology',[39] then, equally, Masson himself found that 'a large quantity of speculative thought has taken, I think, the Materialistic direction – a good deal

---

[36] T. H. Huxley, 'Mr Balfour's Attack on Agnosticism', *The Nineteenth Century*, 37 (1895), 534.

[37] Sir William Hamilton, *Discussions on Philosophy and Literature* (Edinburgh: MacLaughlan and Stewart, 1852; from *Edinburgh Review*, October 1829), 601.

[38] See James C. Livingston, 'British Agnosticism', in Ninian Smart, John Clayton, Stephen Katz and Patrick Sherry (eds), *Nineteenth Century Religious Thought in the West*, Vol. 2 (Cambridge: Cambridge University Press, 1985), 234ff.

[39] Quoted in Livingston, 'British Agnosticism', 262.

remaining within the bounds of Materialism, but some passing on to a kind of Nihilism, which is David Hume's Nihilism over again, though reached by a different method'.[40] Hume returns so insistently as the philosopher of modernity that the Scottish philosopher J. Hutchison Stirling – author of *The Secret of Hegel*, the work which first, in 1864, introduced Hegel to the British public – found Hume's influence on the mid-nineteenth century to be so pervasive that 'Hume is our Politics, Hume is our Trade, Hume is our Philosophy, Hume is our Religion – it wants little but Hume were even our Taste…'[41]

The breadth of Masson's conception of 'Scottish philosophy' in the nineteenth century, and his sense of its centrality to modern thought, contrasts radically with those more recent accounts of the decline of Scotland's intellectual life from the heights of its Enlightenment achievement and influence. And the reason for the difference is that those later accounts treat nineteenth-century Scottish thought in exactly the way that McCosh had done eighteenth-century Scottish thought, by excluding its greatest exponents as not part of the tradition of Scottish thought at all. McCosh himself sees John Stuart Mill as the modern equivalent of Hume, negating in his attack on Sir William Hamilton's philosophy those principles by which the Scottish school had resisted Hume's scepticism:

> Mr J. S. Mill, in his 'Examination of Hamilton' has reproduced to a large extent the theory of Hume, but without so clearly seeing or candidly avowing the consequences. I rather think that Mr Mill himself is scarcely aware of the extent of the resemblance between his doctrines and those of the Scottish sceptic; as he seems to have wrought out his conclusion from data supplied to him by his own father, Mr James Mill, who, however, has evidently drawn much from Hume. The circumstance that Mr Mill's work was welcomed by such declamations by the chief literary organs in London is a proof, either that the would-be leaders of opinion are so ignorant of philosophy that they do not see the consequences; or that the writers, being chiefly young men bred at Oxford or Cambridge, are fully prepared to accept them…[42]

---

[40] Masson, *Recent British Philosophy*, 154.
[41] James Hutchison Stirling, *The Secret of Hegel* (Bristol: Thoemmes Antiquarian Books, [1864] 1990), 'Introduction', lxxiii–lxxiv.
[42] McCosh, *The Scottish Philosophy*, 126–7.

Acceptance of Mill at Oxford or Cambridge is, like Hume's acceptance in Paris, symptomatic of his *un*-Scottish affiliations. The same argument was later made by George Davie when, in the 'Introduction' to *The Scotch Metaphysics*, he identifies 'the English tradition in philosophy' as 'practical utilitarianism, Bentham, John Stuart Mill and his father, Russell, Ryle and Popper'.[43] If the tradition of Hume, as represented by the Mills, is to be treated as not part of the tradition of *Scottish* thought then not only is Scottish philosophy itself radically truncated but Scottish philosophy is wilfully circumscribed to only one side of the debate which Hume's work initiated.

The most striking version of this displacement of Scottish culture is in the work of Alasdair MacIntyre, for whom Hume, the greatest of Scottish thinkers, is the one who brings the tradition of Scottish thought to an end. MacIntyre takes the linguistic argument traditionally levelled at Hume – his concern to avoid Scotticisms in his writing – and turns it into an argument about the social nature of Hume's thought, a social nature which reflects not Scottish *mores* but English ones, with the consequence that the Scottish tradition abolishes itself from within.

> Hutcheson therefore engendered a new type of conflict within Scottish intellectual life, and it is a mark of his importance that he set the terms of debate for that conflict. Just because he did so, it is easy in retrospect to view that conflict as a continuation of the debates internal to Scottish tradition. The participants after all were all Scotsmen. But it was a conflict in which the continuing existence of the Scottish tradition was put in question. What Hume represented in almost every importance respect, what indeed Smith too was to represent, even though he was Hutcheson's most distinguished and well-regarded pupil, was the abandonment of peculiarly Scottish modes of thought in favour of a distinctively English and Anglicizing way of understanding social life and its moral fabric.[44]

The irony of this position is that MacIntyre's analysis of Hume is part of his discussion of the logic of traditions and yet Hume, working in the tradition

---

[43] George Davie, *The Scotch Metaphysics: A Century of Enlightenment in Scotland* (London and New York: Routledge, 2001), 7. Despite its date of publication, this book was written in the 1950s.

[44] Alasdair MacIntyre, *Whose Justice? Which Rationality?* (London: Duckworth, 1996), 280.

established by Hutcheson, becomes the subverter of the very tradition from which he is bred. For MacIntyre, the Scottish philosophical tradition reaches its moment of greatest significance only when it ceases to be Scottish and is incorporated into English culture.

A similar exclusion has also been applied to the third of Masson's great triumvirate of modern Scottish philosophers – Thomas Carlyle – by the insistence that any Scottish thinker who engages seriously with German philosophy has contributed to the undermining of the native tradition. The history of nineteenth-century Scottish philosophy thus becomes the account of its gradual 'Germanising', beginning with Sir William Hamilton's attempt to combine the positions of Reid and Kant, developing through J. F. Ferrier's attempted rejection of the presuppositions of Common Sense in favour of a Hegelian mode of philosophy, and culminating in the neo-Kantianism and Hegelianism of the Scottish Idealists, led by Edward Caird. For Ferrier, for instance, the business of philosophy is 'for the sole purpose of correcting the natural inadvertancies of loose, ordinary thinking', while the Common Sense tradition 'exists for the very purpose of ratifying, and, if possible, systematising these inadvertancies'.[45] Despite this, Ferrier insisted that his philosophy was 'Scottish to the very core; it is national in every fibre and articulation of its frame. It is a natural growth of Scotland's soil, and has drunk no nourishment from any other land.'[46] Nonetheless, Ferrier's interest in Hegel was indicative of the fact that in the latter half of the nineteenth century, as Andrew Seth (later, Pringle-Pattison) phrased it, 'the philosophical production of the younger generation of our University men are more strongly impressed with a German than a native stamp'.[47] And because of Edward Caird's enormous influence in both Scotland and England, the Idealism which he propounded has been treated as a crucial betrayal of the Scottish tradition. Symptomatically, George Davie sees J. F. Ferrier's efforts to find a way of constructing a compromise between the new German philosophy and the Scottish tradition as leading to 'the collapse of the Scottish Enlightenment after 1854' and its ultimate 'blackout':[48] 'The Scottish Enlightenment – which in Ferrier's original form of "German philosophy refracted through a Scottish

---

[45] J. F. Ferrier, *Scottish Philosophy: the Old and the New: A Statement by Professor Ferrier* (Edinburgh: Sutherland and Knox, 1856), 12.

[46] Ibid.

[47] Andrew Seth, *Scottish Philosophy: A Comparison of the Scottish and German Answers to Hume* (Edinburgh: William Blackwood and Sons, 1890), 2.

[48] George Davie, *The Scotch Metaphysics*, 4.

medium" seems to be moving towards a new lease of life – suddenly col-
lapses into a blackout expressed in a series of contradictions which are never
overcome.'[49] For Davie, 'the kind of Hegelianism produced in such quanti-
ties by Caird and his group of disciples was heavy, imitative, and indeed
bibliolatrous, the work of minds which made no secret of their belief that
Hegel had more or less said the last word about everything'.[50] Commitment
to a Germanic style in philosophy is, for Davie, necessarily a refusal to
acknowledge the relevance of the Common Sense tradition, which is 'treated
by Caird as lying absolutely outside "the main stream of intellectual culture"'
since 'no Scottish name later than David Hume passed his lips'.[51] Gordon
Graham, too, accepts that Caird's 'indifference to the national tradition' was
'to signal the end of a philosophical project which had lasted the larger part
of 200 years',[52] although, in his essay on nineteenth-century Scottish philosophy in the *Cambridge Companion to the Scottish Enlightenment*, he suggests that the
tradition lasted another generation, to the work of Pringle-Pattison, whose
work 'marks him out, for all his admiration of Kant, as a philosopher still in
the Scottish tradition – and possibly the last'.[53] Whether it is the empiricisim
of Mill or the idealism of Caird, Scottish philosophy cannot be truly in the
line of Scottish development if it follows the faithless and Anglicising implications of Hume or the Germanising of Carlyle.

In the late nineteenth century, however, in the period when the notion
of a Scottish Enlightenment was first about to be mooted, a very different account of the Scottish tradition was emerging. In the introduction to a
selection of Carlyle's essays published in 1909, Pringle-Pattison declared that:
'Whatever else might be doubtful, Carlyle's intense conviction of the moral
foundations of the universe, vibrating in every page he wrote, communicated
itself to his readers as a tonic force of the most powerful and beneficent
kind.'[54] Carlyle's philosophical as well as literary importance is underscored
by the fact that, for Pringle-Pattison, 'Carlyle's great histories are therefore

[49] George Davie, *Ferrier and the Blackout of the Scottish Enlightenment* (Edinburgh: Edinburgh Review, 2003), 70.
[50] George Davie, *The Scottish Enlightenment and Other Essays* (Edinburgh: Polygon, 1991), 109.
[51] Davie, *Democratic Intellect*, 330.
[52] Graham, 'Scottish Philosophy in the Nineteenth Century', *Stanford Encyclopedia of Philosophy*, http://plato.stanford.edu/entries/scottish-19th.
[53] Broadie (ed.), *Cambridge Companion to the Scottish Enlightenment*, 349.
[54] Thomas Carlyle, *Selected Essays of Thomas Carlyle*, ed. with an introduction by Prof. A. Seth Pringle-Pattison (London: Andrew Melrose, 1909), ix.

as much philosophies of history as history pure and simple'.[55] The most prominent of the Scottish idealists, Edward Caird, was no less certain of Carlyle's importance: no writer 'in this century has done more to elevate and purify our ideals of life' than Carlyle, nor done more 'to make us conscious that the things of the spirit are real, and that, in the last resort, there is no other reality'.[56] For Caird, like Pringle-Pattison, Carlyle's Germanism was not a betrayal of Scottish traditions but, rather, the recovery through philosophy and history of the fundamental principles of the reformed tradition:

> Yet this new ideal, when we came to look at it closely, was, after all, nothing new or strange. It was in new words, words suited to the new time, the expression of those religious and moral principles which all in this country – and especially we Scotsmen – had received into ourselves almost with our mother's milk. It was Puritanism idealised, made cosmopolitan, freed from the narrowness which clung to its first expression, or with which time had encrusted it…Carlyle seemed to change the old banner of the Covenant into a standard for the forward march of mankind towards a better ideal of human life.[57]

Far from representing the Germanising of Scottish philosophy, works such as Edward Caird's *A Critical Account of the Philosophy of Kant* (1877) saw themselves as marching under the Covenanting banner of Carlyle's 'better ideal of human life' and did so because Idealist German philosophy was itself a response to and an attempt to transcend the dilemmas posed by Hume. In adopting the discourse of German philosophy in order to escape the implications of Humean scepticism, such thinkers saw themselves not as negating their Scottishness but as recovering an older Scottish sense of religious conviction and religious commitment in a modern philosophical discourse.

Hume, however, was not to be so easily evaded. In 1885, James Hutchison Stirling published in the journal *Mind* – itself a major Scottish contribution to British intellectual life – a series of articles in which he argued that 'Kant has not answered Hume'.[58] Andrew Seth summarised their implication:

---

[55] Ibid., xii.

[56] Edward Caird, *Essays on Literature and Philosophy* (Glasgow: James Maclehose, 1892), 267.

[57] Ibid., 235–6.

[58] *Mind*, Vol. 9, Issue 36 (October 1884), 531–47, and Vol. 10, Issue 37 (January 1885), 45–72).

Instead of, like Reid, abandoning 'the ideal system' [Kant] elaborately reconstructed it, endeavouring to give it a more rational and tenable form. Kant is, indeed, the very prince of Representationists, and the Representationism of the present day has its roots almost entirely in the Kantian theory.[59]

Reid's response to Hume had been to refuse to take the first steps which scientific rationality seemed to require when it defined our perceptions as intermediaries between ourselves and the world rather than as direct contact with it:

The sceptic asks me, Why do you believe the existence of the external object which you perceive? This belief, sir, is none of my manufacture; it came from the mint of Nature; it bears her image and superscription; and, if it is not right, the fault is not mine: I even took it upon trust, and without suspicion. Reason, says the sceptic, is the only judge of truth, and you ought to throw off every opinion and every belief that is not grounded on reason. Why, sir, should I believe the faculty of reason more than that of perception? – they came both out of the same shop, and were made by the same artist.[60]

Kant, on the other hand, according to Stirling, sought to defeat Hume's metaphysics by elaborating on them, but in the end the fundamental issue which inspired Kant's response – the search for the necessity which we feel to exist between a cause and its effect – proves the undoing of his entire philosophical project: 'Kant's whole work (and what alone led to all the others, Fichte, Schelling, Hegel) rose out of one consideration only. What was – whence was – that very strange and peculiar species of necessity to which Hume has drawn attention in the phenomena of cause and effect'.[61] As a consequence, the whole edifice of the '*Kritik of Pure Reason*, nay, German philosophy as a whole, has absolute foundation in the *whence* or *why* of *necessary connexion*',[62] and on this crux Stirling finds Kant not only to have failed to answer Hume

---

[59] Seth, *Scottish Philosophy*, 149.
[60] Thomas Reid, *An Inquiry into the Human Mind on the Principles of Common Sense*, in Ronald E. Beanblossom and Keith Lehrer (eds), Thomas Reid, *Inquiry and Essays* (Indianapolis: Bobbs-Merrill, 1975), 84–5.
[61] *Mind*, Vol. 10, Issue 37 (January 1885), 48.
[62] Ibid.

but to have realised, belatedly, the significance of his own failure. What Kant could not resolve was how the operation of the 'categories', those structuring principles that shape for us the world of time and space, accounted for the 'necessity' that Hume could not find in our experience of causality. According to Stirling, Kant's category of cause could not be effectively imposed on the world by the mind without the phenomena having already suggested to the categories the ways in which 'real' cases of causation are to be distinguished from mere regular succession. Two different kinds of constant conjunction – the causal kind and that which is simply a matter of regular contiguity – would never be able to be distinguished from one another if the categories themselves *impose* the order of causality on the world, because in order to impose the category of cause on some but not all of these cases there must already be something *in* the phenomena that directs the categories to establishing one as properly causal and the other as not. That which is supposed to be supplied only by the categories in the construction of the world must already be evidenced in the phenomena by the very necessity that only the categories are supposed to provide:

> Kant is found to be suspended here between his two perceptions of the state of the case. He perceives, first, that sense as sense is always contingent. But then he perceives, second, that if a sensation A and another sensation B are to be subsumed under the category and converted into an antecedent and a consequent, they must of themselves have already given us reason to assume for them precisely that quality – precisely that relation! This latter perception we suppose to have come late to Kant; and it is precisely in consequence of this perception that we attribute the cold sweats to him which attend that endless tangle of the Second Analogy where we see only bewildered attempts to renew courage in himself by the constant *refrain*, Necessity of synthesis cannot be due to sense, and must be due to understanding! But the renewed courage must ever fail again . . . [63]

The only way out of this quandary would be 'to conceive that each category, quite unknown to me, without any consciousness on my part, might unerringly scent a case of its own'[64] but then the whole purpose of the categories

---

[63] Ibid., 59.
[64] Ibid., 60.

would be defeated: 'the single purpose they are there for, what they are alone to do, is to give necessity; and this necessity, which they alone are to give, which they alone are to explain, *already exists!*'[65] Stirling can see no conclusion but that 'the vast transcendental machinery is a signal failure'[66] and that Kant's 'position is no better than that of Reid, Beattie, Oswald, and all the rest'[67] who had tried to resist Hume's analysis. The superiority of the Kantian position is entirely undermined, leaving the debate between Humean empiricism and its Scottish opponents of the Common Sense school as intact as ever it had been before the rise of German philosophy.

Hutchison Stirling's argument was to have a profound influence on the course of late nineteenth-century Scottish thought. It is acknowledged by Andrew Seth to be the starting point of his book on *Scottish Philosophy* (1890), subtitled *A Comparison of the Scottish and German Answers to Hume*. In the light of the recognition of the inadequacies of the Kantian response – and the inadequacies of the Hegelian completion of the Kantian project, outlined in Seth's own *Hegelianism and Personality* (1887) – it had become possible to return both to the dilemmas posed by Hume and to Reid's response to them as parts of a continuing – and a continuingly relevant – Scottish dialectic. Significantly, then, in 1898, there appeared in a series entitled 'Famous Scots' – itself a part of the national cultural upsurge of the period, and including as well as poets and novelists, theologians, philosophers, scientists and explorers – parallel studies of *David Hume* (by Henry Calderwood) and *Thomas Reid* (by Campbell Fraser). What the two books between them reveal is a transformation in the historical perception of the relation between their two philosophies.

For Campbell Fraser, the interest of Reid lies precisely in the fact that his philosophy provides a possible alternative, however limited, to a world in which scepticism and doubt have become pervasive:

> It should attract those who, in an age of sceptical criticism, seek to assure themselves of the final trustworthiness of the experience into which, at birth, they were admitted as strangers, ignorant of what the whole means, like the agnostic in Pascal. Who has sent me into this life I know not; nor what I am myself. I find myself chained to one little planet, but without understanding why I am here rather than there; and

---

[65]   Ibid., 65.
[66]   Ibid., 70.
[67]   Ibid., 71.

why this period of time was given me to live in rather than any other in the unbeginning and endless duration. Life with its memories and forecasts looks like a blind venture. The sum of my knowledge seems to be that I must die; but what I am most ignorant of is the meaning of death. One is drawn to Reid by an interest in final questions like these, which the agnostic spirit is now forcing on us.[68]

Against the weight of such agnosticism in an era 'when the fundamental questions of religious thought are at the roots of our doubts and perplexities',[69] Reid's philosophy offers 'Common Sense [as] the final perception of a being who can know the universe of reality only in part, and is therefore needed by man in that indeterminate position in which an absolute beginning or end of things must be to him incomprehensible'.[70] It is the pragmatic basis of this limitation of our ambitions towards knowledge that Campbell Fraser sees as the fundamental value of Reid's work: 'the unjust as well as the just, so far as they live at all, he sees, live by faith in what cannot be either proved or disproved by direct demonstration.'[71]

For Calderwood, on the other hand, contemporary interest in Hume arises precisely from his struggle with doubt, a struggle whose conclusion is not atheism or scepticism but possible faith. Calderwood dwells on Hume's *Dialogues on Natural Religion* as a key text for contemporary readers, because of its debate about scepticism and belief, and while modern readings of Hume's work tend to see in the sceptic, Philo, the character who most closely represents Hume's views, Calderwood emphasises the role of Cleanthes, the seeker after 'a vision of truth in harmony with our fundamental faith in the Divine existence' as 'the hero of the Dialogue',[72] and Hume's true representative. He gives space, therefore, to a footnote added to the second volume of the *History of England* in which Hume regrets his emphasis on 'the mischief which arise from the abuses of religion' as compared with the 'salutary consequences which result from true and genuine piety' because of religion's ability 'to reform men's lives, to purify their hearts, to enforce moral duties

[68] A. Campbell Fraser, *Thomas Reid* (Edinburgh: Oliphant Anderson and Ferrier, 1898), 16–17.
[69] Ibid., 143.
[70] Ibid., 135.
[71] Ibid., 137.
[72] Henry Calderwood, *David Hume* (Edinburgh: Oliphant Anderson and Ferrier, 1898), 108.

and to secure obedience to the laws and civil magistrate'.[73] As a result, Hume can be seen as performing through the very intensity of his doubts a service to belief rather than to scepticism:

> Now that the prejudices against him have in a considerable measure passed away, we can admit that his perplexities may be helpful to us who follow. Faith succeeds doubt, while preparing the way for better thought. A true service is rendered in the history of intellectual and religious development when the common difficulties of our position in the universe are stated with clearness and force. Pioneers, after enduring untold hardships, may have the gratitude of the people.[74]

In consequence, Calderwood hopes that 'readers may be willing to consider afresh the scepticism and the religious faith', with the result that 'they may even be able to find, in Hume, a witness for Christianity whose testimony is in some respects the more valuable since beset by so many and such grave doubts'. Or, at the least, that an understanding of Hume 'may lead us to a fairer interpretation of the attitude of those, in our own day, whose avowed doubts have induced earnest men to classify them amongst the irreligious'.[75] A Hume who can save the irreligious from condemnation and who can lead the doubtful back to faith is a Hume who is no longer the ultimate 'foe' of the Scottish tradition, but an integral part of it.

This reconciliation of Hume and Reid, this return to them as providing, still, the fundamental starting points of modern philosophy in the aftermath of the collapse of the German metaphysic, is what makes possible W. R. Scott's study of Francis Hutcheson as 'a philosopher of the Enlightenment in Scotland'.[76] For Scott, Hume does not stand outside the tradition of Scottish philosophy but completes one phase of it:

> If then Scepticism be accepted as the close of an epoch of thought, and if Scepticism is generally preceded by an Enlightenment, this order holds good in Britain in the first half of the last century. The Realism and Empirical Idealism of the eighteenth century alike, had reached

---

[73]   Ibid., 103.
[74]   Ibid., 107.
[75]   Ibid., 6.
[76]   William Robert Scott, *Francis Hutcheson: His Life, Teaching and Position in the History of Philosophy* (Cambridge: Cambridge University Press, 1900), 257.

their final development. Hutcheson, with many others, constitute the 'Enlightenment,' and the period rounds itself off in the Scepticism of Hume, who turns the arguments of either tendency against the other to disprove the presuppositions of both.[77]

Hutcheson is the subject of Scott's work, but it is Hutcheson as the inspiration of an Enlightenment of which Hume will be the most significant product: 'Is it not strange', Scott asks, 'that in Germany, Hume's claim to have drawn a dividing line across the development of modern Philosophy is admitted, while, in his own country, it is practically ignored?'[78] This rooting of Hume in the intellectual ground of Scotland as enriched by Hutcheson made it possible to identify what was 'national' to the Enlightenment that Hutcheson initiated in Scotland: 'however thorough he imagined his revolt [against Puritanism] to be, it was still Puritanism modified from within, not revolutionised from without, and this fact probably explains the leverage that gave him his influence in Scotland.'[79]

The argument for the continuity of philosophical concerns between Hutcheson and Hume as Enlightenment thinkers was not finally to be completed until 1941, with the publication of Norman Kemp Smith's *The Philosophy of David Hume*, which gave historical contextualisation to the radical rereading of Hume that Kemp Smith had originally published in *Mind* in 1905–6. There, he had insisted that the important issue in Hume's philosophy was not his scepticism but his 'naturalism', involving 'a purely naturalistic conception of human nature by the thorough subordination of reason to feeling and instinct'.[80] In the book, however, he showed how such an interpretation of Hume could be historically grounded in the influence of Hutcheson, because from Hutcheson 'he was led to recognise that judgments of moral approval and disapproval, and indeed judgments of *value* of whatever type, are based not on insight or on evidence, but solely on feeling'.[81] As a result, fundamental – not to say 'common sense' – beliefs, such as 'the belief in the existence of the body is, Hume declares, a "natural"

---

[77] Ibid., 266.

[78] Ibid., 265.

[79] Ibid., 259.

[80] Norman Smith, 'The Naturalism of Hume', *Mind*, NS 54 (April 1905), 150.

[81] Norman Kemp Smith, *The Philosophy of David Hume* (London: Macmillan, [1941] 1966), 15.

belief due to the ultimate instincts or propensities which constitute our human nature. It cannot be justified by reason.'[82] Hume becomes part of a tradition which, as founded on Hutcheson, is no longer fundamentally at odds with Reid, so that all of them can now be participants in that Scottish Enlightenment which W. R. Scott had as presciently descried in the future as in the past.

III Energy and Evolution

What I have called Scotland's 'self-enlightenment' begins in the 1820s and 30s—the very period when the Enlightenment itself is deemed to be over—and gathers momentum towards the conceptualisation of Scotland's eighteenth-century past as itself 'the Scottish Enlightenment'. Is this, however, simply a case of an era in intellectual decline turning to meditate on the greatness of the one that had preceded it and from which it had fallen away? Is such 'self-enlightenment' no more than the epiphenomenon of an underlying decay? That the dominant Scottish philosophies of the mid-nineteenth century faced a crisis, David Masson was in no doubt: it was not, however, a *Scottish* crisis but a crisis of philosophy itself. At the very moment when it seemed possible for the debates between scepticism and common sense, between empiricism and transcendentalism, finally to be resolved, the world which philosophy was called on to understand had been so radically altered by developments in contemporary history that their purchase on reality had dissolved. 'In no age so conspicuously as in our own has there been a crowding in of new scientific conceptions of all kinds to exercise a perturbing influence on Speculative Philosophy. They have come in almost too fast for Philosophy's powers of reception. She has visibly reeled amid their shocks...'[83] Masson dated these shocks to ten years before the announcement of the theory of natural selection, to the year 1848 rather than 1858, 'as if, in that year of simultaneous European irritability, not only were the nations agitated politically, as the newspapers saw, but conceptions of an intellectual kind that had long been forming themselves underneath in the depths were shaken up to the surface in scientific journals and books'.[84] The book whose implications had dominated the latter part of

---

[82] Ibid., 86.
[83] Masson, *Recent British Philosophy*, 117–18.
[84] Ibid., 118.

the 1840s was Robert Chambers's *Vestiges of the Natural History of Creation*, anonymously published in 1844 and sending shockwaves through Victorian culture in the years immediately following. Chambers, one of the brothers who ran the Chambers publishing business in Edinburgh, had laid out starkly in his opening chapter the scale of the universe with which humanity now had to cope: extrapolating from experiments on the distance of stars in the constellation of the Centaur conducted by Professor Henderson of the University of Edinburgh, Chambers suggested that 'we shall readily see that space occupied by even the comparatively small number visible to the naked eye must be vast beyond all powers of conception'.[85] The scale of the development of life on earth was no less disconcerting: in *Explanations*, a riposte to the critics of his original book first published in the edition of 1846 and appended to later editions of *Vestiges*, he states that, 'Fifty years ago science possessed no facts regarding the origin of organic creatures upon earth; as far as knowledge acquired through the ordinary means was concerned, all was blank antecedent to the first chapters of what we usually call ancient history.' In the intervening period, however, 'researches in the crust of the earth' have produced 'a bold outline of the history of the globe, during what appears to have been a vast chronology intervening between its formation and the appearance of the human race upon its surface'.[86] This bold outline 'fully proves that organic creation passed through a series of stages before the highest vegetable and animal forms appeared', providing 'the first hint of organic creation having arisen in the manner of natural order'.[87] Because of the dating of fossil evidence which the understanding of geological strata makes possible, it is clear that there was a period when 'only invertebrated animals now lived', giving 'strong proof that, in the course of nature, *time* was necessary for the creation of superior creatures',[88] and that the 'change in character' of these creatures 'is *a gradual, and not an abrupt one*, and would probably be found more gradual, if we were acquainted, not only with all the forms of animal life which now exist, but also those which have existed in ages long gone by, and are now extinct'.[89]

[85] Robert Chambers, *Vestiges of the Natural History of Creation* (New York: Harper and Brothers, [1844] 1860), 6.
[86] Ibid., 215.
[87] Ibid., 216.
[88] Ibid., 223.
[89] Ibid., 228: in the final sentence Chambers is quoting from a Dr Carpenter in support of his own previous arguments.

In the light of such scientific revelations about the nature of the universe, both physical and biological, the debates of the philosophers are judged to be entirely inappropriate to the issues now confronting them. Human beings were now required to take seriously what Masson describes as 'the notion of *Interplanetary*, or even *Interstellar, Reciprocity* ... a habit of consciously extending [our] regards to the other bodies of our solar systems, and feeling as if some-how *they* were not to go for nothing in the calculation of the Earth's interests and fortunes'.[90] Philosophies which began from the consciousness of the thinker, or even from the whole history of humanity itself, as the most impor-tant fact in the universe, and concentrating on understanding the relationship between subjective consciousness and an objective world, discover that 'no flag-staff ... can we plant at any one spot, however far back in earthly time, and that at that point Humanity is to be considered as beginning':[91]

> Seas, ages, aeons of experience had preceded it, whose essence was conserved and elaborated in its structure; and specimens of the inter-mediate organisms through which this one had been reached, and also the wrecks and shapes of myriads of others, lay strewn about, showing the measureless energy of Nature, and the enormous struggle of sen-tient inventiveness which she had carried in her bosom, during periods anterior to the farthest ken of Man.[92]

The disorientating timescale of such evolutionary perspectives was matched by the terrifying implications of the new science of thermodynamics, which insisted that all work and effort involved a dissipation of the universe's energy which would inevitably result in its disintegration to a condition in which energy was equally spread across space, and activity of all kinds would cease. It was this newly discovered universe, dominated by decay and doomed to the entropic equalisation of heat by 'the tendency of all things to *Ultimate and Universal Collapse*' that Masson believed modern philosophy—committed on all sides as it was, and as, indeed, was Chambers himself, to notions of development and progress—had been confounded:

> By a process which has been named the Equilibration of Forces, and which is slowly going on, it seems to be foreseen that a period will

---

90 Masson, *Recent British Philosophy*, 148.
91 Ibid., 140.
92 Ibid., 141.

come when all the energy locked up in the solar system, and sustaining
whatever of motion or life there is in it, will be exhausted…and all its
parts through all their present variousness will be stiffened or resolved,
as regards each other, in a defunct and featureless community of rest
and death…[Farther, Science] yet sees no other end but that all the
immeasurable entanglement of all the starry systems shall also run
itself together at last in an indistinguishable equilibrium of ruin. Thus,
to something like that Universal Nebula out of which all things are
fancied as evolved does Science, at her utmost daring, conceive of
them as tending to be resolved again. Universal dissolution, universal
rest, universal death, is her last dream of the drift of things in the
infinite future.[93]

Masson is referring here to the implications of the work of William Thomson
(later Lord Kelvin), Professor of Natural Philosophy in the University of
Glasgow, who had published, in 1852, a paper exploring the relationship
between the necessary loss of energy in machines – not all of the available
energy in a machine can be converted into 'work', nor can it be recovered for
useful purposes but is 'dissipated' into the surrounding environment – and
the equivalent implications for the universe as a whole. Thomson argued that
the 'known facts with reference to the mechanics of animal and vegetable
bodies' indicated that the material world was necessarily subject 'to the dissipation of mechanical energy'; that 'any *restoration* of mechanical energy,
without more than an equivalent of dissipation, is impossible'; and that the
earth, therefore, could provide a habitation for humankind for only a limited
period of time.[94] The 'universal' application of this schema would imply, as
Thomson put it in an essay 'On the age of the sun's heat' in 1862, 'a state
of universal rest and death, if the universe were finite and left to obey existing laws'.[95] Thomson's essay was published in *Macmillan's Magazine*, edited
by David Masson, then Professor at University College, London. Masson's
engagement in making public the consequences of Scotland's foremost scientist was to be challenged by London newspapers which suggested that

---

[93] Ibid., 151–2.
[94] William Thomson, 'On a universal tendency in nature to the dissipation of
mechanical energy', *Philosophical Magazine* (series 4), 4 (1852), 304–6; quoted
in Smith and Wise, *Energy and Empire*, 499–500.
[95] William Thomson, 'On the age of the sun's heat', *Macmillan's Magazine*, 5
(1862), 288–93; quoted in Smith and Wise, *Energy and Empire*, 500.

such scientific theories should not be published 'on the ground that, as the catastrophe was so far off, it could concern neither man nor beast to think about it'. For Masson, however, no 'man into whose mind this idea of the exhaustibility of the Sun's Heat, and consequently of the force energizing our system, had once entered, could ever think a thought about anything whatsoever that should not, in shape and colour, be influenced by that idea!'[96]

The implications of Thomson's thermodynamics were to be given general scientific form in 1867 in a book jointly authored by Thomson and Peter Guthrie Tait, who held the chair of Natural Philosophy in Edinburgh: their *Treatise on Natural Philosophy* was designed to achieve nothing less than the overturning of Newtonian physics, replacing 'Newton's *Principia* of force with a new *Principia* of energy', and exemplifying 'the ONE GREAT LAW of Physical Science, known as the *Conservation of Energy*',[97] – a law which, despite its name, actually implied the ultimate dissipation of energy. Thomson and Tait's post-Newtonian physics of energy was one of the great achievements of nineteenth-century science: it redefined the fundamental 'stuff' of the universe as a dynamic fluid rather than as hard, self-enclosed atoms, and it sought to unify the science of fluids with the emergent understanding of magnetism and electricity. Despite its radical challenge to Newtonian physics, however, it was not Thomson and Tait's *Treatise* that was to inaugurate the post-Newtonian era, but a treatise published six years later by Tait's former schoolfellow at Edinburgh Academy, James Clerk Maxwell. Maxwell's *Treatise on Electricity and Magnetism* (1873) is the work which, as his recent biographer, Basil Mahon, described it, 'changed everything'.[98] If Thomson's combination of mathematics and physical experiment allowed him to achieve major technical feats such as inventing a compass which would not be deflected by the metal hull of a steamship (an invention which made him rich), Maxwell's mathematics and natural philosophy were to establish the laws – in the form of Maxwell's 'equations' – which would make possible the modern world, the world of radio and television, of computers and microwaves, of electron microscopy and radio telescopy; the world in which 'electricity, magnetism and light'[99] are simply different aspects of an energy which is the fundamental constituent of our universe. Maxwell, however, had himself

---

[96] Masson, *Recent British Philosophy*, 150.
[97] Quoted in Smith and Wise, *Energy and Empire*, 352, 353.
[98] Basil Mahon, *The Man who Changed Everything: The Life of James Clerk Maxwell* (Chichester: John Wiley and Sons, 2003).
[99] Ibid., 3.

been a concealed force behind Thomson and Tait's *Treatise*, reading it in draft and adding significantly to the radical nature of its new conception of the physical universe, and it was on the basis of this close co-operation that Maxwell's own *Treatise* emerged, the product of a continuous stream of communications between Maxwell in Galloway, Thomson in Glasgow and Tait in Edinburgh. As P.M.Harman has noted, Maxwell acknowledged that his *Treatise*'s geometrical representations of 'magnetic lines of force' and the 'magnetic field' were 'indebted to Thomson's discussion of the mathematical relation between "attraction in electrostatics and the conduction of heat"'; this, he wrote to Thomson, 'I believe is your invention at least I never found it elsewhere.'[100]

The importance of Maxwell's work can hardly be overstated. P.G.Tait's estimate in his review of Maxwell's *Treatise* in 1873–which described his friend as having 'a name which requires only the stamp of antiquity to raise it almost to the level of that of Newton'[101]–is a view which has been upheld by history. As Bruce J. Hunt puts it, 'by the 1890s the four "Maxwell's equations" were recognized as the foundation of one of the strongest and most successful theories in all of physics; they had taken their place as companions, even rivals, to Newton's laws of mechanics'.[102] Indeed, unlike Newton's laws, they survived the arrival of Einsteinian physics entirely unchanged. As Mahon puts it, 'Maxwell's equations were *the* basic laws of the physical world' because 'Einstein's axiom that the speed of light was an absolute constant...was completely determined by Maxwell's theory'.[103] Yet historians of the Scottish Enlightenment treat Maxwell's achievements as though they were isolated afterthoughts to Enlightenment rather than its fulfilment–or, indeed, its transcendence. Arthur Herman, for instance, notes the fact that 'The University of Glasgow laid claim to one of the two most important physicists in Britain' in the nineteenth century, while 'Aberdeen had the other',[104] as though this confluence of the major mathematical physicists of the nineteenth century, who made possible the very infrastructure of twentieth-century technology, were incidental to 'the Scots' invention of

---

[100] P.M.Harman, *The Natural Philosophy of James Clerk Maxwell* (Cambridge: Cambridge University Press, 1998), 77.
[101] Harman, *The Natural Philosophy of James Clerk Maxwell*, 2.
[102] Bruce J. Hunt, *The Maxwellians* (Ithaca and London: Cornell University Press, 1991), 1.
[103] Mahon, *The Man who Changed Everything*, 181.
[104] Herman, *The Scottish Enlightenment*, 347.

the modern world'. Broadie, too, notes that 'Scotland continued to produce world-beaters, most especially James Clerk Maxwell and Lord Kelvin',[105] as though such a combination had not proved as significant to the world as the combination of David Hume and Adam Smith. If there was a period in which Scotland did in truth 'invent the modern world', *our* modern world, it was the period of the 1850s, 60s and 70s when Thomson made long-distance telegraphy possible, when Maxwell produced (in 1861) the first colour photograph, when Bell invented the telephone, and when Maxwell laid the groundwork for Einstein's physics of relativity. These were not 'universally applicable' scientific truths unconditioned by their Scottish environment: as Thomson's biographers note, his projects were specific to the Scottish context (which he refused to leave for a chair at Cambridge), because the 'practical dimension' which 'dominated Thomson's and Tait's conceptualization' was 'closely coupled with the democratic ideals of Scottish education and with the diffusion of useful knowledge'.[106]

James Clerk Maxwell was equally embedded in Scottish intellectual traditions. Since he was only fourteen when his first paper was read to the Royal Society of Edinburgh, it was presented on his behalf by J. D. Forbes, Professor of Natural Philosophy at the University of Edinburgh. Later it was Forbes's lectures that inspired Maxwell's interest in the nature of colour and the fact that the first colour photograph was of a tartan ribbon perhaps underlines Maxwell's indebtedness to such major Scottish figures of the period as Sir William Hamilton, whose lectures on Logic and Metaphysics he also attended at Edinburgh. With Tait (who would later beat him in the contest for Forbes's chair at Edinburgh) he had been friends since his schooldays and Thomson he had met through family connections while still in his teens. Despite their Cambridge educations and their 'Cambridge mathematics', all three were the products of and participants in a Scottish educational system which, whatever its weaknesses, still encouraged its students to see 'philosophy' and 'natural philosophy'—metaphysics and physics—as deeply interdependent. The 'physics' of these scientists was worked out not only in terms of the empirical evidence of experiment but in terms of its cosmological coherence,

---

[105] Broadie, *The Scottish Enlightenment*, 219.

[106] Smith and Wise, *Energy and Empire*, 349. Compare William Ferguson's assumption that 'the reputation won by Scotsmen in science...did little to enhance the culture of their country' because 'science stands independent of national contexts'; *Scotland: 1689 to the Present* (Edinburgh: Oliver and Boyd, 1968), 319.

and, ultimately, in terms of the religious implications of that cosmology. According to Thomson's biographers, 'Thomson and Tait emphasized the consistency between their cosmos and the biblical text',[107] and, as they wrote in their popularising essay on 'Energy', 'dark indeed would be the prospects of the human race if unilluminated by that light which reveals "new heavens and a new earth"'.[108]

Thomson thus regarded the consequences of entropy not, like Masson, as a matter for despair but as the fulfilment of scripture: there was a theology and a cosmology within which the consequences of thermodynamics made sense. What the philosophical training of the Scottish universities encouraged in its scientists was an exploration of the relationship between general truths and empirical evidence, those general truths often shaping the context in which empirical investigation was undertaken. Maxwell, for instance, regarded the traditional methods of mathematics as inadequate because they did not recognise the 'whole' with whose parts they were dealing:

> We are accustomed to consider the universe as made up of parts, and mathematicians usually begin by considering a single particle, and then conceiving its relation to another particle and so on. This has generally been supposed the most natural method. To conceive a particle, however, requires a process of abstraction, since all our perceptions are related to extended bodies, so that the idea of the ALL that is in our consciousness at a given instant is a mathematical method in which we proceed FROM THE WHOLE TO THE PARTS instead of from the parts to the whole.[109]

The 'whole' which Maxwell invoked was both a methodological principle of science and an acceptance of science's place within a greater truth. As Einstein said of the first of these,

> before Maxwell, Physical Reality, in so far as it was to represent the processes of nature, was thought of as consisting in material particles, whose variations consist only in movement governed by total differential

---

[107] Ibid., 535.

[108] William Thomson and Peter Guthrie Tait, 'Energy', *Good Words*, 3 (1862), 606–7; cited in Smith and Wise, *Energy and Empire*, 535.

[109] James Clerk Maxwell, *A Treatise on Electricity and Magnetism* (Oxford: Clarendon Press, [1873] 1881), Vol. 2, 164.

equations. Since Maxwell's time, Physical Reality has been thought of as represented by continuous fields, governed by partial differential equations, and not capable of any mechanical interpretation. This change in the conception of Reality is the most profound and fruitful that physics has experienced since the time of Newton.[110]

For Maxwell, science has to recognise the limits of its abilities: it is 'incompetent to reason upon the creation of matter itself out of nothing',[111] and 'the extent, the order, and the unity of the universe' is something for the scientist to consider while reading the first chapter of the Epistle to Colossians.[112]

The crisis of Scottish philosophy which Masson had identified was, in effect, a crisis induced by a science which was itself testimony not to the *decline* of Scottish culture in the second half of the nineteenth century but to its vitality, to its continued ability not only to engage with new ideas at the very forefront of contemporary thought but to redefine the very terms on which that thought should operate. If Maxwell, Thomson and Tait had been isolated specialists, removed from the general directions of Scottish culture, then perhaps the sense of their being simply the aftermath of an exhausted Enlightenment would be appropriate. But this was far from being the case, as can be seen from the work of William Robertson Smith, remembered if at all in histories of Scotland[113] as the Professor of Theology at the Free Church College in Aberdeen who was dismissed for suggesting that the Bible had to be scientifically studied as a historical text and not simply accepted as the unmediated record of the word of God. Robertson Smith's case is cited by Christopher Harvie, in *Scotland and Nationalism*, as indicative of the decline of Scotland's intellectual life in the nineteenth century:

In the north, religious repression appeared compounded with pseudo-science. Phrenology, centred among Duncan MacLaren's radical friends in Edinburgh, was no improvement on Monboddo's speculations on

[110] Albert Einstein, 'Maxwell and Physical Reality', in *James Clerk Maxwell, A Commemoration Volume 1831–1931* (New York: Macmillan, 1931), 71.
[111] Lewis Campbell and William Garnett, *The Life of James Clerk Maxwell* (London: Macmillan, 1882), 359.
[112] Ibid., 394–5; see Botond Gaál, *The Faith of a Scientist: James Clerk Maxwell* (Debrecen: Istvan Hatvani Theological Research Centre), 21ff.
[113] The event receives two sentences in T. M. Devine's *The Scottish Nation* (384), and is not mentioned in Michael Lynch's *Scotland: A New History*.

evolution and language; Robert Knox on *The Races of Man* (1850) was a disturbing regression. Samuel Smiles's equation of economic progress with a simple set of moral injunctions was scarcely an adequate successor to the work of Adam Smith. H. T. Buckle in 1861 condemned Edinburgh for lapsing into a credulous medievalism, thanks to the deductive methods of Scots philosophy; in 1865 John Stuart Mill settled accounts with the school's last great man, Sir William Hamilton. Even Matthew Arnold, trying to do something for the Celts, pushed them firmly into a commercialised twilight. By the 1880s, as the reformed English universities were gaining momentum in scholarship and research, the Free Kirk was persecuting Robertson Smith, its greatest theologian and a pioneer of social anthropology, for heresy. His move to Cambridge in 1885 seemed a capitulation.[114]

Harvie's bleak analysis of a Scotland where 'the parish was choking, the intermediate level of the nation-state unavailable',[115] makes no mention of Maxwell, who also lost his Professorship in Aberdeen (as a result of the amalgamation of its two colleges), and took up one in King's College, London but then chose to return to his family parish in Galloway to do his greatest work. Harvie also mentions Thomson only in passing, despite the fact that this Ulster Protestant chose his title, Lord Kelvin, from his commitment to his local Scottish culture in Glasgow. Scotland's state of decay is produced by excluding from consideration those thinkers who made the most universal contributions to nineteenth-century intellectual advancement from within Scotland, and by treating all those who left for London or Cambridge or Oxford has having abandoned Scotland. This not only ignores those who, like Masson, chose to return to Scotland, or who, like Caird, moved back and forth between Glasgow and Oxford, but ignores the extent to which someone like Robertson Smith, even after he had taken up his position in Cambridge, remained deeply involved in Scottish intellectual life.

Smith was the son of a Free Church minister who, after proving himself precocious in mathematics at the University of Aberdeen, decided to study theology at New College in Edinburgh. He had already come to the attention of P. G. Tait in winning the Ferguson Scholarship in mathematics, and in 1868, while continuing his study of theology, was appointed as Tait's assistant

---

[114]   Christopher Harvie, *Scotland and Nationalism: Scottish Society and Politics 1707–1994* (London: Routledge, [1977] 1994), 93.

[115]   Ibid., 96.

and laboratory demonstrator. Smith's work for Tait included carrying out experiments to empirically test aspects of Maxwell's work on electricity and magnetism,[116] and his initial publications in the area of mathematical physics suggested a future in which he would become a junior partner in the work of Thomson, Tait and Maxwell. Such a future would not have been inimical to the profound Christian commitments he had learned from his father, because, as Maxwell put it, '…as Physical Science advances we see more and more that the laws of nature are not mere arbitrary and unconnected decisions of Omnipotence, but that they are essential parts of one universal system in which infinite Power serves only to reveal unsearchable Wisdom and eternal Truth.'[117]

Robertson Smith, however, chose to combine science and religion not by scientifically scrutinising the physical world for its demonstration of 'one universal system' but by scientifically scrutinising the source of religious revelation – the Bible – for proof of the divine Wisdom which justified Maxwell's faith. It was by applying the historical modes of analysis developed by the so-called Higher Criticism in Germany to the text of the Bible that Robertson Smith hoped to establish an understanding of the Biblical text as a historical unfolding of religious potentialities whose full significance would only be discernible in Jesus's life and death, an event whose full meaning would in turn only be realised a millennium and a half later with the emergence of the reformed tradition. For Robertson Smith, the relation between God and man was not one in which each encounter between the divine and the human produced an unchangeable ultimate truth. The Word of God was a historicised Word, adapted to the conditions and possibilities of the historical and psychological circumstances of the human beings to whom He spoke. Although still a revelation, it was, nonetheless, both a Word *in* and a Word *of* evolution:

> Now the evolution of God's dealings with man cannot be understood except by looking at the human side of the process. The only idea of moral and spiritual evolution which is possible to us, is that of evolution in accordance with psychological laws. The nexus must always be

---

[116] See Gordon Booth, *William Robertson Smith: The Scientific, Literary and Cultural Context from 1866 to 1881*, PhD Thesis, University of Aberdeen, 2000; available at http://www.gkbenterprises.fsnet.co.uk/index.htm.

[117] P. M. Harman (ed.), *The Scientific Papers of James Clerk Maxwell* (Cambridge: Cambridge University Press, 1991), Vol. 1, 426.

psychological. The teleology of revelation is divine; but the pragmatism of the revealing history must be human.[118]

The challenge which faced contemporary biblical scholars was, for Smith, the effort to 'trace the process of the Old Testament religion completely from the side of psychology and human history', such that,

> the divine elements in the process will take their proper place of themselves, unless with arbitrary rationalism we forcibly thrust them aside. For it is the postulate of all moral religion, that God communicates himself to man in such a way that his revelation is interwoven with history, without violence or breach of psychological laws.[119]

What Robertson Smith proposed, in effect, was nothing less than an evolutionary account of the development of the religious and of the 'spiritual' to match the evolutionary accounts of the biological presented by Chambers, Darwin and Huxley, an account which would be based on a comparative study of early religion and on the identification of the aspects of those religions which made possible the 'higher', properly 'spiritual' developments of later times. The key event on which Robertson Smith focuses is that of sacrifice, where,

> The one point that comes out clear and strong is that the fundamental idea of ancient sacrifice is sacramental communion, and that all atoning rites are ultimately to be regarded as owing their efficacy to a communication of divine life to the worshippers, and to the establishment or confirmation of a living bond between them and their god. In primitive ritual this conception is grasped in a merely physical and mechanical shape, as indeed, in primitive life, all spiritual and ethical ideas are still wrapped up in the husk of a material embodiment. To free the spiritual truth from the husk was the great task that lay before the ancient religions, if they were to maintain the right to continue to rule the minds of men. That some progress in this direction was made, especially in Israel, appears from our examination. But on the whole it is manifest that none of the ritual systems of antiquity was able by mere natural development

[118] William Robertson Smith, 'The Progress of Old Testament Studies', *British and Foreign Evangelical Review*, XXV (July 1876), 487.
[119] Ibid., 486.

to shake itself free from the congenital defect inherent in every attempt to embody spiritual truth in material forms.[120]

Only with Christ's sacrifice would the spiritual truly free itself from the material body, a body which would henceforth be conceived only symbolically.

For this ambitious task of evolutionary exegesis, Robertson Smith was able to call on the work of two other remarkable Scots with whom he became close friends. The first was John Ferguson McLennan (1827–81), an Edinburgh advocate with an interest in ancient history and culture who made the radical suggestion that ancient civilisation was structured on matriarchial rather than on patriarchal foundations. The particular form of this matriarchy required the acquisition of the bride from an alien tribe, because marriage *within* the tribe was forbidden. Exogamous marriage (the term is McLennan's invention) required that the bride had to be extracted from her own tribe or social group, if necessary by force, and installed at the centre of her new family structure. Descent, with all its legal implications, then passed through the matrilineal line, and polyandry (one wife, many husbands) was the likely accompaniment of these arrangements. Such a view, of course, was entirely at odds not only with the contemporary expectations of Victorian society, but with Victorian assumptions about the nature of the development of civilisation. McLennan's challenge to both was to be the beginning of a long line of anthropological studies focused on the implications of the fact that in primitive societies children were assumed to be the offspring of the mother alone. In developing these theories, McLennan provided later anthropologists with one of the key terms – totemism – which would define much of the development of social anthropology in the period up to the First World War. The significance of McLennan's speculations, first published in *Chambers Encyclopaedia* in 1868 and developed in *The Fortnightly Review* in 1869–70,[121] is attested by the fact his terms came to be used in the title of one of Freud's major publications, *Totem und Tabu*, published in 1913.

McLennan's theories were to be developed by the second of Robertson Smith's intellectual colleagues, J. G. Frazer, in articles on 'Totem' and 'Taboo'

---

[120] William Robertson Smith, *Lectures on the Religion of the Semites* (London: Adam and Charles Black, [1889] 1901), 440–1.

[121] 'Totem', *Chambers Encyclopaedia*, 1st edn, Vol. 10 (Supplement), 753–4; 'The Worship of animals and plants', which appeared in three parts in *The Fortnightly Review*, 6, October 1869, 407–27; November 1869, 562–82 and *The Fortnightly Review*, 1870, 7 February, 194–216.

in the ninth edition of the *Encyclopaedia Britannica*, articles which were to lead directly to the writing of *The Golden Bough*, his exploration of the structures of primitive mythology, first published in two volumes in 1890 and expanded to twelve in the third edition of 1915. Robertson Smith cites Frazer's articles as authoritative sources for theories of the savage mind, but it was Smith himself who inspired Frazer to switch from the study of classics to the study of the primitive, and who directed him to McLennan's work as a starting point. Few works had a greater influence on European culture at the turn of the twentieth century than *The Golden Bough*. The roll-call of those who were influenced by, or responded to *The Golden Bough* includes many of the most prominent and radical thinkers of the period, including Malinowski and Durkheim in social anthropology, Bergson and Ryle in philosophy, Freud in psychology, Spengler and Toynbee in philosophical history. The power that Frazer's work held over the European mind is indexed by the fact that Wittgenstein, who had written about it in 1930, was still writing about it as late as 1948.[122] Equally, the search for the ritual and archetypal significance of works of art, initiated in the 1890s by Jane Harrison and Gilbert Murray, who applied the methods of *The Golden Bough* to classical literature, was to culminate in the mid-century in some of the most important of modern approaches to the study of English literature in the work of critics such as Wilson Knight in Britain and Northrop Frye in North America.

Like some volcanic eruption from deep underground, Frazer's accounts of the magic and the legends of primitive peoples, his tracking of the strange origins of familiar Graeco-Roman myths, his explanations of the savage roots of religion and the relation of sacrificial kingship to seasonal rituals, poured across the intellectual landscape, reshaping the ways in which the human mind and human history were conceived. And perhaps *The Golden Bough*'s most enduring legacy was its impact on creative artists, who found in Frazer's work not only a new vocabulary of myth that could be applied to modern conditions but a new conception of the profound and irrational depths of the human mind, depths which could only be expressed through entirely new forms that combined the most adventurous aspects of modernity with the most powerful remnants of the primitive.[123] When T. S. Eliot

---

[122] See John B. Vickery, *The Literary Impact of* The Golden Bough (Princeton: Princeton University Press, 1973) for the most extensive account of the influence of Frazer's work; for Wittgenstein's interest, see 101.

[123] Ibid., 74ff.

declared that, for modern writers, 'the maxim, return to the sources, is a good one' because they 'should be aware of all the metamorphoses of poetry that illustrate the stratifications of history that cover savagery',[124] he was acknowledging what had been learned from Frazer: that underlying the modern world, like a series of archaeological strata, were a variety of savage ones, and that modern civilisation was a thin layer through which it was all too easy to fall back down into those savage origins. When Frazer envisaged the modern world as 'cracked and seamed, sapped and mined with rents and fissures and yawning crevasses', opening onto a primitive belief in magic which 'is very much what it was thousands of years ago in Egypt and India' and remains the environment of the 'ignorant and superstitious classes of modern Europe',[125] he implied the form of works like Eliot's *The Waste Land*, with its underlying structure of powerful myths haunting the facile surface of modern European civilisation. Eliot proclaimed that Joyce, with some help from Yeats, was the inventor of the 'mythic method' which had allowed contemporary writers to make artistic sense of the 'immense panorama of futility and anarchy which is contemporary history';[126] in fact, all of them depended on Frazer, as Eliot himself made clear in his notes to *The Waste Land*: 'To another work of anthropology I am indebted in general, one which has influenced our generation profoundly; I mean *The Golden Bough*; I have used especially the two volumes *Adonis, Attis, Osiris*'.[127] Throughout the development of modernist literature in the first half of the twentieth century, Frazer's writings played a crucial role, providing both some of its key narrative structures – such as the myth of the dying god who must be sacrificed for the return of fertility[128] – and the inspiration for some of its most daring formal innovations, such as the revelation of archetypal myths still operative in contemporary consciousness. Both aspects can be found in many of the works of the major modernist writers of the period – in Conrad, in Yeats, in Eliot, in Joyce, in Woolf – as well as in the work of many of the most important writers of the Scottish Renaissance, from John

---

[124] *Athenaeum* (17 October 1919), 'War Paint and Feathers', 1036.
[125] J.G. Frazer, *The Golden Bough,* one-volume edition (London: Macmillan, 1922), 55–6.
[126] T.S. Eliot, review of James Joyce's *Ulysses*, 'Ulysses, Order and Myth', *The Dial* (1922), 480–3.
[127] T.S. Eliot, 'The Waste Land', *Collected Poems 1909–1962* (London: Faber and Faber, 1963), 80.
[128] See Vickery, *The Literary Impact of* The Golden Bough for a discussion of Yeats's use of this particular aspect of Frazer's account.

Buchan and Lewis Grassic Gibbon to Neil Gunn, Edwin Muir and Naomi Mitchison. Even when Frazer's work had lost much of its original surprise, and its treatment of the primitive had been superseded by later anthropologists, its literary influence continued to be felt in works such Robert Graves's *The White Goddess*,[129] in the poetry of Ted Hughes, in the work of Scottish writers such as Muriel Spark – who sets one of her late novels, *Territorial Rites* (1979), on the banks of the Lake at Nemi where Frazer's narrative opens – and in the novels of Allan Massie, whose depictions of modern European history, as in *The Sins of the Father* (1991), are constantly juxtaposed with elements from Frazer's narrative.

McLennan, Robertson Smith and Frazer laid the groundwork on which the theories of social anthropologists, sociologists, psychologists and cultural historians would build their conception of the nature of humanity in the early years of the twentieth century. No less than Thomson, Tait and Maxwell, these three fundamentally changed the twentieth century's perception of humanity's relationship to the world, and, in particular, of the relationship between civilised modernity and its savage past. If Robertson Smith, true ever to the ideals of the Free Kirk, saw the development of religion as the achievement of higher and more mature forms of spirituality, Frazer, his disenchanted disciple, saw it as a profound mistake: the grand Victorian narrative of the rise of civilisation from savagery is reversed by Frazer to reveal that savagery is the stronger and more permanent condition, and that the beneficent truths of the Christian religion are themselves but the spiritual epiphenomena of a savagery which it is incapable of displacing.

No less than in Thomson's and Maxwell's work, however, it is a new understanding of energy that is the driving force of Robertson Smith's and Frazer's conception of the world: rather than a physical energy, however, it is the transformative power of a protean psychic energy which governs their version of human history. In Robertson Smith's case, this was unleashed in the accumulating energy of God's gradual revelation of himself in forms suited to the historical psychology of a particular historical epoch; in Frazer's case, in the imagination's relentless production of psychological links between

---

[129] Graves attacks Frazer for 'carefully and methodically sailing all round this dangerous subject' because 'what he was saying-not-saying was that Christian legend, dogma and ritual are the refinement of a great body of primitive and even barbarous beliefs' (*The White Goddess*: London: Faber and Faber, 1961, 242); *The White Goddess* states what, in Graves's view, Frazer had declined to state about the consequences of the materials he had discovered.

various natural phenomena that human beings are incapable of separating into the valid and the illusory. In this Frazer depended on a modernised version of Hume's account of the mind as working by processes of association – a conception made contemporary again in the 1850s and 60s by the psychological work of Alexander Bain at the University of Aberdeen, and by the influential article on 'Psychology' in the ninth edition of the *Encyclopaedia Britannica* by Robertson Smith's colleague at Cambridge, James Ward.[130] For Frazer, as for Hume, it is 'regularity in the succession of phenomena' alone which 'breeds in our mind the conception of a cause' and, 'in the last analysis cause is simply invariable sequence'.[131] In the early stages of human experience, however, it is impossible to know what constitutes 'invariable sequence' and Frazer attributes the power of magic and all the mythic structures that go with it to the misapplication of Hume's principles of association: the associations based on 'resemblance' and 'contiguity' are taken, in the primitive mind, to be the same as those of causation, and thus there arises the belief in 'homeopathic magic' – in which things are believed to affect each other because they are similar – and in 'contagious magic' – in which things transfer qualities as a result of coming into contact. The history of humanity, in other words, is the history of a vast and often terrifying organisation of mistaken conceptions about the nature of causation: in *Psyche's Task*, published in 1910, Frazer tried to show how the mistaken causalities of savagery might have assisted 'at certain stages of evolution' the development of 'some social institutions which we all, or most of us, believe to be beneficial', despite the fact that they 'have partially rested on a basis of superstition'.[132] Significantly, it is a very short book, only 81 pages, compared with the six thousand pages into which *The Golden Bough* had grown by its third edition, published between 1911 and 1915, or the four volumes of *Totemism and Exogamy*, published in 1910. However hard he might occasionally have tried to conceive of the material he was analysing as beneficial to humanity, he saw in it primarily 'an unmitigated evil, false in itself and pernicious in its consequences', an evil which 'has sacrificed countless lives, wasted untold treasures, embroiled nations, severed friends, parted husbands and wives, parents and children, putting swords, and worse than swords between them'.[133] As much as his great predecessor, Hume, on whose

---

[130] For a detailed discussion see my *Associationism and the Literary Imagination* (Edinburgh: Edinburgh University Press, 2007), Ch. 4.

[131] J. G. Frazer, *The Worship of Nature* (London: Macmillan, 1910), 2.

[132] J. G. Frazer, *Psyche's Task* (London: Macmillan, 1910), 1.

[133] Ibid.

psychology he relied, Frazer was appalled by the superstition he spent his life charting, because, 'not content with persecuting the living it has pursued the dead into the grave and beyond it, gloating over the horrors which its foul imagination has conjured up to appal and torture the survivors'.[134] If modern civilisation was threatened in the future by the universe's inevitable entropic decline, it was threatened in the present by the equally entropic force that made civilisation much more difficult to sustain than reversion to savagery.

The continuity of these developments of Scottish nineteenth-century thought with its Enlightenment predecessors can be seen in the fact that Robertson Smith's and Frazer's accounts of primitive religion represented a *conjectural history* of the kind that Dugald Stewart believed to be characteristic of Scottish thinkers of the eighteenth century, and a continuation, in some respects, of Hume's speculations in 'The Natural History of Religion'. Indeed, George Davie has suggested that Robertson Smith's thought recapitulates elements of the earlier Smith – Adam Smith's – 'four stages theory [of historical development] and the principle of unintended consequences'.[135] Equally, Frazer's account of the nature of the mind and its relationship to reality recapitulates Hume's theory of how we construct an apparent world from the powers of the imagination. In the first of his Gifford Lectures on *The Worship of Nature*, Frazer describes how,

> ...every one of us is perpetually, every hour of the day, implicitly constructing a purely imaginary world behind the immediate sensations of light and colour, of touch, of sound, and of scent which are all that we truly apprehend; and oddly enough it is this visionary world, the creation of thought, which we dub the real world in contradistinction to the fleeting data of sense. Thus viewed, the mind of man may be likened to a wizard who, by the help of spirits or the waving of his magic wand, summons up scenes of enchantment which, deceived by the very perfection of his art, he mistakes for realities.[136]

The scientist who set out in search of 'realities' discovers that he is a wizard capable of calling up an enchanting but ultimately illusory world. It might seem as though this was a point of view inimical to scientific discovery but

---

[134] Ibid.
[135] Davie, *The Scottish Enlightenment and Other Essays* (Edinburgh: Polygon, 1991), 136.
[136] Frazer, *The Worship of Nature*, 2.

it was a position which also informed Maxwell's natural philosophy. Maxwell used imaginary constructions – to which he would not even give the status of 'hypotheses' – to help him develop those mathematical equations which could predict the workings of the physical world: thus he envisaged atoms as fluid 'vortices' which, as they turned, allowed electrically charged particles to 'flow' through the interstices between them:

> The conception of a particle having its motion connected with that of a vortex by perfect rolling contact may appear somewhat awkward. I do not bring it forward as a mode of connexion existing in nature, or even as that which I would willingly assent to as an electrical hypothesis. It is, however, a mode of connexion which is mechanically conceivable, and easily investigated, and it serves to bring out the actual mechanical connexions between the known electromagnetic phenomena: so that I venture to say that any one who understands the provisional and temporary nature of this hypothesis, will find himself rather helped than hindered by it in his search after the true interpretation of the phenomena.[137]

It was through such a 'fictional' construction of the physical world that Maxwell was to produce his most radical scientific proposal, the one that we now know as 'Maxwell's Demon'.[138] The 'demon' was named such not by Maxwell himself but by Lord Kelvin, because what it claims to show is that the second law of thermodynamics, which requires that heat flow from hotter to colder substances, is not, as Kelvin believed, a necessary outcome of the nature of the universe but simply a statistical probability. Maxwell's demon is a molecule-sized creature who sits between two containers of gases, one hotter than the other. The temperature of the gases is a function of the velocity of the particles of which it consists, but in any gas there will be particles which are faster (hotter) or slower (colder) than the overall average. The demon operates a shutter which allows particles to pass between the two containers but only allows the fastest from the cooler container and the slowest from the warmer container to be exchanged. As a consequence, heat (the

---

[137] James Clerk Maxwell, 'On Physical Lines of Force', *Philosophical Magazine* (March 1861); quoted in Mahon, *The Man who Changed Everything*, 104.

[138] For Maxwell's use of 'analogies', see Richard Olson, *Scottish Philosophy and British Physics 1750–1880: A Study in the Foundations of the Victorian Scientific Style* (Princeton: Princeton University Press, 1975), Ch. 12, especially 300ff.

average speed of particles) 'flows' from the cooler to the warmer chamber, reversing the necessity of the second law and revealing it to be a statistically likely but not a necessary outcome of the exchange of particles between environments of different temperatures. It was an experiment that there was no possibility of testing but it haunted Kelvin's imagination until his final days by its disruption of his sense of scientific truth. It was, in fact, the beginning of what we now know as 'chaos' theory – the operation of systems of such complexity that their outcome cannot be predicted in advance, and which thereby appear to defy the traditional laws of physics on which Kelvin's thermodynamics was founded. Maxwell's 'demon' is a fiction but a fiction which allows us to see how our understanding of reality is always a 'plot', a construction, or, in Frazer's sceptical articulation, the revelation of a 'purely imaginary world' – but one from which we can derive productive 'truths'.

IV   Energy, Spirit and Fantasy

In *Three Rival Versions of Moral Enquiry*, originally delivered as Gifford Lectures in Edinburgh 1988, Alasdair MacIntyre focuses on the ninth edition of the *Encyclopaedia Britannica* as an example of 'rational encyclopaedism', a belief that all areas of human knowledge are governed by the same rationality and that such rationality informs the continuous progress of the sciences. It is this rationality which makes possible the very conception of an encyclopaedia, because the encyclopaedia at one and the same time presents itself as a compendium in which all knowledge forms a single system, while also acknowledging that the progressive development of knowledge demands the encyclopaedia's constant updating to match science's ever-increasing understanding of the universe's knowable reality:

> It was taken to be the outcome of the successful application of methods to facts that there is continuous progress in supplying ever more adequate unifying conceptions which specify ever more fundamental laws. So it is characteristic of genuine science, as contrasted with the thought of the prescientific or non-scientific, that it has a particular kind of history, one of relatively continuous progress.[139]

---

[139] Alasdair MacIntyre, *Three Rival Versions of Moral Enquiry* (London: Duckworth, 1990), 20.

This is an intellectual world with which, according to MacIntyre, we can no longer have any shared presuppositions: 'They assumed the assent of all educated persons to a single substantive conception of rationality; we inhabit a culture a central feature of which is the presence of, and to some degree the debate between, conflicting, alternative conceptions of rationality.'[140] The 'encyclopaedism' of the ninth edition of *Britannica* is a historical remnant, irrelevant to the modern world because its contributors could not have conceived, as we have to, 'that the history of rationality and science might itself *be* a history of ruptures and discontinuities'; for them such discontinuity in the progress of reason was 'an unthinkable thought'.[141] The final editor of that ninth edition, having taken charge after the death of Professor Spencer Baynes of St Andrews University, was William Robertson Smith. According to MacIntyre, the ninth edition 'followed Robertson Smith in using Tylor's concept of survival in order to distinguish what were mere crude survivals from primitivism from what were genuine anticipations of, or already identical with, their own apprehension of what they took to be timeless truths of morality'.[142] Their conception of progress, in other words, led directly to themselves as the instantiation of the now 'timeless' truths which previous history had all along been preparing to reveal.

This, however, glosses over the extent to which Robertson Smith's historical conception of theology is one not of continual progress but rather of dramatic loss and subsequent recovery – in the form, for instance, of the Reformation's recovery of the principles of an earlier Christianity, and of the Free Church's subsequent recovery of those Reformation principles. Far from representing a smoothly objective uncovering of a timeless truth, Robertson Smith presents the history of religion as a profoundly personal engagement with a God whose revelation was always relative to the psychological and historical circumstances of its recipient. What was true in the past – 'God accommodated His work of revelation and grace to the laws of limited human nature, that He unfolded His plan under the conditions of historical development'[143] – was equally true in the present, and what was religiously important was not the achievement of a timeless universality of ultimate truths but the achievement of a *personal* relationship with God:

---

[140] Ibid., 23.
[141] Ibid., 24.
[142] Ibid., 27.
[143] 'On Prophecy' (1876), in John Black and George Chrystal (eds), *Lectures and Essays of William Robertson Smith* (London: A. and C. Black, 1912), 346.

We are to seek in the Bible, not a body of abstract truth, but the living personal history of God's gracious dealing with men from age to age, till at length in Christ's historical work, the face of the Eternal is fully revealed and we by faith can enter into the fullest and freest fellowship with an incarnate God.[144]

Since it is not universally 'abstract truth' that Robertson Smith sought but the personal 'fellowship with an incarnate God', it is a 'truth' which can as easily be lost as found, as the history of religion testifies in the long era which the Reformation brought to an end. History may exhibit progress but far from being guaranteed, progress is dependent on the courageous individualism which was exhibited by the prophets of the Old Testament in their refusal to accept the values of their own society, and by their engagement with 'a new and living power, the utterance of a new life, which because it is a new life, can spring only from the infinite source of all life'.[145] Moral truth is not something that can be discovered by abstract reasoning, and if its history has proved progressive it is not because of the unopposed unfolding of a historical necessity: rather, it is the result of the courageous commitment of individuals to discovering the meaning of a profoundly personal relationship between humanity and God. If there is indeed an evolutionary and 'organic development of history' it is one that can only be known because it has been 'worked out in and through human personality, by a personal redeeming God'.[146]

This anti-objectivist account of the history of religion laid the ground for the 'personalist' philosophies of late-nineteenth-century Scottish idealism: however 'scientific' and 'evolutionary' Robertson Smith's account of the development of religion might be, it recorded a development which would have been meaningless without its more important concomitant in the transformation of Christian ethics as *action* in the present. As George Adam Smith noted in his *Modern Criticism and the Preaching of the Old Testament*, the 'revival of the Prophets in the Scottish pulpit' combined Robertson Smith's historical account of Israel's prophets with the advent of socialism: 'Every department of religious activity felt its effects. Sermons became more ethical: the studies of Bible classes in the Old Testament, instead of being confined to

---

[144] 'What History Teaches', in Black and Chrystal, *Lectures and Essays*, 229–30.
[145] 'On the Question of Prophecy', in Black and Chrystal, *Lectures and Essays*, 189.
[146] Ibid., 165.

the historical books, were extended to the prophetical; and a considerable body of popular literature had appeared, which expounds the teaching of the Prophets and in many cases applies it to modern life.'[147] A truth which was 'personal' and which was evidenced in 'action' is very different from the kind of neutral 'rational superiority'[148] that MacIntyre attributes to Robertson Smith and to Frazer. MacIntyre, in effect, attributes to Robertson Smith the very theory of an objective scientific rationality which Maxwell's Demon, as an imaginative mind-experiment, refutes, and therefore attributes to the whole project of the ninth edition a theory of knowledge which its most prominent contributors – Frazer as much as Maxwell – set out to challenge. Precisely because they took seriously the *historical* understanding of the evolution of knowledge they saw their own knowledge as conditional rather than certain, as provisional rather than conclusive, and not only as inevitably subject to future revision but also as likely to be subject to regression rather than progression.

The provisional and hypothetical nature of truth among these Scottish thinkers, and their use of creative analogies between different areas of research, can be seen in one of the most remarkable publications by its leading scientists, *The Unseen Universe or Physical Speculations on a Future State*, by Peter Guthrie Tait (Kelvin's co-author in the *Treatise of Natural Philosophy*) and Balfour Stewart, one of the leading British experts in thermodynamics. The book was published in 1875 by Macmillan, and went through six editions within its first year of publication and seventeen editions in all before 1886. Its arguments were founded on the new physics of energy as demonstrated in Tait and Thomson's *Treatise*, and the authors therefore accepted that,

> whereas...matter is always the same, though it may be masked in various combinations, energy is constantly changing the form in which it presents itself. The one is like the eternal, unchangeable Fate or *Necessitas* of the ancients; the other is Proteus himself in the variety and rapidity of its transformations... *energy is only of use to us solely because it is constantly being transformed*... [Since] the only real things in the physical universe are

---

[147] George Adam Smith, *Modern Criticism and the Preaching of the Old Testament* (London: Hodder and Stoughton, 1901), 221–2. Quoted in Gillian M. Bediako, *Primal Religion and the Bible: William Robertson Smith and his Heritage*, *Journal for the Study of the Old Testament*, Supplement Series 246 (Sheffield: Sheffield Academic Press, 1997), 261.

[148] MacIntyre, *Three Rival Versions of Moral Enquiry*, 181.

matter and energy, and that of these matter is simply passive, it is obvious that all the physical changes which take place, including those which are inseparably associated with the thoughts as well as the actions of living beings, are merely transformations of energy.[149]

The physics of energy required the dissolution of energy in entropy, an outcome which Tait and Stewart also accepted:

It is absolutely certain that life, so far as it is physical, depends essentially upon transformations of energy; it is also absolutely certain that age after age the possibility of such transformations is becoming less and less; and, so far as we yet know, the final state of the present universe must be an aggregation (into one mass) of all the matter it contains *i.e.* the potential energy gone, and a practically useless state of kinetic energy, *i.e.* uniform temperature throughout that mass.[150]

Nonetheless, however, they attempted, by using Maxwell's Demon as a model, to reverse the consequences of the new physics and to envisage a universe in which energy, instead of being simply dissipated, was being somehow collected in an alternative form which could become the source of new activity:

the law of gravitation assures us that any displacement which takes place in the very heart of the earth will be felt throughout the universe, and we may even imagine that the same thing will hold true of those molecular motions...which accompany thought. For every thought that we think is accompanied by a displacement and motion of the particles of the brain, and...we may imagine that these motions are propagated throughout the universe.[151]

This unproven and untestable 'mind-experiment' allows them then to posit that the dissipated energy of our intellectual activity is actually gathered up in an alternative dimension of the universe, which they identify as the 'invisible body' of our future selves:

[149] Peter Guthrie Tait and Balfour Stewart, *The Unseen Universe or Physical Speculations on a Future State* (London: Macmillan, 1875), 82.
[150] Ibid., 91–2.
[151] Ibid., 156.

…each thought that we think, is accompanied by certain molecular motions and displacements in the brain, and part of these, let us allow, are in some way stored up in that organ, so as to produce what may be termed our material or physical memory. Other parts of these motions are, however, communicated to the spiritual or invisible body, and are there stored up, forming a memory which may be made use of when that body is free to exercise its functions.[152]

As a consequence, it is possible to infer an alternative and invisible universe in which the dissipated energy of our current, 'visible' universe, is collected and reactivated:

there exists now an invisible order of things intimately connected with the present, and capable of acting energetically upon it – for, in truth, the energy of the present system is to be looked upon as originally derived from the invisible universe.[153]

The ultimate dissipation of our physical existence can thus be compensated by its survival in the 'unseen universe' of a pure energy separated from the material forms in which it presents itself to us in our 'seen' universe. No fundamental contradiction exists, therefore, between the new science and the traditional Christian conception of the afterlife – indeed, the transformation of the universe into a Protean series of changing shapes for the same packets of energy makes the eventual transformation of that energy into a purely 'spiritual' existence after death more, rather than less, likely.

Like Maxwell's Demon, Tait and Stewart's *Unseen Universe* is a mind-experiment designed imaginatively to reverse the apparent consequences of contemporary physics. It attempts to validate its speculations by rooting them in a history of humanity's belief in an afterlife from the ancient Egyptians to Swedenborg and spiritualism, a history which they derived in part from the work of Robertson Smith and which, after some critical reviews of the first edition, they asked Smith to improve. *The Unseen Universe* forms a bridge between the anti-Newtonian physics of Thomson, Tait and Maxwell and Robertson Smith's and Frazer's exploration of the 'primitive' mind. In one a speculative fantasy – Maxwell's Demon – changes the nature of truth; in the

---

[152] Ibid., 159.
[153] Ibid., 158.

other, apparent fantasies – the structures of ancient myth – are gathered and searched for their possible truths.

It can scarcely be accidental, then, that Scotland produced in this period some of the most potent and influential 'mind experiments' of the age in the development of the new form of literature that has come to be described in modern criticism as 'fantasy'. As Colin Manlove notes in *Scottish Fantasy Literature*, 'in George MacDonald we have a writer who could fairly be said to be the founder of much modern fantasy',[154] and the emergence of this new literary form in the 1850s, in a Scottish writer who was trained both in religion and in science, underlines, perhaps, why Scots produced some of the most memorable and significant fantasies of the late nineteenth and early twentieth centuries. In MacDonald's own *Phantastes* (1858), in Robert Louis Stevenson's *Jekyll and Hyde* (1886) and in J. M. Barrie's *Peter Pan* (1906), the implications of the new physics are developed in contexts which make accessible and pertinently personal what, in the science, is entirely dependent on dense mathematical formulae.

Phantastes, for instance, begins with a scene of transformation which evokes the new theory of energy that Maquorn Rankine, who held the Chair of Civil Engineering and Mechanics at the University of Glasgow, had described in 1852 as requiring that 'all forms of physical energy, whether visible motion, heat, light, magnetism, electricity, chemical action, or other forms not yet understood, are mutually convertible; that the total amount of physical energy in the universe is unchangeable, and varies merely its condition and locality, by conversion from one form to another, or by transference from one portion of matter to another'.[155] MacDonald, who was sufficiently versed in contemporary developments in science to be able to teach it in colleges in England, used the literary tradition of the German fairy tale to present this new world of transformative energy:

> looking out of bed, I saw that a large green marble basin, in which I was wont to wash, and which stood on a low pedestal of the same material in a corner of my room, was overflowing like a spring; and that a stream

---

[154] Colin Manlove, *Scottish Fantasy Literature* (Edinburgh: Canongate Academic, 1994), 83.

[155] William Maquorn Rankine, paper read to the British Association for the Advancement of Science, 1852, subsequently published in the *Philosophical Magazine*; quoted in Crombie Smith, *Science of Energy: A Cultural History of Energy Physics in Victorian Britain* (London: Athlone, 1998), 142.

of clear water was running over the carpet, all the length of the room, finding its outlet I knew not where. And, stranger still, where this carpet, which I had myself designed to imitate a field of grass and daisies, bordered the course of the little stream, the grass-blades and daisies seemed to wave in a tiny breeze that followed the water's flow; while under the rivulet they bent and swayed with every motion of the changeful current, as if they were about to dissolve with it, and, forsaking their fixed form, become fluent as the waters.

My dressing-table was an old-fashioned piece of furniture of black oak, with drawers all down the front. These were elaborately carved in foliage, of which ivy formed the chief part. The nearer end of this table remained just as it had been, but on the further end a singular change had commenced. I happened to fix my eye on a little cluster of ivy-leaves. The first of these was evidently the work of the carver; the next looked curious; the third was unmistakably ivy; and just beyond it a tendril of clematis had twined itself about the gilt handle of one of the drawers. Hearing next a slight motion above me, I looked up, and saw that the branches and leaves designed upon the curtains of my bed were slightly in motion. Not knowing what change might follow next, I thought it high time to get up; and, springing from the bed, my bare feet alighted upon a cool green sward; and although I dressed in all haste, I found myself completing my toilet under the boughs of a great tree...[156]

MacDonald confronts his readers with a new world in which the substantial 'form' of things has become as 'fluent as the waters' and in which it is impossible to predict 'what change might follow next'. The fluidity of the material of the universe, and the ability of the physical to be transformed into the biological, dramatises the notion of a universe in which physical forms are simply the ephemeral structures for a continuously evolving and dynamic reservoir of energy, and the previously 'unseen universe' of transformative energy is made visible for us in the timescale not of geological change but in that of immediate personal experience.

Transformation, of course, is also the theme of Stevenson's *Jekyll and Hyde*, and while the relationship of Henry Jekyll to his violent alter ego, Hyde, has

---

[156] George MacDonald, *Phantastes: A Faerie Romance for Men and Women* (London: Smith, Elder and Co., 1858), 9–10.

often been read as the consequence of the moral repressions of Victorian society, the consequences of the new physics are equally legible in its structure. Through the Royal Society of Edinburgh, Stevenson's father was closely connected with P. G. Tait and Stevenson had been one of the students that William Robertson Smith took charge of in Tait's laboratory at the University of Edinburgh; indeed, one of the young Stevenson's earliest publication was a scientific paper about energy – 'On the Thermal Influence of Forests'.[157] The entropic nature of the universe that Jekyll inhabits is vividly presented in the cityscapes through which the characters move:

> Mr Utterson beheld a marvellous number of degrees and hues of twilight; for here it would be a glow of a rich, lurid brown, like the light of some strange conflagration; and here, for a moment, the fog would be quite broken up, and a haggard shaft of daylight would glance between the swirling wreaths. The dismal quarter of Soho seen under these changing glimpses, with its muddy ways, and slatternly passengers, and its lamps, which had never been extinguished or had been rekindled afresh to combat this mournful reinvasion of darkness, seemed, in the lawyer's eyes, like a district of some city in nightmare.[158]

The city is decaying towards that 'indistinguishable equilibrium of ruin' that Masson had foreseen as the outcome of entropy, and, like Jekyll attempting to maintain the virtues of his 'higher' being, the energy it expends on lamps cannot prevent – indeed will only hasten – the 'reinvasion of darkness'. As Allen MacDuffie has pointed out,[159] Stevenson's story involves an apparent defiance of the irreversibility of energy expenditure as demanded by the laws of thermodynamics: 'to dream of perfect reversibility is to dream of a world in which events don't matter',[160] and in which actions, therefore, have no consequences. By his transformation, Jekyll is seemingly able to provide himself with a source of immediate energy greater than that to which he has access

---

[157] *Miscellanea, Works of Robert Louis Stevenson* (London: William Heinemann, 1923), Vol. 26, 79–96, originally read before the Royal Society of Edinburgh, 19 May 1873.

[158] Robert Louis Stevenson, *Markheim, Jekyll and the Merry Men* (Edinburgh: Canongate, 1995), 247.

[159] Allen MacDuffie, 'Irreversible Transformations: Robert Louis Stevenson's *Dr. Jekyll and Mr. Hyde* and Scottish Energy Science', *Representations*, 96 (Fall 2006), 1–20.

[160] Ibid., 6.

in his own being, and with the right to commit acts which he can entirely disclaim as his own once the transformation is reversed. Such reversibility of the dissipation of energy, however, is an illusion, because with each expenditure of Hyde's energy Jekyll's future energy resources are being consumed. That is why, at the moment when Utterson and Jekyll's servant Poole enter his locked chamber on the final night, 'the kettle with a startling noise boiled over',[161] underlining the dissipation of energy involved in all the transformations by which Jekyll recreates himself as Hyde and why, towards his end, Jekyll comes to think of 'Hyde, for all his energy of life, as of something not only hellish but inorganic', as though 'the slime of the pit seemed to utter cries and voices; that the amorphous dust gesticulated and sinned; that what was dead, and had no shape, should usurp the offices of life'.[162] In the end, to resist being transformed involuntarily back into Hyde, Jekyll requires not only 'a double dose' of his potion but 'a great effort as of gymnastics'.[163] The energy which Hyde expends leaves Jekyll 'a creature eaten up and emptied by fever, languidly weak in both body and mind',[164] because it is an energy which does not add to life but subtracts from it, an energy whose terminus, like entropy, is not order but disorder, not action but death.

It was the inevitability of such an outcome that Maxwell's Demon had apparently set in doubt. While, for Maxwell, the 'demon' was simply a finite creature, 'very observant and neat fingered',[165] capable of calculating the movement of particles and intervening in their passage, the Demon came to be represented visually as a creature with horns and a tail, and, more often than not, with wings. This flying version of the Demon suggests the presence of Maxwell's theories in J. M. Barrie's *Peter Pan*, and Peter Pan, perhaps, in the evolution of the visual representation of the Demon. Like the Demon, Peter is the guardian of the shutter that keeps two spheres – the sphere of Edwardian London and the sphere of the Neverland – separate, but unlike the Demon, Peter can move between them. At Peter's invitation, however, certain particles – certain children – are allowed to cross from one sphere into the other, thus renewing the energy of the Neverland at the expense of the domestic sphere from which they escape: 'She dreamt that the Neverland had come too near and that a strange boy had broken through from it. He

---

[161] Stevenson, *Markheim, Jekyll and the Merry Men*, 268.
[162] Ibid., 292.
[163] Ibid., 292.
[164] Ibid., 292.
[165] Quoted by Crosbie Smith and M. Norton Wise, *Industry and Empire*, 623.

did not alarm her, for she thought she had seen him before…But in her dream he had rent the film that obscures the Neverland, and she saw Wendy and John and Michael peeping through the gap'.[166] This continual transfer of new energy safeguards Peter's experience of the Neverland from the entropy which haunts his adversary, Captain Hook:

> **Smee** I have often noticed your strange dread of crocodiles.
>
> **Hook** (*pettishly*) Not of crocodiles but of that one crocodile. (*He lays bare a lacerated heart*) The brute liked my arm so much, Smee, that he has followed me ever since, from sea to sea, from land to land, licking his lips for the rest of me.
>
> **Smee** (*looking for the bright side*) In a way it is a sort of compliment.
>
> **Hook** (*with dignity*) I want no such compliments; I want Peter Pan, who first gave the brute his taste for me. Smee, that crocodile would have had me before now, but by a lucky chance he swallowed a clock, and it goes tick, tick, tick, tick inside him; and so before he can reach me I hear the tick and bolt. (*He emits a hollow rumble*) Once I heard it strike six within him.
>
> **Smee** (*sombrely*) Some day the clock will run down, and then he'll get you.[167]

The crocodile that has already begun to consume Hook, like the Hyde who consumes Jekyll, is indicative of the apparent irreversibility of the energy dissipation which Peter, like Maxwell's Demon, is able to defy only by bringing the energy of each new generation of children to recharge the Neverland with the dynamism of a fresh imagination and a new adventure.

The energy of ancient myth, as analysed and collected by Robertson Smith and Frazer, is combined in these tales with the energy of the new physics to defy those accounts of nineteenth-century Scottish culture as one in entropic decline. Scottish physics did not only transform conceptions of material reality but revitalised conceptions of myth and inspired the nation's literary imagination. And far from assuming 'the assent of all educated persons to a single conception of rationality',[168] as Alasdair MacIntyre would suggest, what these works revealed was that our knowledge, like our psyches, are 'not truly one, but truly two'—indeed, multiple, for, as Jekyll declares, 'man will be

---

[166] J. M. Barrie, *Peter Pan* (Harmondsworth: Puffin, 1967; 1912), 23.
[167] J. M. Barrie, *Peter Pan* (London: Samuel French, 1928), 29.
[168] MacIntyre, *Three Rival Versions of Moral Inquiry*, 23.

ultimately known for a mere polity of multifarious, incongruous and independent denizens'.[169] The opposition that MacIntyre constructs between that
'single substantive conception of rationality' and a modernity in which there
is 'debate between conflicting, alternative conceptions of rationality'[170] is an
illusion. Indeed, it is precisely in this period of Scottish scientific and cultural development that the possibility of alternative physical universes – some
ruled by Newtonian laws, some by merely statistical probabilities – and alternative intellectual universes – in which the scientist is merely 'a wizard who, by
the help of spirits or the waving of his magic wand, summons up scenes of
enchantment…he mistakes for realities'[171] – are the subject both of scientific
and philosophic speculation, and it is these multiple universes, seen and unseen,
and the transformative identities which they produce, that are embodied in
the myths – the fantasies of its creative writers, the 'thought-experiments' of
its scientists, and the primitive myths of its anthropologists – that Scotland
contributed to the self-understanding of the modern world.

VI Enlightenment Delayed

Given the international significance of the work of Kelvin, Tait, and Maxwell
in mathematical physics, of McLennan, Robertson Smith and J. G. Frazer in
comparative religion and anthropology, of Edward Caird in philosophy, of
George MacDonald and Robert Louis Stevenson in literature and of David
Masson in literary criticism, it would be difficult to argue that the fifty years of
Scottish culture before 1889, the date of the completion of the great project
of the ninth edition of the *Encyclopaedia Britannica*, was any less vital in itself
or any less crucial to the development of modern thought than had been
the fifty years before 1789. If the metaphysics of Caird and the comparative
religion of Robertson Smith do not engage contemporary thinkers to the
same extent as do the epistemology of Hume and the economics of Adam
Smith, nonetheless the work of Maxwell 'runs all through our daily lives',[172]
Stevenson's *Jekyll and Hyde* continues to have a remarkable provenance as a
metaphor in contemporary scientific and psychological thinking, and Frazer's
Golden Bough is indispensable to an understanding of the development of

---

[169] Stevenson, *Markheim, Jekyll and the Merry Men*, 278.

[170] MacIntyre, *Three Rival Versions of Moral Inquiry*, 23.

[171] J. G. Frazer, *The Worship of Nature* (London: Macmillan and Co., 1926), 2.

[172] Mahon, *The Man who Changed Everything*, 176.

both modern literature and psychology. In this context, W. R. Scott's identification of Hutcheson and Hume as constituting an Enlightenment was, in
effect, the retrospective projection of nineteenth-century Scotland's sense
of its own centrality to the development of modern thought and of the
international significance of the cultural history which made possible its
distinctive modern identity.

Why, then, did it take till the 1970s for W. R. Scott's notion of a Scottish
Enlightenment to gain general acknowledgment and why, when that acknowledgment did come, was it in the context of an insistence on the failure of
Scotland's nineteenth-century culture? In economic and social terms the
most important effect is that of the First World War: Scotland suffered dis-
proportionately in the War, not only in terms of loss of life – Michael Lynch
suggests Scots accounted for 110,000 of the 573,000 deaths in the war,[173]
nearly double its population ratio – but from the concentration of industrial
production which the war required, intensifying Scotland's dependence on
those 'heavy' industries whose collapse after 1920 was to plunge the country
into economic depression for a generation. According to Lynch, Scotland's
unemployment in 1913 was only 1.8 per cent in comparison with London's
8.7 per cent, whereas by 1923 'the positions had been reversed, with 14.3 per
cent out of work in Scotland compared with 11.6 in the United Kingdom as
a whole'.[174] The war depended on and magnified the importance of the heavy
manufacturing base of the British economy in areas such as Scotland;[175] the
peace made it, quite literally, redundant. The most successful and mutually
interdependent areas of Scottish economic activity, in coalmining, steelmak-
ing and shipbuilding – amounting to over a quarter of the total workforce
by the time of the First World War – thus became the most deeply affected
in the 1920s and 30s, with the consequence that the whole trajectory of
nineteenth-century Scottish society seemed to have been founded on a false
promise, and the social experiments which had made cities such as Glasgow
beacons of progressive local management in the 1890s turned into iconic
symbols of social deprivation.

The cost of the war, however, could be measured not only in the loss
of life and loss of economic potential, but in the loss of an intellectual
environment on which much of nineteenth-century Scottish achievement had

---

[173] Lynch, *Scotland: A New History*, 422.
[174] Ibid., 433.
[175] See Peter L. Payne, 'The Economy', in T. M. Devine and R. J. Finlay, *Scotland in the 20th Century* (Edinburgh: Edinburgh University Press, 1996), 16–17.

been built – its relationship, in physics and forestry as much as in philosophy and literature, with German culture. On the basis of the shared culture of the Reformation, Scotland's intelligentsia, from Sir William Hamilton and Thomas Carlyle in the 1820s to Edward Caird and William Robertson Smith in 1870s and 80s, had built many of their cultural projects on their dialogue with developments in Germany. The personal as well as intellectual closeness of this relationship can perhaps be symbolised by the summer of 1871, when the foremost German scientist of the time, Hermann Helmholtz, holidayed with William Thomson [Lord Kelvin] on his summer residence, the yacht *Lalla Rookh*, as Thomson sailed it round the Western Isles. Helmholtz had previously visited Thomson's laboratory in Glasgow in 1863 and had been a correspondent since their meeting at a German spa where Thomson's wife was being treated in 1855. Kelvin and Maxwell's achievments in physics were closely linked with the progress of Helmholtz's work,[176] and he was sufficiently important to them to be given his own unique abbreviation – 'H²' – in the correspondence in which Thomson, Tait and Maxwell exchanged and developed their ideas.[177]

Throughout this period, Scots played key roles in the translation of German ideas for the English-speaking world – from the essays of Thomas Carlyle in the 1820s and Hutchison Stirling's *The Secret of Hegel* in 1865 to the major English editions of Hegel, Kant and Heidegger produced by William Wallace,[178] Norman Kemp Smith[179] and John Macquarrie.[180] The intellectual closeness of the two cultures meant that many Scots spent part of their educational career in Germany: on a visit to Jena in 1879, for instance, Andrew Seth encountered John Haldane, younger brother of Seth's friend R. B. Haldane (who was himself studying with the German philosopher Lotze at Göttingen)[181] and a group of Scots theological students including John Herkless, later principal of St Andrews, and Lewis Muirhead, subsequently

---

[176] See Mahon, *The Man who Changed Everything*, 49, 55.

[177] Ibid., 132.

[178] *Logic of Hegel* (Oxford: Oxford University Press, 1874).

[179] *Immanuel Kant's Critique of Pure Reason* (London: Macmillan, 1929).

[180] Martin Heidegger, *Being and Time* (London: S.C.M. Press, 1962), with Edward Robinson.

[181] Haldane had been sent there on the advice to his family of John Stewart Blackie, Professor of Greek at the University of Edinburgh and a great admirer of the German university system. Haldane became a leading Liberal politician, in charge of the War Office in the years before the First World War.

author of *The Eschatology of Jesus*.[182] Seth was also not unique in finding a wife in Germany, so that the First World War represented more than a challenge to his intellectual allegiances. His youngest son Ronald was killed on the Somme; Ronald's older brother Siegfried – the name itself indicating the family's dual cultural inheritances – was wounded three times in the Allied cause.[183] Although Scottish thinkers like Kemp Smith, John Macmurray and John Macquarrie continued until the 1960s to engage with German philosophy, they became increasingly marginalised in a British philosophical environment that had rejected nineteenth-century German philosophy, and its social and moral consequences, first for the sparser and more specialised work of the Austrian logical-positivists and then for 'ordinary language' philosophy.

The consequences in Scotland of the breach in this hundred-year engagement of the two cultures in each other's philosophical debates – Seth heard the German philosopher Paulsen lecture on Hume's *Dialogues on Natural Religion* in Berlin in 1878[184] – were considerable: the Scots had made a significant commitment, both intellectual and institutional, in a tradition which no longer had its former public resonance[185] and they had, as yet, made only tentative steps to recouping the contemporary value of Scotland's earlier, eighteenth-century traditions. Kemp Smith's study of Hutcheson's influence on Hume was not

---

[182] G. F. Barbour (ed.), 'Memoir of the Author', *The Balfour Lectures on Realism by A. Seth Pringle-Pattison* (Edinburgh: William Blackwood, 1933), 25.

[183] Ibid., 126ff.

[184] Ibid., 22.

[185] See, for instance, Lawrence F. Barmann (ed.), *The Letters of Baron Friedrich von Hügel and Professor Norman Kemp Smith* (New York: Fordham University Press, 1981). Smith writes: 'A number of us are fighting hard to secure the new Professorship of German here for Otto Schlapp who had been the Lecturer for the past 25 years. There is a great deal of ungenerous & narrowminded opposition on account of his German birth. He is a splendid teacher & a very fine man, & highly popular with his students. A majority of the Senate too have signed our memorial in his support. So I think we shall succeed' (57). A few weeks later he adds: 'There has been an extraordinary, & very vulgar-minded, outburst against all things German over Schlapp's candidature, with the most grotesque & weird letters appearing in *The Scotsman* – balanced by some very cogent replies. The result, I regret to say, is that our Principal & others have yielded. It appears certain now that Schlapp will not be appointed. Pringle-Pattison has fought nobly for him, as have many other friends; & the student-body too is strongly in his favour, & what I should describe as the better elements in the Senate. But with a weak Principal & a composite body like the Court, what can be done!' (75).

to appear until 1941 and no book-length study of Thomas Reid appeared between Campbell Fraser's in 1898 and the mid-1970s.[186] Andrew Seth may have been pleased when Norman Kemp Smith, who had been his student at St Andrews, was appointed his successor in Edinburgh in 1919, maintaining the line of continuity back to Campbell Fraser, under whom Seth himself had studied, but Kemp Smith's *Prolegomena to an Idealist Theory of Knowledge* of 1924 never fulfilled its promise – no fully-argued idealist theory, building on Kemp Smith's work, ensued. It took till the 1960s, with the work of George Davie, for the Scottish tradition to be reconstituted, and by then it was reconstituted on the assumption that its Germanic and idealist phase had been a blind alley.

Davie's account of the decline of Scottish philosophy and his rejection of its nineteenth-century Germanic engagements can be seen as a reflection of the 'negative nationalism' of the Scottish Renaissance movement of the 1920s and 30s. Writing in praise of Edwin Muir (at a time when he and Muir were still allies in the Renaissance movement), Hugh MacDiarmid declared that the 'majority of Scottish writers during the past hundred years have been entirely destitute of intellectual equipment adequate to work at international calibre, or even national calibre comparatively considered'; the historical extent of this failure, however, is then suddenly expanded to include every writer back to the fifteenth century:

> Scotland has consequently become insular and has 'fidged fu' fain' on the strength of work that reflected only its national degeneracy and its intellectual inferiority to every other European country. The majority of the Scottish writers held most in esteem by contemporary Scots were (or are) too 'unconscious' even to experience the sense of frustration. They were too completely destitute of artistic integrity. It is in this that Muir is so significantly differentiated from the great majority, if not all, of his predecessors back to the time of the Auld Makars both as a critic and creative artist.[187]

The whole Scottish tradition is blighted with the same disease, a disease which goes all the way back to the Reformation, because 'if the religious and political courses to which we have been committed have not come between

---

[186] Several unpublished theses were written in the 1960s.

[187] Hugh MacDiarmid, *Contemporary Scottish Studies* (Edinburgh: *Scottish Educational Journal*, n.d.), 31.

us and the realisation of our finest potentialities, it is impossible to account for our comparative sterility'.[188]

What MacDiarmid was actually struggling against, however, was not the failure of Scottish literature but its enormous *success* in the previous two centuries in establishing itself as the original foundation and the continuing backbone of English literature. Hugh Blair's *Lectures on Rhetoric and Belles Lettres*, first published in 1783 but delivered in Edinburgh since 1759, aspired to an enlightenment universalism which could traverse Greek, Roman, French, Spanish and English literatures for the best models of literary excellence. In the context of this broad panorama what is striking is the prominence Blair gives to Scottish examples. Blair's elucidation of pastoral, for instance, in a discussion which ranges from Theocritus and Virgil to Pope, concludes: 'I must not omit the mention of another Pastoral Drama, which will bear being brought into comparison with any composition of this kind, in any language; that is, Allan Ramsay's Gentle Shepherd.'[189] No higher accolade could be accorded a Scottish poet than to be reckoned the equal of Theocritus, Virgil and Pope: if, thereafter, Blair notes that it is 'a great disadvantage to this beautiful Poem, that it is written in the old rustic dialect of Scotland, which, in a short time, will probably be entirely obsolete, and not intelligible', he is not *undermining* the relevance of the poem but acknowledging the extent to which, even in a language nearly 'obsolete', there is an achievement that 'would do honour to any poet'.[190] Blair gives similar status to Home's *Douglas* as an example of modern tragedy, because it contains one of the 'most distinguished Anagnorises' and is equal with 'masterpieces of the kind'.[191] And in Macpherson's *Ossian*, which has 'all the plain and venerable manner of the ancient times', is exemplified the highest of all literary achievements – the sublime: 'amidst the rude scenes of nature and of society, such as Ossian describes; amidst rocks, and torrents, and whirlwinds, and battles, dwells the Sublime.'[192] The three languages of Scotland – the Scots of Ramsay, the Gaelic that lies behind Macpherson's Ossian, and the English that is exemplified by poets such as Thomson, whose poetry 'introduces us into society with all nature'[193] – are each asserted by Blair

---

[188] Ibid., 32.

[189] Hugh Blair, *Lectures on Rhetoric and Belles Lettres* (London: W. Strahan, T. Cadell, 1783), 2 Vols, Vol. 2, 352.

[190] Ibid.

[191] Ibid., Vol. 2, 494.

[192] Ibid., Vol. 1, 65.

[193] Ibid., Vol. 1, 331.

to be the equal of the foremost examples of classical literature, and therefore certainly the equal of any English literature.

In Blair's defence of Macpherson's Ossian in his 'Critical Dissertation on the Poems of Ossian' what we see is not the development of an often criti- cised 'Anglocentric' conception of Scottish literature but the assertion of a Scotocentric conception of English (and, indeed, all modern) Literature, one in which Ossianic poetry becomes the model against which modern poetry must be measured: 'Ossian, himself, appears to have been endowed by nature with an exquisite sensibility of heart; prone to that tender melancholy which is so often an attendant on great genius; and susceptible equally of strong and of soft emotions',[194] because 'if Ossian's ideas and objects be less diversified than those of Homer, they are all, however, of the kind fittest for poetry'.[195] Ossian therefore becomes the fulcrum of Blair's aesthetic theory, relating Macpherson's poem to general philosophical and psychological prin- ciples that provide the benchmarks by which other poetry will be measured: 'His poetry, more perhaps than that of any other writer, deserves to be stiled, *The Poetry of the Heart*. It is a heart penetrated with noble sentiments, and with sublime and tender passions; a heart that glows, and kindles the fancy; a heart that is full, and pours itself forth.'[196] Blair's argument was to shape accounts of English literature for a century, both in the conception of poetry as 'pour- ing' from primitive or natural life – which shaped romantic conceptions of the nature of the poet – and in its stress on English poetry's Celtic inspira- tion, echoed in Matthew Arnold's famous insistence on the fact that the Celtic imagination lay behind the best of English literature: 'The Celts, with their vehement reaction against the despotism of fact, with their sensuous nature, their manifold striving, their adverse destiny, their immense calamities, the Celts are the prime authors of this vein of piercing regret and passion, – of this Titanism in poetry. A famous book, Macpherson's Ossian, carried in the last century this vein like a flood of lava through Europe'.[197] To Blair, too, can be traced early accounts of the history of English literature, such

---

[194] Hugh Blair, 'Dissertation on the Poems of Ossian', 1763, in Howard Gaskell (ed.), *The Poems of Ossian* (Edinburgh: Edinburgh University Press, 1996), 352.

[195] Ibid., 357.

[196] Ibid., 356.

[197] Matthew Arnold, 'On the Study of Celtic Literature' (1867), *The Complete Prose Works of Matthew Arnold*, Vol. III, *Lectures and Essays in Critism*, ed. R.H. Super (Ann Arbor: University of Michigan, 1962), 370.

as Henry Morley's *English Writers* (1887), which insists that without its Celtic substratum 'Germanic England would not have produced a Shakespeare'.[198]

In the nineteenth century, because of the influence exerted by the Scottish universities on the earliest English departments in England – those in University College and in King's College in London in the 1820s and 30s – a version of English literature emerged to which the literature of Scotland was central, both in terms of an original Celtic origin for the British imagination but also in terms of the key role of Scots in the historical development of English literature. John Merry Ross, for instance, argued that,

> The influence of Chaucer is felt more powerfully and yields richer fruit in Scotland than in England. Towering high above the group of lay and clerical poets whom we have just named, stand out the splendid figures of King James, Henryson, and Dunbar, whose genius would shed a lustre on any literature, and who are in fact the only great English poets of the fifteenth century. They and their successors in the sixteenth form a real connecting link between the age of Chaucer and that of Spenser, and enable us to measure in some degree the sovereign sway exercised by the great 'Father of English poetry'.[199]

The tradition of English literature is sustained and, indeed, made possible, by the achievements of poets in Scots, thereby allowing Scottish writing not only to claim a contemporary pre-eminence through the work of Burns and Scott, but an equal share in the history of a national British literature. It was an argument acknowledged by early historians of English literature in England and Morley's *English Writers*, for instance, acknowledged the crucial role of Scotland's medieval makers in the creation of the English literary tradition:

> Our North gained vigour by a war for independence, and had, in the fifteenth century, poets and historians who led the way on to a golden time of Scottish Literature. Our South, at the same time, lost vigour by the blight of foreign and domestic wars…From Chaucer's time till the beginning of the sixteenth century our Literature of the North sweeps

---

[198] Henry Morley, *English Writers* (London: Chapman and Hall, 1887), Vol. I, 189–90.
[199] John Merry Ross, *Scottish History and Literature: To the Period of the Reformation* (Glasgow: Maclehose, 1884), 129.

upward. Chief poet of Scotland in the time of Chaucer was John Barbour, of whose chief poem, 'The Bruce', the theme was liberty. [200]

And Thomas Arnold's article on 'English Literature' in the ninth edition of the *Encyclopaedia Britannica* paid appropriate tribute to the Scottish culture which had produced and sustained the *Britannica* itself as one of the major achievements of nineteenth-century British intellectual life: there was no separate article on Scottish Literature – though there was one on 'Celtic Literature' (by W. K. Sullivan of Cork) and even a groundbreaking one on American Literature (by John Nichol of Glasgow University) – because not only did Arnold (younger brother to Matthew) give prominent roles to Dunbar, Henryson and Douglas – 'all of whom, in respect of their turn of thought and the best features of their style, may be properly affiliated to Chaucer'[201] – but a special place was accorded to Burns as 'a man of genius…whose direct and impassioned utterances, straight from the heart' were 'to prepare the English-speaking world for that general break-up of formulas which the tempest of the French Revolution was about to initiate'.[202] The article's culmination is the work of Scott, whose 'strong memory and inexhaustible imagination, joined with a gift for picturesque description, and the faculty…of creating and presenting living types of character',[203] makes him not only the representative novelist of the age but the modern equivalent of Shakespeare. Arnold also includes non-imaginative writing and gives extensive accounts of the works of Francis Hutcheson, David Hume, Adam Smith and Thomas Reid. Even Dugald Stewart is given a key role in the moulding of modern 'English' culture through the wide range of intellectual talents who attended his lectures, many of whom became contributors to those influential organs of a Scoto-English conception of English literature, the *Edinburgh Review* and *Blackwood's Magazine*. Scottish writing in this account forms the very backbone of English literature.

If we return to the Freemason's Tavern in London in 1819, and the festival of commemoration for Robert Burns that aimed to raise enough money to build a 'National Monument to his Memory', what we can see is the emer-

---

[200] Henry Morley, *English Writers* (London: Chapman and Hall, 1887), Vol. VI, 1.

[201] Thomas Arnold, 'English Literature', *Encyclopaedia Britannica*, 9th edn (Edinburgh, 1872–88), Vol. VIII (1878), 415.

[202] Ibid., 428.

[203] Ibid., 433.

gence of an ideology in which Burns's significance is not simply in the quality of his art but in the fact that he stands as the representative of the institutional and personal virtues of the nation itself. For Sir James Mackintosh, the monument which they hoped to erect was not a monument to Burns's poetic genius, because 'no Monument, indeed, was wanting to eternize the name of Burns. His immortality rested on a surer basis—it lived in his Poems, and would flourish as long as human beings felt an interest and a sympathy in a true representation of the history, the cares, the joys, and sorrows of their fellow men.'[204] A national monument, however, would serve a different purpose, because it would remind people that Burns's poetic achievement was only possible because, 'He had enjoyed the benefits resulting from a system of national instruction—he had received an excellent English education, and had industriously availed himself of the resources presented by it'; as a consequence, 'there was no question but that he had read more books than Homer could have read'.[205] The erection of a Monument to the Memory of Burns would stand as a monument to the nation whose educational system and whose religion made his poetry possible, offering Scotland itself as a beacon to the rest of the world:

> [it] would suggest to all who might ever see it, that as it was to the general diffusion of Education in Scotland his inimitable writings owed their origin—so, the same cause, if allowed to operate in other countries, would, in all probability, incalculably augment the common riches of the intellectual world—would open unnumbered mines of mental treasure, which would otherwise lie unsought and unvalued—would unlock and give to society the genius and the talents of ten thousand bosoms, which, but for it, would for ever languish in silence and obscurity.[206]

The *national* monument would reflect not only the achievement of the poet as an isolated genius but as a son of the people, one whose art, despite his detractors, 'afforded intrinsic evidence, that it was in early life, and by his father's fire-side, those seeds of virtue, filial duty, and piety to his Creator,

---

[204] Festival in Commemoration of Robert Burns; and to promote a subscription to erect a National Monument to his Memory at Edinburgh: held at the Freemason's Tavern in London, on Saturday, 5 June 1819, 7.
[205] Ibid.
[206] Ibid.

were implanted, which afterwards grew up and matured into the fruits which would supply powerful and never-failing lessons of moral worth, integrity, and independence.'[207] Burns, the Scottish people and the Scottish nation provided a unique example to the world of the benefits of a presbyterian polity, and the event of the poet's commemoration was in itself a historic one, since it 'was the first instance in the history of the world, of an assembly of Gentlemen called together, and over which a Prince of the Blood presided, for the purpose of erecting a Monument, in the Capital of his Country, to a Peasant of that country'.[208]

What is significant here is not only the *prominence* of Scottish literature in the development of 'English literature' as a discipline but the enormous investment that nineteenth-century Scots made in the Scots language as the distinguishing mark of their cultural identity. Scotland, as a nation, had emerged out of the Wars of Independence in the fourteenth century from which also emerged the first great poems in Scots, Barbour's *Bruce* and Blind Harry's *Wallace*, and if it was only in the nineteenth century that the full richness of the achievement of the Makars could be grasped, that achievement was made significant by the fact that in Burns and, subsequently, in Scott, Scotland had produced writers who had, in the words of Daniel Sandford, chair of the committee for erecting a monument to Scott, 'raised our country to a proud equality of fame with the most renowned nations of ancient and modern times – and they had done more than history itself to throw light and splendour round her annals'.[209] In opposition to the Enlightenment historians' denial of the contemporary significance of the Scottish past, the pre-eminence of Scots in modern literature appeared to justify the continuing relevance of its earlier cultural achievements, and through the impact of the *Edinburgh Review* (founded 1802) and *Blackwood's Edinburgh Magazine* (founded 1819), to make its modern literary achievements central to the taste of a worldwide Anglophone audience. It was in *Blackwood's Magazine* that the original proposal for a national monument to Burns in imitation of a classical temple re-emerged as a proposal for such a temple as a national monument that would symbolise Edinburgh's status as the 'Athens of the North':

---

[207] Ibid., 8.

[208] Ibid.

[209] *Scotsman*, 20 October 1832; quoted in Graeme Morton, *Unionist-Nationalism: Governing Urban Scotland 1830–1860* (East Linton: Tuckwell Press, 1999), 165.

while London must always eclipse [Edinburgh] in all that depends on wealth, power, or fashionable elegance, nature has given to it the means of establishing a superiority of a higher and more permanent kind. The matchless beauty of its situation, the superb cliffs by which it is surrounded, the magnificent prospects of the bay, which it commands, have given to Edinburgh the means of becoming the most *beautiful* town that exists in the world…And thus while London is the Rome of the empire, to which the young, and the ambitious, and the gay, resort for the pursuit of pleasure, of fortune, or of ambition, Edinburgh might become another Athens, in which the arts and the sciences flourished, under the shade of her ancient flame, and established a dominion over the minds of men more permanent even than that which the Roman arms were able to effect.[210]

Edinburgh as the Athens of the North is no casual slogan of neoclassical imitation: in the era in which British arms will create the world's most extensive empire, Edinburgh's role is to provide the 'permanent' spiritual 'dominion' to justify that imperial power. Scottish arts and sciences will have a classical authority over the territory of the *pax Britannica*.

If Hugh Blair had despaired of Allan Ramsay's *The Gentle Shepherd* achieving recognition as the equal of 'any composition of this kind, in any language', because it was 'written in the old rustic dialect of Scotland',[211] a hundred years later Burns's language proved to be no impediment to his being included as one of the greatest of Carlyle's 'Hero Poets':

High Duchesses, the ostlers of inns, gather round the Scottish rustic, Burns;–a strange feeling dwelling in each that they never heard a man like this; that on the whole, this is the man! In the secret heart of these people it still dimly reveals itself, though there is no accredited way of uttering it as present, that this rustic, with his black brows and flashing sun-eyes, and strange words moving laughter and tears, is of a dignity beyond all others, incommensurable with all others.[212]

---

[210] 'On the Proposed National Monument in Edinburgh', *Blackwood's Magazine*, 5 (July 1819), 379–385.

[211] Blair, *Lectures on Rhetoric and Belles Lettres*, 531.

[212] 'On Heroes and Hero-Worship', G. B. Tennyson (ed.), *A Carlyle Reader: Selections from the Writings of Thomas Carlyle* (Cambridge: Cambridge University Press, 1984), 393–4.

Burns stands as one of the heroes of history, comparable to Shakespeare or Dante, but just as importantly, he stands for the continuing identity of the Scottish nation. Carlyle quotes Fletcher of Saltoun's aphorism, 'Let me make the songs of a people and you shall make its laws'[213] and declares Burns to 'have equalled himself with Legislators', because he is 'first of all our Song-writers; for we know not where to find one worthy of being second to him'.[214] Those songs 'are already part of the mother-tongue, not of Scotland only but of Britain, and of the millions that in all ends of the earth speak a British language'. Far from being obsolete because of his use of Scots vernacular, Burns had made Scots the second language of Empire and made it so universally accepted that 'no British man has so deeply affected the thoughts and feelings of so many men, as this solitary and altogether private individual, with means apparently the humblest'.[215] Through the influence of Burns and Scott, through the influence of the Edinburgh journals, the Scottish writer had not only an unparalleled scope for reaching a world-wide audience, but an unparalleled status as representing the modern world's 'classical' culture. As George Saintsbury, David Masson's successor at the University of Edinburgh, put it in an essay on Hogg reprinted in his *Collected Essays and Papers*: 'I do not know to whom the epigram that "everything that is written in Scotch dialect is not necessarily poetry" is originally due, but there is certainly some justice in it. Scotch, as a language, has grand accommodations; it has richer vowels and a more varied and musical arrangement of consonants than English, while it falls not much short of English in freedom from that mere monotony which besets the richly-vowelled contintental languages.'[216] It might seem that the wish of Clerk of Penicuik, one of the foremost antiquarians of the eighteenth century, had been fulfilled: 'Let the two nations', he declared, taking an idea from Book XII of the *Aeneid*, 'each still unsubjected, enter upon an ever-lasting compact under equal terms'.[217] English Literature, at the point of its emergence as a distinctive discipline and at high point of British imperialism, was firmly bound together by its 'unsubjected' Scottish contribution.

---

[213] Thomas Carlyle, *Critical and Miscellaneous Essays: Volume II* (London, 1888), 368.

[214] Ibid.

[215] Ibid.

[216] George Saintsbury, *Collected Essays and Papers* (London: Dent, 1924), Vol. 3, 37.

[217] Quoted in Andrew Hook (ed.), *History of Scottish Literature, Volume 2* (Aberdeen: University of Aberdeen Press, 1987), 40.

That conjoined Scoto-English literary tradition was given its own foundation myth by the publication, in 1815, of *Beowulf*, the previously unknown poem in Anglo-Saxon, discovered and edited by the Icelandic scholar Grim J. Thorkelin. Thorkelin was working on behalf of the Danish government and in search of the Nordic equivalent of Macpherson's Ossian, but the impact of his work was to entirely displace the possible Celtic origins of British literature in favour of Anglo-Saxon origins that could provide a single linguistic tradition stretching from the eighth century to the present. Indeed *Beowulf* came to be endowed with exactly the qualities that Blair had found in Ossian: as the Introduction to *The Cambridge History of English Literature* put it in 1907, '*Beowulf*–romance, history and epic–is the oldest poem on a great scale, and in the grand manner, that exists in any Teutonic language. It is full of incident and good fights, simple in aim and clear in execution; its characters bear comparison with those of the *Odyssey* and, like them, linger in the memory; its style is dignified and heroic.'[218] The emergence of this Anglo-Saxon origin for English Literature initially reinforced rather than undermined the centrality of Scots to the traditions of English literature, since Scots was closer to that origin than modern English. The Scottish Text Society, for instance, at one of its early meetings, 'regretted that too little attention was paid to the language, literature and history of Scotland in the system of education, and that there was no chair of Anglo-Saxon in a Scottish University'.[219] And when the chairs of 'Rhetoric and Belles Lettres' in the Scottish universities became chairs of 'Rhetoric and English Literature' (Edinburgh 1865), or, when new Chairs of English Literature were established (Glasgow, 1862), the possible Celtic origins of English literature had been entirely displaced by these Anglo-Saxon roots. For John Nichol, taking up the Chair in Glasgow, the subject he was about to teach began with Hugh Blair in 1759, but central to it is the study of Anglo-Saxon. Though 'it is only of late years that the researches of Anglo-Saxon scholars have disinterred it, and shown how much it promised', nonetheless 'rude as our Saxon literature was, and scattered as are its fragments, we may be forgiven a certain pride in the reflection that centuries before the "Cid" was written in Spain, or the "Nibelungen Lied" in Germany,...or the Troubadours had sung their earli-

---

[218] A. W. Ward and A. R. Waller (eds), *The Cambridge History of English Literature* (Cambridge: Cambridge University Press, 1907), Vol. 1, *From the Beginnings to the Cycles of Romance*, 4.

[219] Alexander Law, *The Scottish Text Society 1882–1982* (Edinburgh: The Scottish Text Society, 1982), 9.

est lays,…our ancestors had done so much'.[220] For Nichol, Anglo-Saxon is 'our own tongue',[221] the origin of Scots and English, and he quotes David Hume's prophecy, in a letter to the historian Edward Gibbon, that 'our solid and increasing establishment in America' can 'promise a superior stability and duration to the English language' than the French; to Nichol, the truth of this prophecy is evidenced by the fact that 'Shakespeare and Burns are this day read from the banks of the Connecticut and the Columbia river to the sands of Sydney and the Yellow Sea'.[222]

Progressively, however, *Beowulf* was to be read as a purely *English* origin for a purely *English* English literature. Although Scots were prominent contributors to the *Cambridge History of English Literature*, which laid the pattern for much of the development of English Literature in the following half-century or more, and although Scottish writers were given prominence within it,[223] those writers now appear as links in the chain of an unbroken continuity of a self-contained English tradition that starts with *Beowulf*: 'the Englishman of the days of *Beowulf* and *Widsith, The Ruin* and *The Seafarer*, knew what he wished to say, and said it, without exhibiting any apparent trace of groping after things dimly seen or apprehended. And from those days to our own, in spite of periods of decadence, of apparent death, of great superficial change, the chief constituents of English literature – a reflective spirit, attachment to nature, a certain carelessness of "art", love of home and country and an ever present consciousness that there are things worse than death – these have, in the main, continued unaltered.'[224] English literature has become the reflection of an English 'spirit'. When T. S. Eliot and I. A. Richards began to try to define an 'objective' and 'scientific' criticism of literature in the 1920s, Scottish writers did not figure in their conception of the literary tradition, and by the time

---

[220] *Inaugural Lecture to the Course of English Language and Literature in the University of Glasgow*, 17 November 1862, 8, 10–11.

[221] Ibid., 22.

[222] Ibid., 24.

[223] Thus the section on the nineteenth century is opened by a chapter on 'Philosophers' (by W. R. Sorley) which includes James Mill, Thomas Brown, Sir William Hamilton, J. F. Ferrier, John Stuart Mill, William Wallace and the Caird brothers; it also includes a chapter on 'Critical and Miscellaneous Prose' (by Hugh Walker, author of *Three Centuries of Scottish Literature*) which deals, alongside Symonds, Pater and Wilde, with Aeneas Sweetland Dallas, Hugh Miller, W. and R. Chambers, Robert Louis Stevenson and Andrew Lang.

[224] Ward and Waller (eds), *The Cambridge History of English Literature*, Vol. 1, 2.

of F. R. Leavis's *The Great Tradition* (1948), Scottish writers had entirely disappeared from the fabric of what was 'great' in 'English' literature. Ironically, the Scots to which MacDiarmid reverted in the 1920s in his effort to reassert a native Scottish literary tradition was the hundred-year-old Scots of John Jamieson's *Etymological Dictionary of the Scottish Language*, first published in 1808. In using it to get 'Back to Dunbar', MacDiarmid was effectively ignoring, in order to justify an exclusively Scottish tradition uncontaminated by English sources, both the Enlightenment origins of Jamieson's dictionary and its part, through its rooting of Scots in Nordic and Anglo-Saxon sources, in the establishment of what had been a massively successful Scoto-British account of the development of literature in English.

Given the enormous investment which Scots had made in the Scots language from the 1720s to the 1950s, the thinkers of the Enlightenment, as a movement identified with the adoption of the English language and deeply embarrassed by any trace of Scotticisms in their own writings, could not be considered as a focus of Scottish national self-identity. The reconciliation of the Scottish philosophical tradition that paved the way, in W. R. Scott's work, for the concept of the Scottish Enlightenment could not be productive in a Scottish context as long as the investment in the Scots language continued to be central to Scottish cultural self-perception – which is why, perhaps, English and American historians were so prominent in early discussions of the Scottish Enlightenment. In effect, the Enlightenment in Scotland could only become the *Scottish* Enlightenment when the importance of Burns and Scott came to rest not on their contribution to a literature in Scots but – as in Burns's adoption of Adam Smith's 'sympathy' and Scott's dramatisation of the 'stadial history' of Enlightenment historiography – on their continuation of fundamental themes in the thought of the Scottish Enlightenment. As such, however, what they testify to is not the isolation of the Enlightenment from more general Scottish traditions but the incorporation of the Enlightenment as an integral and ongoing part of a still-developing and still distinctively Scottish intellectual history.

3 Beyond Reason: Hume, Seth, Macmurray and Scotland's Postmodernity

I Scotland and the Postmodern

At the Walter Scott conference in Oregon in 1999, Jerome McGann pronounced Scott to be the first postmodernist,[1] a judgment based on Scott's deployment of various metafictional techniques and on his ironic combination of contradictory genres. The proposal was less surprising (to some, at any rate) than it might have been, given how regularly another Scottish novel of the early nineteenth century–James Hogg's *Confessions of a Justified Sinner*–is cited as prophetic of postmodernism in its use of multiple and conflicting narratives. Taken together, the implications of these prescient texts might suggest that there is something inherently *postmodern* about Scottish culture, or something in Scottish culture which leads its writers to exploit those sorts of narrative strategies that we now identify as typical of postmodernism.

It is a possibility that would be substantially endorsed by Scotland's twentieth-century literary history, since many of the earliest examples of recognisably 'postmodern' writing in Britain were produced by Scots. Hugh MacDiarmid's *In Memoriam James Joyce*, for instance, first published in 1955, celebrates a poetry

> … beyond all that is heteroepic, holophrastic,
> Macaronic, philomathic, psychopetal,
> Jerqueing every idioticon,
> Comes this supreme paraleipsis,
> Full of potential song as a humming bird
> Is full of potential motion,

---

[1] 'Scotland and Romanticism', Eugene, OR, July 1999; published as 'Walter Scott's Romantic postmodernity', in Ian Duncan, Leith Davis, and Janet Sorenson (eds), *Scotland and the Borders of Romanticism* (Cambridge: Cambridge University Press, 2003), 113–29.

When, as we race along with kingfisher brilliance,
Seeking always for that which 'being known
Everything else becomes known,'
That which we can only know
By allowing it to know itself in us,
Since 'determinatio est negatio,'
Suddenly 'chaos falls silent in the dazzled abyss.'[2]

The extravagant use of quotation and paraphrase in MacDiarmid's late poems, producing a writing which is a palimpsest of re-iterations and re-inscriptions of previous language, undermines, as thoroughly as poststructuralist theorists such as Derrida or Barthes could have wished, any notion of the author as source and origin of the text. In the same year, W. S. Graham's *The Nightfishing* was published, inaugurating a poetry constructed around the self-referentiality that was to become typical of postmodernist texts. If, as Brian McHale has argued, the historical development of postmodernism involved the replacement of modernist concerns with epistemology by postmodern concerns with ontology,[3] Graham may have been the first British poet to make that transition. In poems such as 'The Constructed Space', alternative ontological levels interact in the 'being' of the poem:

I say this silence, or, better, construct this space
So that somehow something may move across
The caught habits of language to you and me.[4]

The 'I' hovers between the 'I' of the poet who wrote, the 'I' of the reader in the process of reading, and the semantic 'I' that exists only in language itself. As rigorously as Derrida, Graham turns saying into writing and turns the implied origin of a presence in speech into the necessary absence of the speaker from writing. Graham's poetry is often, as here, a commentary upon

---

[2] Hugh MacDiarmid, *In Memoriam James Joyce* (Glasgow: William MacLellan, 1955), 47.

[3] Brian McHale, *Postmodernist Fiction* (London: Methuen, 1987), 9–10: 'the dominant of postmodernist fiction is *ontological*...It is the ontological domination which explains the selection and clustering of these particular features [of postmodernism]; the ontological dominant is the principle of systematicity underlying these otherwise heterogeneous catalogues.'

[4] W. S. Graham, *New Collected Poems* (London: Faber and Faber, 2004), 162.

its own formal attributes and upon the endless deferral of meaning that it enacts.

What Graham was doing in poetry, however, was being done just as radically for the novel by Muriel Spark. In Spark's earliest novel, *The Comforters*, published in 1957, Caroline, the central character, is constantly aware of a typewriter and of voices that anticipate the events of her own life:

> 'But the typewriter and the voices—it is as if a writer on another plane of existence was writing a story about us.' As soon as she had said these words, Caroline knew that she had hit on the truth.[5]

The Comforters, which gestures in the name of one of its central characters—Mrs Hogg—to its connection with James Hogg's *Confessions of a Justified Sinner*, conforms to McHale's conception of conflicting ontological levels but others of Spark's novels, such as *The Prime of Miss Jean Brodie*, 'play' with conceptions of history and of fictionality in ways that fit with Linda Hutcheon's famous definition of the postmodern as 'historiographic metafiction'.[6] If we can say that Scottish writers were very early entrants into the styles that were to become typical of postmodernism, the centrality of those techniques to the representation of modern Scottish experience was established by Alasdair Gray's groundbreaking novel, *Lanark* in 1981. In its (con)fusion of realism, fantasy and science fiction, *Lanark* both fulfilled the postmodernist use of the 'popular' genres for serious purposes and set a pattern that many other Scottish writers—from Iain Banks's *The Bridge* to A. L. Kennedy's *And so I am Glad* and James Robertson's *The Fanatic*—have followed in their representations of modern Scotland.

The characteristics typical of much postmodernist literature, in other words, fit with key elements of the Scottish literary tradition, and do so from long before the invention of 'postmodernism' as a critical term. Alex Clunas's article on Robert Louis Stevenson's 'postmodernity', and Stevenson's influence on later postmodernists such as Borges and Nabokov, revealed a truth that went far wider than its ostensible subject.[7] Indeed, given postmodernism's obsession with varieties of literary illusion, Scottish writing could be

---

[5] Muriel Spark, *The Comforters* (Harmondsworth: Penguin, [1957] 1963), 63.

[6] Linda Hutcheon, *A Poetics of Postmodernism: History, Theory, Fiction* (London: Routledge, 1988).

[7] Alex Clunas, 'Stevenson: a Precursor of the Post-Moderns?', *Cencrastus*, 6 (1982), 9–11.

argued to have been already postmodernist from the moment that James Macpherson, in 1760, presented as a translation of a Gaelic epic a poem of his own construction, and attributed it to an ancient bard by the name of Ossian. The complexities of authorial origin, historical status and generic uncertainty that bedevilled Macpherson's Ossianic poems, even while the vogue for them was sweeping Europe, were perhaps only symptoms of a radical uncertainty about literary forms which postmodernism, two hundred years later, came to replicate – thereby, perhaps, 'authenticating' as its precursor a work whose lack of authenticity has always been held to be the sign of its literary failure.

The source of such prescient postmodernity might be traced to Scotland's tangential relationship to the grand narratives of history whose foundering was, according to Jean-François Lyotard's seminal *The Postmodern Condition*, the necessary prelude to the inauguration of the postmodern. For Lyotard, the grand narratives of the past, whether religious, philosophical or ideological, provided the totalising context in which the events of ordinary life could find their justification, whereas postmodernity is underpinned by what he describes 'as incredulity toward metanarratives'.[8] Such scepticism is the product of mid-twentieth-century economic changes – especially the 'redeployment of advanced liberal capitalism' that has 'eliminated the communist alternative and valorized the individual enjoyment of goods and services'[9] – but in an Appendix to *The Postmodern Condition*, Lyotard holds out an alternative to this *historical* development of the postmodern by suggesting that, in art at least, postmodernity does not develop out of modernity but is, rather, the inherent *ground* of the modern: 'A work can become modern only if it is first postmodern. Postmodernism thus understood is not modernism at its end but in the nascent state, and this state is constant.'[10] Scotland may be postmodernism's 'nascent state', precisely because, as a stateless nation, it never fully entered into the world of modernity. If, as Benedict Anderson has suggested, nationalism was the necessary adjunct of secular modernity, then Scotland's often commented-upon lack of a nationalist movement in the nineteenth century made it a place without a metanarrative of the kind that other 'modern' nations were developing. In that situation, 'incredulity toward metanarrative' was not only possible but became one of the defining

---

[8] Jean-François Lyotard, *The Postmodern Condition*, trans. Geoff Bennington and Brian Massumi (Manchester: Manchester University Press, 1984), xxiv.
[9] Ibid., 37–8.
[10] Ibid., 79.

features of Scottish culture and Scottish writers' use of 'postmodernist' techniques may reflect, therefore, a situation which was itself prescient of the more recent collapse of metanarrative, producing precisely those multiple narratives – as, for instance, in Scott's *Redgauntlet* (1824) or Stevenson's *Jekyll and Hyde* (1886) – and differentiations of multiple ontological levels that became typical of late-twentieth-century writing.

The fit between Lyotard's conception of postmodernism and the way in which Scottish culture developed after 1707 is underlined by the fact that at least three different versions of Scotland's loss of historical metanarrative have been advanced by Scottish critics since the 1970s. The first (and most influential) is Tom Nairn's in *The Break-up of Britain* (1979), which suggests that Scottish culture was profoundly flawed by Scotland's good fortune to have crossed the divide into modernity before the onset of the era of nationalism. As a result, Scotland, like the Britain of which it was a part, remained a fundamentally *pre*-modern culture, and its failure to conform to the metanarrative of modern history – which for Nairn is a Marxist one – produced a necessarily deformed version of the truly 'modern' cultures that were developing in the rest of Europe. Scotland's failure to develop a nationalist movement in the nineteenth century meant that it failed to conform to what had become the standard historical pattern and had lost touch with the metanarrative shaping modern history. The second is Colin Kidd's in *Subverting Scotland's Past* (1993),[11] in which Kidd argues that Scotland's culture imploded as a result of the sceptical demolition of the myths of its own history upon which its claim to separate identity from England had depended. As the historical past of Scotland was revealed to be a series of forgeries (as, for instance, in the Fergusian line of kings which underpinned Scotland's ancient independence) or was challenged as having no political relevance to modern society (as in the case of George Buchanan's view of the constitutional status of kingship), Scotland's independent conception of its own historical trajectory was supplanted by conceptions of English history, producing an 'Anglo-Scottish' ideology which could never find any connection between its own national past and the political realities of its new supra-national political context. Since Scottish historiography had been revealed to be merely fictional, the Scots were thrust early into the arena of historiographic metafiction. The

---

[11] Colin Kidd, *Subverting Scotland's Past: Scottish Whig Historians and the Creation of an Anglo-British Identity 1689–c.1830* (Cambridge: Cambridge University Press, 1993).

third version of this is my own in *Out of History*,[12] published in book form in 1996 though originally appearing as articles in the 1980s. While arguing, like Kidd, that the narrative of Scottish history had been displaced by the narrative of English history, leaving Scotland in a kind of historical limbo, I suggested a less pessimistic outcome than either Nairn or Kidd. Cast into the rapid development of its new commercial, technological and industrial world, and made aware by the Jacobite rebellions of the distinction between the 'primitive' culture of the Highlands and the 'modern' culture of the Lowlands, eighteenth-century Scotland was forced to consider the nature of history – how did it develop, what impelled it, what values were promoted or destroyed by it? The Scottish Enlightenment's enormous contribution to European thought was, in many respects, the development of answers to such questions. But as Scotland was incorporated into a British history to which the Scottish past was irrelevant, the questions posed to Scottish thinkers shifted from those related to developments *within* the processes of history – questions about what shaped historical change and how it related to cultural change – to questions about what was before, beyond or outside of the boundaries of history. Being 'out of history', Scots could question the very nature and value of history, and could initiate the search for the foundations on which history itself was erected, a search that would culminate in the encyclopedic anthropology of J. G. Frazer's *The Golden Bough*, with its exploration of the structures of humanity's *pre*-historical consciousness.

Though the tenor of each of these arguments is very different in their interpretation of the significance of Scotland's loss of metanarrative, what they confirm is a crisis which, by opening up the possibility of competing and contradictory historical narratives, undermines the authority by which any single narrative could claim 'metanarrative' status as representative of the nation as a whole. Such 'incredulity towards metanarrative' is arguably what underlies Scottish literature's famous engagement with doubles and *döppelgangers*,[13] in which are dramatised the conflict between alternative origins for Scotland's social world and alternative teleologies defining the ends to which that history is directed. In this context, Scotland's most important

---

[12] The original argument was presented in 'The Body in the Kit-Bag', *Cencrastus*, 1 (1982), and 'Peripheries', *Cencrastus*, 8 (1983).

[13] See Karl Miller, *Doubles* (Oxford: Oxford University Press, 1985), and Douglas Gifford, 'Myth, Parody and Dissociation', in Douglas Gifford (ed.), *The History of Scottish Literature, Volume 3* (Aberdeen: Aberdeen University Press, 1988), 217–58.

contribution to nineteenth-century literature, Walter Scott's invention of the 'historical novel', can be seen to rest not in the originality of the means by which he represented the historical *reality* of the past,[14] but by his evocation of competing *possible* historical narratives, each of which has, in anticipation, an equal status but only some of which will survive the trial of history to be enacted as realities. Postmodernist theorists such as Hayden White have argued that all history writing is actually shaped by literary genres and that the 'truth' which the historian seeks is always structured according to the dictates of fiction.[15] Scott's historical fictions, on the other hand, invoke 'real' histories but set those histories in generic conflict with one another, so that in *Waverley*, for instance, the Jacobite cause is an ironic tragedy and the Hanoverian an accidental comedy. Postmodernists like White, who are deeply sceptical of our ability to *know* the past because of the necessary rhetorical or imaginative procedures through which it has to be reproduced, read all history-writing as though it was historical fiction, thus making Scott's historical fiction the precursor of postmodernist theory. Indeed, the foundation of Scottish Enlightenment historiography on which Scott drew for his fiction lay in the notion of 'conjectural history', which is defined by Dugald Stewart as allowing that,

> In want of this direct evidence, we are under a necessity of supplying the place of fact by conjecture; and when we are unable to ascertain how men have actually conducted themselves upon particular occasions, of considering in what manner they are likely to have proceeded, from the principles of their nature, and the circumstances of their external situation.[16]

Stewart, like his mentor Adam Smith, thinks such conjecture can be well-founded; postmodernists regard them as inevitably vitiating the truthfulness

---

[14] The revitalisation of Scott's reputation in the 1960s and 70s, after more than half a century of decline, was largely based on such 'realist' readings of his historical novels, pioneered by Georg Lukács's *The Historical Novel* (London: Merlin, 1969).

[15] Hayden White, *Metahistory: The Historical Imagination in Nineteenth-Century Europe* (Baltimore: Johns Hopkins University Press, 1973).

[16] Dugald Stewart, 'Account of the Life and Writings of Adam Smith, LL.D.', in W. P. D. Wightman and J. C. Bryce (eds), *Adam Smith, Essays on Philosophical Subjects, with Dugald Stewart's Account of Adam Smith*, ed. I. S. Ross (Oxford: Clarendon Press, 1980), 293.

of history: both, however, agree that all history is a necessarily imaginative creation in which the 'real' is infused with fictional connections and unverifiable narrative constructions.

As responses to Arthur Herman's book *The Scottish Enlightenment* confirmed, it is now commonplace to view eighteenth-century Scotland as the foundation of the modern world – which means, if we follow Lyotard, that it must also be the cradle of 'nascent postmodernism', and that the crisis of the historical that is central to both should be reflected in other aspects of its intellectual life. The similarities are equally striking, for instance, if we look at theories of language and aesthetics. Postmodern theory relies heavily on Saussure's decoupling of the potential power of the signifier (the arbitrary sound pattern by which we indicate a particular concept) and the signified (the equally arbitrary division of the world into conceptual elements), with the implication that meaning can develop along the multifarious relations of the signifier (the potentiality, for instance, of puns or the multiple meanings of words arising from historical changes in their usage) rather than being determined by the fixity of the signified (the single idea to which they are directed). This is particularly crucial to the ways in which literary texts are both composed and read. Roland Barthes, for instance, proposes the following notion of the 'text' (which acts on the axis of the signifier) as opposed to the 'work' (which acts on the axis of the signified):

> The Text, on the contrary, practises the infinite deferment of the signified, is dilatory; its field is that of the signifier and the signifier must not be conceived as 'the first stage of meaning', its material vestibule, but, in complete opposition to this, as its *deferred action*. Similarly, the *infinity* of the signifier refers not to some idea of the ineffable (the unnameable signified) but to that of *playing*...The logic regulating the Text is not comprehensive (define 'what the work means') but metonymic; the activity of associations, contiguities, carryings-over coincides with a liberation of symbolic energy...[17]

Such a text is 'without closure': it is 'an explosion, a dissemination' of possible meanings which can never be considered complete or finished. This, however, was precisely the nature of text as defined by those Scottish thinkers who

---

[17] Roland Barthes, 'From Work to Text', in Stephen Heath (ed.), *Image— Music—Text* (London: Fontana, [1971] 1977), 158.

were influenced by Hume's conception of the mind as a complex process
of linked associations. Even the terminology of Barthes—associations,
contiguities—echoes those Scottish theorists such as Archibald Alison for
whom the text is, equally, the source of chains of multiple meanings provoked
by the associative connections of a particular mind at a particular moment in
time. By refusing to limit the text to a shared object produced by the public
meanings of words, Alison radically relativises aesthetic experiences, which,
he argues,

> seem often, indeed, to have but a very distant relation to the object that
> at first excited them; and the object itself appears only to serve as a
> hint, to awaken the imagination, and to lead it through every analogous
> idea that has a place in the memory. It is then, indeed, in this powerless
> state of reverie, when we are carried on by our conceptions, not guiding
> them, that the deepest emotions of beauty and sublimity are felt; that
> our hearts swell with feelings which language is too weak to express; and
> that, in the depth of silence and astonishment, we pay to the charm that
> enthralls us, the most flattering mark of our applause.[18]

In Alison, as in the other Scottish aestheticians whose associationist principles derive from Hume, the work of art is only the starting point for the kind
of 'dissemination' of uncontrollable multiplicities of meaning that poststructuralist and postmodernist theory presents as a 'new' revelation of the possibilities of modern literature. The features of openness and indeterminacy
that Barthes takes to be characteristic of postmodern literature's destruction
of 'meta-language'[19] are not only prefigured in the Scottish Enlightenment's
theories of associatively-based aesthetic experience but are carried into practice by the artists influenced by those theories.[20]

Such displacements of 'meta-meaning', applicable equally to the language
of history and the languages of art, are also evident in another displacement
that links the postmodern to the Scottish Enlightenment—the dissolution
of the autonomous self that had been justified by Descartes' *cogito ergo sum*.
For postmodernists, the Cartesian ego is both the foundation for and the

---

[18] Archibald Alison, *An Essay on Taste* (Edinburgh: Archibald Constable,
[1790] 1811), 46.

[19] Barthes, 'From Work to Text', 164.

[20] See my *Associationism and the Literary Imagination* (Edinburgh: Edinburgh
University Press, 2007).

consequence of conceptions of history and of language as hierarchically ordered and providing ultimate, transcendent truths upon which the rest of our knowledge can be grounded. The self in this traditional form cannot survive a situation in which the history of which it is a part and the language through which it is expressed are beyond both knowledge and control. The ousting of 'western man' as thus defined is often associated with Michel Foucault, for whom notions of the 'soul' and 'self' are simply the fictions of a coherent identity which none of us can actually fulfil:

> Where the soul pretends unification or the self fabricates a coherent identity, the genealogist sets out to study the beginning – numberless beginnings whose faint traces and hints of color are readily seen by an historical eye. The analysis of descent permits the dissociation of the self, its recognition and displacement as an empty synthesis, in liberating a profusion of lost events. [21]

The very terms – 'unification', 'fabricates', 'dissociation' – point back, however, to Hume's famous dissolution of the unity of the self into the sequence of its associations, associations from which a supposedly unitary identity can only be a fabrication. For Hume, the 'identity, which we ascribe to the mind of man', is 'a fictitious one'[22] because it is 'nothing really belonging to [our] different perceptions, and uniting them together'; rather, those perceptions are bound together only by 'the smooth and uninterrupted progress of the thought along a train of connected ideas'[23] over which the 'self' has no control. If the disaggregated self of a modern genealogist like Foucault repeats a key element in eighteenth-century Scotland's reduction of the self to its associations, then Scotland's role as that of a 'nascent postmodernism'[24] becomes even more compelling.

---

[21] Michel Foucault, 'Nietzsche, Genealogy, History', in Donald F. Bouchard (ed.), *Language, Counter-Memory, Practice: Selected Essays and Interviews* (Oxford: Basil Blackwell, 1977), 145–6.

[22] David Hume, *A Treatise of Human Nature*, ed. L. A. Selby-Bigge (Oxford: Clarendon Press, 1888), 259.

[23] Ibid., 260.

[24] Given such parallels, the relation between Scotland's divided condition in the aftermath of the defeat of the Jacobites in 1746 and its rise to intellectual eminence in Europe thereafter might usefully be compared with the way in which France, post-1945, sought to replace imperial and economic power with cultural power.

Such *stylistic* and *conceptual* similarities between the Scottish tradition and postmodernism have, however, to be balanced against the fact that many of the recent Scottish writers who are most clearly identifiable as 'postmodern' in their practice are in fact deeply and committedly antagonistic to the world-view which has come to be identified with postmodernism. If we take Lyotard's *Postmodern Condition* as the defining text, then the condition of postmodernity is one in which 'the State and/or company must abandon the idealist and humanist narratives of legitimation in order to justify the new goal: in the discourse of today's financial backers of research, the only credible goal is power'.[25] Postmodernism, in this sense, has come to be identified not as a generic or stylistic issue but as the cultural expression of the changing nature of modern capitalism. As such, postmodernism is nothing other than the power relations of capitalism which function, in the contemporary world, through the processes of Americanisation and globalisation, two words which have been, unfortunately, almost synonymous. As Frederic Jameson puts it: 'What has happened is that aesthetic production today has become integrated into commodity production generally: the frantic economic urgency of producing fresh waves of ever more novel-seeming goods (from clothing to airplanes) at ever greater rates of turnover, now assigns an increasingly essential structural function and position to aesthetic innovation and experimentation.'[26] Postmodern aesthetics can thus be argued to be simply the transfer to the cultural realm of the requirements of contemporary capitalism: just as capitalism has adopted aesthetics – the aesthetics of the 'new', the 'innovative', the 'challenging' – as the means of fulfilling its economic ends, so postmodernist art has adapted itself to being part of the commercial world of consumption.

Scottish writers such as Muriel Spark (who was a Catholic convert), or Alasdair Gray (who declares himself to be anachronistically in favour of a Scottish Co-operative Workers' Republic), are hardly likely to see their own use of postmodernist techniques as implying commitment to such conceptions of the world. It is an opposition we can integrate into a theory of the postmodern by following Linda Hutcheon's suggestion, in *The Politics of Postmodernism*, that the postmodern condition (globalising capitalism) is not identical with postmodernism in art, and that the latter actually develops as

---

25 Lyotard, *The Postmodern Condition*, 46.
26 Frederic Jameson, *Postmodernism, or, the Cultural Logic of Late Capitalism* (London: Verso, 1991), 4–5.

a resistance to, rather than an acceptance of, the postmodern condition. For Hutcheon, 'critique is as important as complicity in the response of cultural postmodernism to the philosophic and socio-economic realities of postmodernity',[27] thereby allowing writers like Spark or Gray to be postmodern*ist* in their opposition to postmodern*ism*. On the other hand, it might be better to say that their style is peculiarly Scottish – rooted in stylistic devices which happen to have become typically postmodernist – and that their resistance is to a world system which sees small and marginal cultures as irrelevant to its logic. And yet, within Lyotard's conception of postmodernism, it is precisely the privilege conferred by the decay of grand narratives that the local can be asserted and celebrated, so that resistant – indeed, national or nationalist – postmodernism would represent the real fulfilment of the postmodern condition. Could it be that Scotland's long maturation of the postmodern was preparation for the fulfilment of a national identity that only the postmodernist decay of grand narratives makes possible, gesturing in defiance to the apparent unification of a world merged into a single, globalised culture?

II   The Kantian Sublime

Postmodernism, no doubt, has become as resistant to a single definition as any other stylistic and historical denominator – such as Romanticism[28] – but there is a strangely recurrent element in discussions of the postmodern which is itself a continuation of Romantic aesthetics – the concept of the 'sublime'. In an Appendix to *The Postmodern Condition*, Lyotard appeals to the 'sublime' as the ultimate explanation of the development of modernist and postmodernist art, and the definition of the sublime that he adopts is that offered by Kant, who is, according to Lyotard's essay on 'The Sign of History', both 'the epilogue to modernity' and 'also a prologue to postmodernity'.[29] Kant's 'prologue' involves the first assertion of what has come

---

[27] Linda Hutcheon, *The Politics of Postmodernism* (London: Routledge, 1989), 26.

[28] Arthur Lovejoy's essay on 'The Discrimination of Romanticisms', in M. H. Abrams (ed.), *English Romantic Poets: Modern Essays in Criticism* (Oxford: Oxford University Press, 1975), has become the *locus classicus* of all such dissolutions of period descriptors.

[29] 'The Sign of History', in Andrew Benjamin (ed.), *A Lyotard Reader* (Oxford: Blackwell, 1989), 393–411, at 394.

to be commonplace of postmodernism: that the world we know is a world which is entirely constructed by the human mind; that it is impossible for us to encounter the world as it *really* is because the world is always already structured and shaped by the categories imposed on it by our own consciousnesses. Kant's 'Copernican revolution' in philosophy required that we can only ever know the *phenomena* of our own sensory experience and never the *noumenon* of the world-as-it-is-in-itself. This may have been transformed by poststructuralism into the assertion that we can never know anything but the world as it is structured by our language, or by the categories of narrative, but the consequence is the same: rather than living in a world where consciousness is in touch with the reality of an external nature, we are forever trapped within a world whose reality is constituted by the nature of our own consciousness.

Lyotard's version of this is that the postmodern condition is one in which we have come to recognise that we are always necessarily involved in 'language games', and that 'truth' is not the discovery of the 'real' out there in the world but the construction of the world according to the rules of a particular game:

> It is useful to make the following three observations about language games. The first is that their rules do not carry within themselves their own legitimation, but are the object of a contract, explicit or not, between players (which is not to say that the players invent the rules). The second is that if there are no rules, there is no game, that even an infinitesimal modification of one rule alters the nature of the game, that a 'move' or utterance that does not satisfy the rules does not belong to the game they define. The third remark is suggested by what has just been said: every utterance should be thought of as a 'move' in a game.[30]

Since the 'social bond is linguistic, but is not woven with a single thread', producing 'at least (and in reality an indeterminate number) of language games',[31] there can be 'no possibility that language games can be unified or totalised in any metadiscourse'.[32] The postmodern conditions of knowledge

---

[30] Lyotard, *The Postmodern Condition*, 10.
[31] Ibid., 40.
[32] Ibid., 36.

as language games may first have been formulated by Wittgenstein, but 'the exploding of language into families of heteronomous language-games is the theme that Wittgenstein, whether he knew it or not, took from Kant'.[33]

The problem that haunted the Kantian project – how could there be a responsible moral act if all events in the world are necessarily structured by the category of cause and effect? – is precisely paralleled in the problem that haunts the Lyotardian scheme – how can one be responsible for one's statements in the language-game in which one is playing if all language games define in advance their own terms of validity? It is not enough that we can posit a noumenon lying beyond the phenomena of experience, we must have some mode of access to it that justifies our belief that we are not simply products of a causality we cannot escape; equally, there must be some means of escaping from the entrapments of language games, some means of switching between them or transforming them that is not simply another move in another language game. The importance of the sublime is that it is the one instance in experience when the mechanism of the Kantian categories fails to operate and by failing confirms the 'beyond' upon which Kant's whole metaphysic depends. For Kant, of course, the key issue was not the sublime – which he regarded as less philosophically significant than the beautiful – but the freedom of moral decision making, in which we step from being creatures of the necessitarian world of cause and effect into the noumenal world in which we are both free and immortal. Since this convoluted escape from the world of causal necessity cost even Kant some doubts, later thinkers have elevated the sublime, rather than moral decision-making, as the experience in which we discover that the categories that normally structure our thought fail, and provide an insight into the unbounded universe that otherwise must always lie beyond the world that is constructed for us by consciousness.

It is this interruption of categorical understanding that Lyotard takes to be crucial in the sublime, and takes to be central to modernist and post-modernist art: real art, that is, sublime art, challenges us precisely because there is no rule to which it adheres; no understanding of previous art that can be mapped on to it to make sense of it; and by breaking the rules it launches us into the experience of the sublime as an assertion of freedom that defies the constraining limits of the existing categories of understanding. If we are to be free beings, if we are to know we are free beings, if we

---

[33] Lyotard, 'The Sign of History', 410.

are not to be entirely encompassed by a totality which claims to shape and control our every act, it is only in our appeal to the sublime that we can be offered any guarantee of escape from the net of causal and categorical necessity. For Lyotard, the aesthetics of modernism is precisely the fulfilment of the Kantian sublime to the extent that its aim is 'to present the fact that the unpresentable exists. To make visible that there is something which can be conceived and which can neither be seen nor made visible: this is what is at stake in modern painting.'[34] In this perspective, however, Lyotard views the aesthetics of literary or visual modernism as a kind of false-consciousness of the sublime, one which gestures to the sublime but never actually confronts it: it is 'an aesthetic of the sublime, though a nostalgic one', because 'it allows the unpresentable to be put forward only as the missing content; but the form, because of its recognizable consistency, continues to offer to the reader or viewer matter for solace and pleasure'.[35] In modernism the terrors of sublimity are made comfortable by a form which continues to operate as a defence mechanism, surrounding the impossibility of graspable meaning with the comfort of 'pleasure'. Postmodernism, however, would be an art which 'puts forward the unpresentable in presentation itself, that which denies itself the solace of good forms, the consensus of a taste which would make it possible to share collectively the nostalgia for the unattainable; that which searches for new presentations, not in order to enjoy them but in order to impart a stronger sense of the unpresentable'.[36]

Lyotard's postmodern is then the fulfilment of the Kantian sublime as the escape from a rule-bound universe, the moment when 'reason' cannot provide a category for the imagined or when the imagined cannot find an explanation through the understanding: 'A postmodern artist or writer is in the position of a philosopher: the text he writes, the work he produces are not in principle governed by preestablished rules, and they cannot be judged according to a determining judgment, by applying familiar categories to the text or to the work. Those rules and categories are what the work of art itself is looking for. The artist and the writer, then, are working without rules in order to formulate the rules of what will have been done.'[37] Like Kant, Lyotard demands a rule-bound world in all its determinacy while maintaining, as the basis of

---

[34] Lyotard, *Postmodern Condition*, 78.
[35] Ibid., 81.
[36] Ibid.
[37] Ibid.

our real humanity, a freedom – the freedom of the sublime – in which we can encounter an experience that has no rules.

It is this potential for defying a deterministic universe that has made the sublime so significant in postmodernism: it holds open the door on a freedom that would otherwise dissolve into the mere banality of playing a different game as a digression from one rule-bound system into another. It is this sense of the postmodern sublime that is invoked by Frederic Jameson in *Postmodernism or the Cultural Logic of Late Capitalism*: the truly postmodern, for Jameson, involves 'the sense that beyond all thematics or content the work seems somehow to tap the networks of the reproductive process and thereby to afford us some glimpse into the postmodern or technological sublime', a glimpse which gives us back our freedom by revealing in their 'distorted figuration' the 'whole world system of present-day multinational capitalism'.[38] The sublime, for Kant, allowed us to escape the determinations of the categories; the sublime, for Lyotard, allows us to defy the existing categories that determine general taste; the sublime, for Jameson, allows us to see – and therefore, at least potentially, to challenge – the economic categories by which we are determined. The sublime thus haunts the postmodern as the last possibility of freedom in a world so structured that freedom as we generally understand it, the freedom of everyday choice and action, can never be more than an illusion; a world where, as postmodernists like Foucault suggest, all change is caused not by the actions of free agents but by the historically determining equivalents of Kantian categories – 'epistemes' which define and delimit all thought and therefore predetermine the limits of all action.[39]

Postmodernism, in other words, is a late-twentieth-century replay of some of the key elements of Kantianism, replacing Kant's transcendental 'categories' with historically-based or linguistically-based determinants of consciousness. Baudrillard's 'simulacra', for instance, are little more than a technological version of Kant's 'phenomena':[40] Famously, of course, Kant's project was inspired by the effort to answer Hume's scepticism, which had 'awakened him from his dogmatic slumbers',[41] and postmodernism's adop-

---

[38] Jameson, *Postmodernism*, 37.

[39] Michel Foucault, *The Order of Things* (London: Tavistock, 1970).

[40] Jean Baudrillard, *Symbolic Exchange and Death*, trans. Iain H. Grant (London: Sage, 1993).

[41] See Manfred Kuehn, 'Kant's Conception of Hume's Problem', *Journal of the History of Philosophy*, 21 (1983), 175–93, for a contextualisation of Kant's famous comment on his relationship to Hume. See also Kuehn's *Scottish*

tion of a Kantian perspective on the nature of knowledge suggests that Kant did indeed answer Hume. As we have seen in Chapter 2, however, as long ago as 1884 J. Hutchison Stirling had argued in articles in the journal *Mind*, that 'Kant has *not* answered Hume'.[42] Hutchison Stirling's case was based precisely on the issue which has required the prominence of the sublime in contemporary theory – the issue of 'necessity' in causal relations, an issue which Hume had put in doubt by claiming that we could never know, except by experience and habit, that one thing is the cause of another. For Kant, causality was 'necessary' because it was a category by which the human mind perceived the world: the necessity that Hume sought, in other words, was already implicit in the very perceptual framework which he had to use in order to ask the question about the nature of causality, so that it could not, justifiably, be doubted. What Hutchison Stirling pointed out, however, was that the Kantian category of causation was involved in an equally profound self-contradiction. If, for Hume, succession could never be proved to be causality because it was possible that one thing which had always been perceived to follow from another might *not* occur in the future (the sun might not rise; flame might not produce heat), for Kant the opposite was true, and causality could never be distinguished from succession, since the category of causality was the inevitable template with which the human mind structured the world that it experienced. If mere succession – it rains, a particular tune is played on the radio – is to be distinguished from causal succession, then the category of causality must be able to distinguish a difference inherent in the successive objects it is experiencing – in which case, the necessity of causality does not derive from the category but from the objects themselves, and we are back in Hume's original (and unresolved) problem.

> That rule, law, order, necessity itself, must already exist in the elements of sense even *for* the categories – that was an afterthought. This afterthought – But how, then, do the categories find their cues ? – coming suddenly upon him in the end, with all his vast labour behind him, must have appalled him like the apparition of a ghost. Ah yes, law can be the product of the understanding alone, no repetition can make this clearer;

Common Sense in Germany, 1768–1800 (Kingston and Montreal: McGill-Queen's University Press, 1987), Ch. ix.
[42] *Mind*, Vol. 9, Issue 36 (October 1884), 531–47; and Vol. 10, Issue 37 (January 1885), 45–72)

but then sense itself must have one necessary order under causality, and quite another necessary order under reciprocity, or how could these categories themselves act without mutual interference and confusion, or how, indeed, could they know when to act at all?[43]

That Kant had not answered Hume on the key issue of the necessity involved in causality undermined, for Stirling and his successors, the whole Kantian schema and, indeed, undermined the whole German tradition in philosophy. And if Kant has not answered Hume then the arguments which lock us into the world as produced by the categories of our own consciousnesses – the structures of our own language, the narrative forms of history writing and so on – is deprived of its authority. The whole edifice, including the need for a sublime which can allow us a momentary escape from those categorial constructions, is without foundation. Postmodernism, we might say, was nothing less than the endless repetition of Kant's failure to address Hume's question about the necessity involved in causation.

III   Beyond Modernity

When Andrew Seth followed Hutchison Stirling in reopening the issue of Kant's answer to Hume by a 'Comparison of the Scottish and German Answers to Hume' in his book on *Scottish Philosophy* (1890),[44] he presented Hume's philosophy as the *reductio ad absurdum* of the philosophical principles introduced by Locke and developed by Berkeley, which substitute the 'ideas' of things as intermediaries between consciousness and the things of which it is conscious, 'ideas' that inevitably lead to doubt about whether they adequately or appropriately represent the real world to which they appear to give us access. Hume's escape from this dilemma, according to Seth, is to abolish objects altogether, and to insist that we are never in contact with anything but 'impressions' and 'ideas', a metaphysical position which cannot

---

[43] Hutchison Stirling, 'Kant has *not* answered Hume', *Mind*, Vol. 10, Issue 37 (January 1885), 63.

[44] Seth's two major books, *Scottish Philosophy* and *Hegelianism and Personality*, were first delivered under the auspices of the Balfour Lectures – funded by the later Prime Minister, Arthur Balfour, himself a philosopher – at the University of Edinburgh. The third lecture series was not published until after Seth's death in 1931 as *The Balfour Lectures on Realism*.

be integrated with the ordinary business of life, as Hume himself seems to acknowledge: 'I dine, I play a game of backgammon, I converse and am merry with my friends; and when, after three or four hours' amusement, I would return to these speculations, they appear so cold, and strained, and ridiculous, that I cannot find in my heart to enter into them any further.'[45] For Seth, this famous passage is Hume's acknowledgment that his philosophy is its own 'self-refutation',[46] and that Hume was unable to find any way beyond the impasse he has created. Kant's philosophy appeared to provide an escape from Hume's dilemma, but if Kant has indeed *not* answered Hume then the focus of attention must turn to the other major response to Hume, that of Thomas Reid, and Reid's attack on the theory of Representative Perception upon which, he claimed, Locke, Berkeley and Hume based their philosophies.

Seth's recuperation of Reid's realism, which maintains our unmediated access to the world against the subjective idealism implied in the theory of Representative Perception, provides Scottish philosophy with an alternative to simply following in the footsteps of Kant, even if the key issues on which Reid alights – such as that the basis of knowledge is not a sensation or an idea but a unit of judgment[47] – are precisely those on which Kant also focused. The outcome in the two philosophies, however, is very different: for Kant, as for Hume, 'we cannot by any conceivable possibility tell how the world of knowledge – ... the phenomenal world – stands related to the world of reality',[48] because 'instead of, like Reid, abandoning "the ideal system", [Kant] elaborately reconstructed it'.[49] Scottish philosophy, on the other hand, 'was fortunate enough ... to escape this danger, by taking up the broad position that, while the principles in question are referable to the constitution of our nature, our nature is, in respect of them, in complete harmony with the nature of things – so that they may, with equal truth, be spoken of as perceived or recognised in things'.[50]

What Reid's analysis underlines, according to Seth, is that 'all principles of explanation ... are derived, and must be derived, from the nature of the

---

[45] David Hume, *A Treatise of Human Nature*, 269; see Seth, *Scottish Philosophy*, 70.

[46] Seth, *Scottish Philosophy*, 66.

[47] Ibid., 96.

[48] Ibid., 136.

[49] Ibid., 149.

[50] Ibid., 161.

explaining Self; they are transcripts, so to speak, of its constitution'.[51] And the nature of the 'Self' becomes, for Seth, the touchstone against which both Hume's original arguments and the neo-Kantian and Hegelian philosophies of the late nineteenth century must be tested, since 'the mere particular and the mere universal are alike abstractions of the mind; what exists is *the individual*'.[52] Thus, though Hegel might have overcome some of the problems of Kant's conception of the categories, Seth's *Hegelianism and Personality* (1887) measured Hegel's shortcomings with reference to his presentation of the 'personality' of both God and Man. For Seth, Hegel's mode of argument 'confounds' logic with ontology or metaphysics and 'ends by offering us *a logic as a metaphysic*',[53] thus reducing the existential self to a set of logical rather than real relations: 'The result of Hegel's procedure would really be to sweep "existential reality" off the board altogether, under the persuasion, apparently, that a full statement of all the thought-relations that constitute our knowledge of the thing is equivalent to the existent thing itself. On the contrary, it may be confidently asserted that there is no more identity of Knowing and Being with an infinity of such relations than there was with one.'[54] Seth insists against Hegel's logical system that 'the meanest thing that exists has a life of its own, absolutely unique and individual, which we can partly *understand* by terms borrowed from our own experience, but which is no more identical with, or in any way like, the description we give of it, than our own inner life is identical with the description we give of it in a book of philosophy'.[55] For Seth, acknowledgment of the limits of our modes of knowing and thinking—logic, psychology, ontology—is the real insight of the Kantian argument, and it is crucial not to confuse the outcomes of one mode of understanding with the possibilities of another. For psychology, the data of sensation in their subjectivity are the basis of understanding: their truth to the external world is not an issue. But this does not mean that their truth to the world is unfounded—any more, in terms of later theories, than we can say that Saussure's deliberate exclusion of 'reference' from the domain of linguistics, as a discipline, means that language has no referent. It is an exclusion necessary to the form of knowledge in question but the grounding

---

[51] Ibid., 109.
[52] Ibid., 174.
[53] Andrew Seth, *Hegelianism and Personality Balfour Philosophical Lectures, University of Edinburgh* (Edinburgh: William Blackwood, 1887), 104.
[54] Ibid., 126.
[55] Ibid.

exclusion which makes one form of knowledge possible must not be taken to be equivalent to a metaphysical truth about the nature of the real. Hegel's procedure, for Seth, involves precisely such a transfer from the abstract conceptions of logic to the ontological requirements of our real existence:

> … we have abundantly seen the impossibility of reaching a real existence by such means. 'The concrete Idea' remains abstract, and unites God and man only by eviscerating the real content of both. Both disappear or are sublimated into it, but simply because it represents what is common to both, the notion of intelligence as such. They disappear, not indeed in a pantheistic substance, but in a logical concept. If we scrutinise the system narrowly, we find Spirit or the Absolute doing duty at one time for God, and another time for man; but when we have hold of the divine we have lost our grasp of the human and *vice versa*. We have never the two together'.[56]

Hegel's Absolute is a logical conception of self-consciousness, 'not an account of any real process or real existence', and is therefore no more an account of a real God than it is an account of real human beings, since 'finite selves are wiped out, and nature, deprived of any life of its own, becomes as it were, the still mirror in which the one Self-consciousness contemplates itself'.[57] 'What other result', Seth asks, 'could we expect than that both God and man, as real beings, would vanish back into their source, leaving us with the logical Idea as the sole reality.'[58]

The Idealism of the neo-Kantians and the Hegelians is, for Seth, a denial of the true meaning of 'personality', for 'if we take away from Idealism personality, and the ideals that belong to personality, it ceases to be Idealism',[59] so that, in a later series of the lectures, Seth proposes the overthrow of Idealism by a Transcendental Realism, one which will combine at an epistemological level the Natural Realism of the Scottish tradition, stemming from Reid, with a transcendentalism that acknowledges the operation of the Kantian categories as the grounding principles of our forms of knowledge: we can escape the confines of the self-enclosed phenomenal world into which Kant plunged us – 'a kind of speculative nightmare … [which]

---

[56] Ibid., 155–6.
[57] Ibid., 162.
[58] Ibid., 191.
[59] Ibid., 193.

had been preparing all through the modern period',[60] by ensuring that we do not mistake the epistemological bases of particular forms of knowledge – which belong, as it were, to particular knowledge games – for the nature of reality itself. Neither should we confuse those epistemological categories with metaphysical truths:

> The problem of knowledge, when it comes into the foreground, inevitably tends to separate the knowing subject from the whole world of objective reality. The philosophical antithesis is no longer between the whole and the part, between the permanent unity and its dependent manifestations, as it is when the line of thought is metaphysical or ontological. The antithesis is now between the subjective consciousness and the world of real things. The subject is, therefore, placed upon one side and the whole trans-subjective universe upon the other, and a chasm is made between them. The knower is practically extruded from the real universe: he is treated as if he did not belong to it, as if he came to inspect it like a stranger from afar. His forms of thought come thus to be regarded as an alien product with no inherent fitness to express the nature of things. Things are rather conceived as in themselves independent of these forms, so that the forms, when applied, are treated as an unauthorised gloss, a distorting medium. A little reflection, however, tells us that to conceive matters thus is to convert the necessary duality or opposition which knowledge involves into a real or metaphysical dualism for which there is no kind of warrant. We are the victims of metaphor, if we allow ourselves to think of the individual knower as standing outside the universe in this way...[61]

The impasse of the modern requires that we escape the 'speculative nightmare' by starting from a different point than that of the isolated knower, who is the abstraction of an independent witness to the world rather than a participant in it. The thoughts of the self-enclosed Cartesian ego may be the foundation of modernity but it is not the *actual* foundation on which our *real* world is built: 'all through the modern period philosophers have been turning the subjectivity of knowledge against its objectivity, and in the last

---

[60] Andrew Seth Pringle-Pattison, *The Balfour Lectures on Realism*, ed. G. F. Barbour (Edinburgh: William Blackwood and Sons, 1933), 255.

[61] Ibid., 255.

resort converting the very notion of knowledge into an argument against the possibility of knowledge.'[62] The consequence is that 'since the time of Hume and Kant' philosophy 'has largelý created the difficulties which it finds it so hard to surmount'.[63] Seth, in other words, identifies the contradictions of the modern which would have to be surmounted if we were ever to be able to reach the 'post-modern', but in doing so reveals how deeply rooted is 'post-modernism' in the very crises and contradictions of the 'modern'. Far from being truly *post*-modern, postmodernism is modernism caught in a repetitive loop in which Kant and Hume continually undermine one another.

What Seth achieved by his critical account of the philosophy of the previous two hundred years, and by his testing of the Kantian tradition against the Scottish tradition, was a clearing of the ground, a breaking free both from the Representative Theory of Perception as developed by Hume and the determining structure of Kant's categories. What was needed was a starting point which did not lead to such mutually negating philosophical outcomes, and four key suggestions are made by Seth to specify an alternative starting point that could escape the contradictions bedevilling modern philosophy. The first is that we must not conceive the Self as the isolated knower, but as a being among others:

> If a mere individual, as we are often told, would be a being without consciousness of its own limitations – a being therefore, which could not know itself as an individual – then no Self is a mere individual. We may even safely say that the mere individual is a fiction of philosophic thought. There could be no interaction between individuals unless they were all embraced within one Reality; still less could there be any knowledge by one individual of others, if they did not all form parts of one system of things.[64]

The Self, for Seth, is both a 'unique existence, which is perfectly *impervious*...to other selves'[65] and, at the same time, dependent on the otherness of other selves to know itself as a Self. The second is that the Self is a personality and that personality is related to the *will* rather than to self-conscious knowledge:

---

[62] Ibid., 184–5.
[63] Ibid., 185.
[64] Seth, *Hegelianism and Personality*, 215–16.
[65] Ibid., 216.

I have a centre of my own – a will of my own – which no one shares with me or can share – a centre which I maintain even in my dealings with God Himself. For it is eminently false to say that I put off, or can put off my personality here. The religious consciousness lends no countenance whatever to the representation of the human soul as a mere mode or efflux of the divine. On the contrary, only in a person, in a relatively independent or self-centred being is religious approach to God possible.[66]

And, since will is the fundamental characteristic of the Self as personality, the third suggestion is that the Self is not known primarily through its *consciousness of* the world – not, in other words, through reflective *knowledge* – but through action:

It is in action that we have the surest clue to the early stages of the animal and the human consciousness. Knowledge in such creatures exists simply in a practical reference. Consciousness would be a useless luxury unless as putting them in relation to the surrounding world and enabling them to adapt their actions to its varying stimuli.[67]

And it is as action, fourthly, that we should think of knowledge itself. Instead of the world presenting itself to a passive consciousness, or presenting itself in the necessary forms of the Kantian categories, the world is known only in and through action:

Knowledge means nothing if it does not mean the relation of two factors, knowledge *of* an object *by* a subject. But knowledge is not an entity stretching across, as it were, from subject to object, and uniting them; still less is knowledge the one reality of which subject and object are two sides or aspects. Knowledge is an activity, an activo-passive experience of the subject, whereby it becomes aware of what is not itself.[68]

The establishment of a philosophy of the Self as a Personality which knows itself in action rather than in contemplation, which understands itself as part of the world rather than set over against it, and which discovers its unique

---

[66] Ibid., 218–19.
[67] Seth, *Balfour Lectures on Realism*, 189.
[68] Ibid., 193.

individual identity through the will rather than through the universal and empty *cogito*, is, for Seth, the basis for transcending the contradictions of the modern and, therefore, from our later perspective, the basis for a properly *post*-modern philosophy.

In Seth's effort to create a post-modern philosophy by a return to Scottish traditions and by a critique of the whole Kantian-Hegelian tradition we can see a prefiguration of the most important Scottish philosophy of the twentieth century, that of John Macmurray, which set itself the task of overturning the whole tradition of modern philosophy whose failures Seth had identified:

> Modern philosophy is characteristically *egocentric*. I mean no more than this: that firstly, it takes the Self as its starting-point, and not God, or the world or the community; and that, secondly, the Self is an individual in isolation. This is shown by the fact that there can arise the question, 'How does the Self know that other selves exist?' Further, the Self so premised is a thinker in search of knowledge. It is conceived as the Subject; the correlate in experience of the object presented for cognition.[69]

The answer to the 'speculative nightmare' of modernity – for it is Kant whom Macmurray identifies as 'the most adequate of modern philosophies'[70] – must reverse the 'Copernican revolution' by which Kant had made the world depend upon the knower: 'If we make the "I think" the primary postulate of philosophy, then not merely do we institute a dualism between theoretical and practical experience, but we make action logically inconceivable – a mystery, as Kant so rightly concludes, in which we necessarily believe, but which we can never comprehend.'[71] A truly post-modern philosophy will be one that starts from the entirely different basis that the Self is first an agent rather than a thinker, and that that agent inhabits a social world of persons rather than a mechanical world of objects or a dynamic world of organisms. The failure of modern philosophy from Hume to Kant and to Hegel lies in the inadequacy of its conception of the human *person* rather than simply the human being or the human thinker:

---

[69] John Macmurray, *The Self as Agent*, Vol. I of *The Form of the Personal* (London: Faber and Faber, 1957), 31.

[70] Ibid., 39.

[71] Ibid., 73.

Any 'self' – that is to say, any agent – is an existing being, a person … The idea of an isolated agent is self-contradictory. Any agent is necessarily in relation to the Other. Apart from this essential relation he does not exist. But, further, the Other in this constitutive relation must itself be personal. Persons, therefore, are constituted by their mutual relation to one another. 'I' exist only as one element in the complex 'You and I'. We have to discover how this ultimate fact can be adequately thought, that is to say, symbolized in reflection.[72]

The extent to which Macmurray's philosophy succeeded in fulfilling its ambition of transcending the modern may be debated, but it proposes a post-modernism radically different from the postmodernisms that remain within the Kantian frame. The question of agency is precisely the issue that postmodern theory either negates or sidesteps, since there is neither a place for an encounter with the 'real' in postmodern theories nor a conception of a human individual who can exert purchase upon that reality. As Fitzhugh and Leckie have argued, there is no way out of 'the relentless logic of the postmodern's incompatibility with any attempt to reconcile it with agency'.[73] Macmurray's philosophy of the 'self as agent' opposes postmodernism precisely by providing a means of going beyond the modern and therefore of fulfilling a real post-modernity. And it is Macmurray's form of the post-modern, I suggest, rather than in the Kantian postmodernism of Lyotard or in the poststructuralism from which such postmodernisms derive, that we find 'symbolized in reflection' in the works of Scottish postmodernist writers. Indeed, uncovering the 'You and I'[74] in the isolated individual of modernity has been the driving force of precisely those Scottish writers who are most often associated with the stylistic gestures of postmodernism, from Muriel Spark and Alasdair Gray to A. L. Kennedy, Janice Galloway and Iain Banks. One quote from James Kelman, however, will have to suffice as illustration of Scottish novelists' concern with this issue:

---

[72] Macmurray, *Persons in Relation*, 24.

[73] Michael L. Fitzhugh and William H. Leckie, Jr, 'Agency, Postmodernism, and the Cause of Change', in David Gary Shaw (ed.), *Agency after Postmodernism*, in *History and Theory: Studies in the Philosophy of History*, Vol. 40, No. 4 (December 2001), 76.

[74] For a discussion of the sources of Macmurray's argument see Frank G. Kirkpatrick, *Community: A Trinity of Models* (Washington, DC: Georgetown University Press, 1986).

Fuck it man he switched on the radio, lifted out the cassette. Sometimes the voices drowned ye out. The incredible lives being led elsewhere in this poxy country, like a fucking fairy story. Ye couldnay believe yer ears at some of the stuff ye heard. Ye go about yer business, eating yer dinner and all that, washing the dishes; and ye listen to these voices. Ye think fucking christ almighty what the fuck's going on. Sammy couldnay even see. He couldnay fucking see man know what I'm talking about, and he still had to listen to them, these fucking bampot bastards.[75]

Sammy, who is (apparently) blind, has become an isolated consciousness to which the external world is no longer 'real' – it is 'like a fucking fairy story'. In this isolation, 'others' are not persons-in-relation but simply mechanically reproduced voices which require no response, except disbelief: 'Ye couldnay believe yer ears at some of the stuff ye heard'. Displaced from the 'You and I' of real relationships, first, second and third person pronouns become involved in a dance of substitution that makes their referents uncertain. Sentences become suspended between a narrative commentary on what we, the readers, are hearing (can we believe what we hear from Sammy?) and Sammy's response to the world around him, a world he now encounters through his ears. So, 'He couldnay fucking see man know what I'm talking about' starts as though in the third-person voice of the narrator but ends as though the 'he' has been Sammy referring to himself as a third person, just as the 'ye' of 'Ye go about yer business' is Sammy describing his own condition. What that self-referring 'ye' underlines, however, is that Sammy's self-consciousness—despite his apparent isolation in the narrative—is in fact a 'self' which can only know itself in relation to a 'you', and in the lack of an external 'you' attempts to externalise itself as a substitute for relationship. The isolation of Kelman's character thus replicates the isolation of the Cartesian–Kantian ego, but the linguistic structure and its invocation of 'you' implies an entirely different conception of the self, one which is always in relation with the Other. Kelman's novel, like Muriel Spark's *The Driver's Seat* (1974) or Alasdair Gray's *Lanark* (1981), dramatises the ways in which the egoistic self of modernity, a self whose isolation is even more pronounced in its postmodern version, is unsustainable, and points towards the ways in which an alternative sense of the self might begin to be acknowledged.

---

[75] James Kelman, *How late it was, how late* (London: Secker and Warburg, 1994), 119.

IV   The Slave of the Passions

Tucked into the conclusion to *The Postmodern Condition* is a challenge by Lyotard to one of the most influential alternatives to postmodernist and poststructuralist thought – Habermas's conception of 'communicative reason'. Refusing to accept that the Enlightenment's trust in truth and justice was misplaced, Habermas presents communicative reason as an escape from the 'subject-centred' rationality of past philosophy, and a means of giving new impetus to the 'unfinished project of modernity'.[76] Lyotard, however, finds in Habermas's argument only the continuation of the notion of 'humanity as a collective (universal) subject' to which we are each, as individuals, necessarily subordinated. It is against what he sees as the totalitarianism of Habermas's revitalised Kantian rationality that Lyotard invokes the Kantian 'sublime' as that which must always escape from the dictates of reason. The argument between them, in other words, is carried out entirely within the framework of a Kantian philosophy, making it inevitable that the 'modern' – the Enlightenment as the development of a rational conception of human history – and the postmodern – anti-Enlightenment refusal of any such metanarrative – represent neither a specific historical development, nor an intellectual opposition, but rather a successive dialectic, oscillating between two sides of the same philosophical schema. The emphasis swings from the unknowable Kantian 'thing-in-itself' to the universal Kantian rationality and back again, but the centrality of reason is never in doubt. In salvaging from Hume's critique the necessity involved in causation, Kant was salvaging the significance of reason itself as our means to the discovery of truth, and Lyotard and Habermas follow in his footsteps. For Lyotard, scientific rationality provides the model for social rationality, since in scientific rationality 'consensus is a horizon that is never reached';[77] for Habermas, social rationality provides the model for scientific rationality, since 'reason is by its very nature incarnated in contexts of communicative action and in structures of the lifeworld'.[78] Insofar as Kantian rationality is central to our conception of the Enlightenment (as well as to the

---

[76] For a discussion of Habermas's relation to poststructuralist and postmodernist thinkers, see Christopher Norris, *Deconstruction and 'the Unfinished Project of Modernity'* (London: Athlone Press, 2000).

[77] Lyotard, *The Postmodern Condition*, 61.

[78] Jürgen Habermas, 'An Alternative Way out of the Philosophy of the Subject: Communicative versus Subject-Centred Reason', in *The Philosophical Discourse of Modernity* (Cambridge, MA: MIT Press, 1987), 322.

anti-Enlightenment of postmodernity), and yet is built on the failed foundations of Kant's response to Hume, we might wonder if the nomenclature of
the 'Scottish Enlightenment' is misleading, for the real challenge that Hume
laid down was not simply the dissolution of our notions of causality but
the radical assertion that far from being the sovereign power of the human
mind, 'reason is and ought to be the slave of the passions, and can never pre-
tend to any other office than to serve and obey them.'[79] If we take Hume to
be the central figure of eighteenth-century Scottish thought, it would, given
its refusal of the power of reason, make more sense to describe this as a
'Scottish romanticism',[80] but the whole opposition between Enlightenment
and Romantic, as between modern and postmodern, is one which cannot be
mapped onto the Scottish context.

Hume's *Treatise* corresponds to traditional conceptions of Enlightenment
rationality to the extent that he adopts the scientific model of Newton's physics and seeks to apply it to the workings of the human mind: what he discovers, however, is that the reason by which he investigates the mind is undone
by what he discovers *about* the mind – that the mind does not work on rational
principles but by 'irrational' associative processes and on the basis of unverifiable natural beliefs. If we identify 'Enlightenment' with the rationalism of the
Kantian tradition then, in the earliest stages of the Enlightenment, Hume's
philosophy undoes its fundamental concept. To nineteenth-century Kantian
interpreters of Hume, such as the English Idealist T. H. Green, this Hume was
invisible: Green represents Hume as having reduced psychological experience
to impossible atomic units which only the categories of Kantian philosophy
could reconstruct into a valid conception of the human mind. But it was to
Hume's insistence on reason's 'slavish' role that Norman Kemp Smith reverted
in his 1941 study of *The Philosophy of David Hume*. Kemp Smith, who was Seth
Pringle-Pattison's successor at Edinburgh University, and Macmurray's predecessor, and who, as we saw in Chapter 1, was a distinguished translator of
Kant, applied to Hume the lesson of Seth's re-reading of Scottish philosophy
and located Hume not in relation to Locke and Berkeley but in relation to
Francis Hutcheson, from whom, Smith claimed, Hume learned that 'judgments of moral approval and disapproval, and indeed judgments of *value* of
whatever type, are based not on rational thought or on evidence, but solely

---

[79] Hume, *Treatise of Human Nature*, 415.
[80] See Norman Kemp Smith, *The Philosophy of David Hume*, 59–61 for the ways
in which Hume extends Newton's doubts about 'hypotheses' and focuses
on the fact that 'what is ultimate' rests on 'factors which are occult'.

on feeling'.[81] Hume's radical move was to apply this insight to all forms of knowledge not purely axiological:

> …what is central in his teaching is not Locke or Berkeley's 'ideal' theory and the negative consequences, important as these are for Hume, which follow from it, but the doctrine that the determining influence in human, as in other forms of animal life, is feeling, not reason or understanding, i.e. not evidence whether *a priori* or empirical, and therefore also not ideas – at least not 'ideas' as hitherto understood. 'Passion' is Hume's most general title for instincts, propensities, feelings, emotions and sentiments, as well as for the passions ordinarily so-called; and belief, he teaches, is a passion. Accordingly the maxim which is central to his ethics – 'Reason is and ought to be the slave of the passions' – is no less central to his theory of knowledge, being there the maxim: 'Reason is and ought to be subordinate to our natural beliefs'.[82]

The crisis of the *Treatise*, when Hume seems to despair of his own metaphysical speculations at the end of Book 1, is not, therefore, the *reductio ad absurdam* of Hume's philosophy – as Seth believed – but Hume's dramatisation of the necessary failure of reason to be able to address the issues with which it is confronted. The isolated rational consciousness is incapable of making sense of the world because the sense of the world lies in human – and animal – passion, rather than in reason. Kant's critical philosophy, as an effort to establish the appropriate limits of reason while leaving open the needs of faith, is, from a Humean point of view, entirely misguided: the real issue is to establish the ways in which reason must subordinate itself to feeling and to establish the consequences for our conceptions of knowledge that flow from that subordination.

Hume, in other words, displaces Enlightenment rationality as effectively as the Romantics sought to do and subverts it as radically as Nietzsche claimed to do.[83] Hume, we might say, is already post- or anti-Enlightenment insofar as Enlightenment is identified with the rationalism of the Cartesian

---

[81] Kemp Smith, *The Philosophy of David Hume*, 13.

[82] Ibid., 11.

[83] For certain strands of postmodernism, Nietzsche is the key formative influence; see, for instance, Allan Megill, *Prophets of Extremity: Nietzsche, Heidegger, Foucault, Derrida* (Berkeley and Los Angeles: University of California Press, 1985).

and Kantian traditions; or, alternatively, Hume and those thinkers of the 'Scottish Enlightenment' closest to him, such as Adam Smith, propose such a different conception of Enlightenment that it leads beyond modernity rather than towards it, and therefore prefigures a different kind of 'post-modernity'. Beyond the isolated *cogito*, beyond the reasoning self, what Hume insists upon is the self as fundamentally *social*. The distressed philosopher must learn that 'since reason is incapable of dispelling these clouds' pro-duced by metaphysical speculation, he must trust to nature and be deter-mined not to 'seclude myself … from the commerce and society of men, which is so agreeable'.[84] It is in our interaction with other human selves that our passions come into play, and the reason that 'is and ought to be the slave of the passions' mistakes its own role when it seeks to separate itself from that passional existence, when it reduces the self to a thinking thing instead of a social agent. As Hume puts it in the *Treatise*, 'reason alone can never produce any action or give rise to volition' and therefore 'nothing can oppose or retard the impulse of passion, but a contrary impulse':[85] the reasoning self is a constricted, limited creature which seeks to ignore the fact that the real self is the passional self, and since the passions require will and action, the real self is the self as agent.

When Macmurray, in his broadcast talks on *Reason and Emotion*, pub-lished in 1935, argued that 'every activity must have an adequate motive, and all motives are emotional' because they 'belong to our feeling, not to our thoughts',[86] he cited Plato, rather than Hume, as the only major phi-losopher who believed that 'reason is primarily an affair of emotion, and that the rationality of thought is the derivative and secondary one'.[87] It may be, then, that Kemp Smith's re-reading of Hume was itself a response to the 'personalist' philosophies of Seth and Macmurray, but it retrospectively makes Hume the precursor of the effort to get beyond the contemplative reason of the thinking ego and to reach a post-modern rationality based in the emotions. No 'affection', Hume argued 'can be call'd unreasonable' except 'when a passion, such as hope or fear, grief or joy, despair or security, is founded on the supposition of the existence of objects, which really do not exist',[88] that is, when it is mistaken about its object. It is precisely this that

---

[84] Hume, *Treatise of Human Nature*, 269–70.

[85] Ibid., 414, 415.

[86] John Macmurray, *Reason and Emotion* (London: Faber and Faber, 1935), 23.

[87] Ibid., 26.

[88] Hume, *Treatise of Human Nature*, 416.

Macmurray takes to be the 'rationality' of the emotions. Reason, he argues is 'the capacity to behave consciously in terms of the nature of what is not ourselves...to behave in terms of the nature of the object';[89] it is therefore equally possible to distinguish between rational and irrational emotions in terms of their adequacy to their object, a distinction which does not depend on the reason precisely because reason, as in Hume, is necessarily subordinate to the passions:

> The emotional life is not simply a part or an aspect of human life. It is not, as we so often think, subordinate, or subsidiary to the mind. It is the core and essence of human life. The intellect arises out of it, is rooted in it, draws its nourishment and sustenance from it, and is the subordinate partner in the human economy.[90]

Rationality, therefore, for Macmurray must arise not out of the Cartesian–Kantian thinking ego but out of the real cause of our actions, the emotions themselves:

> The rationality that appears in thought is itself the reflection of a rationality that belongs to the motives of action. It follows that none of our activities, not even the activities of thinking, can express our reason unless the emotions which produce and sustain them are rational emotions.[91]

For Macmurray, as for Hume, the quality of our social life is dependent not on the development of 'reason', nor on our submission to some Kantian universal law, but on the education of the emotions, an education that begins with the recognition that our emotions bind us into a world which is not the world of cause and effect describable by scientific rationality but a world of human intentions. It is the world of 'intentions' that Macmurray describes as the 'personal' world, as opposed to the mechanical or organic worlds of physics and biology. The isolated ego of the Cartesian-Kantian tradition treats itself as though it were independent of the world – or, at least, as though the world is dependent upon it. Macmurray, on the other hand, insists

---

[89] Macmurray, *Reason and Emotion*, 19.
[90] Ibid., 75.
[91] Ibid., 23–4.

on the self as 'dependent'[92]–dependent in infancy in ways which are quite different from the dependence of almost all other creatures, and dependent in adulthood not only on the whole network of society but on the existence of others through whom it achieves and maintains the significance of being a person. As Kemp Smith declares of Hume, it is *sympathy*–the 'propensity we have to receive by communication [the] inclinations and sentiments' of others[93]–which is the 'universal influence' that 'renders man the specific type of creature he is, namely, a creature so essentially social that even in his most self-regarding passions sympathy keeps others no less than the self constantly before the mind'.[94] As Macmurray puts it, 'the self cannot exist in isolation' because 'without an other there can be no self'.[95]

If Macmurray's philosophy is truly post-modern precisely because it challenges both the modern and postmodern of the Cartesian–Kantian tradition, it does so by following–or by running in parallel with–the Hume who is given to us by Kemp Smith, a Hume whose philosophy has to be read not in terms of the metaphysical isolation of the thinker of Book 1 of the *Treatise*, on which earlier commentary had focused, but on the 'sympathetic' self of Books 2 and 3. By revealing how 'dependent' that isolated consciousness is in its real social relations, Hume subverted in advance the Kantian rational ego just as effectively as his theory of causation subverts the Kantian categories, paving the way for a 'post-modernism' in Scotland that sought truly to reach beyond those limitations of the modern upon which late-twentieth-century postmodernism remained impaled. This tradition of Scottish thought can be seen emerging in contemporary debate in the work of Alasdair MacIntyre. For MacIntyre, human beings are 'dependent rational animals'.[96] As someone who believes that a return to Aquinas is the true route for contemporary moral thinking, his 'postmodernity' is, like Macmurray's, a 'post-modernity', one for which, as for a whole tradition of Scottish thought from Hume to Seth, 'the

---

[92] Macmurray, *Persons in Relation*, 42.
[93] Kemp Smith, *The Philosophy of David Hume*, 170.
[94] Ibid., 175.
[95] Macmurray, *The Self as Agent*, 142.
[96] See Alasdair MacIntyre, *Dependent Rational Animals: Why Human Beings Need the Virtues* (London: Duckworth, 1999). In his preface, MacIntyre underscores that 'the positions I have taken involve a rejection of Lockean accounts of personal identity, of Kantian or quasiKantian views of perception' (xii), and, like Macmurray, argues that 'neither the modern nation-state nor the modern family can supply the kind of political and social association that is needed' (9).

mere individual is a fiction of philosophic thought';[97] or, as Macmurray puts it, 'human behaviour is comprehensible only in terms of a dynamic social reference; the isolated, purely individual self is a fiction'.[98] If Scottish fiction shows all the marks of stylistic postmodernism it is perhaps because, from the very inauguration of the modern, Scottish thought was searching for an alternative to that 'purely individual self' which is a 'fiction of philosophic thought', mirroring the rational consciousness of the philosopher rather than the passional existence of the person. Hume's crisis – 'we have, therefore, no choice left but betwixt a false reason and none at all'[99] – and the self-negating structure of his *Treatise* prefigure the characteristic traits of a literature that is committed to going beyond reason in order to escape from the madness to which the isolated rational consciousness – like Hogg's Robert Wringhim or Stevenson's Dr Jekyll – inevitably leads.

---

[97] Seth, *Hegelianism and Personality*, 216.
[98] Macmurray, *Persons in Relation*, 38.
[99] Hume, *A Treatise of Human Nature*, 268.

4   Intended Communities: MacIver, Macmurray and the Scottish Idealists

I   Personal Communities

Ian Hamilton Finlay's garden at Little Sparta is not only devoted to the memory of earlier gardens, but to the recollection of the Second World War: amidst the greenery lurk aircraft carriers, warships, panzer tanks, and memorials of the battle of Midway. Like many Scottish artists of his generation, Finlay's work is deeply marked by his experiences during the War, in which he served for three and a half years with the Royal Army Signals Corps. *Betula Pendula*–the Latin name for Scotland's silver birch tree–is the inscription beneath a picture of the raised gun of a tank disguised with foliage;[1] and John Milton's 'Of famous Arcady ye are' is juxtaposed with the outline of a ghostly tank among trees. This is a garden with a modern war in it: what might be a slate-black standing stone by a lake is named 'nuclear sail', revealing itself to be the conning tower of a submarine thrusting up through the landscape of Scotland, a country which, through the Cold War, was home to one of the world's largest nuclear arsenals.

In the dark days at the beginning of the Second World War, an American philosopher, Ruth Nanda Anshen, brought together a collection of essays entitled *Freedom: Its Meaning*, which was published by Harcourt Brace in New York. 'The passionate concern' of the book, Anshen wrote in her introduction, was with 'the freedom of Man, the autonomy of the rational being developing to ripe maturity and achieving self-fulfilment'.[2] And its aim was 'to bring about a correlation of those contemporary ideas which are concerned not with sense data and logical universals, but with the status of values and the bearing of these values on conduct'.[3] To these ends Anshen

---

[1] Abrioux, *Ian Hamilton Finlay*, 169.

[2] Ruth Nanda Anshen, *Freedom: Its Meanings* (London: George Allen and Unwin, 1942), 4.

[3] Ibid., 2.

had assembled a list of contributors that is a roll-call of the major figures of the arts and sciences in the first half of the twentieth century: Albert Einstein, Henri Bergson, Thomas Mann, Jacques Maritain, Alfred North Whitehead and Bertrand Russell, to name but half a dozen. But amongst them were two Scottish contributors: Robert Morrison MacIver, Professor of Sociology at Columbia University in New York, and John Macmurray, Professor of Philosophy at University College London. Their inclusion is acknowledgment not only of their status as major contributors to debates about the nature and direction of contemporary society in the 1930s and 40s, but indicative of their being at the forefront of what Anshen describes as the 'synthetic clarification of modern knowledge', a clarification that requires 'a reinterpretation of the fundamental values of mankind'.[4] The fact that both are thinkers who have, subsequently, been almost entirely neglected by Scottish sociologists and philosophers[5] – even if Macmurray received a brief flurry of popular attention when it was discovered his works had been the main reading of Tony Blair's student days – is symptomatic of how little tended Scotland's past still is.

MacIver (1882–1970) had taken degrees in Edinburgh and Oxford and taught in the philosophy department at the University of Aberdeen before the First World War, where he introduced what was one of the earliest courses in sociology in any British university. He left in 1915 for the University of Toronto after a disagreement with his head of department, the philosopher and subsequently Vice-Chancellor of the University of Leeds, J. B. Baillie, apparently over a review in which MacIver attacked the Hegelianism of which Baillie was a leading proponent.[6] In Toronto he became head of social sciences on the retiral of another influential Scottish emigré, James Mavor (1854–1925) – who had been an assistant of Patrick Geddes's in Edinburgh – before moving on to a chair at Columbia University in New York, where he became one of the leading figures of American sociology in the 1930s, being elected President of the American Sociological Association in 1940.

---

[4] Ibid.

[5] There are signs of a recent revival in interest in Macmurray, inspired in part by John E. Costello's biography (2002) and by David Fergusson and Nigel Dower's collection of essays, *John Macmurray: Critical Perspectives* (Oxford: Peter Lang, 2002).

[6] See John Brewer, '"We must protest that our inheritance is within us": Robert Morrison MacIver as sociologist and Scotsman', *Journal of Scottish Thought*, Vol. 1, No. 1, 1–24.

MacIver's original degree was in classics, as was John Macmurray's (1891–1976), who went from Glasgow to Oxford in 1913 but volunteered for the Army Medical Corps almost as soon as war broke out, and subsequently transferred to a fighting unit. Wounded in the Battle of Arras in 1918, he completed his studies after the war, going to posts at Manchester University, Balliol and University College London before returning to Scotland in 1944 to the Chair of Moral Philosophy at Edinburgh University. MacIver's major works included *Community: A Sociological Study*, written at Aberdeen in 1913 but not published till 1917, *The Modern State* (1926) and *Society: Its Structure and Changes*, one of the standard textbooks of sociology, first published in 1931, revised in 1937 and extended (with C. H. Page) in 1949. Macmurray published seven books and a host of articles in the 1930s, including *Freedom in the Modern World* (1932), *Reason and Emotion* (1935), *Creative Society: A Study of the Relation of Christianity to Communism* (1935) and *The Clue to History* (1938).

After the War, MacIver produced a series of works on the nature of democracy in the modern state – *The Web of Government* (1947), *Democracy and the Economic Challenge* (1952), *Power Transformed* (1962) – at a time when Macmurray was formalising his philosophical arguments in two major books stemming from his Gifford lectures in Glasgow in 1953–4: *The Self as Agent* (1957) and *Persons in Relation* (1961).[7] Both men were not only leading academics in their field but prominent public intellectuals. A series of talks on philosophy by Macmurray, broadcast by the BBC between 1930 and 1932, set the model for the BBC's efforts to bring serious thought to a mass audience, and the producer, Charles Siepmann, recalled that 'few would have expected that at the height of a beguiling summer and at the unlikely hour of eight of the evening twelve broadcast talks on Philosophy would have produced a miniature renaissance among thousands of English listeners'.[8] In the United States, MacIver was one of the leading campaigners for racial equality in American society and was also a leader in the fight for academic freedom in the McCarthy era. His standing in the post-war era is reflected in another project of Ruth Nanda Anshen's, a publication entitled 'The Credo Series': in 1961 she invited him to join the editorial board, which included W. H. Auden, Werner Heisenberg, Paul Tillich, C. P. Snow and Michael Polanyi – and insisted, in a letter to him of 15 April 1961, that 'yours will be

[7] For a full bibliography of their works see Robert M. MacIver, *Politics and Society* (New York: Atherton Press, 1969), ed. David Spitz, 533ff., and John E. Costello, *John Macmurray: A Biography* (Edinburgh: Floris, 2002), 424ff.
[8] Quoted in Costello, *John Macmurray*, 180.

one of the first nine volumes to be published in the Series, the others being by Kenneth Galbraith, Erich Fromm, Werner Heisenberg, C. P. Snow, James Sweeney, Paul Tillich, René Dobos, Fred Hoyle'.[9]

MacIver and Macmurray do not seem to have known one another, but the brief intersection which brought them together as contributors to Anshen's *Freedom: Its Meaning*, reveals how closely connected are their concerns with issues of freedom and determinism, of agency and moral responsibility, and of the relation of the individual to the organisation of the modern state. For both – as for Benedict Anderson – the crucial concept is that of 'community' but the crucial failing of modern political theory, for both of them, is its confusion of community with the State. This, for MacIver, was the fundamental mistake of Hegelian and neo-Hegelian philosophers, a mistake he would have identified only too clearly in Benedict Anderson's Hegelianised Marxism. It is a confusion which, as David McCrone has pointed out,[10] is deeply embedded in modern consciousness but the very need for the hyphenated term the 'nation-state' is indicative of an unresolved contradiction. Political states and national communities may co-exist, but the relations which they produce are different. In society as constituted by the state, people 'co-operate', according to Macmurray, 'to achieve a purpose which each of them, in his own interest, desires to achieve, and which can only be achieved by co-operation'. In that situation, however,

> the relations of its members are functional; each plays his allotted part in the achievement of the common end. The society then has an organic form: it is an organization of functions; and each member is a function of the group. A community, however, is a unity of persons as persons. It cannot be defined in functional terms, by relation to a common purpose. It is not organic in structure, and cannot be constituted or maintained by organization, but only by the motives which sustain the personal relations of its members.[11]

'Organic' is still associated in modern thought with 'unity' and 'whole-ness' – and indeed with the workings of the imagination as invoked by Anderson – but organic unity is, for Macmurray, still merely a functional unity

---

[9] Robert Morrison MacIver, Correspondence, Box 8, Butler Library, University of Columbia.

[10] McCrone, *The Sociology of Nationalism*, 85.

[11] John Macmurray, *Persons in Relation*, 157–8.

which cannot explain the relations of people who value one another not as a means to an end but as an end in themselves. Macmurray illustrates this by 'two types of association', the 'partnership', which is underpinned by a single common end and which finishes when that end is achieved or fails, and 'friendship', which generates new ends out of the mutual commitment of individuals to one another. The language of 'association' in this example directly mirrors MacIver's distinction in his first book, *Community*, which proposed that 'an association is an organisation of social beings (or a body of social beings as organised) for the pursuit of some common interest',[12] whereas 'a community is a focus of social life, the common living of social beings'.[13] It is for this reason that for MacIver, too,

> The State must, therefore, be clearly distinguished from the community which creates it. Community is the common life of beings who are guided essentially from within, actively, spontaneously, and freely (under the conditions prescribed by the laws they make) relating themselves to one another, weaving for themselves the complex web of social unity.[14]

In the context of the State, people are functionaries: as Ernest Gellner put it, the nation-state is constituted by 'two propositions: (1) Every man a clerk. (Universal literacy recognised as a valid norm.) (2) Clerks are not horizontally mobile, they cannot move from one language-area to another'.[15] Gellner attributes this functionalism to the nation, but for MacIver and Macmurray it derives only from the State. The State may appeal to and may try to reinforce the communal – or the 'national' – relations of its members in order to strengthen its own internal cohesion but the State can never be a community: 'the State, unlike community, is exclusive and determinate. Where one State ends, another begins; where one begins, another ends. No man can without contradiction owe allegiance to two States, any more than he can serve two masters, but he can enter into the life of as many communities as his sympathies and opportunities will allow'.[16] For Gellner and Anderson, people's commitment to their nation is a profound puzzle – why should they

---

[12] R. M. MacIver, *Community: A Sociological Study* (London: Macmillan, [1917] 1920), 23.
[13] Ibid., 24.
[14] Ibid., 34.
[15] Hutchinson and Smith, *Nationalism*, 56.
[16] Ibid., 29.

value so highly this rag-bag of invented traditions? MacIver and Macmurray perhaps provide an answer: the nation-as-community is one of the contexts in which people feel valued simply in their own being, simply *for being*. Family life, pre-eminently, can provide such a context, as can religion, and the territorialisation of religion in the aftermath of the Reformation, with the creation of national churches, is one of the foundations of nationalism which the modernist theorists, with their emphasis on politics and economics, tend to ignore. The creation of the Church of Scotland or the Church of England translate a sense of a shared value before God – indeed, a sense of shared election – into the sense of a recognition of mutuality based simply on a common territory, a common community of origin.

To treat others as ends and not as means is, for both MacIver and Macmurray, to recognise them as persons, and to value them for what is personal to them. What distinguishes community from state is its creation of a context for the development of the 'personal' and of 'personality', a context which does not require a retreat by the individual from the social in order to maintain the personal but one in which the development of the personal and communal go hand in hand: 'the laws of community are laws revealing the connection between the evolution of social forms and the increase of human life or personality'.[17] As a result, 'community is simply common life, and that common life is more or less adequate accord-ing as it more or less completely fulfils in a social harmony the needs and personalities of its members'.[18] For both thinkers, therefore, the relation-ship between 'community' and 'personality' is such that 'the widening of community is itself one result of the growth of personality'.[19] Rather than submergence in Anderson's 'unisonance', the achievement of community lies in the development of *difference*, of increased differentiation of the per-sonal, and the evolution of community is achieved not by the submersion of debate, resistance and opposition but on their development within the recognition of underlying shared interests:

> For every individual there is always present the necessity of choice between conflicting interests of his own; for every community there is always a conflict of interest among its members, its associations and groups. Intra-individual conflict and harmony of interests is relative to

[17] MacIver, *Community*, 177.
[18] Ibid., 171.
[19] Ibid., 208.

the unity of the individual being, social conflict and harmony to the like-
ness to one another of the members of the community.[20]

The development of community is towards increasing 'difference in unity',
an increasingly diversified unity, and increasingly differentiated forms
of the personal. The development of the community and the person
therefore represent a single process: 'It is in the attainment of personality,
the progressive union of sociality and individuality, that community is
fulfilled.'[21] If we put this person-in-community rather than the individual-
in-the-state at the core of our thinking then 'the only justification of any
individualism or any socialism is the furtherance of personality which its
adoption would ensure'.[22] As MacIver puts it, 'All values are finally personal,
values of personality, and in the service of personality alone are the laws and
institutions justified'.[23] A society has to be judged in terms of its ability to
sustain 'persons' who are ends in themselves, rather than mere functionaries
of the system: 'If the whole be such as to have an end which is realized
otherwise than as the fulfillment of the ends of its parts or persons, then
personality is in so far an illusion; for it rests on the being of each as an
end in itself, and all its striving is understandable only on the supposition
that each person and the other persons for whom also he strives are ends
in themselves.'[24]

These differences between the state and the community can be understood in their very different relations to 'intention', and to the nature of
our 'intending'. In his contribution to *Freedom: Its Meaning*, Macmurray insists
that,

> The exact difference between society and community and the proper
> relation between them are best recognized by reference to the intentions
> involved. The intention involved in society lies beyond the nexus of
> relation which it establishes. In community it does not.[25]

[20] Ibid., 118.
[21] Ibid., 333.
[22] Anshen, *Freedom: Its Meaning*, 223.
[23] MacIver, *Community*, 95.
[24] 'Personality and the Suprapersonal', *Politics and Society*, 155; originally pub-
       lished 1915.
[25] John Macmurray, 'Freedom in the Personal Nexus', in Anshen, *Freedom: Its
       Meanings*, 187.

The difference between a human being who is a person and a human being who is a function is that one is free—and is able to *intend* his or her actions—and the other is not. This is why MacIver and Macmurray are deeply concerned, both at a social and at a metaphysical level, with the issue of agency. For MacIver, the business of sociology is defined by the fact that 'there is an essential difference, from the standpoint of causation, between a paper flying before the wind and a man flying from a pursuing crowd. The paper knows no fear and the wind no hate, but without fear and hate the man would not fly nor the crowd pursue.'[26] MacIver's account of the nature of the social sciences emphasises two different forms of knowledge, facts which 'we know only from the outside' and facts which 'we know, in some degree at least, from the inside':

> Why did the citizens turn against the government? Why did the union call a strike? To answer these questions we must project ourselves into the situations we are investigating. We must learn the values and the aims and the hopes of human beings as they operate within a particular situation. There is no inside story of why a meteor falls or why liquid freezes.[27]

The difference between the two forms of knowledge rests on agency, an agency which we understand precisely because each of us is an agent, experiencing our actions not as the products of an external necessity but directed by our own intentions, because, in the end, 'the self is a purposive self-conscious self whose acts are attempts to attain an end so related to the self that it conceives their fulfilment as a self-realization'.[28] As Macmurray puts it,

> The association of persons in a unity is constituted by practical relations; by the ways in which the associates *act* in relation to one another. A relation of agents can never be mere matter of fact. It must be a matter of intention.[29]

[26] Robert Morrison MacIver, *Society: A Textbook of Sociology* (New York: Farrar and Rinehardt, 1937), 376–7.
[27] 'The Social Sciences', *Politics and Society*, 17; first published 1938.
[28] 'Ethics and History', *Politics and Society*, 77; written in 1908, previously unpublished.
[29] Macmurray, *Persons in Relation*, 148.

The world of the personal and the communal is only distinguishable from a world of objects and events because it is a world of actions governed by *intention* – because, in the end, its object is an *intended* world.

It is important to grasp the ontological implications of this: for MacIver and Macmurray the world that is *real* to human beings is the world of human relations produced by intention; the world revealed to us by science is produced by a narrowing and thinning of that reality in order to reduce it to a world of order without intention, and thereby to produce a world of predictable 'events'. But it is precisely predictability which is impossible in the realm of the personal and communal because

> the distinction we have drawn between a personal and an 'objective' knowledge of one another rests upon this, that all objective knowledge is knowledge of matter of fact only and necessarily excludes any knowledge of what is matter of intention. What is intended is never matter of fact, though it may be a fact that I intend it. For what is intended is always future, and there are no future facts...[30]

The world that persons inhabit is an *intended* world. Like the garden which is its earliest image, it is a world not of 'facts' and 'events' but of 'intentions': as such, it can never be complete or completed because intentions always go beyond the immediate to invoke the possible – or, indeed, the impossible.

This emphasis on the *intentionality* of the personal world has significant consequences for the nature of the communal world that is the nation. In an essay on 'The Foundations of Nationality', written in 1915, MacIver argued that 'the sentiment of nationality proper emerged when men again sought...to realize and distinguish the claims of the complete community to which they felt themselves to belong',[31] claims which were expressed equally in 'the growth of nationality and the growth of democracy'.[32] Nationalism, like democracy, is 'the spirit of protest against political domination', but 'to attain the demand of nationalism is not to achieve these interests, it is to have built the foundation only' because 'nationality is not the end but the beginning':

---

[30] Macmurray, *Persons in Relation*, 39.
[31] 'The Foundations of Nationality', *Politics and Society*, 222.
[32] Ibid.

Hence we have to realize very carefully the limits of the ideal of nationality. It is the failure to realize these limits which perverts that ideal from
a savor of life into a savor of death. *Nationality can be a true ideal only so
long as and in so far as nationality itself is unrealised.* As soon as it is attained,
as soon as a nation is a unity free from alien domination, a new ideal
must take its place.[33]

The nation, in effect, can never be realised: it is an intention which, as soon
as fulfilled, generates a new ideal, a further intention, because the real end
towards which we strive is the enhancement of community and its consequent enriching of personality, a process which is endless in both senses of
that word – endless in being without limit, and endless in being without a
predefined outcome. We do not live in an imagined community of the kind
described by Benedict Anderson, a community of anonymous functionalism, but in real communities, one of whose possible forms is our intended
nation. The problems with many modern theories of the nation is that
they try to treat nations as 'facts', as objects in a world of causally constituted events, when nations are, if MacIver and Macmurray are correct, the
products of agents and of their 'intentions', intentions which evolve and
change as they are fulfilled or thwarted. Nationality, in this sense, can never
be realised: it is an ideal because it is always an intention awaiting fulfilment,
one which nevertheless survives because 'the deepest antagonisms between
interests are not so deep as the foundations of community'[34] – and for a
very simple reason: human beings are social creatures who cannot survive
without community.

It is often suggested by 'postmodern' critics that the nation has become a
redundant category: as Michael Billig put it in *Banal Nationalism*,

It is as if the whole business of nationhood is being unravelled...no
longer is the national territory *the* place from which identities, attachments and patterns of life spring...In place of the bordered, national
state, a multiplicity of *terrae* are emerging. And those, who see their
identities in terms of gender of sexual orientation, are...bound by no
earthly *terra*, restricted by no mere sense of place. Thus, a new sensibility – a new psychology – emerges in global times.[35]

[33] Ibid.
[34] MacIver, *Community*, 117.
[35] Michael Billig, *Banal Nationalism* (London: Sage, 1995), 134.

This would neither have surprised nor discomfited MacIver and Macmurray: the nation is merely the vehicle, at a particular historical moment, of the impulse of community – for community is where persons flourish, and the most effective community is that which allows persons to flourish most fully. The idea that the nation has ceased to provide such a location was, as we have seen, the burden of nation theory in the 1960s and 1970s: the nation outlasted them, as it has now outlasted the fashion for postmodern cosmopolitanism, because even gender communities of the kind that Billig points to still have to exist in relation with other communities in a space which is defined by the laws of nations, and by their mutual pressure upon one another. Their community – like may others – may be broader than the nation, but that does not release it from engagement with the other communities of the nation.

If postmodernism invoked globalisation as its justification for the irrelevance of nations, then nations, at the beginning of the twenty-first century, can invoke the ecological crisis as an alternative justification – each human community representing a way of ordering and of understanding the world which is valuable because, like the diversity of natural lifeforms, it is a resource which may prove to be of crucial value to the development or survival of the species at some point in the future. Its maintenance is not a reactionary refusal of the outside world, because it is the very medium through which we encounter the world outside: its cultivation is an acknowledgment that we all, as persons, can only become ourselves in and through communities, and that the nation remains, for the time being, one (but only one) of those communities, but in terms of our co-operative agency, the most significant. It remains, in our contemporary world, the principal medium through which our intentions are turned into actions and so into realities, and remains, therefore, the shaping context of our existing and our possible communities.

II Communities of Persons

Just as Finlay's garden helps us grasp, retrospectively, a buried Scottish past in the nation's gardening traditions, so the parallels in the work of MacIver and Macmurray allow us to grasp another dimension of the Scottish past that has been all but obliterated from view – the Scottish philosophy of the late nineteenth and early twentieth centuries to which both were introduced at Edinburgh and Glasgow universities. It is a philosophy often described as 'British' idealism, though it was a Britishness consisting of a disproportionate number of Scottish contributors.[36] MacIver and Macmurray both exhibit the typical characteristics of this idealist tradition in their commitment to linking academic knowledge with public action, and in their commitment to finding a contemporary justification for the traditional 'spiritual' values of their Christian past.[37] But the work of both is much more deeply rooted in Scottish tradition than has been generally recognised.[38] When MacIver applied for a post at Toronto, for instance, after his time teaching in Aberdeen, his referee was James Seth, who had been appointed as Professor of Moral Philosophy at Edinburgh in 1898 after periods at Dalhousie, Brown and Cornell universities in North America. Seth's emphasis in his essays is on harnessing Christianity to the solution of the new problems of modern industrial societies: 'All this belongs to the education of the modern Christian conscience', he writes in 'The Christian Ethic', 'to the new sense of social responsibility of the individual, as a member of the community, as a citizen of the State, for the economic, social, and political conditions which means so much for the moral as well as the material well-being of mankind.'[39] Sociology, as the means of understanding the organisation of modern societies, is, in effect, a

---

[36] See David Boucher (ed.), *The British Idealists* (Cambridge: Cambridge University Press, 1997), xxxiv–xliii, for brief biographies of the leading figures: no less than six of the nine listed were born in Scotland and one, Henry Jones, born in Wales, was professor at St Andrews and Glasgow.

[37] The spiritual underpinnings of both these accounts of human societies is indicative of thinkers whose background is steeped in the religion of Calvin, even if both were in revolt against the narrowness and repressiveness of their childhood experiences of that religion: 'The elder MacIver became a successful merchant, though his real vocation, according to his son, was for the Free Church of Scotland...', Leon Brason (ed.), *Robert Morrison MacIver on Community, Society and Power: Selected Writings* (Chicago: University of Chicago Press, 1970), 3; 'This Calvinist culture that shaped a firm, even militant, way of life in Scottish society clearly formed the character of its children, including the young John Macmurray', Costello, *John Macmurray*, 21.

[38] In the best collection of essays on Macmurray, Fergusson and Dower (eds), *John Macmurray: Critical Perspectives*, Jack Costello refers to Macmurray's article, 'The Influence of British Philosophy during these Forty Years', as providing a knowledgeable account of 'the British Idealists, Green, Bosanquet, Caird, Bradley, McTaggart, Ward, Baillie and Henry Jones' (14), but that hinterland of Macmurray's engagement with his predecessors is unexplored in the rest of the volume.

[39] James Seth, *Essays in Ethics and Religion*, ed. A. Seth Pringle-Pattison (Edinburgh: William Blackwood and Sons, 1896), 67.

Christian duty, as is Socialism, because it is a politics dedicated to 'social and political reforms, in the rectification of economic injustice':[40]

> While it seems to me that the application of the Christian ideal to the modern social conditions was undreamt of by the Founder of Christianity, this social and practical application is implied in that ideal, as the consummation of the aspirations of the Old Testament Prophets for the reign of social righteousness, in the concern of Christ for the material needs of suffering humanity, and in his making social service the criterion of discipleship…Thus modernised – that is, interpreted in the light of modern conditions – the Christian ideal, on its human side, is identical with the ideal of contemporary Socialism'.[41]

The emphasis on 'community', and on the necessity of addressing economic inequality if spiritual equality is to be a reality, is equally evident in the philosophy of Henry Jones, who was professor at Glasgow when Macmurray was a student. For Jones, the conflict between the Individualist and the Socialist is a false antithesis:

> The contention that 'Socialism is already upon us' is true, if by that is meant that the method of organised communal enterprise is more in use; but it is not true if it means that the individual's sphere of action, or his power to extract utilities, that is, wealth, out of his material environment has been limited. It is being overlooked that the displacement of the individual is but the first step in his reinstalment; and that what is represented as the 'Coming of Socialism' may, with equal truth, be called the 'Coming of Individualism'. *The functions of the State and City on the one side and those of the individual on the other, have grown together.* Hence it is possible that here, once more, the principle is illustrated according to which the realisation of the self, whether on the part of the individual or of the State, is at the same time the realisation of the self's opposite. It is possible that the State as a single organism grows in power, even as its citizens acquire freedom; and that the more free and enterprising the citizens, the more sure the order and the more extensive the operations of the State.[42]

---

[40] 'Christianity and Socialism', in Seth, *Essays in Ethics*, 114.

[41] Ibid., 'Christianity and Socialism', 115.

[42] Henry Jones, 'Individualism, collectivism and the general will', in Boucher, *The British Idealists*, 205–6.

It is characteristic of the Idealists of this period to resolve apparent oppositions – self and society, individualism and socialism – by showing that both
develop *in relation* to each other: that the development of the social – even
to the extent of socialism – is in fact the environment in which the self can
flourish, and that the ultimate test of such developments is the test of 'personality': 'It follows', Jones argues, 'that this social problem is material and
economical only on the surface. In its deeper bearings it is ethical: it is the
question of the rights of personality.'[43] It is on the development of 'personality' that the judgment has to be made between individualism and socialism:

> Private property may, as is alleged, give occasion for cupidity, competi-
> tion, aggression, and untold miseries of extreme poverty, and the no less
> tragedy of unjust, profligate, and irresponsible wealth. Nevertheless it
> is the condition of the opposite virtues – of loyal service, of justice, of
> generosity, of manhood itself. The means of doing right are the same
> as the means of doing wrong. There must be choice between them, and
> the choice must be real: and that is not possible unless personality has its
> own sphere and inalienable station in the outer world.[44]

The significance of 'personality' as the ground which allows us to resolve the
apparent conflict between the social and the individual into a relationship of
mutuality within community is fundamental: the 'rights of personality' are,
in the end, the rights on which all community and society are based, and that
form of social organisation is best which best encourages the development
of 'personality'.

Thus, in his *Study of Ethical Principles* (which went through sixteen editions
between 1894 and 1926), James Seth focuses on 'personality' as the key distinguishing feature of human as against organic life:

> When we wish to describe the characteristic and peculiar end of human
> life, we must either use a more specific term than self-realisation, or we
> must explain the meaning of the human self-realisation by defining the
> self which is to be realised. And since man alone is, in the proper sense,
> a self or person, we are led to ask, What is it that constitutes his per-
> sonality and distinguishes man, as a person, from the so-called animal or

---

[43] Ibid., 198.
[44] Ibid., 200.

impersonal self? The basis of his nature being animal, how is it lifted up into the higher sphere of human personality?[45]

The answer lies in the fact that it is 'self-consciousness, this power of turning back upon the chameleon-like, impulsive, instinctive, sentient or individual self, and gathering up all the scattered threads of its life in the single skein of a rational whole, that constitutes the true selfhood of man. This higher and peculiarly human selfhood we shall call "personality", as distinguished from the lower or animal selfhood of mere "individuality".'[46] Seth's ethical ground – the human characteristic of 'personality' – is the foundation of MacIver's sociology, which starts from the 'axiom that ultimate value can attach to persons alone – "persons" being here employed as inclusive of all conscious beings that in any degree can strive toward what they conceive as good and so become ends in themselves.'[47] Equally, Seth's argument prefigures Macmurray's assertion that 'the Self is neither a substance nor an organism, but a person'.[48]

   It was not James Seth, however, who made the 'personal' the key concept of late-nineteenth-century Scottish idealism, but his brother Andrew, later known, for family reasons, as Andrew Seth Pringle-Pattison.[49] In *Hegelianism and Personality*, published in 1887, Pringle-Pattison (then mere Andrew Seth, and Professor in St Andrews) argued against the idealist tradition's answer to the problems set by Hume, insofar as the logical outcome of Kantianism was Hegel's metaphysics, a metaphysics which had no place for the 'personality' either of God or of human beings. As we have seen in Chapter 3, Pringle-Pattison attributed the 'radical error both of Hegelianism and of the allied English doctrine' to 'the identification of the human and the divine self-consciousness, or, to put it more broadly, the unification of consciousness in a single Self'.[50] Hegel's conception of a universal spirit, manifesting itself

---

[45] James Seth, *A Study of Ethical Principles* (Edinburgh and London: William Blackwood and Sons, [894] 1898), 198.

[46] Ibid., 200.

[47] 'Personality and the Suprapersonal', in *Politics and Society*, 153.

[48] John Macmurray, *The Self as Agent*, 37.

[49] A distant family relative left Seth an estate in the Borders as long as he continued the name of the Pringle-Pattisons. I will refer to him in this chapter as Pringle-Pattison, even when the individual works were published under the name of Andrew Seth, since this will distinguish clearly between his works and those of his brother.

[50] Andrew Seth, *Hegelianism and Personality*, 215.

in and through the individual, denied, for Pringle-Pattison, the existential reality of individual selfhood: 'Each of us is a Self: that is to say, in the technical language of recent philosophy, we exist *for* ourselves or are objects to ourselves. We are not mere objects existing only for others.'[51] The 'Self is a unique existence, which is perfectly *impervious*...to other selves',[52] and must be if the relation of human being to divine creator is to be a relationship of individuals and not merely a mirroring of identities: 'only in a person, in a relatively independent self-centred being is religious approach to God possible. Religion is the self-surrender of the human will to the divine. "Our wills are ours to make them Thine." But this is a *self*-surrender, a surrender which only self, only will, can make.'[53] This is precisely the argument that MacIver will remake, citing Pringle-Pattison, in 'Personality and the Suprapersonal', in 1915:

> Hegel was on the whole willing to sacrifice personality to his Absolute, but *his* successors have latterly been evincing the desire both to have and eat their cake. The world is spoken of as a place where personality manifests itself, where souls are made, but the making is unreal after all; for nothing remains in the Absolute save that mysteriously detached 'content' with which the self was filled, the 'content' of timeless being ...[54]

It is on this basis that MacIver insists that there is no transcendent spirit or superior willpower that is over and above the wills of the individual human beings who make up a community: the 'fundamental fallacy' of all such views is that 'we think of a system of persons as a person, a system of organisms as an organism, a system of minds as a mind; but the identification is in every case fallacious'.[55] All such identifications are 'really a disguised form of an absolute-idea theory', which suggest that 'it is possible to work for humanity otherwise than by working for men, to serve nationality otherwise than by serving the members of a nation', and in so doing treat 'the end and value of society...as other than the ends and values of its members taken as a whole', with the consequence that the individual is reduced to a 'means to an end

51 Ibid., 215.
52 Ibid., 216.
53 Ibid., 217–18.
54 'Personality and the Suprapersonal', in *Politics and Society*, 159.
55 Ibid., 153.

which is beyond, not merely each as individual, but all as collective'.[56] Against such negations of the personal, MacIver insists that,

> Persons or selves are bound up in contemporaneous no less than in historic interdependence, and here we reach the facts which most of all reveal the nature of superindividual unity. For the relations we are now to consider, unlike those already considered, are *reciprocal* relations. Herein persons are united in common dependence upon one another ... For whose is the wider, greater welfare that we seek, if not that of a whole of persons, and how can we seek their welfare unless we conceive it as of like nature to our own?[57]

Persons in Relation is the title of Macmurray's second volume of Gifford lectures, but the notion that *persons* in *reciprocal relation* constitutes the fundamental ground of human experience is not only already present in MacIver's essay of 1915 but in Pringle-Pattison's account of the relation of the human and divine. His critique of Hegelianism underlines that the human and the divine can only be a *relation* if it is an encounter between different personalities, and if God is to have a personality, and so be capable of a personal relation, it can only be in relation with a human being as a person and not as a mere reflection of the divine mind: Hegel's theory denies the *relation* of human and divine because it 'deprives man of his proper self, by reducing him, as it were, to an object of a universal Thinker' and 'leaves this universal Thinker also without any personality'.[58] The realm of the personal is necessarily the realm of *relations* of difference rather than of unities of the same.

Exactly that argument, though directed at Kant rather than at Hegel, is the foundation of Macmurray's effort to overthrow the western tradition since Descartes by making the 'self as agent' primary and the 'self as thinker' secondary in our construction of the subject:

> ... the adoption of the 'I think' as the centre of reference and starting-point of [Kant's] philosophy makes it formally impossible to do justice to religious experience. For thought is inherently private; and any philosophy which takes its stand on the primacy of thought, which defines

---

[56] Ibid., 155.
[57] Ibid., 164, 165.
[58] Pringle-Pattison, *Hegelianism and Personality*, 222.

the self as Thinker, is committed formally to an extreme logical individualism. It is necessarily egocentric…in recognizing the existence of a
multiplicity of persons, it must treat them all as identical instances of the
'I think', whose differentiation is, for theoretical purposes, accidental.[59]

Macmurray's argument repeats Pringle-Pattison's: a real *relation* is necessarily
a relation of differences; the 'I think' reduces all persons to duplications of
one another, 'who must be represented as a multiplicity of "I"'s'.[60] Such a system violates what Macmurray takes to be fundamental to the very nature of
the 'I' – that it requires a 'you': 'any philosophy which takes the "I think" as its
first principle, must remain formally a philosophy without a second person;
a philosophy which is debarred from thinking the "You and I".[61] A world
of persons no less than a theology of persons requires relations, requires
difference, requires a 'You' who is not identical with, who has a different
personality from but is capable of a personal relation with, the 'I'.

Macmurray's alternative account of the self – of the self conceived first
of all as an agent and only secondarily as a thinker – is equally rooted in
Pringle-Pattison's critique of his predecessors. In 'The "New" Psychology
and Automatism', for instance, one of the essays in his collection *Man's
Place in the Cosmos*, first published in 1897, Pringle-Pattison challenges
recent developments in German psychology for returning us to a similar
conception of the mind as that proposed by David Hume, one in which
the subject becomes a mere spectator of its own ideas: 'The individual self
is reduced, as with Hume, to groups and sequences of ideas; it is an object
in consciousness – an object, presumably, for this impersonal spectator-
subject'.[62] Such a spectatorial conception of the self fails to acknowledge
that 'ideas in themselves are pale and ineffective as the shades of Homeric
mythology; they are dynamic only as they pass through the needle's eye of the
subject. It is the subject which acts upon its appreciation of the stimulus, and
the emotional attitude of welcome or repulse is what is meant by feeling'.[63]
Feeling, in such an analysis, is not a passive response to the environment

---

[59] Macmurray, *The Self as Agent*, 71.

[60] Ibid.

[61] Ibid., 72.

[62] A. S. Pringle-Pattison, 'The "New" Psychology and Automatism', in *Man's
Place in the Cosmos and Other Essays* (Edinburgh: William Blackwood and
Sons, [1897] 1902), 68.

[63] Ibid., 73.

but the very 'driving-power in all life',[64] stimulating the organism to action, such that 'feeling-prompted action –*i.e.* action which is germinally purposive, germinally voluntary,– is … the first in the order of nature'.[65] In Hume as in the German psychologists, 'All real action, all real causality, is eliminated',[66] and that reduction means that they fail to realise that 'it is not in knowledge … but in feeling and action, that reality is given'.[67]

As we have seen, MacIver acknowledges Pringle-Pattison's account of Hegel and, in an essay written when he was at Oxford (though not published until 1969), it seems that MacIver is also drawing on Pringle-Pattison's account of feeling and action. 'Emotion', he writes, 'is not simply feeling, but at the least a feeling-activity, a reaction or response borne to its object', so that 'our emotions are ourselves in action',[68] and he criticises those of the Humean tradition, like Alexander Bain, for failing to recognise 'the great role of the emotions in the formation of all primary ends of action'.[69] MacIver's tentative definition of emotion is that it is 'the spontaneous reaction of the self toward an object realized as significant' because emotions are 'activities which, in so far as they produce further activities, are called motives'.[70] This conception of the self-in-action underlies MacIver's account of the nature of sociology: sociology is the study of the relations which selves form through their actions, relations which derive directly from 'personality': 'Understand individuals as concrete beings whose relations to one another constitute factors of their personality, and you realise that these *are* society, these and these alone – and the metaphysical confusion which leads you to look for something beyond this, something beyond these unsummable social individuals, passes away.'[71] The discipline of sociology is the study of community, and community 'is nothing but wills in relation, if we understand by will no abstract faculty but mind as active'.[72]

These active 'wills in relation' clearly prefigure Macmurray's 'persons in relation' but they do so by recuperating Pringle-Pattison's account of the falsity of a metaphysical tradition which 'laid stress, designedly or not,

[64] Ibid., 74.
[65] Ibid., 75.
[66] Ibid., 82.
[67] Ibid., 87.
[68] 'The Passions and their Importance in Morals', in *Politics and Society*, 123.
[69] Ibid., 125.
[70] Ibid., 128, 127.
[71] MacIver, *Community*, 91.
[72] Ibid., 128.

upon the intellectual; and the result was, that the real activity of the subject was discarded'.[73] In *The Self as Agent*, Macmurray's argument against post-Cartesian philosophy is precisely against the privacy of its intellectual source, its emphasis on the self-as-thinker:

> It is that any philosophy which takes the 'Cogito' as its starting point and centre of reference institutes a formal dualism of theory and practice; and that this dualism makes it formally impossible to give any account, and indeed to conceive the possibility of persons in relation, whether the relation be theoretical – as knowledge, or practical – as co-operation. For thought is essentially private. Formally, it is the contrary of action; excluding any causal operation upon the object which is known through its activity, that is to say, upon the Real. If we make the 'I think' the primary postulate of philosophy, then not merely do we institute a dualism between theoretical and practical experience, but we make action logically inconceivable.[74]

Overturning this logical inconceivability of action within the Cartesian tradition, understanding the self as agent and agency as a necessary relatedness between self and object, between self and self, makes it possible to envisage a community of persons (or 'wills') in relation which, for both MacIver and Macmurray, constitutes the true terrain of social understanding and social improvement.

Macmurray has often been portrayed as a 'revolutionary' thinker, and to this end a comment by the Scottish theologian, Thomas Torrance, is regularly invoked: 'John Macmurray is the quiet giant of modern philosophy, the most original and creative of savants and social thinkers in the English speaking world. If his thought is revolutionary, as it certainly is, the kind of revolution he has in view is not revolt but the reconstruction of the foundation of life and knowledge with a view to a genuinely open and creative society for the future.'[75] Macmurray might have been 'revolutionary' in virtue of the radical nature of his challenge to the organisation of the modern world, but as the parallels with MacIver make clear, he was building on a philosophical

---

[73] Pringle-Pattison, 'The "New" Psychology and Automatism', 89.

[74] Macmurray, *The Self as Agent*, 73.

[75] Quoted, for instance, by Kenneth Barnes in the foreword to Jeanne Warren, *Becoming Real: An Introduction to the Thought of John Macmurray* (York: The Ebor Press, 1939).

foundation in which his thought was far from revolutionary, in which the key concepts – selves in relation, community, the self as agent – had already been developed in the work of Pringle-Pattison and the other Scottish idealists of the late nineteenth and early twentieth centuries. 'Ideas in themselves are nothing', Pringle-Pattison writes,

> and the analysis of knowledge as knowledge can never give us reality. If we were to recast Descartes's formula, in the light of all that has come and gone in philosophy since his day, not *Cogito ergo sum*, but *Ago ergo sum* is the form his maxim would take.[76]

'I act therefore I am' is the ground from which both MacIver and Macmurray's thought grows.

It is an assertion which would become fashionable in the post-Second World War period with the popular dissemination of existentialism, but it is significant that in John Macquarrie's *Existentialism*, published in 1972, the presentation of the existential subject – who 'is not only a thinking subject but an initiator of action and a centre of feeling'[77] – is conducted not through the work of Heidegger or Sartre but through the work of John Macmurray: 'It is through free and responsible decisions that man becomes authentically himself. In John Macmurray's language, the "self as agent" provides the central themes for existentialism.'[78] Sometimes one's own garden, even if a small one, is more important than other people's, because what existentialism does not provide, despite its talk of 'being-with-others', is the necessary implication of the self in a community – or, rather, since the self can only become a self through its participation in community, of the community in the self. The philosophical tradition which informs the work of MacIver and Macmurray makes 'community' – the sphere in which human beings meet as intentional creatures and not as the outcomes of external causes – the foundation and not the consequence of the self's ability to develop and differentiate itself from

---

[76] Pringle-Pattison, 'The "New" Psychology and Automatism', 89.

[77] John Macquarrie, *Existentialism* (London: Penguin, 1972), 15; Macquarrie was himself, of course, the inheritor of the Scottish tradition of engagement with Kantian and Hegelian philosophy; born in Renfrew, he was educated at the University of Glasgow, and *Existentialism* is dedicated to the memory of 'Charles Arthur Campbell, formerly Professor of Logic University of Glasgow'.

[78] Ibid., 16.

others. The self is not 'thrown' into the world in an existential isolation from which it has to reach out towards the world: the self is possible only in and through the sustenance of community, only in and through learning selfhood from its community. There are, of course, many forms of community, but because the world we inhabit has come, increasingly rather than decreasingly, to be defined in terms of the nation, the nation-as-community is the one through which the self develops, the one with which, at some stage, it has to engage. The question that this particular Scottish tradition of philosophy would ask is, does the nation-as-community provide an appropriate context for the development of individual and differentiated personality? Can the individual flourish in, and in flourishing, enhance this community? Is it a place where we meet as intentional creatures, creating the future, or merely as functionaries, determined by external forces?

Which kind of community, which kind nation, it would ask, do we intend?

III   Intended Communities

Hamilton Finlay's 'Nuclear Sail', which features on the cover of this book, was actually produced in conjunction 'with John Andrew', just as many of Finlay's most striking artworks have been produced in collaboration 'with' other artists – 'with Gary Hincks', 'with Nicholas Sloan', 'with Annet Stirling', 'with Alexander Stoddart', to name but a few. This is not incidental to Finlay's decision to make a garden the focus of his art for the garden is an image of art not as the product of isolated genius but as a necessarily collaborative effort. In Finlay's 'Homage to Pop Art' ('with Sydney McK. Glen'), the aggressive domination demanded by modernism's new visual culture – 'Treat nature as the cube, the cone, and the cylinder' – is visually re-enacted in images of an Oxo cube, an ice-cream cone and a ice-cream wafer (known in some parts of Scotland as a 'slider'): 'Treat Nature as the Cube, the Cone and the Slider' is the ironic subtitle.[79] The declarations of an abstract universalism are subverted by meanings which are shared by and can only be immediately recognised by a particular, 'popular' community. No matter how abstract and 'universal' art aspires to be, in the end it has its origin and its being in a community of shared knowledge and expectation. So Finlay's various works deriving from

---

[79] Abrioux, *Ian Hamilton Finlay*, 162.

the names and identification numbers of fishing boats[80] produces an apparently abstract art in turning those names and numbers into visual images – as in 'Sea Poppy', for instance, which uses the lettering from ships to form the petals of a poppy. Our knowledge of the origin of those letterings, however, means that they cannot help but invoke the fishing communities from which they derived and the (now merely historical) communal meanings of which they were a part. But in this they enact the art which we find in Finlay's garden, which celebrates the community of the living and the dead, a community in which the words and the intentions of the dead are reintegrated into the fabric of our immediate experience – as in 'The Henry Vaughan Walk', with its plaque announcing that

> The
> Contemplation
> of *death* is
> an obscure
> melancholy
> *walk*[81]

We take that walk with Henry Vaughan, despite his death over four hundred years ago, just as we can encounter Apollo lurking in the undergrowth,[82] for the garden is a community in which the ancient and the exotic mingle with the local and the contemporary.

If MacIver and Macmurray help us to see better the ways in which late nineteenth-century Scottish philosophy developed, and the significance of what it was trying to achieve, they provide us as well, perhaps, with a context in which to understand the insistence on the primacy of community that continues to run through some of the major productions of Scottish artists in the latter part of the twentieth century. Their displacement of the isolated, individual thinker of the Western philosophical tradition, their emphasis on the primacy of agency and mutual dependence, is echoed in Finlay's rejection of 'autobiography and biography (both), because it seems to me that *much* of one's life is only nominally related to oneself'.[83] Such a displacement of the originating self as the source of creativity opens the way to new forms

---

[80] See Abrioux, 198ff.
[81] Ibid., 103.
[82] Ibid., 64.
[83] Ibid., 159.

of art – art-in-action, art-in-community – which are represented in Hamilton
Finlay's various designs for public gardens.

It was not the values of the Scottish Enlightenment that shaped the ethos
of twentieth-century Scotland, but the values of the Scottish Idealists, which
suffused the early Labour movement in the 1880s and 1890s as well as galvanising the social mission of the Scottish churches. The Idealists' emphasis on
the necessary relation between self and community can be traced in the works
of many of Scotland's major writers, from Nan Shepherd and Neil Gunn in
the 1920s and 30s to Alasdair Gray and Janice Galloway in 1980s and 90s,[84]
works which emphasise in their linguistic style as well as in their narratives
the dependence of the self on its community. And they can be traced in
the Scottish Constitutional Convention's blueprint for a Scottish parliament,
which declared that 'the powers of the Scottish parliament will enable it to
develop the type of high quality public services to individuals which are the
measure of a civilised community'.[85] The choice of 'civilised community'
rather than 'civilised society' was significant, since, for Macmurray, society
was the realm of the functional while community was the realm of the personal. It was a distinction which Margaret Thatcher thought she was invoking
when she declared, in that same year, that 'there is no such thing as society',[86] and which she defended to Ian Lang (later Scottish Secretary, 1990 till
1995) by quoting Macmurray: '"Society is a socialist concept," she intoned,
while she scanned the pages, "community is Christian."'.[87] Thatcher mistook
the nature of Macmurray's distinction but it was perhaps appropriate that a
Convention aimed at establishing a Scottish parliament and inspired in part
by a refusal of Thatcher's individualist philosophy should defiantly return to
the language of community which she had tried to co-opt.

For the Convention, and all who supported it, the words embossed on the
cover of Alasdair Gray's satirical account of Thatcherite values, *Poor Things*
(1992), were only too appropriate: 'Work as if you live in the early days of a
better nation',[88] it said. Otherwise, *intend* a better community.

---

[84] See my *Modern Scottish Novel* (Edinburgh: Edinburgh University Press, 1999),
     86ff.

[85] http://www.almac.co.uk/business_park/scc/scc-rep.htm#Serving_the_
     people_of_Scotland (accessed December 2008).

[86] Interview with Douglas Keay, *Woman's Own*, 31 October 1987.

[87] 'Who inspired Thatcher's most damaging remark? Tony Blair's Favourite
     guru', *The Spectator*, 24 August 2002, by Peter Oborne.

[88] *Poor Things: Episodes from the Early Life of Archibald McCandless M.D. Scottish
     Public Health Officer* (London: Bloomsbury, 1992).

5 Telephonic Scotland: Periphery, Hybridity, Diaspora

I Geography Undone by History

> A strong recommendation of the study of Natural Philosophy arises from the importance of its results in improving the physical condition of mankind. At no period of the world's history have the benefits of this kind conferred by science been more remarkable than during the present age…Who would have believed…that our messages should now be communicated for thousands of miles by sea or land, literally with the speed of lightning?[1]

In 1858 the first attempt to lay a telegraph cable between Europe and North America ended in disaster: after an initial transfer of some 700 messages, the signals faded, became unintelligible and ended. William Thomson, Professor of Natural Philosophy at the University of Glasgow, had been an adviser to the project but his advice had been ignored by the managing engineer, Wildman Whitehouse, who did not have Thomson's expertise in the theoretical aspects of the transmission of electronic currents. After a parliamentary investigation into the failure, Thomson was put in charge of a second attempt in 1865 and eventually succeeded in 1866 not only in laying a cable from Ireland to Nova Scotia but in establishing a consistent contact that linked continent to continent in an almost instantaneous circuit of information.

With the establishment of the intercontinental telegraph distance was, as far as information was concerned, effectively abolished. The telegraph became, for Britain, the nervous system of Empire, binding the centre and its most farflung margins so that nowhere could be beyond the horizon of

---

[1] William Thomson, 'Introductory Lecture', 1846; quoted in Smith and Wise, *Energy and Empire*, 649.

almost immediate perception. Marshall McLuhan suggested that the report-
ing of the Crimean War by William Howard Russell for the *Times* produced a
political storm in England in 1854–5 because, for the first time, the events on
the battlefield were also the events at the breakfast table, and those digesting
their breakfasts had to consume, at the same time, the fact that *their* troops
were dying of starvation at the front. It is the image of Empire as an organic
self-conscious unity, core and periphery linked in an immediate reciprocity
of instantaneous responsiveness.[2]

The telegraph, in a prefiguration of what will only intensify in the eras of
radio and television, *short-circuits* spatial relations, makes location irrelevant
and foregrounds contemparaneity as the defining context of our experience.
It is the world which Benedict Anderson invoked in *Imagined Communities*, a
world in which meaning is produced by mere 'temporal coincidence':

> What has come to take the place of the mediaeval conception of
> simultaneity-along-time is, to borrow again from Benjamin, an idea of
> 'homogeneous, empty time', in which simultaneity is, as it were, trans-
> verse, cross-time, marked not by prefiguring and fulfilment, but by
> temporal coincidence, and measured by clock and calendar. (*IC*, 24)

The modern nation can exist because we imagine, and trust our imagining
of, our immediate relationship in a shared present with our fellow nationals:
'An American will never meet, or even know the names of more than a
handful of his…fellow-Americans. He has no idea of what they are up to
at any one time. But he has complete confidence in their steady, anonymous,
simultaneous activity' (*IC*, 26). Our relations with the world are defined not
by connections of past, present and future, but by synchronicity, by our
shared awareness of and dependence upon what is happening now, at this
moment, anywhere in the world. For Anderson, it is this world which was
already prefigured by the invention of the newspaper:

> What is the essential literary convention of the newspaper? If we were
> to look at a sample front page of, say, *The New York Times*, we might find
> there stories about Soviet dissidents, famine in Mali, a gruesome murder,
> a coup in Iraq, the discovery of a rare fossil in Zimbabwe, and a speech

---

[2] Marshall McLuhan designates the telegraph as an extension of the nervous
system: see, *Understanding Media*, Ch. 25, 337–8.

by Mitterand. Why are these events so juxtaposed? What connects them to each other? Not sheer caprice. Yet obviously most of them happen independently, without the actors being aware of each other or of what the others are up to. The arbitrariness of their inclusion and juxtaposition (a later edition will substitute a baseball triumph for Mitterand) shows that the linkage between them is imagined.

This imagined linkage…is simply calendrical coincidence. The date at the tops of the newspaper, the single most important emblem on it, provides the essential connection – the steady onward clocking of homogenous empty time. (*IC*, 33)

The date, however, is precisely *not* 'the single most important emblem' on the newspaper's front page: it is *place* which is crucial – these times are the '*New York* Times'. The newspaper is not simply the juxtaposition of things which happen to happen at a particular point in calendrical time: it is the organisation of events from the perspective of a particular place, from the point of view of a particular community in space. What real newspapers attest to is not calendrical time (yes, of course, today's are all produced on the same day) but location in space, which defines what will count as important within the *geographical* horizon from which the world is seen. The linkages may be 'imagined' but they are parts of a narrative which *takes place* from a certain point of view, which happens in space, and which connects 'here' to a variety of possible 'theres'.

This suppression of space in *Imagined Communities* was to become the guilty unconscious which drove the development of Anderson's later work. As Chapter 1 pointed out, Anderson's conception of 'imagined community' was introduced through a novel by José Rizal, now 'regarded as the greatest achievement of modern Filipino literature' (*IC*, 26). In a footnote a further hundred pages on we are told that that work, *Noli Me Tangere* (1887), is typical of 'many other nationalist novels' in its geography – for although 'some of the Filipino characters have been to Spain (off the novel's stage), the circumambience of travel by any of the characters is confined to what, eleven years after its publication and two years after its author's execution, would become the Republic of the Philippines' (*IC*, 115). From this we might deduce that Rizal, an indigenous writer – his was also the first novel by an 'Indio' (*IC*, 26) – whose characters are limited in their journeys to the boundaries of the emergent nation, was himself a writer whose life is circumscribed by the geography of what would become his nation. What we learn from Anderson's later work, *Under Three Flags* (2005),[3] however, is that far from being a writer limited by national geography, Rizal wrote his major works during nearly ten years when he was travelling and living in France, Germany and England, with briefer forays to Japan and the United States, and that his biography is an example of what Anderson calls 'The Age of Early Globalisation' (*UTF*, 233). And his execution, too, was a consequence of global forces, since it was ordered in the fear of a nationalist uprising in the Philippines to take advantage of the fact that the Spanish were already engaged in suppressing resistance to their rule in Cuba.

In *Under Three Flags*, therefore, Rizal the nationalist is also Rizal the globalist; Rizal the writer of the periphery is also Rizal the traveller between cultural centres–corresponding in several languages, influenced by French and German literature, working with other Filipinos and Philippine specialists who are resident in Spain, France, Germany or Belgium. He is also Rizal the proto-anarchist, since many of those with whom he was connected were part of an international anarchist movement that was attempting to resist the global effects of imperialism. The Rizal of *Under Three Flags*, in other words, is very different from the Rizal to whom we thought we had been introduced in *Imagined Communities*. For this Rizal, space – global space – is significant, and the establishment of the nation which he seeks has to be approached by way of journeys through the core cultures responsible for its peripheral repression, journeys which are not defined by the shared 'unisonance' of a nationalist movement but by its internal conflicts, its secessions, its founding of many conflicting newspapers whose content is not defined by 'homogeneous empty time' and 'calendrical coincidence' but by competing visions of the (possible) nation's (possible) future. This intended community can only be approached, however, by recognising the *space* – the space of imperialism, of capitalism – which resists its coming into existence. Rizal the global traveller is a Rizal who has learned that his imagined community is not 'hundreds of unnamed people who do not know each other, in quite different parts of Manila, in a particular month of a particular decade' (*IC*, 27) but a community whose possible existence is prevented by the exploitative spatial relations in which it is trapped.

Anderson's emphasis on the space through which Rizal's nationalism came to be defined was part of a general development in left-wing thought in

---

[3] Benedict Anderson, *Under Three Flags: Anarchism and the Anti-Colonial Imagination* (London: Verso, 2005). Hereafter cited in the text as *UTF*.

the 1980s and 90s, driven by the recognition not only of the economic failings of 'actually-existing' Marxist states but by their undeniably nationalist ethos. Marxism's failings, it was argued by the most prominent revisionist of Marxist theory, Immanuel Wallerstein, were due to its failure to recognise the fundamentally spatial nature of capitalism. Instead of the class-based structures of traditional Marxism, operating within the boundaries of a single society, Wallerstein analysed what he called 'the world system' in terms of 'cores' and 'peripheries', which are involved in a mutually defining structural relationship: cores aggrandise and enrich themselves precisely by enforcing peripherality on those whose resources they require. A world-wide division of labour forces peripheral areas of the world economy into supplying the requirements of core areas, and the states in the periphery, as a consequence, are always relatively poorer and much more politically unstable than those of the core. Whereas Marxists had seen the key to history as the inevitable conflict between the proletariat and the bourgeoisie, which would initially be fought out within the borders of existing nations, Wallerstein saw the key as the conflict between the core economies of the world and the rest of the world which they exploited, whether directly (by imperialism) or indirectly (through economic coercion).[4]

It was an argument to which the example of Scotland proved to be particularly important. In 1980, Wallerstein challenged the lessons to be learnt from eighteenth-century Scottish history as offered by Scotland's leading historian, T. C. Smout: according to Smout, Scotland's eighteenth-century industrial take-off was a case of a 'dependent economy' finding no 'disadvantage from its initial dependency' in its progress into modernisation. What Scotland showed was how 'progress' could be achieved 'in the way traditional economists assumed it would, benignly, and to Scotland's advantage', and thereby underlined how capitalist development leads to an economic convergence in which, if 'the rich will get richer' then 'the poor will also get richer as well, probably in relative and certainly in absolute terms'.[5] For Wallerstein, such benign economic development was an illusion: Scotland as a whole did not 'develop' and those parts of Scotland which did, did so only as a result of 'development by invitation' – 'the privilege (or the luck) of a very few, a case which offers few policy lessons for other states since it cannot be imitated at

---

[4] See Immanuel Wallerstein, *Politics of the World Economy: the States, the Movements, the Civilisations* (Cambridge: Cambridge University Press, 1984).

[5] *Review: A Journal of the Fernand Braudel Center for the Study of Economies, Historical Systems and Civilizations*, Vol. III, No. 4 (Spring 1980), 631–2.

will'.[6] For Scotland's 'fortune' only illustrates others' misfortune (in Ireland, for instance), because 'it is never possible for *all* peripheral zones to move "upward"' in a world economy determined by the geographical distribution of physical labour (peripheral economies provide cheap basic resources and commodities), and the increasing concentration of intellectual labour (core economies progress by exploiting the advantages of new technologies). Liberal economists who believe in the benign operation of 'development' in underdeveloped countries make the same mistake as Marxists who believe in the revolution of the proletariat in individual countries: both ignore the world-wide structure of a capitalism whose effectiveness depends on creating and maintaining the exploitative relationship that transfers value from the periphery to the core. As a consequence, the proletariat of the core can no longer be depended on to provide the revolutionary impetus to overthrow capitalism: their own economic standing is dependent on maintaining their exploitative relationship with the peoples of the periphery – which is why the promised Marxist revolutions in advanced economies never took place and why, instead, Marxism became the revolutionary discourse of the agrarian peripheries.

In an editorial in the magazine *Cencrastus* in which an essay by Wallerstein was published, Geoff Parker suggested that both liberal and Marxist accounts of economic development could be traced back to the structures of Scottish Enlightenment thinking, since the 'stadial histories' characteristic of the work of David Hume and Adam Smith provided a justification for the fact that all countries would go through the same stages of development, from primitive pastoralism to modern commercialism, even if not necessarily at the same speed. The effect is 'the subordination of geography to History',[7] on the assumption that History will (eventually) bring all areas of the world into the same condition of harmonious economic modernity and polite social civility. History is the eradication of difference, an ideology all too effectively promoted by what was taken to be the Scottish Enlightenment's commitment to assimilate backward Scots to the culture of progressive England. Wallerstein's argument reversed that Enlightenment expectation of benign economic imitation by showing how geography, in the form of the distribution of core and peripheries, remained resistant to such historical assimilation.

---

[6] Ibid., 633.
[7] Geoff Parker, *Cencrastus*, 17 (1984), 2.

This reconceptualisation of the geographical thrust of capitalism did not, however, unleash a new form of global resistance to its dominance. For Wallerstein, the core–periphery relation might have displaced the bourgeois– proletarian opposition of traditional Marxism, but whatever peripheries might *think* of their own cultural values, their only place within Wallerstein's world system was as local and temporary disruptions of the hegemonic power of capitalism. Whether your cultural value was peripheral nationalism, trades-union socialism, feminism, Muslim or Hindu resistance to westerni- sation, or ecopolitics, its *function* in the system was simply as an irritant to the overwhelming trajectory of capitalism. Such 'antisystemic' movements, resisting the world system in which they were inevitably caught, might, at some future point, allow an entirely new and as yet unimaginable socialist world system to come into existence, but individual antisystemic movements could not, themselves, form the basis of that future non-exploitative soci- ety. As Alberto Moreiras put it: 'There is no cultural-ideological praxis that is not always already produced by the movements of transnational capital, which is to say, we are all factors of the global system, even if and when our actions misunderstand themselves as desystematising ones.'[8] As rigorously as traditional Marxism, Wallerstein envisaged humanity's salvation as a salvation through history that would be achieved by the withering away of the cultures which people had inherited from an earlier set of geopolitical relations. The causes for which people fought *now*, as resistance movements to global capi- tal, would be rendered redundant when capitalism was finally overthrown. Their efficacy was purely negative: they might help derail global capitalism but their positive content would be irrelevant to the ideology by which capi- talism would, eventually, be replaced.

It is this tragic contradiction – the contradiction of a geographically determined world whose exploitative and destructive economy can end only in some entirely unimaginable future history – that lay behind Benedict Anderson's return to the writings of José Rizal in *Under Three Flags*, and the judgment that the novel which now best represents the nature of the mod- ern nation is not *Noli Me Tangere*, through which 'imagined community' had been illustrated, but Rizal's second novel, *El filibusterismo* (1891), which had not even been mentioned in *Imagined Communities*. The immediate generic difference between them is that while *Noli Me Tangere* 'can be said – up to

8 Alberto Moreiras, 'Global Fragments: A Second Latinamericanism', in Frederic Jameson and Masao Myoshi (eds), *The Cultures of Globalization* (Durham, NC: Duke University Press, 1998), 92.

a point – to be realist in style' (*UTF*, 31) and, therefore, typical of Rizal's nineteenth-century environment, *El filibusterismo* is much stranger, because 'nothing in "real" Philippine history remotely corresponds' (*UTF*, 31) to its characters or its events – it is, in effect, prescient of the kind of 'magic realism' that will be typical of a later generation of non-Spanish Hispanic writers. This style Anderson attributes to Rizal's sense of the imminence of the success of Philippine nationalism: 'Not there yet in reality, but, since already imagined, just like his nation, on the way' (*UTF*, 121). The novel he describes, however, is one in which events in Spain – at the metropolitan centre of the imperial world – are translated back into the Philippines as an image of the future which the colony will necessarily encounter: by 'a massive, ingenious transfer of real events, experiences, and sentiments from Spain to the Philippines, which then appear as shadows of an imminent future' (*UTF*, 121). The future for the periphery, in other words, is to suffer a repetition of the destructive past history of the centre.

Anderson's sympathetic identification with the Rizal of *El filibusterismo* reveals his changing attitude to nationalism in the 1990s – if only because he is less convinced about its alternatives. In a section punningly entitled 'What is Left?' in *The Spectre of Comparisons*, nationalism is recognised as now the only viable resistance to imperialism and global capitalism, and therefore as the only location of the utopian impulse which had once belonged to Marxism. This is why 'it is both possible and necessary, against, one might say, the evidence, to think well of nationalism around the time of its two-hundredth birthday'.[9] The tragedy of nationalism is, however, that its utopian promise will always be undone by the reality of its implementation, because what it actually achieves is simply the repetition at the periphery (as in *El filibusterismo*) of an earlier stage of the centre's economic development. Successful nationalisms trade political 'autonomy' for economic servitude – which is why it is Rizal's interest in anarchism which Anderson finds most interesting: only those who, like the anarchists, altogether reject the teleology of history, can offer a real alternative in the present to the overwhelming force of imperial capitalism. What history promises to aspirant nationalisms – like those of Eastern Europe in the aftermath of the collapse of communism – is simply the repetition at the periphery of an earlier stage of existence at the centre. Not the freedom of a newly imagined national community,

---

[9] Benedict Anderson, *The Spectre of Comparisons: Nationalism, South-East Asia and the World* (London: Verso, 1998), 26.

or of an imaginably different future, but the shackles of a history which is only ever the repetition of its own destructive trajectory. History's sameness everywhere obliterates the differences of geography.

It is an irony embedded in the very nature of Rizal's writing, for his presentation of life on the periphery is carried out in Spanish, so that the language of the centre is quite literally overwriting experience at the periphery. The author from the periphery can no longer stand as the representative of his culture because his art necessarily mimics – as in the very intention of the writing in that Western form, the 'novel' – the pre-existing structures of the centre. The problem of Rizal's changing role in Anderson's works is not simply the result of Anderson's increasingly detailed research but that he is dealing with a writer who has crossed the line between periphery and centre. Such writers are like a crossed line in a telephone connection: who are they speaking to, speaking for? Which culture do their works represent? Which network are they a part of? Where, in a telegraphic world, are their messages inscribed?

II   Border Crossings

The Rizal of Anderson's works who metamorphoses from peripheral realist, bound within the territory of his local nationalism, to cosmopolitan border crosser, lurking unseen within the metropolises of the imperial centres, is not simply a nineteenth-century figure: he is also a reflection of a significant change in left-wing British culture in the 1980s and 90s. Rizal, indeed, forms a strange mirror-image to the career of one of the most influential of British left-wing thinkers between the 1950s and 1980s – Raymond Williams. Williams's reputation was based on a series of theoretical and critical works – *Culture and Society* (1958), *The Long Revolution* (1961), *The Country and the City* (1973) – which self-consciously positioned themselves as responses to, and continuations of, a distinctively English tradition in literary and cultural criticism developed, in the previous generation, by F. R. Leavis. At the end of *The Country and the City* – often referred to as his 'masterpiece' – Williams notes that his analysis has been traced in 'what I believe to be these major processes, in their major variations, within a single literature and society: a literature, English, which is perhaps richer than any other in the full range of its themes of country and city; and a society which went through a process of historical development, in rural and then industrial and urban economies and communities very early and very thoroughly; still a particular history but one which has also become, in some central ways, a dominant mode of development in many parts of the world.'[10] The word 'country' here refers only to the world of nature (agriculture) as over against society (urban/ industrial): it has no overtones of 'country', as in 'nation', although the opening paragraph of the book had stressed that 'in English, "country" is both a nation and a part of a "land"; "the country" can be the whole society or its rural area'.[11] From the anglocentric focus of Williams's discussion it would have been almost impossible to guess that he was, in fact, Welsh, and yet by 1981, in an interview with the editors of *New Left Review* (who included Benedict Anderson's brother Perry), Williams was to claim that being Welsh had been, for him, the crucial discovery of the 1960s: 'a big change started to happen from the late sixties. There was a continuity in a quite overwhelming feeling about the land of Wales…But then I began having many more contacts with Welsh writers and intellectuals; all highly political in the best tradition of the culture, and I found a curious effect. Suddenly England, bourgeois England, wasn't my point of reference any more. I was a Welsh European…'[12] Williams's interviewers quickly changed the subject, but the tensions he is referring to can be felt in an early and partly biographical essay of 1958, 'Culture is Ordinary', in which he describes his first encounters with the 'culture' of Cambridge: 'I was not, by the way, oppressed by Cambridge. I was not cast down by old buildings, for I had come from a country with twenty centuries of history written visibly into the earth.'[13] 'Country' here is never specified: it might simply be a 'countryside' rather than a 'country'. The specifically Welsh background, as opposed to a working-class background, is never invoked, and when 'nation', 'society', 'culture' are called into play it is always in the context of 'English traditions', which are the foundation of '*our* society', '*our* lives'.[14] And yet retrospectively Williams was to interpret his own work – especially his work as a creative writer – as shaped by the fact that 'unconsciously my Welsh experience was operating'.[15] Just as Anderson's Rizal, the apparently local recorder of Philippine 'national' society, turned

---

[10]   Raymond Williams, *The Country and the City* (London: Chatto and Windus, 1973), 291–2.

[11]   Ibid., 1.

[12]   Raymond Williams, *Politics and Letters: Interviews with New left Review* (London: Verso, 1979), 295.

[13]   'Culture is Ordinary', in John Higgins (ed.), *The Raymond Williams Reader* (Oxford: Blackwell, 2001), 12.

[14]   Ibid., 21.

[15]   Raymond Williams, *Politics and Letters*, 113.

out to be an unacknowledged metropolitan wanderer, so Williams, the apparently anglocentric metropolitan Marxist, turns out to have been, all along, a secret Welsh localist whose universalising terms, like 'community', were actually founded on specific national experiences: 'The way I used the term community actually rested on my memories of Wales'.[16]

The Welshness, and the Welsh commitments, of Williams have hardly entered into critical discussions of his work, despite J. P. Ward's account of him, in 1981, as one of the 'Writers of Wales'.[17] Terry Eagleton's introduction to *Raymond Williams: Critical Perspectives* is typical in taking Williams's Welsh working-class experience as the foundation of his antagonism to English bourgeois values but in seeing that 'national' experience as a 'deprivation' which Williams had to overcome: 'He never underestimated the value of the intellectual tools of which his own people had been deliberately deprived: it was just that he took the instruments which he had been handed and turned them against the educators.'[18] Williams's development is based not on his Welsh community experience but on the 'tools' he learned in his English education, tools put to purposes of 'rational enquiry' that the English had never envisaged for them. The end-point of Williams's journey is therefore one which aligns him with the rationalism of Marxism – ('Cultural materialism', he declared cautiously, was 'compatible' with Marxism)[19] – and to which, in the end, the emotional attachments of Wales and Welshness are irrelevant. The nation may be part of the experience but it is not necessary to the theory. In this, Eagleton and others are in fact following a crucial contradiction in Williams's own work: whatever its resonance in his creative writing, Wales has no *theoretical* significance in his criticism. In his essay on 'The Writer: Commitment and Alignment', for instance, from 1980, the issue of the nation is never raised: 'alignment' may be a matter of being 'born into a social situation, into social relationships, into a family, all of which have formed what we can later abstract as ourselves as individuals',[20] but the *nationality* of that family is not one of its 'relations'. Williams's usual level of

---

[16] Ibid.

[17] J. P. Ward, *Raymond Williams* (Cardiff: University of Wales Press, 1981). This lack has now been challenged by Daniel Williams in his edition of Raymond Williams's writings on Wales, *Who Speaks for Wales: Nation, Culture, Identity* (Cardiff: University of Wales Press, 2003).

[18] Terry Eagleton (ed.), *Raymond Williams: Critical Perspectives* (Cambridge: Polity Press, 1989), 5.

[19] Ibid., 6.

[20] Higgins, *The Raymond Williams Reader*, 216.

abstraction may here be concealing his own personal reference to his Welsh background but Wales itself is not present as part of the argument, and any English reader could read the sentences unproblematically with reference to him- or herself. Equally, in *The Country and the City*, Williams's account of the childhood experience that lies behind his novel *Border Country* gives it no national location – it is simply 'the village in which I had grown up', a place whose history he had to understand by going back to 'read, as if for the first time, in George Eliot and Hardy and Lawrence',[21] as though its meaning was not only socially integral to but culturally indistinguishable from the tradition of the English novel.

This lack of a theoretical account of the role of the nation is clear in his essay on 'Region and Class in The Novel', which concludes by focusing on the 'Welsh industrial novel' as an instance of the 'regional' novel and of the difficulties of providing, within a regional context, 'any full realization of class relations'.[22] The relations of Wales to England, of English language writing in Wales to Welsh-language writing, or of Welsh writers' access to publication, disappears into the formal issue of how to represent dramatically the conflict of class in an area in which the real owners of capital are socially invisible. Important though this issue is (and it is an important issue in the Scottish novel), it is an issue which is not, as the rest of Williams's discussion of the possible meanings of 'the regional novel' makes clear, specific to the Welsh situation: Wales, in this context, is no different from Nottingham, Tyneside or the Mearns. Lacking any conceptual framework for the 'national', the *regionality* of Welsh working-class writing can simply be taken for granted.

When Williams did address the problems of language and of the literary traditions possible within a bilingual national environment in a related essay on 'The Welsh Industrial Novel', the strains on his theoretical perspectives are clear: what he finds in the Welsh industrial novel 'is, I believe, within the general category of the industrial novel, a specifically Welsh structure of feeling'.[23] 'Structure of feeling' was Williams's term for the interplay of cultural inheritances within which each of us has to find a meaningful relationship between the past and the future, but it is not a category to which Williams had ever assigned a 'national' meaning, or which he had attempted to develop in terms of 'national' interactions. It had always been the means of identify-

---

[21] *The Country and the City*, 298, 299.
[22] Raymond Williams, *Writing in Society* (London: Verso, 1983), 236.
[23] Raymond Williams, *Problems in Materialism and Culture* (London: Verso, [1980] 1997), 221.

ing a particular *class* formation whose national situation had never been at issue because it was always assumed to be internal to English culture – or, at least, if we wish to generalise it more broadly, internal to a culture sufficiently substantial to require no reference to any culture outside its borders for the definition of its internal class relations. Thus the chapter on 'Structures of Feeling' in *Marxism and Literature* concludes with some examples of 'the complex relations of differentiated structures of feeling to differentiated classes', which are instanced by the case of 'England between 1660 and 1690', by the case of the emergence of 'a new structure of feeling...related to the rise of a class (England, 1700–60)' and by 'contradiction, fracture, or mutation within a class (England, 1780–1830 or 1890–1930)'.[24] No non-English examples are offered, and the concept is not tested against any other 'national' context. As Williams's own discussion makes clear, however, such purely *internal* analysis is impossible in the case of the Welsh novel: it is part of a culture which operates, necessarily, in the shadow of its dominant neighbour, in the shadow of a history of cultural subordination which Williams himself, as the product of an English-language grammar school and a Cambridge education, experienced but which, through much of his earlier career, he repressed or ignored: 'What I did not perceive at the time but I now understand is that the grammar schools were implanted in the towns of Wales for the purpose of Anglicisation.'[25]

This asymmetry, which allows English cultural products to be examined purely in terms of English class categories while Welsh cultural products have to be examined in relation to their involvement with, or resistance to, English models, is never incorporated into Williams's theoretical account of the nature of culture and society, or country and city. What stands in its place is Williams's insistence on his own existential situation as someone who has always lived on the border between Welsh and English cultures: 'I was born in a remote village, in a very old settled countryside, on the border between England and Wales.'[26] Behind the 'impersonal procedures, in description and analysis' of the literary critic, there is 'this personal pressure and commitment'.[27] The personal pressure, however, remains personal: it has no place in the analytic structure. What it does do, though, is allow Williams to claim

[24] Raymond Williams, *Marxism and Literature* (Oxford: Oxford University Press, 1977), 134.
[25] Williams, *Politics and Letters*, 25.
[26] Williams, *The Country and the City*, 2.
[27] Ibid., 3.

a level of objectivity in his analysis that derives from his not being fully and *personally* implicated in the culture he is analysing. By being a 'border' intellectual, his critique can aspire to an 'impersonality' whose ground may be his own unique personal experience but it is the experience of being *undetermined* by either of the cultures on whose border he has developed.

Williams's influence on the development of cultural criticism has been profound, both by setting an agenda which others tried to complete and by setting an example which others could repeat. The need to extend Williams's analysis beyond its English territory was underlined by Palestinian critic Edward Said in a conversation between the two at a conference on 'Cultural Studies, Media Studies and Political Education' in London in 1986:

> **Said**: I remember a moment in *Politics and Letters* where…one of the questioners asks Raymond: you talk about culture in nineteenth-century England for the most part, but what about Empire? He is taken to task about not discussing the relationship of the two, and Raymond I think you related that to the unavailability at the time of your Welsh experience…And for me, though perhaps I am putting it too strongly, culture has been used as essentially not a cooperative and communal term but rather as a term of exclusion.[28]

That omission in Williams's account of 'culture' was to form the basis of Said's own *Culture and Imperialism* (1993), in which Williams's historical account of the notion of culture and of country and city within a single tradition is replaced by a 'geographical inquiry into historical experience',[29] one in which 'our critical consciousness' of past theories of culture, such as Carlyle's or Ruskin's, has to take account of 'the authority that their ideas simultaneously bestowed on the subjugation of inferior peoples and colonial territories'.[30] To Terry Eagleton's *Raymond Williams: Critical Perspectives*, published shortly after Williams's death, Said contributed an essay on 'Jane Austen and Empire', which was to become a key chapter in *Culture and Imperialism*. In it he emphasised his indebtedness to Williams's *The Country and the City* while suggesting

---

[28] Raymond Williams, *The Politics of Modernism: Against the New Conformists*, ed. Tony Pinkney (London: Verso, 1989), 'Appendix: Media, Margins and Modernity', 177–97, 196.

[29] Edward W. Said, *Culture and Imperialism* (London: Chatto and Windus, 1993), 6.

[30] Ibid., 12.

that its failure to engage with empire was a serious weakness, and proposed a theoretical perspective in which the internal history of a dominant culture could be made to intersect with the imperial geography with which it was, in political fact and of economic necessity, deeply implicated: 'After Lukács and Proust, we have become so accustomed to regarding the novel's plot as constituted mainly by temporality that we have overlooked the fundamental role of space, geography and location.'[31] The geographical mode of reading which Said proposed in *Culture and Imperialism* was not, however, one based on reading *from* the periphery, from a particular location, in opposition to the imperial centre: what he proposed was a reading that moved back and forth between the centre and the periphery in a process that he called a 'contrapuntal reading':

> As we look back at the cultural archive, we begin to reread it not uni-vocally but *contrapuntally*, with a simultaneous awareness both of the metropolitan history that is narrated and of those other histories against which (and together with which) the dominating discourse acts.[32]

The reader, in other words, can retrospectively position him- or herself both at the centre and at the periphery. If the economic and political impact of imperialism appeared to distance centre and periphery from one another, the procedures of cultural understanding can produce a reversal that allows them to be understood in their mutual interaction. Indeed, the destructive and disruptive forces that ravage the periphery for the aggrandisement of the centre can be reversed to produce, at least at the level of reading, a form of cultural harmony:

> In the counterpoint of Western classical music, various themes play off one another, with only a provisional privilege being given to any particular one; yet in the resulting polyphony there is concert and order, an organized interplay that derives from the themes, not from a rigorous melodic or formal principle outside the work. In the same way, I believe, we can read and interpret English novels, for example, whose engagement (usually suppressed for the most part) with the West Indies or India, say, is shaped and perhaps even determined

---

[31] Eagleton (ed.), *Raymond Williams*, 154.
[32] Said, *Culture and Imperialism*, 59.

by the specific history of colonization, resistance, and finally native nationalism.[33]

By reading back and forth across the core–periphery divide, a transcendent order emerges which re-establishes the value of 'culture' not as the imposition of power but as the domain of a revitalised humanism, able to generate 'an imaginative, even Utopian vision which reconceives emancipatory (as opposed to confining) theory and performance'.[34]

   This 'emancipatory' performance, however, requires a reader who is trapped neither by the dominating culture of the centre nor the resistant culture of the periphery, a reader who has, in effect, moved beyond the cultures of either core or peripheral nations. Who, though, might represent this post-nationalist 'human community'? Who can escape from the orders of the nation, either core or peripheral, to achieve such contrapuntal elevation? The answer is, quite literally, those who have left their nation behind but not yet acquired a new one: the utopian vision of a new humanity belongs to the migrant and the exile:

> It is no exaggeration to say that liberation as an intellectual mission, born in resistance and opposition to the confinements and ravages of imperialism, has now shifted from the settled, established, and domesticated dynamics of culture to its unhoused, decentred, and exilic energies, energies whose incarnation today is the migrant, and whose consciousness is that of the intellectual and artist in exile, the political figure between the domains, between forms, between homes, and between languages.[35]

By being the inhabitant of both the culture of the periphery and the culture of the centre, the exile and the migrant have the stereoscopic equipment to hear the counterpoints to which the monocultural is necessarily deaf. It is no accident, of course, that *Culture and Imperialism* announces itself in its 'Introduction' as 'an exile's book', written by someone who, by accident, 'belonged to both worlds, without being completely *of* one or the other'.[36]

---

[33] Ibid., 59–60.
[34] Ibid., 337.
[35] Ibid., 403.
[36] Ibid., xxx.

In Said's work, Williams's borderer, standing at the touching point of core and periphery, becomes a Rizal-type traveller, moving back and forth between core and periphery like a continuously circulating telegraphic message. The continuities which link Williams to Said are indicative, as Ajiz Ahmad has pointed out,[37] not of the nature of the formerly colonised cultures, nor of the nature of the colonising cultures – nor, indeed, of the ambiguities of the globalisation process that has planted American 'international' culture in the territory of nation and region – but of the collapse of any ultimate source on which critical values can be founded. The critic's right to judgment is no longer based on values deriving from an argued philosophy or from a cultural tradition: it is based instead on the ability of the critic to stand beyond the boundary of culturally conditioned value systems. Those who are 'purely' inside a culture cannot know that culture properly because they are 'totally' shaped by it: those who would aspire to escape such intellectual determination, therefore, and who would aim at independence of judgment, can only be those who look back at their culture from a point 'beyond' its borders. To see the world from *within* a culture, and through the lens of that culture, is to see the world falsely: to see truly is to find a position outside of one's originating culture without involving submission to the interiority of another culture. In the collapse of the intellectual positions which could call on religious or Marxist or humanist value systems to interrogate contemporary society in terms of a 'truth' which could not simply be assimilated to a local cultural determination, the only position left is that in which the individual is released from the determination of one culture without having (yet) submitted to the determination of another.

It is an argument given a much broader and more radical application in the work of Homi Bhabha, for whom the exile and the migrant make it possible for us not only to comprehend the relation of the core to the periphery but to unravel that relation and reveal that, despite the apparent disparity in power which they represent, they are in fact mirror images of one another. Our understanding of the core–periphery dynamic, Bhabha suggests, has been built on the assumption of the coherence of the core and the fragmentation of the periphery. In the modern world, however – the world of many different migrations and diasporas – the unity of the core is no less disrupted and fractured by the communities of migrants which are the inevitable

---

[37] Ajiz Ahmad, 'The Politics of Literary Postcoloniality', in Padmini Mongia (ed.), *Contemporary Postcolonial Theory: A Reader* (London: Arnold, 1996), 276–93.

consequence of the population flows released by capitalism and imperialism. Instead of a coherent core culture opposing itself to a fragmented periphery, the core comes to be an image-in-reverse of the very fragmentation which was once the weakness of the periphery. Instead of the nation representing a 'community' of shared value, 'community' comes to be the term which identifies those – the 'black community', the 'Asian community', the 'Polish community' – who are *not* part of the nation's traditional self-perception: 'Community is the antagonistic supplement of modernity: in the metropolitan space it is the territory of the minority, threatening the claims of civility; in the transnational world it becomes the border-problem of the diasporic, the migrant, the refugee'.[38] What Williams and Said take to be a primarily individual experience, the experience of continual oscillation between core and periphery, Bhabha transforms into a general cultural condition in which the communities of the exiled undermine the very foundations of the unity of the nation:

> The transnational dimension of cultural transformation – migration, diaspora, displacement, relocation – makes the process of cultural translation a complex form of signification. The natural(ized), unifying discourse of 'nation', 'peoples', or authentic 'folk' tradition, those embedded myths of culture's particularity, cannot be readily referenced. The great, though unsettling, advantage of this position is that it makes you increasingly aware of the construction of culture and the invention of tradition.[39]

The final phrase locates Bhabha's argument within the Gellnerite conception of the nation as a modern fabrication of ancient lineage but it is the 'you' of that sentence which is troubling: who is 'you', and what is 'this position'? As with Williams and Said, 'you' is the border crosser, the disrupter of the myths of the nation, except that instead of being the person who can look in both directions from the border country, or who can contrapuntally play one set of cultural meanings against another, this 'you' has become the representative of a new culture, a previously unknown culture infused with the cultures of both core and periphery. Thus Bhabha applauds that 'range of contemporary critical theories' which 'suggest that it is from those who

38 Homi K. Bhabha, *The Location of Culture* (London: Routledge, 1994), 172.
39 Ibid.

have suffered the sentence of history – subjugation, domination, diaspora, displacement – that we learn our most enduring lessons for living and think-ing'.[40] Those who live lodged as an alien element within a dominant culture, who do not move back and forth *between* cultures but produce a new compos-ite culture of multiple origins, are the models for the modern culture-critic, since 'it is from this hybrid location of cultural value – the transnational as the translational – that the postcolonial intellectual attempts to elaborate a historical and literary project'.[41] Where Williams and Said continued to see cultures as fundamentally separate from one another, and only the individual as in motion between them, Bhabha envisages a world in which cultures dissolve, deliquesce and lose their boundaries: the 'hybrid', produced by the mutual incorporation of previously separate cultures into something distinct from either of its origins is, for Bhabha, the truly creative and, indeed, the culturally procreative location of culture in the modern world.

III   Escaping Essentialism

A key component of Bhabha's conception of the hybrid derives from the theories of Mikhail Bakhtin, the Russian theorist whose works became avail-able in the West in the 1960s and 70s and for whom hybridity is a defining feature of the language of the novel. In answer to the question, 'What is a hybridization?', Bakhtin replies,

> It is a mixture of two social languages within the limits of a single utterance, an encounter, within the arena of an utterance, between two different linguistic consciousnesses, separated from one another by an epoch, by social differentiation or by some other factor.[42]

In a Scottish context, Bakhtin provided for many analysts the theoretical basis for challenging the long-standing criticism that Scotland's literatures have been undermined by the lack of a single and unitary linguistic environ-ment. Instead of being a weakness, the division of Scotland's literary heritage between a variety of languages and cultural traditions can be presented as

---

[40] Ibid.
[41] Ibid., 173.
[42] Mikhail Bakhtin, *The Dialogic Imagination*, ed. Michael Holquist (Austin, TX: University of Texas Press, 1981), 358.

its strength, and interaction between Scotland's languages and dialects produces the kind of creative speech that, in Bakhtin's terms, 'belongs, by its grammatical (syntactic) and compositional markers, to a single speaker, but that actually contains mixed within it two utterances, two speech manners, two styles, two "languages", two semantic and axiological belief systems'.[43] The celebration of Scotland's hybridity, of Scotland's *Bakhtinianism*, became, in the 1980s and 1990s, Scottish criticism's version of Bhabha's reversal of the valuation of the hybrid. The 1993 conference on 'Bakhtin and Scottish Literature' at St Andrews was perhaps the high point of this conjunction, celebrated in Robert Crawford's article on 'Bakhtin and Scotlands' in 1994. Crawford suggests that 'a nation whose culture is under pressure often clings to traditional notions of itself, since change seems to threaten a dissolution of identity' and that Bakhtin provides a conception of 'identity not as fixed, closed, and unchanging, but as formed and reformed through dialogue'.[44] Bakhtinian dialogic identity challenges what Crawford describes as 'notions of an essentialist Scotland', opening the possibility that 'various Scotlands may enter into dialogue', characterised by awareness of 'other tongues', of 'one speaker using and reaccenting elements from another's speech, and of the fructifying impurity' that comes from being aware that 'one's own language is never a single language'.[45]

The literary context of this Bakhtinianism was the rediscovery of Scottish vernacular speech as major mode literary experiment in the work of Tom Leonard, Liz Lochhead, James Kelman and Irvine Welsh (to name but four). There is, Crawford argues, a 'mutual awareness of cultural differences (primarily between various native tongues)' that 'is quite different in Scotland or in Wales from the overall awareness in Britain'. Bakhtin's theories, in other words, are not simply a culturally neutral account of the workings of literary language but an account particularly appropriate to the context of 'linguistic and cultural pluralism' that results in Scotland being 'significantly removed' from the linguistic condition 'of England or of Britain as a whole'.[46] Bakhtin's emphasis on the possibility of there being 'two social languages within the limits of a single utterance' justifies Scottish writing that exploits the interplay between the forms of written English and the orality of Scots speech. Bakhtinian hybridism thus provided a means of *accepting* rather than *regretting*

---

[43] Ibid., 304.

[44] Robert Crawford, 'Bakhtin and Scotlands', *Scotlands*, 1 (1994), 55–65, 57.

[45] Ibid., 60.

[46] Ibid.

the nation's mixed linguistic and cultural history while at the same time shaping a strategy that aligned Scottish writing with those 'postcolonial' cultures of mixed linguistic origins which were producing some of the most theoretically inspiring contemporary writing. If literature in English was underpinned by the need for the Empire to *write back* to the colonising centre,[47] and to resist the homogenising force of the old colonial culture in order to accept its own hybrid nature; if, as Wilson Harris argued, 'hybridity in the present is constantly struggling to free itself from a past which stressed ancestry, and which valued the "pure" over its threatening opposite, the "composite"',[48] then the assumption that Scotland was actually a hybrid allowed critics not only to distance Scottish writing from the 'purity' of English cultural traditions but to make it a major contributor to postcolonial resistance to English cultural imperialism. The 'belatedness' of Scotland's nationalist resistance to English culture, its failure to produce a romantic nationalism in the nineteenth century, could thus be represented as Scotland's prophetic anticipation of the terms of the postcolonial.

It was a parallel that James Kelman asserted in the published version of his acceptance speech for the Booker Prize in 1994 (headlined 'The speech he had no time to make at the Booker ceremony'), in which he situated his own writing as part of the movement 'towards decolonisation and self-determination' based on 'the validity of indigenous culture' and 'the right to defend it in the face of attack'.[49] And it is a parallel emphasised by Michael Gardiner, in one of the few theoretically informed discussions of Scotland and the postcolonial, when he argues that while Scotland was not 'in any sense postcolonial',[50] the reading strategies of postcolonial criticism were, nonetheless, particularly appropriate to Scotland, because those reading strategies 'foreground questions of race and nation' and 'questions of race and nation are already foregrounded in situations where they have been uncleanly and indecisively split between national centres'.[51] For critics such as Gardiner, Scotland, as a place characterised by exactly the kinds of 'ambivalent post-

---

47 See Bill Ashcroft, Gareth Griffiths and Helen Tiffin, *The Empire Writes Back: Theory and Practice in Post-colonial Literature* (London and New York: Routledge, 1989).

48 Quoted in *The Empire Writes Back*, 35–6.

49 *The Sunday Times*, 16 October 1994, 21.

50 Michael Gardiner, 'Democracy and Scottish Postcoloniality', *Scotlands*, 3.2 (1996), 24–41, 36.

51 Ibid., 39.

colonial agencies' that Bhabha defines, may not itself be *post-colonial* (in the sense of having been directly colonised), but its cultural products are so profoundly responsive to *postcolonial* modes of interpretation that it 'is *already* implicated in postcolonial theory'.[52]

The fact that Gardiner focuses on a specifically *textual* notion of the postcolonial, just as Crawford focuses on a narrowly *linguistic* notion of hybridity, emphasises how problematic is Scotland's adoption into the language of the postcolonial hybrid. Both are concerned with those elements of Scotland's *internal* cultural situation that conform to the requirements of hybridity theory: neither is concerned with the fact that Scotland is indeed only too truly *post*-colonial – in the historical sense of having come (almost) to the end of being a colonising nation. Concentration on the nation's *internal* hybridity emphasises what Scotland is assumed to have in common with the colonised of the English speaking world – the interaction of local language or dialect with standard English, the interplay of local mythology and literary tradition with the 'standard' literature of the English cultural imperium – and represses the fact that it was Scottish writers such as Walter Scott from whom the colonised had to learn in order to acquire the imperial language and culture.

The compromises and silences involved in this view of Scottish culture are evident if one compares it with what has been happening in Irish criticism in the same period. Much more easily able to identify their history as the history of the *colonised* and to refuse to accept any direct complicity in the process of colonisation (despite the Union which made Ireland part of the United Kingdom from 1801 till 1922, and despite the significant presence of the Irish in imperial organisations such as the East India Company), Irish critics have, since the 1990s, evolved a breathtaking redefinition of Irish literature as the original postcolonial culture, and as the original embodiment of the Bakhtinian hybridity which will come to characterise postcolonial cultures. In *Inventing Ireland*, for instance, Declan Kiberd describes Oscar Wilde as a writer whose 'identity was dialogic' because 'the other was also the truest friend, since it was from that other that a sense of self was derived'.[53] In Kiberd's construction of the history of Irish literature, Irish precedence in – indeed, Irish prescience of – the dialogic terms of postcolonial literature is what gives it its fundamental significance. The culture which has lived in the margins of

---

[52] Ibid.
[53] Declan Kiberd, *Inventing Ireland* (London: Janathan Cape, 1995), 48.

English literature becomes, ironically, the centre from which all later marginal literatures derive the structure of their identity:

> Davis's description of the Irish as 'a composite race' had been borne out yet again. What had been billed as the Battle of the Two Civilizations was really, and more subtly, the interpenetration of each by the other: and this led to the generation of the new species of man and woman, who felt exalted by rather than ashamed of such hybridity.[54]

This 'mixed' nature of the Irish, as both the earliest victims of colonisation and the 'first modern people to decolonize in the twentieth century', is what makes them 'so representative'.[55] By being the archetypally *hybrid* culture, Ireland is the model from which all the postcolonialisms of the post-Second World War environment of decolonization are copied:

> Were the Irish a hybrid people, as the artists generally claimed, exponents of multiple selfhood and modern authenticity? Or were they a pure, unitary race, dedicated to defending a romantic notion of integrity? These discussions anticipated many others which would be heard across the 'Third World': in Ireland, as elsewhere, artists celebrated the hybridity of the national experience, even as they lamented the underdevelopment which seemed to be found alongside such cultural richness.[56]

With the severity of the Irish experience of colonisation, of course, Scotland cannot compete but, by a further reversal of the role of margin and centre, Robert Crawford has challenged the Irish pre-eminence in the role of postcolonial mentor by presenting Scotland as not only the site of resistance to English cultural hegemony but as the very source of the cultural hegemony that postcoloniality has to resist. If Ireland is the first nation of postcoloniality in its resistance to linguistic and cultural imperialism, then Scotland had already, in the eighteenth century, made a more radical move by seeking to define from the margin what the centre itself ought to represent, by seeking to shape the very nature of English literature in advance of its imposition on the rest of the imperial territory. If English Literature in the

---

[54] Ibid., 162.
[55] Ibid., 5.
[56] Ibid., 7.

modern world is best represented by postcolonial writers and critics, English Literature in its historical origins is no less a product of the peripheries, since it was invented and defined by the Scots, who not only initiated the university discipline of English Literature but were the first, in the words of William Barron, to insist that 'there is nothing, therefore, in the nature of the thing that should hinder the language of England from being written well in India or America'.[57]

Crawford's *The Scottish Invention of English Literature* thus proposes an even more ambitious claim than Kiberd's *Inventing Ireland*, making Scotland the source of both canonical English literature *and* of postcolonial opposition to it. If literature in Ireland can be presented as the outcome of the miscegenation of English Literature and the Celtic imagination, then English *literature* itself is a product of the marriage of Scottish criticism and English writing. English Literature, as originally evolved in Scotland, is a hybrid construction, generating 'heteroglot and multicultural kinds of writing which form not a peripheral exception to but a model for international writing in the English-speaking world in the nineteenth and twentieth centuries'.[58]

Crawford's revisionary account of the history of Scoto-English literature leads to an equally deconstructive account of modern Scotland, in which Bakhtinian hybridity encourages us to resist 'an essentialist position which assumes some sort of unaltering Scotland or Wales or Canada',[59] and to celebrate the emergence of multiple 'Scotland' to replace the Scotland of old:

> So we have Catholic Scotland, which means not only those constituent individuals and areas of Scotland which might be identified as Catholic, but also the views of Scotland which the Catholic community holds, and which are likely, in some ways at least, to differ from those of Islamic Scotland or Protestant Scotland. So we have Gaelic Scotland, whose vision is constructed through and by the Gaelic language, we have Scots Scotland, Urdu-speaking Scotland, English-speaking Scotland. And there are Scotlands beyond our national boundaries, yet which construct their own Scotland that in turn influence our state.[60]

---

[57] Robert Crawford (ed.), *The Scottish Invention of English Literature* (Cambridge: Cambridge University Press, 1998), 15.

[58] Ibid., 6–7.

[59] Ibid., 13.

[60] Crawford, 'Bakhtin and Scotlands', *Scotlands*, 1 (1994), 56–7.

Hybridity allows us to get away 'from the pressure for pure Scottish canons and for one essentialist Scotland that have tended to plague us'.[61] The historical irony of such Bakhtinianism, however, is that it is precisely Scotland's divided and plural past which has 'tended to plague us', rather than any one notion of an 'essentialist' Scotland. Scotland is the exemplar of the *failed* unity of the nation, its whole literary history back to the eighteenth century fraught with doubles, fratricides and outcasts representing the fractured, uncompletable project of national unity. Crawford's litany of modern, multiple Scotlands could be repeated of the Scotland of any period of its history so that hybridity could scarcely have represented a *new* configuration in our understanding of Scottish culture.

Importantly, however, Crawford's use of Scotland's modern linguistic 'hybridity' to celebrate anti-essentialist notions of the 'self' ignores the canons of Scottish culture itself, since a 'dialogic' conception of the self has been a fundamental aspect of Scottish thought at least since the Enlightenment. The notion of the dialogic self is not one which happens to be *accidentally* parallel to the theories of Adam Smith but has been, from Smith's conception of the 'spectatorial self' in *The Theory of Moral Sentiments* (1759)[62] to John Macmurray's conception of the self as 'heterocentric'[63] – that is, directed towards the other – crucial to Scottish conceptions of individual identity. Scottish philosophy has been engaged, since the eighteenth century, in examining and exploring the multiplicities rather than the unity of the self. Crawford points to Charles Taylor's *Sources of the Self: The Making of Modern Identity*[64] as a possibly useful resource for understanding Scottish identity because it incorporates elements of Bakhtin's theories, but to imply that it is only through the ideas of Russian or American intellectuals that one can grasp the real nature of the Scottish condition is to continue Scotland's submission to cultural imperialism, reproducing the inferiorism by which Scotland is always the *object* of an understanding that can only come from outside Scotland itself, never a *subject* capable of understanding itself.

---

[61] Ibid.

[62] Adam Smith, *The Theory of Moral Sentiments,* ed. D. D. Raphael and A. L. Macfie (Indianapolis: Liberty Fund, 1984), 22: 'as nature teaches the spectators to assume the circumstances of the person principally concerned, so she teaches this last in some measure to assume those of the spectators'.

[63] Macmurray, *Persons in Relation*, 158.

[64] Taylor was a Canadian who was at Cambridge with Raymond Williams and was a co-founder of the journal *Universities and Left Review* which, after it merged with the *New Reasoner*, became the *New Left Review*.

IV   Hybridity

In Robert Young's *Colonial Desire: Hybridity in Theory, Culture and Race*, Robert Louis Stevenson's *Strange Case of Dr Jekyll and Mr Hyde* is used as an index of the fear and longing of the West for its repressed, colonised 'Other': 'Many novels of the past have also projected such uncertainty and difference outwards, and concerned with meeting and incorporating the culture of the other, whether of class, ethnicity or sexuality, they often fantasize crossing into it, though rarely so completely as when Dr Jekyll transforms himself into Mr Hyde.'[65] *Jekyll and Hyde* is the fictional transposition of the fear of degeneration that will result from miscegenation between the superior human specimens of white, western culture and any of the lesser races with which it comes into contact in the process of colonisation – of the terror of what Kipling called 'the monstrous hybridism of East and West'.[66] Such fear may have been given mythic expression in the work of an Edinburgh author in the 1880s but it had its roots in the Edinburgh of the 1820s and 1830s, where Robert Knox – famous as a pioneer anatomist and the surgical entrepreneur who engaged the services of grave robbers Burke and Hare – developed theories of racial evolution that were deeply to influence Victorian culture. The different races of humanity were, for Knox, different species, the products of whose cross-breeding – like the product of the mating of a horse and a donkey after which the *mulatos* of the Caribbean were named – would produce a sterile outcome, 'by that physiological law which extinguishes mixed races…and causes the originally more numerous one to predominate, unless supplies be continually drawn from the primitive pure breeds'.[67] The hybrid is the biological equivalent of the 'entropy' of Kelvin and Clerk Maxwell's energy science of the same period, producing a decline in the potential energy of the species. In Stevenson's *Jekyll and Hyde*, Young implies, is reflected the final outcome of mutual self-destruction which flows from sexual contamination between the 'higher' and 'lower' species of humanity.

---

[65] Robert J. C. Young, *Colonial Desire: Hybridity in Theory, Culture and Race* (London and New York: Routledge, 1995), 3.

[66] Quoted in Young, *Colonial Desire*, 3.

[67] Robert Knox, *The Races of Men: A Philosophical Enquiry into the Influence of Race over the Destinies of Nations* and *An Inquiry into the Laws of Human Hybridité* (London: Henry Renshaw, 1862), 48–9. See 503ff. for a summary of Knox's theory of race difference and its relation to hybridity.

The importance of a Scottish thinker like Knox to the development of nineteenth-century theories of race and hybridity suggests a concern some-how embedded in the very nature of Scottish culture. One might see in Knox's genetics of racial purity a response to what Colin Kidd has identified as the problematic nature of Scottish culture's construction of its origins from the early medieval period onwards – the deliberate assertion, despite the many ethnic and cultural elements that went to the making of Scotland, of a single cultural and racial origin, which remained the unique source of Scotland's continuing independent identity:

> The various peoples who composed the emerging kingdom, includ-ing the Dalriadic Scots, Picts, Strathclyde and Galwegian Britons, and Northumbrians, as well as Anglo-Norman and Flemish immigrants, were gradually amalgamated under a Scotic umbrella identity as the *regnum Scottorum*. Although the Scottish regnal line included some Pictish as well as Dalriadic-Scottish kings, the monarchy which was to form the core of Scottish identity was clearly linked to the early history of Dalriada. The Scottish War of Independence firmly established the Scotic identity of the nation. In particular, the Anglo-Scottish propa-ganda warfare of the late thirteenth and early fourteenth centuries linked Scottish independence to the ancient autonomy of the Dalriadic Scots as a means of rebutting the claim derived from the Brutus legend that the Plantagenet monarchy enjoyed suzerainty over the whole island of Britain. The history of the Gaelic Scots had become the national history of all-Scotland; indeed, this particular ethnic past justified the sovereignty of the whole. [68]

Hybridity represents an underlying threat to Scottish culture because any compromise to the purity of its 'Celtic' origins undermines its refusal to accept English suzerainty. At the same time, Scottish development since the Wars of Independence, focused on the Lowlands and on the *Inglis* lan-guage, increasingly marginalised and devalued the very culture – Gaelic – on which the nation's independence was based. The nation was forced to assert the purity of its original Gaelic roots at the same time as distancing itself from the actual Gaelic culture which derived from those roots. According to

---

[68] Colin Kidd, *British Identities before Nationalism: Ethnicity and Nationhood in the Atlantic World, 1600–1800* (Cambridge: Cambridge University Press, 1999), 123–4.

Kidd, Scotland's 'Lowlanders inherited distinctively non-Gaelic manners and speech together with a history whose content was Gaelic. This unusual combination of inherited cultural characteristics formed the identity of Scottish Lowlanders, a people untroubled by an ethnic schizophrenia in large part because political discourse was not driven by an ethnic imperative.'[69] By the nineteenth century, however, such a hybrid identity seemed, to Knox at least, to have become profoundly uncomfortable. The conception of the Scottish past described by Kidd is overthrown by Knox to produce a history in which Celt and Saxon are entirely incompatible races maintaining an unmixed genealogy and separate historical trajectories:

> To me the Caledonian Celt of *Scotland* appears a race as distinct from the Lowland Saxon of the same country, as any two races can possibly be: as negro from American; Hottentot from Caffre; Esquimaux from Saxon…The Caledonian Celtic race, not Scotland, fell at Culloden, never more to rise; the Boyne was the Waterloo of Celtic Ireland. If the French Celt recovers from the terrible disaster of 1815 it will cause my surprise.[70]

The Saxonising of Lowland Scotland, its absolute separation from the *national* inheritance of a Celtic past, required not only that the races of Scotland had never become hybrid, however mixed its culture might sometimes have been, but that the nation itself was redundant. The impure nation had to be dissolved back into the constituents of its racial types, allowing history to be rewritten *not* as the story of the nation but as the story of the pure races who were either genetically predisposed to political liberty (the Saxons) or to submission to tyranny (the Celts).

It is ironic, therefore, that when Kidd, in an earlier book, undertook to explain the failure of Scottish national culture in the eighteenth century, he proposed that its weakness lay precisely in the fact that it was a *hybrid* culture, which, in adopting English values, had produced a hyphenated 'Anglo-British' identity:

> Anglo-Britishness is almost as pervasive in Scotland as in the English heartland of the United Kingdom. This ready acceptance of English

---

[69] Ibid., 140.
[70] Knox, *The Races of Men*, 14–15.

ideals in Scottish political culture is almost certainly connected to an ideological non-occurrence in Scotland's modern history whose causes pose a second historical problem for this study. During the nineteenth century, the Scots, unlike the Irish, Italians, Hungarians, Poles and most of the other historic nations of Europe, who, at that stage, lacked full political autonomy, missed out on the development of a full-blown 'romantic' nationalism.[71]

Scotland's failed *national* identity for Kidd may be based on legal and cultural assimilation to Englishness but its separation of *Anglo*-Scotland from the leftover remnant of the rest of Scotland has precisely the same effect as Knox's Saxonising of the Lowlander in opposition to Celtic Highlanders: Scotland's *national* integrity is destroyed and its future lies in its assimilation to the stronger and purer tradition of its southern neighbour. The hybrid nature of Kidd's conception of Scottishness after the mid-eighteenth century is emphasised by his adoption of a nomenclature used by no Scot of that or any other period:

> It might be objected that this chapter has ignored the rise of North British identity among eighteenth-century Scots. Rather that is exactly what has been described, though termed Anglo-British on the basis of its historical content. North Britishness was a Scottish version of English whig identity, based on a commitment to English constitutional history. North Britishness involved the appropriation of English whig materials in an attempt to construct a more inclusive and properly British whig culture. North Britishness was an aspiration towards full British partici-pation in English liberties; a set of intellectual approaches to the history of English liberty; and a celebration of the growing contribution made by post-Union Scots to the domestic security and imperial expansion of the new British state.[72]

Scotland's Anglo-British identity is incapable of maintaining its own histori-cal vigour, and hybridity, as with Jekyll and Hyde, becomes both Scotland's characteristic feature and its inherent failure, its claim to special significance and the negation of its cultural efficacy in the world.

---

[71] Kidd, *Subverting Scotland's Past*, 1.
[72] Ibid., 214.

Kidd's analyses are only one strand of the long effort by Scottish cultural theorists since the 1960s to make sense of Scotland's 'mongrel' identity. For some, like Kidd, the hyphenated Anglo-Scottish tradition of the Enlightenment is both the great achievement of Scottish culture and the inevitable destroyer of any conceptions of an autonomous and authentic Scottish culture; for others, like Tom Nairn in *The Break-up of Britain*, the deformed offspring of a Scoto-Celtic coupling has generated the 'vast tartan monster' of Scottish popular culture.[73] In all such theories the fundamental weakness of Scotland's cultural history is its hybrid formation, a hybridity that undermines its capacity for reproduction and prophesies its eventual extinction as, in Knoxian terms, it enters terminal degeneration or is assimilated back into one of the pure forms from which it originally derived.

Despite its positive implications, a similar outcome is produced by Homi Bhabha's deployment of 'hybridity' for, as Anthony Easthope has argued,[74] hybridity is, to Bhabha, a fundamentally negative concept, one in which it is much clearer to see what hybridity is being mobilised *against* than what it means in itself. In effect, hybridity is for Bhabha what *différance* is for Derrida, that which destabilises the structured hierarchies of traditional Eurocentric thought. The most important element of the Eurocentric tradition is the nation, whose values are inscribed in and, at the same time, justified by its traditional culture. The hybrid, according to Bhabha, 'destroys this mirror of representation in which cultural knowledge' is usually couched, and 'challenges our sense of the historical identity of culture as a homogenizing, unifying force, authenticated by the originary Past, kept alive in the national tradition of the People'.[75] It is towards the destabilisation of the unitary nation that hybridity is directed, a nation whose 'political unity . . . consists in a continual displacement of its irredeemably plural modern space, bounded by different, even hostile nations, into a signifying space that is archaic and mythical, paradoxically representing the nation's modern territoriality, in the patriotic, atavistic temporality of Traditionalism'.[76] Hybridity undoes the process by

---

[73] Nairn, *The Break-up of Britain*, 162. Hyphenated hybridities proliferate in Nairn's account of the Scottish past, which is home to a 'cultural sub-nationalism', an 'Id-culture' with 'an extraordinary blatant super-patriotism – in effect, a kind of dream-nationalism' (162–3).

[74] Antony Easthope, 'Bhabha, hybridity and identity', *Textual Practice*, 12.2 (1998), 341–8.

[75] Bhabha, *The Location of Culture*, 37.

[76] Ibid., 149.

which the nation turns 'Territory into Tradition,...the People into One', and thereby reveals that 'cultural difference is no longer a problem of "other" people' but a 'question of the otherness of the people-as-one'.[77] The national subject is, by this means, split and fragmented in order to undo 'any supremacist, or nationalist claims to cultural mastery',[78] making it impossible to 'hark back to any "true" national past'.[79] In the backward glance of the hybrid, the national cultures of the European world are simply aspects of that 'invention of tradition' by which ancient authenticity and authority are invoked to justify what are entirely modern and pragmatic constructions of political power.

The value of hybridity, to Bhabha, then, is that it undermines the false unities of the national subject, providing 'counter-narratives of the nation that continually evoke and erase its totalizing boundaries – both actual and conceptual – and disturb those ideological manoeuvres through which "imagined communities" are given essentialist identities'.[80] Even in the most well-established nation, Bhabha sees a conflict between the 'pedagogic' nation – the nation as it is taught to us on the basis of the nation's past – and the 'performative' nation – the nation that discovers itself through its contemporary actions, because those actions will always escape the unifying totality of the pedagogic narrative.[81] As a consequence, 'the liminal figure of the nation-space would ensure that no political ideologies could claim transcendent or metaphysical authority for themselves',[82] since any claim to transcendent or metaphysical authority would inevitably run foul of that 'discursive ambivalence that emerges in the contestation of narrative authority between the pedagogical and the performative'.[83] Nationalism, in other words, is always doomed to failure because its political claim rests on a conception of the nation that invokes an imaginary unity of the past which the nation, in its contemporary actions, will always fracture. In defiance of the nation as imagined by nationalisms, the inhabitants of the nation always live in an 'in-between' condition, in a 'beyond' that represents an 'interstitial

[77] Ibid., 150.
[78] Ibid.
[79] Ibid., 152.
[80] Ibid., 149.
[81] This is itself a renaming of Williams's account of the conflict between 'residual', 'dominant' and 'emergent' structures of feeling, the 'dominant' providing the 'pedagogic' structure of a singular identity which is resisted by the 'performative' development of the 'emergent' culture.
[82] Ibid.
[83] Ibid., 148.

passage between fixed identifications' and 'opens up the possibility of a cultural hybridity that entertains difference without an assumed or imposed hierarchy'.[84]

That nationalism should thus be posed as the antithesis of hybridity is deeply ironic, both in fact and in theory. Hybridity is presented as the alternative to nationalist theories of the unity of the nation, to that notion, as Ernest Renan put it, that the nation is 'a soul, a spiritual principle'.[85] But, as is clear from Robert Young's *Colonial Desire*, conceptions of national and racial purity are themselves a *response* to the perceived problem of mixed cultures: it is the issue of cultural hybridity which leads to the search for cultural purity rather than the reverse. Thus, for Renan, the importance of Irish Celtic culture is – in direct contradiction of recent constructions of Irish culture as fundamentally hybrid – that it represents one of the few cases in the world of cultural purity, where a race remains unmixed with foreign blood. Renan's Celticism, like that of Matthew Arnold (who drew heavily on his views), is a nostalgic escape from a world of the 'hybrid' – the world of the modern British and French nations – to the possibility of the revival of pure cultural and racial forms. Knox's 'scientific' explanation of how any human hybrid will always revert to one or other of its contributory racial forms is equally characteristic of this process: hybridity is the apparently overwhelming condition of the modern world against which a continuing purity has to be defended. National histories, Knox argued, ignored the fact that most nations were constituted of several races and that, as a consequence, nations themselves were fundamentally unstable. The modern nations of the world were mixed entities which would, in time, revert to their pure racial forms and the boundaries of those purified racial territories. Equally, Knox believed that colonialism would always fail, since the colonisers could never sustain their dominion where their racial type would steadily decay through miscegenation with the local population and under the effects of an environment hostile to their racial characteristics. In the great experiment in both colonialism and hybridity that was the United States, Knox expected Anglo-Saxon domination to wane as the strength of the race was sapped by climate and by cross-breeding, just as he expected the Anglo-Saxon domination of South Africa to fail for the same reasons.[86]

---

[84] Ibid., 4.

[85] Ernest Renan, trans. Martin Thom, 'What is a Nation?', in Homi K. Bhabha (ed.), *Nation and Narration* (London: Routledge, 1990), 19.

[86] See Knox, *An Inquiry into the Laws of Human Hybridité*, Ch. III, 532ff.

The nation, for Knox, is the antithesis of the racially and culturally pure just as much as, for Bhabha, the nation is the antithesis of the culturally and sociologically hybrid. Bhabha, in other words, attributes to the nation precisely the characteristics of an originary purity that Knox attributed to race, while Knox attributed to the nation precisely the characteristics of plurality and hybridity that Bhabha denies to it. The contradiction underlines the problem of the nature of the nation as we have inherited it, both from the traditions of nineteenth-century nationalism and from contemporary nation-theory. The notion of the nation as a 'pure' cultural form, each race having its own organic process of development that is ensconced in its national being, is usually attributed to the first stirrings of German nationalism and, in particular, to Johann Gottfried Herder. As Anthony Smith states it – following the arguments of John Breuilly – Herder's account of the nature of the nation rested on the fact that,

> Thought, therefore, like language, was group-specific and unique; so was every other cultural code – dress, architecture, music – in tandem with the society in which it developed. In its original state of nature, as created by God, each nation is both unique and 'authentic'. The task of the nationalist is clear: to restore his or her community to its natural, authentic state … [which] can only be done by realising the cultural nation as a political nation, thereby reintegrating what modernity had sundered.[87]

This interpretation ignores, however, the fact that Herder asserted the importance of cultural authenticity only in the context of resistance to imperialism, and a rejection of the enforced combination of 'native' and 'alien' forms of culture of the kind that would impose French 'liberty' on Germany. For Herder 'natural' culture – which was also national culture – was not distinguished by some original purity but developed precisely by a process of 'grafting' and cross-breeding, by the same kind of cultivation that produces new forms of organic life in the world of nature. What Herder pitched against each other were not the 'pure' and the 'hybrid' but the 'organic' (as that which is cultivated) and the 'artificial' (as that which is

---

[87] Anthony D. Smith, *Nationalism and Modernism: A Critical Survey of Recent Theories of Nations and Nationalism* (London: Routledge, 1998), 87. Smith is paraphrasing John Breuilly's *Nationalism and the State* (Manchester: Manchester University Press, 1993).

imposed), the 'chosen' against the 'enforced'. To attribute to the nation and to nationalisms a fundamental belief in the purity of the nation – whether racial or cultural – may therefore reflect on some of the ideological assertions of particular nationalist movements (and certain imperialisms), but it does not characterise either the founding statements of romantic nationalism or the nature of the nation *per se*. Indeed, for Herder, it is not race or even language which *defines* the nation; in the words of F. M. Barnard, it is,

> (i) the land of the *Volk*'s common heritage
> (ii) the law of the constitution, as a covenant freely entered upon
> (iii) the family or clan origin, fostered and perpetuated by
> (iv) reverence for the forefathers.[88]

The nation is first and foremost an *institutional* environment, one which subsequently finds its unique expression through the language of the people, but which begins in the institutions that are the carriers of a sense of national community. Neither, for Herder, was nationalism the isolationism of the purified: it was the development of the maximum diversity and inter-relationship of human cultures:

> A world of 'organic' nation-States, in which political government in the orthodox sense was replaced by centrally unco-ordinated autonomous *ad hoc* institutions, presupposed, therefore, not only a highly developed sense of social co-operation within individual States, but also an unusual degree of international harmony in the relations between States. Herder visualized the attainment of such national and international conditions as the outcome of the tendency which he held to be inherent in human society no less than in nature: the tendency of diversity towards unity.[89]

The problem with the language of hybridity is that it refuses the continual interchange between diversity and unity as the fundamental dynamic of the nation – the mutual development, as Robert Morrison MacIver or John Macmurray would have put it, of the personal and the communal. There can be no hybrid forms unless there are pure forms, unadulterated species, whose

---

[88]   F. M. Barnard, *Herder's Social and Political Thought: From Enlightenment to Nationalism* (Oxford: Clarendon Press, 1965), 62.

[89]   Ibid., 86.

cross-breeding will produce a mixed and impure outcome. It is only possible to characterise *any* human culture as hybrid if it is possible to characterise *some* human culture as *not* hybrid. But for Bhabha, however true it may be that all cultures are grafted, crossed, mixed, and that there is, therefore, *nothing but* hybridity, the pure has to be insistently reintroduced in order to justify the language of hybridity, and if it cannot be discovered at the level of the 'real nature' of societies then it must be discovered at the level of 'ideology'. Whatever their actual origins or contemporary complications, core cultures (for Bhabha) continue to believe themselves to be, and continue to assert themselves to be, in some sense 'pure'. In maintaining the language of 'hybridity', however, Bhabha does not challenge this presumption on the part of the core culture but effectively underwrites it, because if all cultures are truly hybrid then the term itself becomes redundant. By insisting on the significance of the hybrid – as the form of the culture of the marginal and peripheral – Bhabha also insists on maintaining the very 'purity' against which, in social and political terms, he is in revolt. The problem with Bhabha's theory, and with all theories which assert the positive value of 'hybridity', is that they unavoidably require the continual re-identification and re-assertion of the very 'purity' that they were deployed to overthrow.

V   Global Scotland

In 1844 the Church of Scotland in Canada split into an Established and a Free Church, in a replication of the Disruption in Scotland in the previous year. This long-distance imitation of events in Scotland – for which there was little or no local justification – is indicative of how globalised Scotland had become by the mid-nineteenth century. It had not just exported large numbers of people to those areas of the globe ruled by the British Empire, it had also exported its own national institutions, creating versions of Scottish churches, Scottish universities, Scottish schools, Scottish publications and Scottish industries from long-established places such as Princeton in New Jersey – where John Witherspoon, graduate of Edinburgh University and signatory to the American Declaration of Independence, was responsible for rebuilding the college after the War of Independence in the 1770s – to newly established Dunedin in New Zealand, which was founded in 1848 as a Scottish Free Church settlement. It was in this 'global Scotland' that much of the popular infrastructure of modern Scottish culture was to be established, from the promotion of Burns as a national icon[90] to the celebration of St Andrew's Day as a 'national' event. If the nation was indeed a spiritual and not a material, territorial entity, constituted by what Renan described as its 'rich legacy of memories' and the 'will to perpetuate the value of the heritage that one has received',[91] then Scotland was, in effect, a globalised nation. The fact that it was Scottish science which made possible the laying of the first transatlantic telegraph cable was a symbolic representation of Scotland's ability to inscribe itself across the globe, from the street patterns of Dunedin – named after the streets of Edinburgh's New Town – to 'Bonny Doon' in California, the Scottish context of whose Burnsian nomenclature is continued to this day in the title of its local newspaper, *The Highlander.*

A spiritual, global nation made up of migrants and colonisers, exiles and transient travellers, the territorial nation of its homeland was also increasingly composed of immigrants, first from post-famine Ireland, and then from those countries of Eastern Europe to which Scots had themselves, over many centuries, been migrants. Scotland was both a centre and a periphery – was both peripheral (in the United Kingdom) and yet central (to many communities around the world who identified themselves with it). Scotland was a new kind of nation: at once ancient and rooted and yet, at the same time, modern and dispersed; at once local – and often accused of being parochial – and yet at the very forefront of the technologies which were producing a world as globalised as its people. It was a 'nation' for which 'nation theory', in the twentieth as much as the nineteenth century, had no explanation. If it was an ancient nation, it yet showed no serious symptoms of a desire to reclaim its national political independence; if it was a diaspora, it was a diaspora which did not, like the Jews, lack a homeland and was not, like the Irish, motivated towards the 'freeing' of the homeland from foreign occupation. What made Scotland such a difficult case for theorists of the nation was that already, by the mid-nineteenth century, Scotland was a place prophetic of a world where national identity would be the product not of territorial and cultural unification but of the retroactive and retrospective impact of cultural dispersal; of a froing and toing between centres and peripheries, in which the nation could, at one and the same time, be both a centre – the centre of a cultural iconography and a cultural commitment – and a periphery – an economic and

---

[90] The project for the establishment of a national monument to Burns referred to in earlier chapters was first suggested and funded by Scots in Bombay.

[91] Ernest Renan, 'What is a Nation?', 19.

cultural periphery to those coming from New York, or Toronto, or, indeed, London.

Given the dispersed nature of this nation, it was symbolically appropriate that its achievements in intercontinental telegraphy were rapidly followed by the invention of the telephone. Alexander Graham Bell had only emigrated six years before he first demonstrated his telephone at the Centennial Exhibition in Philadelphia in 1876 but the invention of the telephone was more than just the accidental collision of a talented emigré and a technology which many believed was not only possible but could not be long delayed. Bell was steeped in sound, and steeped in sound because of the particular cultural conditions of Edinburgh in the nineteenth century. As James Clerk Maxwell was to note in a public lecture of 1878,[92] the telephone was not just the creation of Alexander Graham Bell, but of his father, Melville Bell, who had earned his living as an elocution teacher in Edinburgh, training Scottish voices to be able to pronounce themselves in English. (Maxwell made this part of his address in a broad Scots accent and declared that he wished he had taken lessons from Bell when he lived in Edinburgh.) Bell's experience of turning Scots voices into English voices led him to develop a 'universal alphabet', designed to provide a sign-system for all the possible sounds of the human voice, and his family's emigration was in part to promote that alphabet in North America. The expert in *sounding* the universal alphabet was Alexander Graham Bell, who had been called on to give demonstrations of it from a young age, and had used his experience to become an innovative teacher of the deaf. A universal knowledge of the capacities of the voice, a specific knowledge of the failures of the ear – these, rather than technical expertise in electrical circuitry, were the basis of Bell Jr's priority in the creation of the telephone. Indeed, the many lawsuits against his patent emphasised his lack of technical expertise, but none of his competitors had the advantage of coming from a culture obsessed with the sound of the voice and with its social register in the ears of listeners from another culture. The universality of the alphabet designed by the father, on the basis of a local concern with what was expressed by the sound of the voice, became the universality of a means of transmission that would allow voices of very different inflections to communicate with one another. Bell's achievement was the product of a culture which was, because of its concern with accent, and because of its diasporic mobility, inherently concerned with communication-at-a-distance – inherently *telephonic*.

---

[92] Mahon, *The Man who Changed Everything*, 162.

The difference between the telegraph and the telephone is immense. The telegraph produces a universal message which is everywhere the same: it works only by virtue of a code that makes no concession to the local. The telephone, by contrast, transmits difference: the voice—even the voice of Standard English—is always local, is always particular. The telephone joins voice to ear not as placeless universality but as local identification or as distinctive difference. Indeed, in eliminating distance it increases the awareness of difference. The difference between telegraph and telephone, despite the chronological closeness of their invention, is also the difference between two different phases of world capitalism, or two different theoretical perspectives on capitalism's consequences. The telegraph represents the first stage of economic and communicative globalisation: by incorporating the whole of the world into its division of labour, into its communicative system, it intensifies the economic opposition between centre and periphery—rapid communication makes exploitation more efficient—while, at the same time, exporting an 'international' culture which negates the differences *between* centre and periphery. It is what Roland Robertson describes as 'a massive twofold process involving *the interpenetration of the universalization of particularism and the particularization of universalism.*'[93] The cultural distinctions of the peripheries are erased, and difference at an economic level—the acquisitions of the centre at the cost of the periphery—is concealed behind sameness at a cultural level; the message of the centre is inscribed on the culture of the periphery—McDonald's, Starbucks—as though there were a *shared* culture when in fact the passivity of the periphery to such inscription is simply surrender to, or complicity with, an imperious commercial domain in which the periphery has no active role. That mirror-image in which peripheral cultures mimic the culture of the centre—effectively, in our time, their Americanisation or their Westernisation—produces the appearance of a shared rather than a divided world; equally, the postmodern relativism of the metropolitan centre in which all the peripheries are represented—if only as sites of culinary consumption—means that everyone can claim 'we are all marginals now'. From the perspective of the centre, 'globalization has meant a decentering and proliferation of differences',[94] but differences which comply with an underlying

---

[93] Roland Robertson, *Globalization: Social Theory and Global Culture* (London: Sage, 1992), 100.

[94] Frederic Jameson, 'Notes on Globalization as a Philosophical Issue', in Frederic Jameson and Masao Myoshi, *The Cultures of Globalization* (Durham, NC: Duke University Press, 1998), 66.

code which is everywhere the same. Like Wallerstein's world systems theory, however, this version of postmodern diversity is based on an implicit universalism – capitalism not only dominates the world, it is inherently *singular* and everywhere the same. The technical and technological knowledge that drives its development is also universal and singular, mirrored in the spread of English as the *lingua franca* of international technical and commercial communication. These are 'systems' precisely to the extent that they are orderly, and, within the necessarily incomplete limits of current knowledge, predictable in their operation – thus the emergence of 'futures' markets which negotiate between the openness of the future and the predictability of humanity's needs for certain resources. The telegraph is the prophecy of the world of orderly sameness.

The telephone, by contrast, emphasises particularity: it generates localisms which are untranslatable into universal codes; it encourages the expression of difference in the voice and the recognition of difference in the ear. As Claud S. Fischer pointed out, it is often assumed that the telephone destroys the local, that it is 'an antidote to provincialism', but the most extensive research into the topic insists that the impact of the telephone was 'to augment local ties much more than extralocal ones and that calling strengthens localities against homogenizing cultural forces, such as movies and radio'.[95] We treat telephonic communication as a private relationship, as an escape from the rule-bound hierarchies of the external world. Our telephonic voices do not need to bend themselves to the 'rules' of public broadcast, or our texting to the requirements of a public discourse. Thus the localised conventions by which text messages reduce the number of characters in a communication creates an alternative, local language that is the textual equivalent of vernacular speech. The power of the telephonic is that it foregrounds voice over content, feeling over meaning, interaction over statement: the telephonic vernacularises, we might say, what the telegraph standardises, the universality of its technology enabling, rather than destroying, the particularity of the local.

This disjunction reveals the extent to which, in the traditions of Western culture, it is assumed that we can move from the particular to the universal and from the universal to the particular without changing the fundamental categories by which we order and understand our experience: man is made

---

[95] Claud S. Fischer, *America Calling: A Social History of the Telephone to 1940* (Berkeley: University of California Press, 1992), 25. The quotation is from Malcolm Willey and Stuart Rice, *Communication Agencies and Social Life* (New York: McGraw-Hill, 1933).

in God's image; peripheries are all versions of the same core; classes are, in the end, everywhere the same. This easy transition between 'particularity' and 'universality' is, however, little less than an ideology. As Josué V. Harari and David F. Bell put it in their introduction to a selection of the work of Michel Serres,

> Until recently, science had convinced us that in the classification of the spaces of knowledge the local was included in the global, in other words that a path always existed between one local configuration and another, that from local configurations one could always move without break or interruption to a more encompassing global configuration. Clearly this assumption implied a homogeneous space of knowledge ruled entirely by a single scientific or universal truth that guaranteed the validity of the operation of passage. Such a space differs qualitatively from a more complex space in which the passage from one local singularity to another would always require an arduous effort. Rather than a universal truth, in the more complex case one would have a kind of truth that functions only in the context of local pockets, a truth that is always local, distributed haphazardly in a plurality of spaces.[96]

The local, in effect, is the habitation of truths which escape universalisation; the universal an illusion achieved by ignoring the evidence which disrupts and disturbs the applicability of a 'truth' under all conditions. Thus Newtonian physics works, but works only by ignoring its own limitations. As Ian Stewart describes it, 'One of the common idealizations of Newtonian mechanics is to consider hard elastic particles. If two such particles collide, they bounce off at well-determined angles and speeds. But Newton's laws are not enough to fix the outcome of the simultaneous collision of *three* such particles.'[97] This was the problem that Poincaré showed in 1890 could not be solved within Newtonian physics,[98] opening the way to 'chaos theory' – the study of nonlinear systems in which the magnitudes of cause and effect do not correspond as they do in Newtonian physics. This became famous as the 'butterfly

---

[96] Michel Serres, *Hermes: Literature, Science, Philosophy*, ed. Josué V. Harari and David F. Bell (Baltimore: Johns Hopkins University Press, 1982), xiii.

[97] Ian Stewart, *Does God Play Dice? The New Mathematics of Chaos* (Harmondsworth: Penguin, [1989] 1990), 33.

[98] Jules Henri Poincaré, 'Sur le problème des trois corps et les équations de la dynamique', *Acta Mathematica* (1890), 13, 1–270.

wing' account of the forces involved in the production of weather[99] but what chaos theory in general asserts is that far from being the exception, such chaotic systems are in fact a normal state of nature. Michel Serres's presentation of the ways in which classical science emerges through the suppression of the possibility of chaos, by emphasising the constructed repeatability of experiment in time rather than the unrepeatability of happenings in space, presciently suggests how, in the words of N. Katherine Hayles, 'the sciences of chaos make the local/global relation problematic in a way which it was not in older paradigms', because, 'with the onset of chaos, different levels tend to act in different ways, so that locality intrudes itself as a necessary descriptive feature, defeating totalization'.[100] The desire to construct an *order* out of core–periphery relations is just such a totalisation: it is equivalent to the effort to impose a Newtonian model on the weather. The kind of knowledge required to understand the workings of peripheries is one which acknowledges the asymmetry of the global and the local, the universal and the particular; one in which, as Serres argues, 'the global does not necessarily produce a local equivalent, and the local itself contains a law that does not always and everywhere reproduce the global'.[101] That asymmetry is precisely what is represented by the telephone, in which an apparently universal technology encourages the disruptive force of the local as a chaotic productivity which it cannot control. That chaos is where peripheries survive and renew themselves, always resistant to incorporation within the assumed universality of the centre. It is a lesson which the world's dominant powers have failed, painfully failed, to learn since the end of the Second World War.

VI   Taking the Call

In the aftermath of the SNP's victory in the Scottish elections in May 2007, the question with which political journalists were obsessed was, when would the UK Prime Minister, Gordon Brown, telephone the new Scottish First Minister, Alex Salmond, to congratulate him on his victory? Before the election Brown had declared that he would not work with an SNP-led Scottish

---

[99] Edward Lorenz, 'Deterministic Nonperiodic Flow', *Journal of the Atmospheric Sciences*, 20 (1963), 130–41.

[100] N. Katherine Hayles, *Chaos Bound: Orderly Disorder in Contemporary Literature and Science* (Ithaca: Cornell University Press, 1990), 210.

[101] Michel Serres, *Hermes V: Le Passage du nord-ouest* (Paris: Minuit, 1980), 75.

executive; now, the issue was, could the British Prime Minister, who had been appointed as Tony Blair's successor and had not yet submitted himself to the test of an election, speak – on the phone – to the democratically elected leader in Scotland? Why, for the media, was that phone call so symbolically charged? According to Marshall McLuhan, 'the phone is a participant form that demands a partner'.[102] The call would demand partnership between two men whose intentions for Scotland could not have been more divergent. The intimate privacy of the phone call might set at risk their public dispute while at the same time demanding a public answer to the question devolved government could not avoid – whose voice spoke for Scotland, the leader of a minority government in Scotland itself or the leader of the majority party in the UK? By reducing geographic and political distance to the distance between a mouthpiece and an earpiece, by making them, however briefly, intimates in a personal relationship, the telephone call threatened the relationship of centre and margin on which devolution itself was premised. 'The separation of powers had been a technique for restraining action in a centralist structure radiating out to remote margins', McLuhan wrote, but 'in an electronic structure there are, so far as the time and space of this planet are concerned, no margins'.[103] The Brown–Salmond telephone call took on such symbolic import because it revealed how tenuous in a devolved political arrangement was the relationship of centre and margin on which British cultural life had been constructed since the Union, and which devolution had originally been designed to maintain: on the telephone, however, there can 'be dialogue only among centres and among equals',[104] or, perhaps, between the equally peripheral.

[102] McLuhan, *Understanding Media, The Extensions of Man,* 360.
[103] Ibid., 365.
[104] Ibid.

6   Identifying Another Other

I   The Mirror of Otherness

In *Strangers, Gods and Monsters* (2003),[1] Richard Kearney set out on an ambitious exploration and critique of the role of the 'Other' in Western thought, and especially as it has developed in modern 'Continental' theory. Though it is hardly crucial to the overall scope of his argument, England and Ireland are offered as antitheses which represent a defining instance of the process of 'othering':

> Most Western discourses of identity…are predicated upon some unconscious projection of an Other who is not 'us'. At the collective level of politics, this assumes the guise of an elect 'nation' or 'people' defining itself over against an alien adversary. Witness the old enmities between Greek and Barbarian, Gentile and Jew, Crusader and Infidel, Aryan and non-Aryan. Even modern 'civilized' nations have not always been immune to such stigmatizing practices. For example, the English defined themselves for colonial purposes as an elect people (*gens*) over against the Irish considered as a 'non-people' (*de-gens*). And this strategy of separating pure from impure was subsequently employed with regard to the subject races of overseas colonies in Africa, Asia and the Americas. (*SGM*, 72)

England as 'self' and Ireland as 'other' is, in this interpretation, the foundation of all later forms of the colonial construction of the 'other' that stemmed from the impact of British imperialism. In *Inventing Ireland* (1995),[2] Declan Kiberd had made a similar claim:

---

[1]   Richard Kearney, *Strangers, Gods and Monsters: Interpreting Otherness* (London: Routledge, 2003), hereafter cited in the text *SGM*.

[2]   Hereafter cited in the text as *II*.

In centuries to come, English colonizers in India or Africa would impute to the 'Gunga Dins' and 'Fuzzi-Wuzzies' those same traits already attributed to the Irish. The fact that the Irish, like the Indians, can on occasion be extremely cold, polite and calculating was of no great moment, for their official image before the world had been created and consolidated by a far greater power. (*II*, 15)

Such constructions of England and Ireland as mutually defining 'others' have been fundamental to the assertion of the 'postcolonial' significance of modern Irish writing. If Ireland, historically, is the first modern nation to overthrow colonial rule, it is the precursor and predicter of all later such relationships so that the Ireland-England opposition represents a defining version of the opposition of 'self-other', 'same-different' within colonial and postcolonial writing.

This 'universalising' of the Ireland-England opposition is then completed by being read through the lens of Freudian psychology, so that the ways in which 'the national *We* is defined over and against the foreign *Them*' (*SGM*, 65) produces a complex process of mutual exchange in which, Kearney suggests, 'we find creatures of our own repressed unconscious returning to haunt us as phantom "doubles" – *frères ennemis*. The divided self seeks to protect itself against its own inner division by projecting its "other self" onto someone other than itself' (*SGM*, 74). Similarly, Kiberd suggests that 'every great power evolved its own opposite in order to achieve itself' (*II*, 37–8), so that, 'if England and Ireland had never existed, the Irish would have been rather lonely. Each nation badly needed the other, for the purpose of defining itself' (*II*, 2). What this implies, for Kiberd, is that 'Ireland also began to appear to English persons in the guise of their Unconscious', so that 'the *effect* of official policy was the creation of *a secret England called Ireland*' (*II*, 15). Ireland is both England's 'other' and its 'double', its opposite and its unconscious, a repressed sameness masked by the assertion of difference. And the process of repression and projection means that no one is closer to us than those from whom we claim the greatest distance: 'identity', Kiberd suggests, 'was dialogic; the other was also the truest friend, since it was from that other that a sense of self was derived'; thus it was that 'Wilde loved England as genuinely as Goethe loved the French' (*II*, 48). England-Ireland is a fundamental binary of opposites and, at the same time, a comprehensive and all-inclusive totality – 'self' *and* 'other', 'conscious' *and* 'unconscious' – in which each both negates and completes the other.

It is an argument that has significant parallels with Jacques Derrida's auto-biographical meditation on otherness in *Monolingualism of the Other* (1996),[3] in which he presents himself as both 'other' to French – an Algerian Jew who had never visited France – and, at the same time, as a 'self' constituted by the French language; and yet also one for whom, paradoxically, it was met-ropolitan France which was 'other': '*First and foremost*, the monolingualism of the other would be that sovereignty, that law originating from elsewhere, certainly, but also primarily the very language of the Law' (*MO*, 39). From the perspective of the colonial Algerian, the Other is the French Law under which he lives, and yet it is the French language which constitutes the 'self' who is Derrida. Before beginning to speak about oneself, Derrida insists, 'it is necessary to know already in what language *I* is expressed, and I *am* expressed' (*MO*, 28). For Derrida, whatever his ethnic or national origin, the language of the self is French:

> My attachment to the French language takes forms that I sometimes consider 'neurotic'. I feel lost outside the French language. The other languages which, more or less clumsily, I read, decode or sometimes speak, are languages I shall never inhabit... Not only am I lost, fallen, and condemned outside the French language, I have the feeling of honoring or serving all idioms, in a word, of writing the 'most' and the 'best' when I sharpen the resistance of *my* French, the secret 'purity' of my French... its relentless resistance to translation. (*MO*, 56)

At the same time, of course, as always for Derrida, one can never be 'at one' with a language because language precedes its speaker, escapes a writer's or speaker's control, and is always more than (any)one can manage: 'I have only one language and it is not mine; my "own" language is, for me, a language that cannot be assimilated. My language, the only one I hear myself speak and agree to speak, is the language of the other' (*MO*, 25). The colonial subject who is 'other' to the French becomes 'self' *in* French but in doing so reveals that French is always already other to itself, and its speakers inevitably 'other' to it: French may be Derrida's home, but we are all homeless in language.

From the perspective of postcolonial resistance to the imposed languages of imperialism, one might expect such a deconstructive transformation of

---

[3] Jacques Derrida, *Monolingualism of the Other, or, The Prosthesis of Origin*, trans. Patrick Mensah (Stanford, CA: Stanford University Press, [1996] 1998), hereafter cited in the text as *MO*.

self into otherness, otherness into self, to be the opening for a displacement of or resistance to the power of the language of the coloniser. But for Derrida the colonial experience re-inscribes the difference – not to say the *différance* – that separates French from other languages. Indeed, Derrida (however gently) mocks those Algerian-French writers who still claim to have a 'mother' tongue that is not French:

> Abdelkebir Khatibi speaks of his 'mother tongue'. It is certainly not French, but he speaks about it. He speaks about it in another language. In French, precisely. He makes this little secret public. He publishes his words in our language. In order to say of his mother tongue that – and that is a little personal secret! – it has 'lost' him. (*MO*, 35)

Derrida can claim no such 'mother tongue' because French, the language of the 'other' rather than the mother (though it was, in fact, the language of his mother), cannot perform for him the role of a lost origin, of a displaced innocence in which language and world are one. Those who indulge themselves in the 'bilingualism' of writing in French about their lost mother tongue are enacting not so much the defeat of the colonised by the hegemony of the coloniser (however painful that might be) but the metaphoric loss of a language in which one can be 'at home'. Such nostalgia is, of course, for Derrida an illusion: there is no such language, and the (sentimental) bilingualism of the colonised simply encourages the false conception of a language which one might 'inhabit' as though one were truly 'at home' within it. The 'monolingualism of the other' is the condition in which one is forced to confront the ultimate fact that language itself, even a language which is one's only habitation, will always be a place in which one can never be at home. It is therefore the condition, one might say, of Irish people who speak only English – a condition characteristic of many of the most influential Irish writers in the twentieth century and the driving force behind many of their most spectacular achievements.

By deconstructing the supposed opposition between (native) 'mother tongue' and (learned) 'written language', and therefore the supposed superiority ascribed to the 'hybrid' in postcolonial theory, Derrida effectively reinscribes the monolingualism of the French speaker/writer as superior to the bilingualism of the colonised, because it is a condition which is not haunted by a false sense of language's ability to redeem one from otherness by cocooning oneself in 'motherness'. The colonial from the margins for whom French is the first and only language is redeemed from the falsehoods of believing in a language of 'origins' while continuing to be able to make use of the power of cultural tradition to which a language like French gives one access. Whatever the ontological status of all languages in terms of their relationship to the 'real', French remains the language of power, not only the colonial power to which Derrida was subject in Algeria but the power of the cultural capital which that colonial domination made possible. And Derrida has acquired that cultural capital by assimilating himself to what, as an Algerian Jew, was 'other' to him in his childhood: 'one entered French literature only by losing one's accent' (*MO*, 45), he declares, and with all the insistence of a convert acknowledges, 'I cannot bear or admire anything other than pure French' (*MO*, 46). However 'other' French might be, in other words, it is an 'otherness' which reinscribes and retains a perfection – the purity of the medium – to which 'other' languages cannot aspire, and it is the repository of a completeness (even in its necessary incompleteness) which other languages are incapable of matching. However 'other' Derrida might have been to French, however 'other' French might be to itself (as all languages are), nonetheless French remains central to culture-in-general in a way that other languages cannot be: Derrida is the inheritor of a power which, if embraced, is able to turn other into self:

> The obscure chance, my good fortune, a gift for which thanks should be given to goodness knows what archaic power, is that it was always easier for me to bless this destiny. Much easier, more often than not, and even now, to bless than curse it.... Everything I do, especially when I am writing, resembles a game of blindman's buff: the one who is writing, always by hand, even when using machines, holds out his hand like a blind man seeking to touch the one whom he could thank for the gift of a language, for the very words in which he declares himself ready to give thanks. (*MO*, 64)

A 'mother tongue' requires an act of translation between self and other, but for Derrida, French self-other, his own writing has to be so French that it not only resists translation into other languages but resists translation even into 'another such French' (*MO*, 56). The power of powerlessness, the centrality of being marginal: writing – writing as deconstruction – is only made possible by the power of a French which can give access to the tradition of Western culture – the canon by which our identity has been constructed – and, at the

same time, makes possible its deconstruction, its transformation into otherness. Within French, in other words, self and other can endlessly change
places in a series of deconstructive inversions: like Kearney and Kiberd's
'Ireland-England' they form a union (no matter what the politics) in which
each mimics the other, in which 'otherness' is simply a projection of an
unacknowledged version of the self. Algeria-France and Ireland-England are
binaries in which opposition turns out to be sameness, in which otherness
turns out to be selfhood, and – ironically – in which the superior power of the
dominant language is relentlessly reasserted no matter how often its works
are subject to deconstruction, precisely because it makes that deconstruction
possible.

It is for this reason – and against the grain of much Irish criticism – that
Kiberd's hyphenated version of Ireland-England lays so much importance
on the role of the Anglo-Irish, both in Irish literature and in the construction
of modern Irish identity: if Ireland-England are mutually reflecting others,
then it is the Anglo-Irish who most richly fulfil in themselves and in their
writing the 'othering' by which the Irish self comes into existence. They,
more than any other, perform in their very personalities the Ireland-England
dialectic by which both countries are defined: 'The project of inventing a
unitary Ireland is the attempt to achieve at a political level a reconciliation
of opposed qualities which must first be fused in the self' (*II*, 124). As with
Derrida, the colonial 'other' becomes, through being *at one* with the language
of the coloniser, the equal of, if not a projection of, the colonising self. Self
and other exchange places, and exchange cultures in an economy in which
apparent loss (otherness) becomes profit (a new assertion of selfhood), in
which apparent opposition (self-other) becomes unity (self-reflection). The
self-other opposition is transformed – 'After a while, neither the colonizer
nor the colonized stood on their original ground, for both – like Prospero
and Caliban – had been *deterritorialized*' (*II*, 279) – and is revealed to be
fundamentally illusory: self and other, as in Derrida, turn out to be versions
of the same, allowing the colonised to acquire the powers of the coloniser
(pre-eminence in literature in English) without losing their identity as the
colonised.

It is by such an exchange that W. B. Yeats becomes, for Kiberd, the first
truly modern poet, because he is the first decolonising poet to accept his
monolinguality within the imperial language. The consequence is that Yeats's
poetry is a poetry without reference: it is directed at an object – Ireland – which
does not yet exist or, later, when it does exist, does not correspond to the

Ireland that Yeats wishes to address. The outcome is a writing that asserts its nationality through the refusal of past traditions, through the creation of a new style which has no foundation either in the self or in the nation:

> Synge wrote as if he were Adam and this the first day of creation: so did Whitman and so, at times, did Yeats. Their problem was that the worlds which they created existed only as linguistic constructs and solely for the duration of the text. Each artist had, strictly speaking, no subjective self preceding the book as predicate; and so the text had no time other than that of its enunciation. (*II*, 126)

The danger of such a style is that it might not be able to 'reproduce itself in the material world' and 'may become an end in itself' (*II*, 127): formal invention thus becomes a means to 'celebrate the nation's soul, while at the same time insisting that it has yet to be made' (*II*, 128). The nationalist poet of the nation-yet-to-be-invented must work, therefore, with a language which has no content: 'it is possible to fake a nation into existence via a style' (*II*, 308). Poetry (in English) that addresses the (Irish) nation as an 'imagined community' which never, in the past or the future, can have the status of a real referent, thereby prefigures Derrida's 'monolingualism of the other': 'The monolingual of whom I speak speaks a language of which he is *deprived*. The French language is not his. Because he is therefore deprived of *all* language,…he is thrown into absolute translation, a translation without a pole of reference' (*MO*, 61). Yeats's Irishness and his monolingualism, his composite English-Irish self, his nationalism without a national referent, his traditionalism without a nation which shapes his tradition, makes language itself the object of his art, and thus transforms the marginal, nationalist poet into the archetypal 'modernist' poet in whose work we can see a prefiguration of the 'linguistic turn' in modern thought that made deconstruction itself possible.

II   Science's Other

Yeats's status as the first modern poet might be justified, on this account, because his contentless style – resulting from the specific historical circumstance of his 'monolingual otherness' – confirms what came to be, in the very years when Ireland as a nation was turning into a real referent, the basis of the most influential account of the nature of poetry in the modern critical tradition – C. K. Ogden and I. A. Richards's *The Meaning of Meaning* (1923).[4] For Ogden and Richards poetry is language to which 'reference' is irrelevant: poetic language and scientific language are as 'other' as Ireland and England since, for poetry, 'the truth or falsity' of a statement 'matters not at all', for 'provided that the attitude or feeling is evoked the most important function of such language is fulfilled' (*MoM*, 259). Since poetry represents 'the *emotive* use' (*MoM*, 257) of language, we cannot test it by the referential procedures of science; we can test it only by how it fits within the attitudes which structure our response to the world:

> As science frees itself from the emotional outlook, and modern physics is becoming something in connection with which attitudes seem rather *de trop*, so poetry seems about to return to the condition of its greatness, by abandoning the obsession of knowledge and symbolic truth. It is not necessary to know what things are in order to take up fitting attitudes towards them... (*MoM*, 271)

Ogden and Richards's argument is one which has been regularly used to justify Yeats's work since the 1920s. From W. H. Auden's famous elegy which defended the poet from his politics – 'For poetry makes nothing happen/ ...it survives/A way of happening, a mouth'[5] – to deconstructive analyses of Yeats's poems which assume that there is 'no outside to text', Yeats's 'mythologies', his belief in magic and spiritualism, his encounters with ghosts, have been condoned on the basis that they require no 'truth content', that they belong to a different order of discourse from those which can be scientifically or logically tested. Poetry is the expression – or the creation – of the self; science its reference-bound other.

Yeats himself gave credence to the Ogden and Richards view when he suggested that the mythology presented in *A Vision* was designed primarily as 'stylistic arrangements of experience comparable to the cubes in the drawings of Wyndham Lewis',[6] but if one looks back to the science in which

---

[4]   C. K. Ogden and I. A. Richards, *The Meaning of Meaning: A Study of the Influence of Language upon Thought and of the Science of Symbolism* (London: Kegan Paul, 1923), hereafter cited in the text as *MoM*.

[5]   W. H. Auden, *Collected Shorter Poems 1927–57* (London: Faber and Faber, 1966), 142.

[6]   W. B. Yeats, *A Vision* (London: Macmillan, [1925] 1962), 25.

Yeats grew up in the last quarter of the nineteenth century the opposition between Yeats's theories and scientific reality is not as great as this argument would suggest. Take, for instance, what is often considered to be Yeats's most 'anti-modern' statement, his essay on 'Magic', first published in 1900. In it, Yeats makes three key assertions:

> (1) That the borders of our mind are ever shifting and that many minds can flow into one another, as it were, and create or reveal a single mind, a single energy.
>
> (2) That the borders of our memories are as shifting, and that our memories are a part of one great memory, the memory of Nature herself.
>
> (3) That this great mind and great memory can be evoked by symbols.[7]

The apparently arcane nature of such beliefs have led critics to see Yeats as deliberately constructing theories in defiance of contemporary science, and indeed Yeats dramatised himself as determinedly opposed to modern thought: '… if some philosophic idea interested me, I tried to trace it back to its earliest use, believing that there must be a tradition of belief older than any European Church, and founded upon the experience of the world before the modern bias.'[8] But the ideas proposed in 'Magic' are in fact very closely based on theories that were at the forefront of both nineteenth-century theoretical physics and contemporary empirical psychology.

First, the notion of minds that 'flow into one another' can be traced in the most important contribution by a British thinker to the development of the discipline of 'psychology' – James Ward's article on 'Psychology' in the ninth edition of the *Encyclopaedia Britannica* (1871–88). Ward's article is sometimes claimed to initiate the discipline of psychology, and what is distinctive about it (and which also reflects on contemporary philosophical dilemmas) is its effort to find a way of combining the empirical approach of the British tradition (in which everything in the psyche derives from sense experience) with the transcendental theories of German philosophy (for which everything derives from the categories which shape how we experience the world). Ward's response was to treat the mind as a historical and evolutionary phenomenon,

---

[7] W. B. Yeats, 'Magic', *Essays and Introductions* (London: Macmillan, 1961), 28.

[8] Yeats, 'Hodos Chameliontos', *Autobiographies* (London: Macmillan, 1955), 265.

whose content in its contemporary manifestation was produced neither from a Lockean *tabula rasa* nor as the outcome of Kantian transcendental categories. In *Heredity and Memory*, a lecture delivered in 1912, he argued that, 'provided we look at the world from what I would call a spiritualistic and not from the usual naturalistic standpoint, psychology may shew us that the secret of heredity is to be found in the facts of memory'.[9] Memory, for Ward, was not merely personal: the workings the 'law of habit' – that is, the gradual mechanization of action by repetition until it becomes a skill which needs no conscious reflection – makes possible 'the inheritance of the permanent achievements of one generation by the next'.[10] Evolution works by transforming the acquired skills of one generation into bodily and mental capacities that are passed on to succeeding generations. As Ward explains it in his article in the *Encyclopaedia Britannica*,

> What was experienced in the past has become instinct in the present. The descendant has not consciousness of his ancestors' failures when performing by 'an untaught ability' what they slowly and painfully found out. But if we are to attempt to follow the genesis of mind from its earliest dawn it is the primary experience rather than the eventual instinct that we have first of all to keep in view.[11]

Ward proposed that we should think of the whole of humanity as being like a single Lockean individual: it began in a *tabula rasa* but gradually acquired habits which became unconscious abilities. Kantians are, therefore, correct in believing that the mind is structured by categories which have never been part of the (modern) individual's experience; they are wrong in thinking, however, that these are universal and transcendental categories to which the human mind is necessarily subject. Those categories are, rather, the historical and contingent habits produced by memories which are passed on from one generation to another. These psychological inheritances Ward called 'engrams'[12] – memories written into the body and which had been

---

[9] James Ward, *Heredity and Memory, being the Henry Sidgwick Memorial Lecture delivered at Newnham College, 9 November 1912* (Cambridge: Cambridge University Press, 1913), 6.

[10] Ibid., 12.

[11] James Ward, 'Psychology', *Encyclopaedia Britannica*, 9th edn, Vol XX (Edinburgh: A. and C. Black, 1886), 44–5.

[12] Ward attributes the term 'engram' to 'Professor R. Semon of Munich' in *Die*

laid down by the 'sensational' experiences of our distant ancestors. The 'doctrine of the inheritance of acquired characters' is, Ward insists, 'not only Aristotle's and Lamarck's, but Darwin's as well',[13] and Ward accuses evolutionary theorists of having neglected this fact. This 'psychological or mnemic theory of heredity'[14] underpins the notion of an 'organic memory'[15] inherent in the body. In this context, Yeats's 'Great Memory' is no myth: it is that evolutionary deposit which allows each of our minds access to a much greater experience than our own limited lives can accumulate; so, too, his symbols are 'engrams' and his 'Anima Mundi' – the world memory – the storehouse of hereditary capabilities. Yeats's use of 'magic', therefore, disguises in an apparently anti-scientific formulation an account of the mind which is largely consistent with the most advanced empirical psychology at the end of the nineteenth century.

Secondly, critics have regularly pointed to Yeats's rejection of the materialism of Huxley and Tyndall – 'I am very religious, and deprived by Huxley and Tyndall, whom I detested, of the simple-minded religion of my childhood, I had made a new religion, almost an infallible Church of poetic tradition'[16] – as proof of his rejection of contemporary science. Such an argument fails to take account, however, of the fundamental debates going on within nineteenth-century science. Huxley – 'Darwin's bulldog' – may have adopted a thoroughgoing materialism as the consequence of the Darwinian account of evolution but the co-discoverer of the theory of natural selection, Alfred Russel Wallace, had, within seven years of the announcement of that theory, declared that natural selection could *not* account for the higher faculties of human beings and that these were produced by an alternative spiritual influence. Wallace's theories in effect paved the way for the kind of panpsychism that Madame Blavatsky was to popularise and that underpinned Yeats's own experiments in spiritualism. That this dualistic theory of humanity's relationship to evolution was not simply Wallace's individual eccentricity is clear from the fact that Tyndall's materialism was equally opposed by William Thomson

---

Mneme als erhaltendes Prinzip im Wechsel des organischen Gechehens (1908), though the notion of 'organic memory' he attributes to 'Professor Ewald Hering in a lecture, *Concerning Memory as a general function of Organized Matter*, delivered at Vienna in 1870' (*Heredity and Memory*, 27).

[13] Ibid., 20.
[14] Ibid., 42–3.
[15] Ibid., 43.
[16] W. B. Yeats, *Autobiographies*, 116.

(later Lord Kelvin) and Peter Guthrie Tait, co-authors of the *Treatise on Natural Philosophy* (1867), which was, as we have seen, designed to overthrow the accepted Newtonian physics of force and replace it with a physics of energy. To Thomson and Tait, the issue was not simply a matter of rejecting Tyndall's challenge to the status of religion, but of Tyndall's failure to realise that his 'materialism' had been made scientifically redundant by their science of energy.

That this 'energy' was fundamentally spiritual, however, was, as we saw in Chapter 2, the argument of Tait and Stewart's *The Unseen Universe*.[17] 'energy', they stated, 'has as much claim to be regarded as an objective reality as matter itself [for] while matter is always the same, though it may be masked in various combinations, energy is constantly changing the form in which it presents itself.' (*UU*, 115). Agreeing with Wallace, they believed that mind-energy indicated 'that there exists now an invisible order of things intimately connected with the present, and capable of acting energetically upon it – for, in truth, the energy of the present system is to be looked upon as originally derived from the invisible universe, while the forces which give rise to the transmutations of energy probably take their origin in the same region' (*UU*, 199). The consequence is a psychical universe running parallel to, and gradually supplanting, the 'physical' one, and from such a physics could be derived a theoretical justification for the immortality of individual personality because, 'thought conceived to affect the matter of another universe simultaneously with this may explain a future state' (*UU*, 199–200). These were the arguments not of mystical cranks but, as in case of Wallace, of serious scientists. Yeats's 'spiritualism' would, in the 1870s and 80s, not have been 'other' to science but at one with some of science's own most radical and innovative speculations about the nature of reality. If the 'reference' of such scientific theories has since proved illusory – like the 'ether' which was assumed to allow action at a distance – that does not mean that they were not *intended* referentially, and the parallel between Yeats's poetic reference to similar entities would bring Yeats's poetry – at least in its historical context – much closer to science than the Ogden-Richards view would imply.

Thirdly, one of the consequences of this revision of Newtonian physics was a re-envisaging of the nature of the atom by Thomson and Tait's brilliant junior colleague, James Clerk Maxwell: developing Kelvin's theories on energy, Maxwell presented the atom not as a solid, fixed particle but as a

---

[17]　Tait and Stewart, *The Unseen Universe*, hereafter cited in the text as *UU*.

vortex of liquid energy, with electricity as the output of these vortices as they spin in opposite directions, generating flows of energy between them:

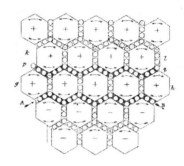

Clerk Maxwell's diagrammatic representation of the atom as vortex (left) and of the interaction of atoms as intertwining vortices generating energy (right)

Ezra Pound's 'vorticism' of the 1910s gets its metaphorical energy from Maxwell's reconstruction of the universe's energy as produced from these vortices, and their structure is replicated in Yeats's own theory of the 'gyre'. However individualistic Yeats's theories may seem, they had in fact much in common with contemporary scientific speculation.

The Unseen Universe was one of the most successful books published by Macmillan (who became Yeats's publisher), and given its prominence in late-nineteenth-century discussions of the spiritual it is unlikely that he had not encountered it. However, he was certainly familiar with another Macmillan publication, J. G. Frazer's *The Golden Bough* (first published in 1890). Frazer had attended Thomson's lectures at Glasgow as an undergraduate, taking from them, 'a conception of the physical universe as regulated by exact and absolutely unvarying laws of nature expressible in mathematical formulas', and that conception he declared to have been 'a settled principle of my thought ever since'.[18] It was then James Ward who encouraged Frazer towards anthropology (Frazer was, as we saw in Chapter 2 a classicist) and it was Ward's psychological theories which underpinned Frazer's analysis of the primitive mind. A key element in Ward's psychology was its incorporation of the theory of the 'association of ideas', an account of the mind that had been given renewed impetus as a result of the work of John Stuart Mill and Alexander Bain. Their associationist explanation of the mind was to provide the basis of the new and influential evolutionary psychology of Herbert Spencer. For Frazer, magic

---

[18] Robert Ackerman, *J. G. Frazer: His Life and Work* (Cambridge: Cambridge University Press, [1987] 1990), 14.

could be explained scientifically as a product of the association of ideas, while
the theory of psychological association gave Yeats an empirical basis for the
operation of spiritual powers: 'All sounds, all colours, all forms,' he declared in
1900, 'either because of their pre-ordained energies or because of long association, evoke indefinable and yet precise emotions, or, as I prefer to think, call
down among us certain disembodied powers, whose footsteps over our hearts
we call emotions'.[19] Yeats and Frazer, coming from opposite directions, are
both engaged in translating magic into psychological association, association
into magic: 'long association' becomes for Yeats a 'disembodied power' while,
for Frazer, homeopathic and contagious magic are nothing else but 'different
misapplications of the association of ideas'.[20]

Yeats's engagement with Frazer, and with the scientific contexts of
The Golden Bough, was not, however, simply an engagement with a science
which was far from poetry's 'other', it was an engagement with the specifically *Scottish* thought of the late nineteenth century, since *The Golden Bough*
was, as we have seen, one of the most distinctive products of a group of
Scottish thinkers[21] which included John Ferguson McLennan and William
Robertson Smith, as well as Kelvin and Maxwell. The ways in which Yeats's
thought shadows the work of these thinkers confirms what I have argued
elsewhere:[22] that far from Ireland-England being 'self' and 'other' in Yeats's
'Anglo-Irish' project, Scotland played a crucial role, representing 'another
other', one that offered an alternative way of envisaging both the Irish past
and an Irish future. Scotland's status in Yeats's conception is clear from his
account of the Scottish writer with whom he might seem to have the least in
common – Thomas Carlyle:

> When once a country has given perfect expression to itself in litera-
> ture, has carried to maturity its literary tradition, its writers, no matter
> what they write of, carry its influence about with them, just as Carlyle
> remained a Scotsman when he wrote of German kings or French rev-
> olutionists, and Shakespeare an Elizabethan Englishman when he told

---

[19] Yeats, 'The Symbolism of Poetry', *Essays and Introductions*, 156–7.
[20] Frazer, *Golden Bough* (1922 edn), 12.
[21] For an account of this group, see my 'Introduction' to the Canongate Classics
     edition of Frazer's *The Golden Bough* (Edinburgh: Canongate, 2004).
[22] 'National Literature and Cultural Capital in Scotland and Ireland', Liam
     McIlvanney and Ray Ryan (eds), *Ireland and Scotland: Culture and Society*
     (Dublin: Four Courts Press, 2005).

of Coriolanus or of Cressida. Englishmen and Scotsmen forget how much they owe to mature traditions of all kinds – traditions of feeling, traditions of thought, traditions of expression – for they have never dreamed of a life without these things. They write or paint or think or feel, and believe they do so to please no taste but their own, while in reality they obey rules and instincts which have been accumulating for centuries; their wine of life has been mellowed in ancient cellars, and they see but the ruby light in the glass.[23]

Carlyle, as much as Shakespeare, is for Yeats the inheritor of 'traditions of feeling, traditions of thought, traditions of expression' which 'have been accumulating for centuries', and the fact of such an independent culture existing and prospering on England's doorstep is what makes the Ireland he dreams of creating a real possibility. In Scotland Yeats identified another other to England, one whose different 'otherness' interrupts the self-other binary of the England-Ireland to which Kearney and Kiberd attempt to return Irish writing.

III   Another Self

If there is indeed, for Yeats, the possibility of identifying 'another other' in a Scotland which is differently antithetical to England, what does this imply about the theories within which Kiberd and Kearney construct their Ireland-England binary? It is notable that Scotland is not mentioned in the index of Kiberd's book: Walter Scott receives one passing reference as does a 'Celtic' David Hume; Burns receives none and there is no mention of the Fiona Macleod with whom Yeats was initially besotted in the 1890s. Ireland-England, it would appear, exhausts all possible relations, reducing even American developments to mere imitations of the hyphenated totality in which 'Irish experience seems to anticipate that of the emerging nation-states of the so-called "Third World"' (*II*, 4). Neither self nor other, Scotland becomes invisible even when Scottish traditions are being lived – as in the poetry of the Ulster Weavers – on the island of Ireland, and even when one of the political and intellectual heroes of Kiberd's narrative – James Connolly – was

[23] 'Irish National Literature, I: from Callanan to Carleton', *The Bookman*, July 1895, in John P. Frayne (ed.), *Uncollected Prose by W. B. Yeats, 1, First Reviews and Articles 1886–1896* (London: Macmillan, 1970), 360.

born and brought up in Scotland.[24] Instead of Derrida's 'monolingualism of the other', Kiberd's account is a 'monoculism of the other' in which Ireland stands as representative of all others over against whom the imperial centre is defined.

For Kearney, such binarism is inscribed in all accounts of otherness because they derive from fundamental structures which have informed the whole tradition of Western thought: 'ever since Western thought equated the Good with notions of self-identity and sameness, the experience of evil has often been linked with notions of exteriority. Almost invariably, otherness was considered in terms of an estrangement of the pure unity of the soul' (*SGM*, 65). If estrangement of an original 'pure unity' means that the Other was once a portion of the Self, it also means that the Other is necessarily as singular as the self-identity from which it emerged. It is a partition of the world which is replicated in that founding move of the modern Western tradition, the Cartesian *cogito*, in which the world is divided between the 'I think' and everything else over against which it is counterposed. As Kearney notes,

> This definition of alterity in relation to sameness is revisited by the modern movement in phenomenology … In *The Phenomenology of Spirit*, Hegel historicizes the problem in terms of the master-slave dialectic. Here, he argues, the self only expresses itself as a sovereign subject in so far as it struggles with, and is eventually recognized by, its Other (*das Andere*). But it is Husserl who brings the phenomenological dialectic to its logical conclusion in the Fifth *Cartesian Meditation* when he claims that the other is never absolutely alien but is always and everywhere recognized as other precisely as other-than-me, that is, by analogy and appresentation. (*SGM*, 16)

It is an opposition that was to be reinforced in Sartre's philosophy of the nothingness of the self, since the self is an act of negation which ensures

---

[24] Connolly's Scottish origins are mentioned only indirectly: 'Even more depressing was the fact that an otherwise advanced thinker such as James Connolly did not develop a generalized anti-racist or anti-imperialist philosophy. Immediate realities in Scotland and Ireland were just too pressing' (*II*, 259). The fact that Scotland is introduced only in the context of *failings* in Connolly's otherwise laudable ideology is significant, as is the reference to the fraudulent tradition of kilt-wearing (*II*, 151).

that whatever the self is confronted with is simply *not-self*: 'the Other is the one who is *not-oneself*.'[25]

For Kearney, this absolute opposition of 'self' and 'other' is the 'problematic' which 'informs...the entire metaphysical paradigm of self-and-other running from Plato and Aristotle to Hegel and the modern philosophy of consciousness' (*SGM*,16), and his own work represents an effort to find a way through the 'enigma of the other' as presented in 'religious anthropology (Eliade, Girard, Lévi-Strauss) and psychoanalysis (Freud/Lacan/Kristeva), and running on into deconstruction (Derrida/Lyotard/Caputo), phenomenology (Husserl/Heidegger/Levinas) and hermeneutics (Gadamer/Greisch/Ricoeur)' (*SGM*, 11–12). Kearney believes that we can escape the oppositions that haunt the Western tradition if we give primacy to the fact that 'the human self has a narrative identity based on the multiple stories it recounts and receives from others' (*SGM*, 231), and by foregrounding the fact that 'we are narrative beings because the shortest road from self to self is through the other' (*SGM*, 231). As a result, he insists, there are 'certain narrative footbridges which may help us negotiate both the dizzy peaks of alterity and the subterranean chasms of abjection' (*SGM*, 231) and thereby 'make us more hospitable to strangers, gods and monsters without succumbing to mystique or madness' (*SGM*, 18).

If we start, however, on this particular ground, and within this particular tradition, the binary of the self-other opposition is always going to be waiting at the other end of the bridge, whichever end one decides to make for – since, as Derrida insists, every route 'is repetition, return, reversibility, iterability, the possible reiteration of the itinerary' (*MO*, 58). The metaphysics of the self-other opposition as invoked by this tradition – even when presented as an *anti*-metaphysics – is so insistent and so wide-ranging that it makes Kearney's project of being 'able to critically discriminate between different kinds of otherness' (*SGM*, 67) absolutely impossible. However much he may insist on the importance of finding a way 'between the *logos* of the One and the *anti-logos* of the Other' in order to discover a 'practice of dialogue between self and other' (*SGM*, 18), he finds it impossible to escape from these extremes except by mere assertion: 'It simply doesn't have to be like this. All or nothing' (*SGM*, 187). There is no *theoretical* way out of the same-other dialectic, only a refusal to submit to its consequences by asserting that 'the ultimate

---

[25] William Ralph Schroeder, *Sartre and his Predecessors: The Self and the Other* (London: Routledge and Kegan Paul, 1984), 239.

response (though by no means solution) offered by practical understanding is to *act against evil*' because 'action turns our understanding towards the future in view of a *task* to be accomplished' (*SGM*, 101), transferring 'the aporia of evil from the sphere of theory (*theoria*) – proper to the exact knowledge criteria of logic, science and speculative metaphysics – to the sphere of a more practical art of understanding (*techne/praxis*)' (*SGM*, 100–1).

Kearney's choice of the so-called 'Continental' tradition as both the ultimate expression of the (post)modern condition and the context for developing his own theoretical position is, of course, itself part of a 'binary' which pits the English language tradition of modern philosophy (the 'Anglo-American' tradition) against the 'Continental' tradition: they are, in effect, philosophical 'others'. And Kearney's choice of where he locates himself, as an Irish philosopher, just like Kiberd's situating of his criticism within a postcolonial framework, is the expression of a resistance to 'English' hegemony. Continental theory and postcolonial criticism define philosophy and literature in Ireland as not-England. But if, as I have suggested in relation to Yeats, Scotland might represent for Ireland another other, then in the Scottish philosophical tradition there might be also be another other, an alternative starting point for confronting Kearney's dilemma of how 'to acknowledge a difference between self and other without separating them so schismatically that *no* relation at all is possible' (*SGM*, 9). In his introduction, Kearney quotes approvingly the words of Julia Kristeva, that today 'the media propagate the death instinct' and that 'nationalisms, like fundamentalisms, are screens in front of this violence, fragile screens, see-through screens, because they only displace that hatred, sending it to the other' (*SGM*, 8–9). The 'death' instinct, of course, is a fundamental element of Freud's later psychology, but it is one which was the target of an influential book – *The Origins of Love and Hate*[26] – published in 1935 by Scottish psychologist Ian D. Suttie, in which he disputed Freud's account of the mind because it 'postulates conflict, struggle and repression as inevitable and indeed as the welder of society' (*OLH*, 116).

The inadequacy of Freud's theories, Suttie argued, derived from his insistence on 'a primary, independent, instinct for destruction – a hatred stimulated from within like hunger, and having no reference to external provocation or purpose' (*OLH*, 198), which results in a view of society as

---

[26] Ian D. Suttie, *The Origins of Love and Hate* (London: Kegan Paul, 1935), hereafter cited in the text as *OLH*. This is a tradition which has been analysed by Gavin Miller; see his *R. D. Laing* (Edinburgh: Edinburgh Review, 2004).

'absolutely broken up into individuals each seeking its own ends exclusively' (*OLH*, 239). Suttie finds it difficult to believe that 'any successful species can be born with useless and even self-conflicting dispositions' (*OLH*, 238) and proposes an alternative: 'The important thing to remember, however, is that consciousness of *self* as isolated from and independent of the rest of the world is probably associated with some measure, however trivial, of anxiety and resentment from the very beginning, but on the other hand (in my view, as against Freud's) it is also associated with loving feelings towards others as well as with angry claims upon them' (*OLH*, 27). For Suttie, love is the foundation of identity because he regards love 'as social rather than sexual in its biological function, as derived from the self-preservative instincts not the genital appetite', so that sociability is fundamental to the individual psyche – rather than 'an aim inhibited sexuality' – and culture, the defining context of human life, is 'derived from love as a supplementary mode of companionship (to love) and not as a cryptic form of sexual gratification' (*OLH*, 36).

Where the tradition of Western thought has begun from the self as thinker, to which the world is other, Suttie begins from a situation in which 'the bodily self acquires a value over and above its capacity for yielding sensory satisfactions *in so far as it is the object of the mother's interest*, and the first plaything *shared* with her' (*OLH*, 37). We begin, in other words, as the 'other', and become a 'self' through *sharing*: the 'self' does not project 'the other' from its own autonomous individuality, but learns its selfhood through sharing its otherness. The failure of Freudian psychology lies in its 'obstinate determination to leave out of account social situations and hypothetical social motives. They wish to account for the whole process of mental development in terms of what goes on within the individual mind itself' (*OLH*, 40). Freudians fail to acknowledge the fundamentally *social* nature from which individual experience begins.

> I consider that the germ of goodness or of love is in the individual (of every species which has evolved a nurtured infancy) from the very beginning, and that our traditional method of upbringing frustrates this spontaneous benevolence and substitutes a 'guilt-anxiety' morality for natural goodness. I consider further that the traditional attitude is so deeply ingrained in Freud and Adler's outlook on life that they cannot admit the existence of love as other than a prudent avoidance of the anger of others. (*OLH*, 52)

We do not begin in self-assertion: the baby 'not only starts life with a benevolent attitude, but the Need-to-Give continues as a dominant motive throughout life' (*OLH*, 53); our psychoses are not the product of the frustration of sexual instincts but of the frustration of our need to love, and be loved, so that psychotherapy in practice is 'nothing but the *overcoming of the barriers to loving and feeling oneself loved*, and not as the removal of fear-imposed inhibitions to the expression of innate, anti-social, egoistic and sensual desires' (*OLH*, 53–4).[27]

Suttie was one of several Scottish psychologists who challenged Freudian theory, a challenge climaxing in the 1960s and 70s in the anti-psychiatry of R. D. Laing. Laing's most famous book was *The Divided Self*,[28] a phrase invoked in Kearney's discussion of Julia Kristeva: 'the stranger is neither a race nor a nation…we are our own strangers–we are divided selves' (*SGM*, 76). For Kristeva, the 'divided self' 'expresses the universal experience of a deep unconscious malaise with "others" arising from our repressed rapport with the internally housed "primal scene" that informs our psyche' (*SGM*, 76). That 'primal scene'–Freud's account of the original killing of the father by his sons as the origin of the Oedipus complex–is, for the Scottish tradition, a fiction, the outcome of Freud's refusal to engage with human beings as social, and, therefore, as caring beings: as Suttie summarises it, Freudian psychology 'ignores the mother for the father'; 'denies tenderness–filial and parental–and universalises sex'; 'interprets socialization in man as *merely* the overcoming of *sex* jealousy by coercion and fear'; 'regards hate as spontaneous, ineradicable appetite and all motive as egoistic' (*OLH*, 235). By putting the mother back into the story of the psyche, the primal scene is transformed from one of violence and destruction to one of love and mutuality. Kearney's discussion is focused on 'Strangers, Gods and Monsters' because these are terrifying versions of an Other from which one is estranged, but for Suttie the real monsters are the creations of modern psychology–'these "mythical monsters", independent individuals' (*OLH*, 112)–who can be believed to exist only in the conceptions of theorists who ignore the fact that human life is characterised from its beginning (and in its ending) by dependency on one

[27] This had been the anti-Darwinian argument of *Evolution* (London: Williams and Norgate, 1911) by Patrick Geddes and J. Arthur Thomson, which argued that the success of human beings as evolutionary creatures was their capacity for co-operation based on love.
[28] R. D. Laing, *The Divided Self* (Harmondsworth: Penguin, [1959] 1990), hereafter cited in the text as *DS*.

another. As the Scottish philosopher John Macmurray put it[29] in developing Suttie's ideas, 'the most obvious fact about the human infant is [its] total helplessness' (*PR*, 47): it 'is, in fact, "adapted" to being unadapted, "adapted" to complete dependence on an adult human being' (*PR*, 48). The primal scene is that a human child 'is made to be cared for... born into a love-relationship which is inherently personal' (*PR*, 48). As a consequence the Other is, for Macmurray, the very antithesis of the alien and the monstrous:

> We have seen that the form of the child's experience is dependence on a personal Other; and that this form of experience is never outgrown, but provides the ground plan of all personal experience, which is constituted from start to finish by relation to the Other and communication with the Other. (*PR*, 154)

The self, for Macmurray, is not the isolated ego of Cartesian or Sartrean tradition: the self is a person in relation with others. Neither is the self the narrative self that Kearney invokes: the self is an *agent* and it is precisely through its agency in the world that it is in contact with the other:

> in acting I am not 'over against' an object, but in contact with the Other. In acting I meet the Other, as support and resistance to my action, and in this meeting lies my existence. Consequently, I am aware of the Other, and of myself as dependent upon and limited by the Other. This awareness is knowledge, for it is awareness of the existence of the Other and of my own existence in dynamic relation with the Other. (*PR*, 209)

Starting from the self-reflective 'I', the thinking self, the Western tradition has projected the 'Other' as unknowable and therefore alien, and in so doing has created the Other as monstrous: Suttie, Macmurray and Laing, on the other hand, start from the 'I and you' as the fundamental structure of experience. As Laing puts it in attacking traditional Freudian psychology:

> Instead of the original bond of *I* and *You*, we take a single man in isolation and conceptualize his various aspects into 'the ego', 'the superego', and 'the id'. The other becomes either an internal or external

---

[29] Macmurray, *Persons in Relation*, hereafter cited in the text as *PR*. Macmurray acknowledges the influence of Suttie's work, *PR*, 45.

object or fusion of both. How can we speak in any way adequately of the relationship between me and you in terms of interaction of one mental apparatus with another? (*DS*, 19)

'The science of persons', Laing argues, 'is the study of human beings that begins from a relationship with the other as person and proceeds to an account of the other still as person' (*DS*, 21). The phrase 'divided self', which Laing took from Macmurray, has a very different significance in this context than in Kristeva's (or Kearney's) usage: it is the self which seeks autonomy and independence, the self of philosophical self-consciousness, that is sick; the healthy self knows both its dependence on the other and the necessary inner division that comes from being, in part, a part of the other: 'It is out of the earliest loving bonds with the mother that the infant develops the beginnings of being-for-itself. It is in and through these bonds that the mother "mediates" the world to the infant in the first place' (*DS*, 190). The individual self, as a product of (m)othering, always remains dependent on the other and, in its development, on many another, thereby beginning to answer Kearney's quandary about how we can avoid treating 'the other as so exterior or estranged that it becomes utterly alien'.

IV   Another Other

For Richard Kearney, the problem with which the philosophical tradition leaves us is that of finding a passage from the outcomes of 'speculative theory' to our need to 'act against evil' (*SGM*, 101), an act for which 'speculative theory' can give us no valid justification. In the end, Kearney offers us as a middle way the possibility that we can 'muddle through' with 'a certain judicious mix of phronetic understanding, narrative imagination and hermeneutic' (*SGM*, 187). From the perspective of the Scottish tradition that I have been outlining, however, Kearney's dilemma is unresolvable precisely because it begins from the priority of 'speculative theory'. For John Macmurray, on the other hand, 'the Self exists only as an Agent' and, therefore, 'the Self exists only in dynamic relation with the Other' (*PR*, 17). If 'speculative theory' is a *consequence* of action rather than its foundation, if engagement with the other has priority over the effort to recognise the other, then it may be possible to construct an alternative 'middle way' which is not simply a 'muddle way'.

In this sense, the Scottish traditions I have been exploring do not constitute merely an alternative to or a supplement to the Ireland-England binary – or, indeed, to the opposition between Anglo-American and Continental philosophy – but a critique of the very bases on which the self-other dialectic has been constructed within those traditions. The practical task of how we can encounter and deal ethically with the Other, of how we can resist reducing the Other to the irredeemably alien, is given philosophical and psychological grounding by challenging the fundamental isolation of the self-as-thinker from which the Cartesian tradition begins. The argument of this Scottish tradition is that we do not encounter the world as alien and subsequently try to find a way of relating to it: 'the personal conception of the world', as Macmurray puts it, 'is not the result of personifying what is first recognized as non-personal' (*PR*, 221). We begin as other-related creatures and thus 'the personal conception of the Other is original' (*PR*, 221), in the sense that it has an existential and logical priority over all other forms of understanding. Since 'the Self is constituted by its relation to the Other' (*PR*, 17) there can be no isolated 'ego' to which the Other is inherently alien: it is only through the Other that the Self exists, and the most important component of the Other is 'other persons': 'Persons, therefore, are constituted by their mutual relation to one another' (*PR*, 24). Otherness in the personal world is, in other words, always plural: if it is the case that '"I" exist as only one element in a complex "You and I"', the 'you' in that 'you and I' is not 'you' as in the 'I-Thou' of Buber's version of our relation with God. That can only ever be an address to one unique individual, whereas the 'I-You' of the infant's relationship with the mother is an opening out on to a multiplicity of 'I-you' relationships: 'I exist as an individual only in a personal relation to other individuals' (*PR*, 28). The binary of Self and Other is a linguistic illusion: in the real world there are only 'selves and others', selves whose very being and identity as selves is defined in their relations with multiple others.

In relation to the earlier parts of this chapter, three things follow: first, the world as revealed by science from which the young Yeats recoiled, may be threatening and disturbing but it is not the *antithesis* of our ordinary human experience: science is a subtraction from the world of the personal, a deliberate reduction of the world of the personal by the elimination of what is defining of persons – their intentions. For science the world is a place in which 'everything in it *happens*; nothing is ever *done*; and none of its constituent elements is capable of reflection' (*PR*, 219). Science treats the world as though it were without intentions but can do so only on the basis of the unacknowledged intention of the scientist. From this perspective, we can see in Yeats's grappling with the science of his time (as, indeed, in the speculative work of scientists like Tait and Stewart) an effort to bring the scientific and the personal back into relation, and by resisting the reduction of the personal to the scientific to give the personal again priority in our encounter with the Other.

Secondly, the historical perspectives opened up by the anthropological theories that lie behind *The Golden Bough* provide an alternative to the Freudian account of why human beings are as they are. In this version, Strangers, Gods and Monsters are not symbols of the threat of the unreachably alien but of the potential of love to regain the relationship with the other on which all selfhood was originally based. It is a perspective whose evolutionary significance had already been explored in the theories of 'totem and taboo' developed by J. F. McLennan and Robertson Smith, which emphasised how different were the value systems of societies which were matriarchal rather than patriarchal, and in the evolutionary theory of Patrick Geddes and J. Arthur Thomson, which emphasised the evolutionary value of co-operation – that is, of love – rather than Darwinian notions of individual struggle. The flaw in Freud's account of the mind, in Suttie's view, comes from the fact that he is insufficiently historical – or anthropological – in his understanding of the psyche; he accepts the structures of his own culture as universal and 'dismisses the great and mysterious Mother-cults of antiquity' (*OLH*, 137). In so doing he loses sight of the real evolutionary impetus of human communities and, unlike those 'Mother-cults', is 'unwilling to admit the existence of any positive, primary, "other-regarding" feeling' (*OLH*, 116). In the Freudian animus against 'other-regarding' feeling we can descry, perhaps, 'a puritan intolerance of tenderness' (*OLH*, 96) which resists recognition of our indebtedness to the other – an attitude all too familiar in many areas of our nation-based cultural studies.

Thirdly, if we think of our national 'self' as being like our individual self, then we can think of it as defined not by its confrontation with a hostile Other (even if some Others are hostile), or determined by an exclusive Self-Other binary (even if a particular Other weighs heavily on us), but as constituted by the (many) crossing points of our other-relatedness. Adding Ireland–Scotland to Ireland–England (and, indeed, Scotland–England) then provides us with 'another other' that can release us not only from the repressions of past history, but from some of the repressions and distortions of modern theory. We might then take as an emblem of the aim and purpose of comparative studies that refuse the binaries of England–Ireland or Scotland–England Suttie's account of the difference between Celtic Christianity and its mainstream alternatives:

> Pelagius, who resisted the Augustinian doctrine of eternal damnation of unbaptized infants, was an Irish monk. Duns Scotus, who later upheld similar views, was, as his name indicates, a Scotsman. The spread of Christianity in these regions and early times was by persuasion (i.e. mission work) rather than by conquest and coercive 'conversion'. The tolerance of this strain of Christianity was further indicated by their treatment of pagan myth and festivals – new saints borrowing the harmless celebration (and sometimes even the names) of the old deities. (*OLH*, 153)

As Macmurray puts it, 'the fear of the Other is, at bottom, the fear of life' (*PR*, 165) – and if we are to do justice to the nature of our cultures as living and creative environments, we have to accept how dependent they are on otherness, and acknowledge that their identity develops not by resistance to or withdrawal from the 'Other' but precisely from the complexity of their relatedness to many others. We have to cease constructing them as binary engagements of Self and Other and accept that their identity depends always on the possibility of Another Other.

Afterword

In the 1980s, when Hamilton Finlay's garden was coming to maturity, another Scottish poet created an institution aimed at regaining poetry's relationship with the natural world. The International Institute of Geopoetics in Paris was launched in 1989 by Glasgow-born Kenneth White, then Professor of Twentieth-Century Poetics at the Sorbonne. Geopoetics was a response to the fact that 'it was becoming more and more obvious that the earth (the biosphere) was in danger and that ways, both deep and efficient, would have to be worked out in order to protect it', and that what was required was a return to 'the richest poetics' which 'came from contact with the earth, from a plunge into biospheric space, from an attempt to read the lines of the world'.[1] White linked his project to a tradition which included Patrick Geddes, but through Geddes 'geopoetics' was linked to a much longer tradition of Scottish environmentalism that went back to Scottish concerns with the consequences of deforestation, an issue that became urgent in many parts of the British Empire. as a result of the ruthless exploitation of natural resources.

One of the most important contributors to the understanding of deforestation was John Croumbie Brown, born in Haddington (1808–95), who started to research the impact of deforestation while a missionary in South Africa in the 1840s, and wrote numerous books[2] on forestry after returning to Scotland to train in botany. Brown's theories had a significant impact on influential botanists such as Joseph Hooker, whose father had been Professor of Botany at Glasgow University from 1820 till 1841, and who followed his father as head of Kew Gardens in 1865. Hooker spent the summer of 1877 in California, collecting plant speciments with John Muir (born Dunbar, 1838–1914), who had just begun his career as an

---

[1] http://geopoetics.org.uk/pages/what-is-geopoetics.php (accessed December 2008).

[2] Including *Schools of Forestry in Europe* (1877) and *Introduction to the Study of Modern Forest Economy* (1884).

environmental campaigner and who, by the early 1900s, would convince US President Theodore Roosevelt to establish National Parks to protect the 'wilderness' and the ancient sequoia forests of California. Six years earlier, in 1871, Muir had been visited by America's greatest writer and thinker, Ralph Waldo Emerson, at a time when Muir was living in isolation in the Californian forests: 'I have everywhere testified to my friends, who should also be yours,' Emerson wrote, 'my happiness in finding you – the right man in the right place – in your mountain tabernacle'.[3] The meeting resulted in Emerson adding Muir his list of 'My Men', a list which began with Thomas Carlyle, whom Emerson had travelled to Scotland to find in 1833 after reading Carlyle's early works.[4] Indeed, Emerson's response to Muir was to identify him with Carlyle's 'heroes', those who appear when 'Nature itself' can produce 'a Hero-soul'.[5]

Muir's campaign to save 'God's First Temples',[6] the redwood forests, began in 1876, the same year that Alexander Graham Bell demonstrated the telephone at the Centennial Exhibition in Philadelphia, an invention which was dwarfed, both literally and in the public imagination, by the vast Corliss steam engine – 39 feet tall, 680 tons in weight – which powered the mechanical exhibits in 'Machinery Hall'. Muir's determination to prevent that machine-society from destroying the natural world of California was a commitment echoed in France by Kenneth White's geopoetics, which sought an escape from the 'the motorway of Western civilisation' to find a route by which the human future could travel *with* rather than against the world of nature. For Geddes, for Muir, for White, as for many in the tradition of Scottish gardeners, botanists and environmentalists, the engagement with the natural world was a reminder that we are not only creatures of human history but creatures who can, and need to, relate ourselves to a different, natural temporality:

> this is today
>   raised out of history[7]

---

[3] Frederick Turner, *John Muir: From Scotland to the Sierra* (Edinburgh: Canongate, [1985] 1997), 215.

[4] Ibid.

[5] 'The Hero as Poet', *A Carlyle Reader*, 388.

[6] Title of Muir's first published essay, 9 February 1876, in the Sacramento *Record-Union*.

[7] Kenneth White, 'The Chaoticist Manifesto', *Open World: The Collected Poems 1960–2000* (Edinburgh: Polygon, 2003), 551.

Index

Abrams, M. H. 156
Abrioux, Yves 21n, 25n, 200n, 278n
Adams, William Howard 23
Ahmad, Ajiz 219
Aiton, William 29
Alison, Archibald 153
Anderson, Benedict 41–8, 49–51, 148,
    182, 183, 184, 188, 204–6
  Imagined Communities 41–8, 49–50,
    204–5
  The Spectre of Comparisons 210
  Under Three Flags 206
Anderson, John 56
Anderson, R. D. 65–6
Anshen, Ruth Nanda 179–80, 181, 186
  Freedom: Its Meaning 179–80
Aristotle 255
Arnold, Matthew 135, 234
  The Study of Celtic Literature 135
Arnold, Thomas 137
Ascherson, Neal 7–9
Ashcroft, Bill 223n
Auden, W. H. 181, 252
Ayer, A. J. 64–5

Baillie, J. B. 180
Bain, Alexander 115, 257
Bakhtin, Mikhail 221–3, 224, 226–7
Baldick, Chris 85n
Banks, Iain 147, 171
Banks, Joseph 29, 33, 34
Bannatyne Club 85
Barbour, John 137, 139
Barman, Lawrence F. 132
Barnard, F. M. 236
Barrie, J. M. 124, 126–8

Peter Pan 124
Barron, William 226
Barthes, Roland 146, 152–3
Baudrillard, Jean 160
Baynes, Spencer 119
Beattie, James 19, 95
Bediako, Gillian M. 124n
Bell, Alexander Graham 239, 272
Bell, Eleanor 11, 55–60
Bell, Melville 239
Beowulf 142
Bergson, Henri 112, 180
Berkeley, George 174
Beveridge, Craig 56–61, 63–8
  The Eclipse of Scottish Culture 56, 64
  Scotland after Enlightenment 56, 57, 58
Bhabha, Homi K. 219–21, 224, 232–5,
    237
  The Location of Culture 232–3
Billig, Michael 188
Blackwood's Edinburgh Magazine 137,
    139–40
Blaikie, Thomas 29–32
Blair, Hugh 19, 134–5, 140
  'Critical Dissertation on the Poems of
    Ossian' 18, 135
  Lectures on Rhetoric and Belles Lettres 134
Blair, Tony 180, 243
Blavatsky, Madame 255
Bold, Alan 52n, 53n
Booth, Gordon 109n
Boucher, David 190
  The British Idealists 190
Braque, Georges 23
Breuilly, John 235
Broadie, Alexander 22, 83, 84, 105

Cambridge Companion to the Scottish Enlightenment 83
The Scottish Enlightenment 105
The Tradition of Scottish Philosophy 22
Brown, Gordon 243–4
Brown, John Croumbie 271
Brown, Robert 33–4
Bryson, Gladys 77
Buber, Martin 267
Buchan, John 18, 20, 113–14
    Witchwood 18, 20
Burns, Robert 14, 15–16, 25–6, 28, 137–41, 143, 144, 259
Bute, John Stuart, Third Earl of 29

Caird, Edward 11, 90–1, 92, 129, 131
Calderwood, Henry 95, 96–7
Caledonian Horticultural Society 31
Cambridge History of English Literature 142–3
Campbell, R. H. 77
Carlisle, Andrew 31
Carlyle, Thomas 86, 87, 90, 91–2, 132, 140, 218, 260–1, 272
Cencrastus 147n, 208
Chalmers, Thomas 83
Chambers, Robert 100, 110
    Vestiges of the Natural History of Creation 100
Chitnis, Anand 1, 78
Clerk of Penicuik, John 141
Clive, John 80
Clunas, Alex 147
Coleridge, Samuel Taylor 43
Colvin, Calum 22
Common Sense Philosophy 96–7
Connolly, James 259
Conrad, Joseph 113
Continental philosophy 64–5, 245, 262
Corbusier, Le 23
Costello, John E. 190
Craig, Cairns
    Associationism and the Literary Imagination 153n
    History of Scottish Literature 22
    Out of History 5, 150
Craig, David 16, 17
    Scottish Literature and the Scottish

People 16
Crawford, Robert 222, 224, 225–6
    The Scottish Invention of English Literature 225–6
Cunningham, Andrew 20n

Dacre, Lord *see* Trevor-Roper, Hugh
Darwin, Charles 86–7, 110, 255
Davidson, John 35
Davie, George 56, 58, 61, 65–6, 82, 84, 89–91, 116
    The Democratic Intellect 82
    The Crisis of the Democratic Intellect 58
    The Scotch Metaphysics 89
    The Scottish Enlightenment and Other Essays 116
Davis, Leith 145n
Derrida, Jacques 146, 232, 247–51, 261
    Monolingualism of the Other 247–51, 261
Descartes, René 154, 265, 267
Devine, Tom 5n, 6–7, 23, 79–80, 130n
    The Scottish Nation 6–7, 23, 79
    Scotland's Empire 7
Dickinson, W. C. 85n
Douglas, Gavin 137
Dunbar, William 14, 15, 85, 86, 136, 137
Duncan, Ian 145n
Durkheim, Émile 112

Eagleton, Terry 58, 213, 217n
Easthope, Anthony 232
Edinburgh Review 137, 139
Einstein, Albert 33, 106, 180
Eliot, T.S. 24, 60, 112–13, 143
    'Tradition and the Individual Talent' 60
    The Waste Land 113
Emerson, Ralph Waldo 272
Encyclopaedia Britannica (ninth edn) 112, 115, 118–19, 129, 137, 253
Engels, Friedrich 6–7
Ewing, Winifred 4

Fanon, Frantz 56
Ferguson, Adam 11, 77
Ferguson, William 2, 105
Ferrier, J. F. 90–1
Finlay, Alec 25
Finlay, Ian Hamilton 13–14, 18, 20–2,

25–8, 36, 51, 52, 74, 179, 189, 200, 271
'Autumn Poem' 27
Glasgow Beasts, an a Burd 13
'More Detached Sentences on Gardening' 25, 26
Nature Over Again After Poussin 25
'Nuclear Sail' 200
Poor. Old. Tired. Horse. 13
Proposal for a Garden Built on a Slope 23
Wave, Solitary Wave, Great Wave of Translation 51
Finlay, Richard 6, 13, 130n
Finlay, Sue 13–14, 18, 21, 36
Fischer, Claud S. 241
Fitzhugh, Michael L. 170
Fletcher of Saltoun, Andrew 141
Flint, Robert 12
Forbes, Duncan 77–8
Forbes, James D. 105
Foucault, Michel 154, 160
Fraser, Campbell 95–6, 133
Frazer, J. G. 111–16, 121, 123, 128, 129, 150, 257–8, 268
The Golden Bough 112–14
Psyche's Task 115
Totemism and Exogamy 115
The Worship of Nature 116
Freud, Sigmund 111, 112, 262–5
Totem und Tabu 111
Frézier, Amédée-François 54–5
Fry, Michael 5–6
Frye, Northrop 112

Gaál, Botond 107n
Galbraith, Kenneth 182
Galloway, Janice 171
Gardener's Magazine 32
Gardenesque 36
Gardiner, Michael 223
Gay, Peter 81
Geddes, Patrick 28, 73–5, 202, 273
Gellner, Errnest 37, 43, 48, 65, 183, 220
Nations and Nationalisms 37
Thought and Change 37
Words and Things 65
George IV 31
Gibbon, Lewis Grassic 114

Gifford, Douglas 150n
Gloag, John 32–3
Gordon, James of Rothiemay 29
Graham, Gordon 82, 84, 91
Graham, W. S. 146–7
'The Constructed Space' 146–8
The Nightfishing 147
Graves, Robert 114
The White Goddess 114n
Gray, Alasdair 22, 147, 155, 156, 171
Lanark 22, 147, 172, 202
Gray, Iain 3
Green, T. H. 173
Grieve, C. M. *see* MacDiarmid, Hugh
Griffiths, Gareth 223n
Grove, Richard 34n
Gunn, Neil 14, 114

Habermas, Jürgen 58, 172–3
Haldane, R. B. 131
Hall, John A. 48n
Hamilton, Sir William 86, 87, 88, 90, 105, 131
'Philosophy of the Unconditioned' 87
Harari, Josué V. 242
Harman, P. M. 104, 109n
Harris, Wilson 223
Harrison, Jane 112
Harvie, Christopher 4n, 174n, 107–8
Scotland and Nationalism 4n, 176n
Hayles, N. Katherine 243
Hearn, Jonathan 12
Hector, James 35
Hegel, G. W. F. 88, 131, 161, 164–5, 170, 260
Heidegger, Martin 64, 131
Heisenberg, Werner 181, 182
Helmholtz, Hermann 131
Henryson, Robert 86, 136, 137
Herder, Johann Gottfried 235–6
Herman, Arthur 2, 78, 82, 104–5, 152
Hobsbawm, Eric 40n, 58
Hogg, James 141, 178
Confessions of a Justified Sinner 145
Home, John 134
Hook, Andrew 141n
Hooker, Joseph 271
Hope, John 34

Howatson, Alexander 31
Hughes, Ted 114
Hume, David 5, 11, 61, 77, 81–2, 87–90,
    91, 92–3, 96–9, 105, 115, 129, 130,
    137, 143, 153, 154, 161–2, 163, 167,
    170, 173–8, 196, 208, 259
    Dialogues on Natural Religion 96–7
    Natural History of Religion 116
    Treatise of Human Nature 154–5, 173–6,
    177, 178
Hunt, Bruce J. 104
Hunt, John Dixon 24
Husserl, Edmund 260
Hutcheon, Linda 155–6
    The Politics of Postmodernism 155–6
Hutcheson, Francis 84, 97–8, 130, 137
Hutchinson, John 49
Huxley, T. H. 87, 110, 255

Jameson, Frederic 155, 160
    *Postmodernism, or, the Cultural Logic of
    Late Capitalism* 155
Jamieson, John 144
Jencks, Charles 25
Johnson, Samuel 18
    *A Journey to the Western Islands of
    Scotland* 18
Jones, Henry 191–2
Joyce, James 113

Kant, Immanuel 92–5, 131, 158–62, 163,
    166–7, 169–70, 174
    Kritik of Pure Reason 93
Kearney, Richard 245–6, 250, 259–2, 264,
    266
    Strangers, Gods and Monsters 245–6,
    260–2, 264, 266
Kedourie, Elie 37
Kelman, James 171–2, 222, 223
    How late it was, how late 171–2
Kelvin, Lord *see* Thomson, William
Kennedy, A. L. 147, 171
Kew Gardens 29, 33
Khatibi, Abdelkebir 248
Kiberd, Declan 224–5, 245–6, 250–1,
    259–60, 262
    Inventing Ireland 224–5, 246, 259
Kidd, Colin 2, 149, 229–32

British Identities before Nationalism 229
    Subverting Scotland's Past 149, 230–1
Kipling, Rudyard 228
Kirkpatrick, Frank G. 171
Knight, G. Wilson 112
Knox, John 16, 85
Knox, Robert 108, 228, 230, 232, 234–5
    The Races of Men 108, 228
Kristeva, Julia 264, 266
Kuehn, Manfred 161

Laing, David 85–6
Laing, R. D. 56, 264–6
    Divided Self 265–6
Lamarck, J.-B. 255
Lamb, Keith (and Patrick Bowe) 35n
Law, Alexander 84, 142
Leavis, F. R. 15, 144, 211
Lecky, William H. 170
Lee, James (of Lee and Kennedy) 30
Lehmann, W. C. 77
Leonard, Tom 222
Lindsay, Maurice 53
Little Sparta *see* Stonypath
Livingston, James C. 87n
Lochhead, Liz 22, 222
Locke, John 174
Lorenz, Edward 242
Loudon, John Claudius 32–3, 34, 35–6
    Encyclopaedia of Gardening 33
    The Gardener's Magazine 32
    The Green-House Companion 33
    *Observations on laying out Farms in the
    Scotch Style* 32
    *Suburban Gardener and Villa
    Companion* 33
    *The Utility of Agricultural Knowledge to
    the Sons of the Landed Proprietors of
    England* 32
Louis XIV 54
Lovejoy, Arthur 156
Lukács, Georg 151n
Lyell, Sir Charles 87
Lynch, Michael 5, 130, 431
Lyndsay, David 21
Lyotard, Jean-François 148–9, 152, 155,
    156–60, 172–3
    The Postmodern Condition 148, 155

Mabberley, D. J. 33n
McArthur, Colin 9
McCleery, Alistair 14n
McConnell, Jack 78
McCosh, James 81, 88–9
   The Scottish Philosophy 81
McCrone, David 12, 49n, 61–2, 63–73,
   182
   The Sociology of Nationalism 49n, 62, 182
   Understanding Scotland 12, 62, 68–70
MacCunn, Hamish 19
MacDiarmid, Hugh 9, 14–15, 17, 19–20,
   52–3, 80, 133–4, 144, 145–6
   Contemporary Scottish Studies 17, 133–4
   'The Glen of Silence' 14–15
   In Memoriam James Joyce 145–6
   The Voice of Scotland 15, 17
MacDonald, George 124–5, 129
   Phantastes 124–5
MacDonald, Murdo 25–6
MacDuffie, Allen 126
McGann, Jerome 145
McGuffie, Jessie 52
McHale, Brian 146
   Postmodernist Fiction 146n
McIlvanney, Liam 27, 258n
Maciness, Allan I. 5n
MacIntyre, Alasdair 56, 57, 58, 59, 61,
   89–90, 118–21, 128–9, 178
   After Virtue 59, 60
   Dependent Rational Animals
   Hume's Ethical Writings 57
   Three Rival Versions of Moral Enquiry 57,
   118–19
   Whose Justice? Which Rationality? 89
MacIver, Robert Morrison 180–9, 190,
   193, 236
   Community: A Sociological Study 181, 182,
   183–5, 188, 197
   Politics and Society 186, 187, 193, 194–5,
   197
   Society: A Textbook of Sociology 186
   Society: Its Structure and Changes 181
Mackay, James Townsend 35
Mackay, Sheila 22n, 32n
MacKenzie, John 30
Mackintosh, James 138
McLennan, John Ferguson 111–12, 114,

129, 258, 268
Macleod, Fiona 259
McLuhan, Marshall 50, 204, 244
   Understanding Media 50, 204
Macmillan, Duncan 22
Macmurray, John 11, 132, 169–71, 174,
   175–8, 180–9, 190, 193, 227, 236,
   264–5, 266, 267, 269
   Persons in Relation 37, 181, 227, 264,
   265, 267, 269
   Reason and Emotion 175–6
   The Self as Agent 169, 181, 193, 196,
   198
Macpherson, James 19, 134, 142, 148
   Poems of Ossian 19, 134, 135
Macquarrie, John 131, 132, 199
Mahon, Basil 103n, 129n
Mairet, Philip 73n
Malinowski, Bronislaw 112
Malmaison 30
Manlove, Colin 124
Mann, Thomas 180
Mansel, H. L. 87
Maritain, Jacques 180
Marxism 207–8
Massie, Allan 114
Masson, David 85, 86, 90, 99–103, 106,
   129, 141
   British Novelists and their Styles 85
   Recent British Philosophy 86, 99–103
   'Scottish Contribution to British
   Literature' 85
Masson, Francis 29
Mavor, James 180
Maxwell, James Clerk 12, 66, 103–9, 114,
   117–18, 123, 129, 131, 239, 256–7,
   258
   'Maxwell's Demon' 117–18
   Treatise on Electricity and Magnetism 103
Megill, Allan 175
Melville, Robert 34
Mill, John Stuart 86, 88–9, 91, 257
Millar, James Hepburn 86
Miller, Gavin 262n
Miller, Karl 150n
Miller, Philip 29
Milton, John 179
Mind 92–5, 161–2

Mitchison, Naomi 114
Mitchison, Rosalind 80
Moore, Charles 35
Moore, David 35
Moreiras, Alberto 209
Morgan, Edwin 52
Morison, Robert 33
Morley, Henry 136–7
Morton, Graeme 139n
Muir, Edwin 9, 16, 17, 114, 133
   John Knox 16
   'Scotland 1941' 16
   Scott and Scotland 17
   Scottish Journey 19
Muir, John 271–2
Mumford, Lewis 73–4
Murray, Gilbert 112

Nairn, Tom 9, 38–40, 47, 53–4, 55, 60,
   150, 232
   The Break-up of Britain 38–40, 232n
Neish, Alex 52
New Left Review 212
Newton, Isaac 103, 104
Nichol, John 137, 142–3
Nicoll, Laurence 63–7
Nietzsche, Friedrich 175
Niven, Ninian 35
Noble, Andrew 27
Norris, Christopher 172n
'North British' 231

Ogden, C. K. 252, 256
   The Meaning of Meaning 252
O'Hagan, Andrew 9–10, 13
   Our Fathers 13
Olson, Richard 117n
Orléans, Duc d' 31, 33, 34

Parker, Geoff 208
Payne, Peter L. 130n
Pelagius 268
Phillipson, Nicholas 78, 80
Picasso, Pablo 23
Plato 175
Poincaré, Henri 242
Polanyi, Michael 181
Porter, Roy 78

Pound, Ezra 257
Pragmatism (American) 81
Pringle-Pattison, A. S. *see* Seth, Andrew
Purser, John 22
Ramsay, Allan 27, 134, 140
   The Gentle Shepherd 134, 140
Ranger, Terence 40n
Rankin, Ian 22
Read, Herbert 20
Reid, Thomas 90, 93, 97, 99, 133, 137,
   163–4, 166
Renan, Ernest 234, 238
Richards, I. A. 143, 252, 256
   The Meaning of Meaning 252
Rizal, José 45–6, 205–6, 209–11, 212, 219
   El filibusterismo 209–10
   Noli Me Tangere 45–6
Robertson, Forbes W. 28n, 31n
Robertson, James 147
Robertson, John 5n, 77–8
Robertson, Roland 240
Robinson, Daniel Somner 81
Robinson, Tim 34n
Rocheford, Jorevin de 28
Rohan, Henri Duc de 28
Roosevelt, Theodore 272
Roseberry, Lord 84
Ross, John Merry 86, 136
Ross, Stephanie 23n
Ross, Thomas 28
Rousseau, Jean-Jacques 29
Roxburgh, William 34, 35
Runrig 22
Ruskin, John 216
Russell, Bertrand 180
Russell, William Howard 204
Ryan, Ray 258n
Ryle, Gilbert 112

Said, Edward 216–19, 220–1
   Culture and Imperialism 217–18
Saintsbury, George 141
Salmond, Alex 3, 243
Sandford, Daniel 139
Sartre, Jean Paul 260, 265
Saussure, Ferdinand de 152, 165
Schoene, Berthold 63
Schroeder, William Ralph 260n

Scott, Walter 20, 40, 85, 137, 139, 141,
144, 145, 149, 151, 259
Redgauntlet 149
Waverley 151
Scott, W.R. 84, 97–9, 130
Scottish Enlightenment 1–4, 8–9, 53,
77–84, 88, 90, 97–9, 116–17, 130–1,
144, 150, 152–3, 173, 202, 208, 227
Scottish Football Association 69, 71–2
Scottish History Society 84
Scottish International 53
Scottish National Party 1, 4, 37–9
Scottish National Portrait Gallery 84
Scottish Renaissance 14, 52–3, 80
Scottish Text Society 84, 142
Scotus, Duns 22
Serres, Michel 242–3
Seth, Andrew (Pringle-Pattison) 11, 90,
91–2, 95, 131, 133, 162–9, 174, 178,
193–9
The Balfour Lectures on Realism 164,
166–7
Hegelianism and Personality 163, 164–6,
168, 193–4, 195
Man's Place in the Cosmos 196–7, 198,
199
Scottish Philosophy 163, 164–5
Seth, James 190–1, 192–3
Essays in Ethics and Religion 190–1
Study of Ethical Principles 192–3
Shaw, David Gary 170n
Sheeler, Jessie 18
Siepmann, Charles 181
Skinner, Andrew 77
Skinner, Quentin 78
Smith, Adam 8, 11, 78, 105, 116, 129,
137, 144, 151, 175, 208, 227
Theory of Moral Sentiments 227
The Wealth of Nations 8
Smith, Anthony D. 37n, 39, 235
Smith, Crosbie 66, 102n, 103n, 105, 106,
124, 203n
Energy and Empire 66, 102n, 103n
Science of Energy 124
Smith, George Adam 120–1
Smith, Norman Kemp 12, 98–9, 132–3,
174, 176
Philosophy of David Hume 98, 132–3

*Letters of Baron Friedrich von Hügel and
Professor Norman Kemp Smith* 132
*Prolegomena to an Idealist Theory of
Knowledge* 133
Smith, William Robertson 107–12, 114,
115, 119–21, 123, 126, 128, 129, 131,
258, 268
Lectures on the Religion of the Semites 111
Lectures and Essays 119, 120, 121
Smollett, Tobias 19
Smout, T.C. 6, 82–3, 207–8
Snow, C.P. 181, 182
Sorenson, Janet 145n
Spark, Muriel 114, 147, 155, 156, 171
The Comforters 147
The Driver's Seat 172
The Prime of Miss Jean Brodie 147
Territorial Rites 114
Speirs, John 15
The Scots Literary Tradition 15–16
Spencer, Herbert 87, 257
Spengler, Oswald 112
Stephen, Jeffrey 5n
Stevenson, Robert Louis 61, 124–7, 129
Strange Tale of Dr Jekyll and Mr Hyde 61,
124–7, 129, 149, 178, 229
Stewart, Balfour 121–4, 255–7, 267
The Unseen Universe 123–6, 258–9
Stewart, Dugald 3, 116, 137, 151
Stewart, Ian 242
Stirling, J. Hutchison 88, 92–5, 131,
161–2
The Secret of Hegel 131, 161
Stonypath (Little Sparta) 13, 21, 179
Sullivan, W.K. 137
Suttie, Ian D. 262–5, 268–9
The Origins of Love and Hate 262–4,
268–9
Synge, John Millington 251
Szporluk, Roman 48

Tait, Peter Guthrie 103, 105, 106–9, 114,
121–4, 126, 129, 131, 255–7, 267
Treatise on Natural Philosophy 103, 255
The Unseen Universe 123–6, 258–9
Taylor, Charles 58, 61, 227
Taylor, Patricia 29, 30
Thatcher, Margaret 4, 202

Thom, Martin 234n
Thomson, E. P. 7
Thomson, James 134
Thomson, William (Lord Kelvin) 66,
    103–9, 114, 117–19, 121, 129, 131,
    203, 255–6
  Treatise on Natural Philosophy 103–4,
    121
Thorkelin, Grim J. 142
Tiffin, Helen 223n
Tillich, Paul 182
Tilly, Charles 49
Torrance, T. F. 12, 198
Toynbee, Joseph Arnold 112
Trevor-Roper, Hugh (Lord Dacre) 1, 2,
    3–4, 9, 40, 77–8
Turnbull, Ronald 56–61, 63–8
  The Eclipse of Scottish Culture 56, 64
  Scotland after Enlightenment 56, 57, 58
Tyndall, John 253

Union (Ireland) 224
Union (Scotland–England, 1707) 2, 5, 38

Vickery, John B. 112n, 113

Walker, Hugh 86
Wallace, Alfred Russel 87, 255, 256
Wallace, William 131
Wallerstein, Immanuel 207–9, 240
Ward, J. P. 213
Ward, James 115, 253–5, 257
  Heredity and Memory 254–5
  'Psychology' 253
Warnock, Geoffrey 64–5
Welsh, Irvine 22, 222
Whatley, Christopher A. 5n

White, Hayden 151
White, Kenneth 271–2
Whitehead, Alfred North 180
Whitehouse, Wildman 203
Wilde, Oscar 224, 246
Williams, Daniel 213n
Williams, Raymond 211–16, 219, 220–1,
    233n
  Border Country 214
  The Country and the City 211, 214, 215
  Culture and Society 214
  'Culture is Ordinary' 212
  The Long Revolution 214
  Marxism and Literature 215
  Politics and Letters 212, 215
  Problems in Materialism and Culture 214
  Writing in Society 214
Wilson, Woodrow 12
Wise, M. Norton 66, 102n, 103n, 105,
    106, 124, 203n
  Energy and Empire 66, 102n, 103n
Withers, Charles 1
Witherspoon, John 237
Wittgenstein, Ludwig 112, 157
Womack, Peter 19
Wood, Paul 1, 3
Woolf, Virginia 113
World Systems Theory 207–9
Worringer, Wilhelm 20

Yeats, W. B. 113, 250–1, 252, 253, 255,
    257–8, 259, 262, 267
  Autobiographies 253, 255
  Essays and Introductions 253, 258
  A Vision 252
Young, Robert 228
  Colonial Desire 228, 234